The Effects of the Mass Media on the Use and Abuse of Alcohol

Research Monograph No. 28

THE EFFECTS OF THE MASS MEDIA ON THE USE AND ABUSE OF ALCOHOL

Edited by:
Susan E. Martin, Ph.D.,
with the assistance of Captain Patricia Mail

U.S. DEPARTMENT OF HEALTH AND HUMAN SERVICES
Public Health Service
National Institutes of Health
National Institute on Alcohol Abuse and Alcoholism
6000 Executive Boulevard
Bethesda, MD 20892-7003

NIH Publication No. 95-3743

This monograph is based on the Working Group on the Effects of the Mass Media on the Use and Abuse of Alcohol sponsored by the National Institute on Alcohol Abuse and Alcoholism (NIAAA) that met on September 24-25, 1992.

About the Editor: Susan E. Martin, Ph.D., is a health science administrator in the Prevention Research Branch, Division of Clinical and Prevention Research, NIAAA.

NIH Publication No. 95-3743
National Institutes of Health

TABLE OF CONTENTS

FOREWORD

Alcohol appears frequently in the mass media. Viewers may see beer ads in televised sports events, spirits ads in magazines, TV programs that take place in bars, and product placements in movies. Despite the conventional wisdom that advertising must have an effect on viewers' attitudes and behavior toward drinking, scientific knowledge in this area is limited.

The contents of this volume represent a renewed effort by the National Institute on Alcohol Abuse and Alcoholism (NIAAA) to assess the current state of knowledge and identify directions for additional research that may contribute to the ongoing policy debates on the presentation of alcohol in the mass media. The papers herein presented were initially prepared for discussion at the Workshop on the Effects of the Mass Media on the Use and Abuse of Alcohol that was held in September 1992. The richness of the dialogue that ensued has led to publication not only of those papers but of the edited comments of discussants and a synthesis of the discussion itself.

There are many interesting questions about alcohol and advertising, but the one that dominates the discussion is whether advertising accelerates or otherwise contributes to the initiation of drinking by youths. This debate ranges from the view stated by many representatives of the alcohol beverage industry and the media that advertising only affects brand preference to the prevention and consumer activists who assert that alcohol advertising promotes drinking by underage youths. The Executive Branch, Congress, State policymakers, local citizens' groups, and national organizations all have entered the policy debate at one time or another, and it is likely that the debate will continue for some time. Despite the high profile of this policy debate, science has few answers due, in large part, to the methodological and measurement difficulties described in this volume. These problems are likely to grow rather than diminish with the shift of marketing resources from traditional radio, TV, and print advertising to integrated marketing tactics and mechanisms. Yet our need for findings has never been greater given the conflict between common sense and scientific evidence in addressing the issue.

The issue of alcohol and the mass media is one in which science might make an important contribution to public policy, although it has not done so thus far. This volume is intended to stimulate such policy-relevant research by synthesizing knowledge, identifying methodological limitations and alternative research designs, and suggesting more creative ways to address important research questions.

Clearly, NIAAA does not endorse all of the statements that appear in this volume; these statements represent the opinions and views of the diverse group of individuals who participated in the workshop. Nevertheless, we believe that there is value in exposing the exchange of ideas and perspectives to a wider audience and hope that they might take up the scientific challenge that this issue poses.

Enoch Gordis, M.D.
Director
National Institute on Alcohol Abuse and Alcoholism

INTRODUCTION

Susan E. Martin[1]

There is a widespread belief among the general public that alcohol advertising affects the initiation and amount of drinking. Yet despite many studies, scientific evidence supporting these assumptions is very weak; the effects of alcohol advertising, promotion activities, and mass media presentations involving alcohol on attitudes toward drinking, actual consumption, and alcohol-related problems remains unclear. Similarly, evidence concerning the effectiveness of counteradvertising efforts and health promotion campaigns in reducing alcohol initiation, use, and problems also is limited.

The inconclusive findings appear to be due to the nature of the questions that have been addressed, data availability limitations, and flaws in research designs. Data that might help resolve questions often are not available. In particular, many surveys have been challenged for inadequacies related to their samples; experimental findings have been faulted for their questionable generalizability; and econometric models have been challenged due to specification errors. Studies of the effectiveness of various counteradvertising initiatives by public health advocates also have been limited in number and subject to many of the same methodological flaws. During the last decade, there appear to have been a diminishing number of studies of the effects of both advertising and counteradvertising, making it difficult to shed new light on an important policy question.

Nevertheless, obtaining better evidence on the impact of alcohol advertising continues to be of great interest to many communications researchers and policymakers concerned with the initiation, use, and misuse of alcohol by youths, vulnerable populations (i.e., pregnant women, alcoholics, and persons taking prescription drugs), and other relevant segments of the population.

To assess the current state of knowledge and stimulate further research on these important issues, the National Institute on Alcohol Abuse and Alcoholism (NIAAA) convened a Working Group on the Effects of the Mass Media on the Use and Abuse of Alcohol that met on September 24–25, 1992. More specifically, the Working Group had the following goals:

1. To critically review current knowledge of the effects of alcohol advertising, promotion, entertainment programming, and public service messages on attitudes, expectancies, and

[1]Prevention Research Branch, National Institute on Alcohol Abuse and Alcoholism, 6000 Executive Blvd., Rockville, MD 20892

behaviors related to

- alcohol initiation and use among youths,
- alcohol use by vulnerable populations, and
- high-risk drinking in the general adult population;

2. To assess the methodologies and data sets on which these findings are based;

3. To explore how individuals, groups, and communities perceive and respond to alcohol advertising, promotional practices, and health promotion messages; and

4. To identify key research questions and promising strategies—including potential new research designs, analytic techniques, data sets, and methodologies—to more effectively assess the immediate and longer term effects of advertising, sponsorships, media programming, and health promotion campaigns on alcohol consumption and abuse.

Participants included a group of 18 scholars from a wide variety of substantive fields who were deliberately chosen to have diverse research perspectives. Review papers were prepared for discussion at the meeting, and other invitees served as discussants for specific papers in their respective areas of expertise.

In addition to the authors and discussants, members of the larger community, including representatives of other Federal agencies, the alcohol beverage industry, and public advocacy groups, as well as alcohol-focused researchers, were invited to observe. The result was a stimulating, lively, and scholarly discussion of the state of knowledge, methodological approaches, and future directions for research related to advertising, other marketing practices, program content, and public health communications related to alcohol. (A list of attendees is included in the appendix.)

OBJECTIVES AND THEMES

In publishing this collection of articles based on presentations at the Working Group meeting, NIAAA has several objectives. The first is to provide a comprehensive review of the literature on alcohol advertising and mass communications for researchers and policymakers concerned with learning what we really know. The second is to acquaint the broad constituency of alcohol researchers with the world of advertising and marketing and to acquaint those in the latter fields with some of the issues related to research on alcohol, a unique commodity that raises particular concerns for public health. The third is to widely disseminate the menu of research issues that emerged from the workshop discussion so that these ideas may stimulate new studies that ultimately will be useful in understanding media effects and shaping public policy.

The authors of the central thematic papers included in this volume were requested to assess the methodologies used in existing studies and the validity of findings relevant to a specific issue or research approach. They also were asked to identify key questions and promising directions for further study. The volume additionally includes briefer articles that are based on the remarks of the discussants at the meeting. Some focus primarily on the paper to which they are directed; others use the stimulus paper as a basis for explaining the authors' own perspectives.

This monograph begins with an overview of the place in American culture of both the mass media (including advertising) and alcohol. Next, it turns to what we really know about relationships between media presentations and alcohol-related attitudes and behavior. Included are detailed reviews and critiques of the research literature on alcohol advertising, looking respectively at experimental and survey studies, econometric studies, the development of alcohol expectancies and their relationship to advertising, and analyses of the content of mass media programming and how the audience interprets what it sees and hears. The focus then shifts to general examinations of the nature and effects of advertising and of nontraditional marketing in which the authors explore how advertising is designed so as to affect viewers and why such effects have not been heretofore measured by alcohol researchers. These are followed by examinations of the nature, effectiveness, and obstacles to mass communication by public health advocates. The final article in the volume is a synthesis of the major themes that emerged from the lengthy discussions that followed each pair of presentations at the Working Group and the concluding general discussion.

SUMMARY OF CONTENTS

The first chapter, George Gerbner's "Alcohol in American Culture," provides a critical introductory overview of the place of alcohol, the mass media, and advertising in contemporary culture. It also examines the problems faced by agencies and groups that are trying to control possible deleterious effects of industry advertising. Gerbner discusses current laws, government regulatory policies, and their implementation; alcohol industry and media self-regulation; and the role of citizen action groups. The author contends that advertisements are "stories that sell," and that for the first time in modern history it is impossible for Americans to avoid the positive images of alcohol portrayed in the mass media, particularly television. Children learn about the world and its social norms and values from this "compelling media environment of stories" that do not come directly from family, church, or community and that provide a picture of alcohol that is glamorized and distorted.

In response to the increased centralization and power of the mass media, Gerbner calls for the development of alternative strategies to prevent and control the harmful effects of alcohol. These include producing more diverse images and role models and saturating the community with health information. Such an effort also requires new mechanisms of public participation in cultural policymaking and financing, more diversity of health-related representations, and the recognition that "what has to be addressed is not just isolated messages or media, but the very structure of a seamless and coherent total cultural environment that has drifted out of democratic reach" (page 22).

Joseph Gusfield's commentary focuses on why advertising and the media have become topics of interest, as evidenced by the Working Group. He observes the ambivalent and diverse views of alcohol in American culture and identifies several factors that contribute to researchers' concerns with alcohol advertising and with its presentation in the mass media. It is a problem deemed worthy of study, Gusfield asserts, because it neatly fits existing research paradigms, because the media tend to exaggerate alcohol use in programming in order to heighten drama, and because concern with advertising provides a convenient diversion from looking at deeper policy conflicts related to alcohol.

In "Survey and Experimental Research on Effects of Alcohol Advertising," Charles Atkin provides a detailed review and critique of reported findings and conclusions drawn from field surveys and experimental and laboratory studies. For each of the 12 experimental studies he scrutinizes, he reviews the underlying theoretical rationale, appropriateness of the methodology, threats to external validity, adequacy of the sample, and generalizability of the findings to "the real world." Atkin finds that these studies have resulted in contradictory and ambiguous findings due primarily to "methodological deficiencies, compounded by the lack of conceptualization underlying the design of most experiments." Field survey studies avoid the problem of unnatural laboratory settings but have other limitations including the lack of a control group, reliance on self-report data, and uncertainty regarding causality.

Atkin's review of survey studies concludes that despite divergences in measurement techniques, the research suggests that TV beer ads slightly increase the consumption of beer. However, studies examining alcohol-misuse outcomes were inconclusive. Based on both experimental and field survey findings, Atkin concludes that "it appears that advertising is a contributing factor that increases drinking to a modest degree . . ."

In the final section of his chapter, Atkin maps out an ambitious research agenda designed to better inform policy processes. Such research should both "pinpoint the precise extent of impact" and "identify the theoretical processes that account for this outcome" by (1) answering key questions such as the strength of the causal impact of advertising and the role of the other independent and intervening variables that amplify or attenuate the influence of advertising; (2) specifying the differential effects on various audience segments; (3) isolating influential message content and stylistic factors in ads; (4) comparing the relative impact of varying quantities of advertising and public service messages; and (5) examining inoculation strategies for educational messages designed to counteract alcohol advertisements.

The next commentary, by John Lastovicka, "A Methodological Interpretation of the Experimental and Survey Research Evidence Concerning Alcohol Advertising Effects," expands on some of the methodological issues raised by Atkin and suggests an alternative research strategy. He calls for an expansion of field experimental studies, which he acknowledges are more costly and complex but promise to more effectively address the issue of causality. Lastovicka uses a study that he and colleagues recently completed to illustrate both the difficulties of mounting a split-cable television advertising experiment and the greater certainty of findings from such experiments. They can identify the effects of specific kinds of advertising (in this case beer ads targeted at young men) on specific types of alcohol-related behaviors (drinking and driving).

In "Alcohol Advertising and Alcohol Consumption: Econometric Studies," economist Henry Saffer reviews prior econometric work on alcohol advertising and provides a simple but innovative economic model of how advertising affects demand. He then uses his model to interpret and reconcile the different conclusions of previous studies regarding the effects of alcohol advertising. Saffer's review of econometric studies of both alcohol and cigarette advertising finds that advertising expenditures show little effect on consumption. However, studies of bans on advertising indicate that the bans do reduce consumption. And econometric studies that estimate the effects of counteradvertising consistently find that counteradvertising is an effective method of reducing consumption. These results support Saffer's model of advertising effects. For example, he attributes the absence of an advertising effect in most advertising expenditure studies to the fact that there was very little variation either in the level of advertising (which was uniformly high) or the level of demand in these studies. Saffer identifies three areas for future econometric research on alcohol advertising: studies of advertising that use data sets that maximize the variance in the advertising data, including new internationally-based advertising ban studies; studies of counteradvertising; and studies of the effects of targeted advertising and targeted counteradvertising.

Victor Tremblay's "Comments" on Saffer's paper call attention to the need to go beyond advertising and counteradvertising by considering policy alternatives, including taxation and public education. He also identifies several of the limitations of econometric research on the relationship between advertising and alcohol consumption that leave many of the important questions unanswered.

Joel Grube's discussion of "Television Alcohol Portrayals, Alcohol Advertising, and Alcohol Expectancies Among Children and Adolescents" addresses the question of whether exposure to televised alcohol portrayals and advertisements influences youths' alcohol expectancies and intentions to drink. According to Grube, previously published cross-sectional studies have not addressed the influence of such exposure nor directly assessed expectancies. Moreover, experimental studies have presented highly artificial situations. Grube's ongoing research, some of which is reported in this paper, attempts to surmount some of these methodological and conceptual shortcomings.

As the theoretical foundation for his research, Grube uses an information processing model of media effects that posits that advertising has significant effects on knowledge, beliefs, intentions, and behaviors only when the advertisements are attended to and remembered. Thus, Grube focuses on awareness of advertising rather than simple exposure, and he addresses the issue of directionality of media effects by using nonrecursive modeling techniques. To explore the reciprocal relationships among exposure, awareness of advertising, and drinking intentions, beliefs, and knowledge, Grube collects and examines data from fifth and sixth graders. His findings show that after controlling for the reciprocal effects of knowledge and beliefs on awareness of advertising, children who are more aware of TV beer ads have more favorable beliefs about drinking and intend to drink more frequently as adults. On the basis of his findings, Grube suggests that reducing the appeal of alcohol ads to children as well as their exposure to them should be part of a broad prevention strategy.

In response to Grube's suggestion, Lorraine Collins proposes "Prevention as Skills Training: An Approach to Lessening the Impact of Alcohol Advertising." She observes that children are curious about alcohol and that those who do not get sufficient information about it at home frequently turn to TV. Since drinking is legal, normative, and portrayed with reasonable accuracy in advertisements, the author asserts that it would undermine the credibility of health educators in the eyes of children to portray all drinking as harmful. Instead, she advocates a skills training approach to prevent alcohol problems by enabling youths to learn about drinking nonabusively. Such a program might resemble that used in training youths to drive.

Jane Brown and Trevy McDonald shift the focus from advertising to the content of television in "Portrayals and Effects of Alcohol in Television Entertainment Programming." Content analyses of the frequency of alcohol portrayals in TV programming find that the proportion of all drinks consumed that contain alcohol is much greater than that proportion is in the real world. Whether such portrayals cause more drinking, however, is uncertain. Correlational studies that find an association between drinking and television viewing raise questions of the direction of causality. According to Brown and McDonald, support for the "cultivation hypothesis" of Gerbner and associates (i.e., that frequent TV viewers are more likely than light viewers to adopt the world view offered by television) also is limited.

The content analyses reported by Brown and McDonald document variations in TV portrayals of drinking that are related to the drinker's gender, character attributes, and age; to the situations in which drinking occurs; and to the consequences of drinking (which rarely are negative). The authors praise recent initiatives of public health experts to institute "cooperative consultations" with TV producers as a promising tactic. They note that these efforts have affected presentations of alcohol on television, but caution that their effects on viewers still have not been studied.

Brown and McDonald suggest that future research should address the content and consequences of portrayals of alcohol by examining the effects of portrayals on the audience rather than focusing only on program content. Such research should include qualitative studies and should treat viewers as complex information processors who attend to and interpret information, rather than as passive recipients of media messages.

In his commentary entitled "Viewers' Interpretation of Television Images of Alcohol," Anders Hansen expands on Brown and McDonald's paper. He asserts that to understand the symbolic environment created by television, it is necessary to go beyond entertainment programs to examine factual portrayals in news, documentaries, and current affairs programs. Using his research on adolescent TV viewers in Great Britain, Hansen illustrates how viewers interact with and interpret media presentations by drawing on two frames of reference: their personal experience and their knowledge of the conventions of the format and presentation of the TV genre. Like Brown and McDonald, the author emphasizes the importance of looking beyond content analysis to the complexities of television images and audience interpretation of them. He is less sanguine about the effectiveness of cooperative consultation but asserts that it can be valuable in providing balance since, "in an informed democracy, citizens should have ready access to images, portrayals, and information on the full range of pleasures *and* problems associated with alcohol use . . ."

In "Studies of the Effects of Alcohol Advertising: Two Underexplored Aspects," Esther Thorson identifies two key areas of advertising research that she believes should be examined before it is concluded that alcohol advertising has no effects. The first area is the role of strategic planning and execution that underlies alcohol advertising; the second area is the way that alcohol ads portray and affect cultural meanings. Thorson observes that much of the experimental literature on advertising and alcohol behavior ignores the content and message in the advertisements shown to subjects. To do so is to overlook what advertisers do when designing an advertising campaign. Such campaigns are always strategically targeted at a particular audience with a message specifically chosen to reach them through a particular medium and aired with consideration of time, place, and circumstances in which the messages will be seen and heard. Illustrating her second point, Thorson analyzes a series of alcohol advertisements to identify the cultural meanings connoted by their messages. Finally, she suggests that alcohol researchers should design experimental studies to measure the presence and strength of shared cultural myths related to alcohol and to assess their impact on purchasing and consumption behavior.

Jerome Williams' commentary, "Advertising Principles, Practices, and Outcomes: Applicability to Alcohol Marketing," observes that advertising researchers and alcohol researchers have different goals and research objectives that lead to the use of different dependent measures. These differences, in turn, may account for a portion of the conflicting results reported by each group. The author also suggests that researchers too frequently leap from advertising exposure to alcohol consumption, bypassing consideration of intervening variables. Rather than making a direct exposure–consumption link, he urges researchers to put more emphasis on understanding *how* intervening variables mediate relationships between exposure and consumption. In addition, he calls for more longitudinal research, greater attention to context, and the application of a wider range of general theories (e.g., cognitive dissonance and commodity theories) in understanding the effects of alcohol advertising.

In "Nontraditional Media and Promotions in the Marketing of Alcoholic Beverages," David Stewart and Ronald Rice discuss the increasingly wide range of marketing strategies that are now being used to promote and sell a variety of products, the ways these techniques have been employed by the alcohol industry, and the limitations of the research that attempts to measure their effects. The authors note that the distinctions between advertising and other forms of promotion have become blurred due to technological, social, and economic changes. These changes have led to the rise of nontraditional vehicles for advertising and promotion. Nevertheless, across the fragmented and heterogeneous media environment, audiences increasingly control the media to which they are exposed. Marketers have responded by tailoring messages to specialized audiences and by using a variety of nontraditional media (e.g., computer bulletin boards, 900 phone numbers, and specialized cable TV channels). They are also using nontraditional marketing approaches such as product placement techniques and event marketing. Responses to the changing media environment that characterize the advertising world at large are also evident among alcohol marketers.

Stewart and Rice observe that empirical research on the effectiveness of these newer forms of advertising and promotion has been even more limited than research on traditional forms. While some data suggest that these new media approaches may influence brand selection and consumption decisions, it is less clear whether promotions, sponsored events, or nontraditional advertising have effects beyond those obtained with traditional ads. Nontraditional advertising may be more carefully targeted at specific groups of consumers (e.g., mall shoppers), but it seems to have a direct effect only when it involves lower prices or increased availability. Other less salient forms of communication (e.g., a logo on a shirt) are less likely to have an influence on aggregate alcohol consumption, although they may influence brand choice and the circumstances of consumption. The authors conclude that the central research question is not whether nontraditional media are more effective than traditional approaches but rather which strategies are most effective for communicating with a particular audience.

Michael Mazis' commentary, "Conducting Research on Nontraditional Media in the Marketing of Alcoholic Beverages," begins by challenging several of the myths related to nontraditional media (e.g., advertisers are able to target their efforts to legal-age drinkers). He then identifies several of the difficulties in conducting research on nontraditional media, asking, for example, how it is possible for a researcher to study exposure of subjects to teeshirts or to simulate an "event" in a laboratory. To address the research questions of interest, Mazis recommends developmental studies that emphasize the processes used by adolescents and children in learning about alcoholic beverages. Such studies should be based on theories about how a particular medium is likely to work, and they should examine intermediate variables such as perceptions rather than behavioral outcomes like alcohol consumption.

In "Reconceptualizing Alcohol Advertising Effects: A Consumer Psychology Perspective," Joel Cohen recommends exploring six different object–concept associations, then examining how these associations affect behavior toward alcohol as the object. For example, advertisers sometimes seek to foster the association between their product and a social identity (e.g., the product and a rugged individualist or "macho" image). He argues that the link between object–concept associations and behavior toward the object is well established and that alcohol researchers should proceed on the same premise followed by advertising researchers in explicitly examining individual ads or categories of ads. By determining "what has been conveyed and the effect on related beliefs and attitudes (assuming the subsequent probabilistic link to behavior)," alcohol researchers will be better able to measure the likelihood of an advertising effect and to identify portrayals that are problematic.

The paper by Lawrence Wallack and William DeJong, "Mass Media and Public Health: Moving the Focus From the Individual To the Environment," shifts the focus in this volume from commercial advertising and program content to the activities of health educators and public health advocates. Wallack and DeJong identify three general approaches to using the media to prevent alcohol-related problems: public service announcements (PSAs), comprehensive health communication campaigns, and media advocacy. They assert that PSAs rest on the view that a lack of knowledge is the source of unhealthy behaviors such as drinking and driving. This approach reinforces the view that such behaviors are personal problems solved through individual behavior change, thereby minimizing government responsibility for addressing the underlying social and economic conditions. According to Wallack and DeJong, comprehensive community-based health campaigns show more promise than the individual approach, although the results have been mixed. In designing and implementing such campaigns, health communicators are amassing knowledge about the resources, expertise, and commitment required for success. Media advocacy, which complements health campaigns, rests on the view that public health problems are the result of social, economic, and political conditions. The twin goals of media advocacy are (1) to gain access to the media to tell a particular story and (2) to frame that story so that it focuses on the policy issues rather than the unhealthy behavior of individuals.

Sally Casswell's "The Nature and Effectiveness of Media Advocacy, Counteradvertising, and Health Promotion Messages" provides a cross-cultural perspective on health communication efforts. Echoing Thorson's emphasis on the synergistic impact produced by the combination of the elements in a strategic plan, Casswell illustrates the dynamic effect of involving both community workers and the mass media in New Zealand's alcohol-problem prevention campaign. She also observes that emphasizing environmental changes (e.g., drunk driving enforcement) may reinforce individual change efforts (e.g., by providing formerly heavy drinkers with an acceptable reason for drinking less). Casswell suggests that promising research related to media advocacy should include documenting both the process by which media advocacy campaigns develop and qualitatively assessing the likely outcome of those campaigns.

The final chapter, "Alcohol and the Mass Media: Issues, Approaches, and Research Directions," is the editor's synthesis of key points and central themes raised by the discussion that took place during the 2 days the Working Group convened. Among those themes were questions about what we really know about the effects of alcohol advertising and marketing on consumption in general and on specific vulnerable populations like youths under 21 years of age; the application of general advertising and marketing techniques to *alcohol* marketing; measurement issues, particularly the question of appropriate endpoints or outcome variables and ways to address issues of causality; how to determine what audiences perceive and understand from mass-media portrayals of alcohol; research priorities for the next generation of alcohol-advertising studies; and policy implications emerging from research related to alcohol and the mass media. From the diversity of perspectives on the value and limits of research on the presentation of alcohol in the mass media emerged a rich array of suggestions for future studies that may ultimately lead to more effective policies.

ACKNOWLEDGMENTS

This volume has been the work of many people who deserve grateful acknowledgment here. I want to commend the authors who wrote the articles, both for their ideas and their patience during the publication process. Jan Howard, Chief of the Prevention Research Branch at NIAAA, deserves credit for guidance and support throughout the process. Captain Patricia Mail helped review the conference papers, provided invaluable support in finding and checking elusive references, and took the initial steps in editing the conference transcripts and identifying important themes. Nancy Colladay's skill in planning and managing the logistics of the original Working Group were essential. I am also grateful to Diana O'Donovan, who managed the contract for publishing this volume, and to Beatrice Kessler and her staff at Cygnus Corporation, who were responsible for the copy editing, typesetting, and artwork.

The Mass Media, Alcohol, and Culture: An Overview

Chapter 1

Alcohol in American Culture

George Gerbner[1]

Alcohol and other drugs have a long history of remedial, recreational, and ceremonial functions. The industrial and media revolutions swept away most of the traditional controls of scarcity, custom, and ritual. Except where ideological, political, and other (usually religious) inhibitions limit or forbid their uses, alcoholic beverages are now commodities sold in unlimited quantities to serve individual desires and to further competitive institutional and geopolitical interests. No longer homemade and community-bound, beverage alcohol is now part of a mass production and marketing process.

Culturally supported behaviors that undermine health, such as the misuse of alcohol, claim many more lives than could be accounted for through lack of access to good medical care or unsuspected environmental hazards.[2] Yet alcohol presents a difficult prevention problem. It is legally obtained and widely used and enjoyed. While its devastation is vast, its lethal toll is highly concentrated. Six-and-a-half percent of drinkers consume 50 percent of all alcoholic beverages (National Institute on Alcohol Abuse and Alcoholism 1987). Nearly one-third of all drivers involved in fatal crashes in the early 1980's were estimated to be drunk, and a 1989 estimate is that one-fourth of all traffic fatalities are intoxicated at the time (National Highway Traffic Safety Administration 1989).

The cost in lives, health, troubled families, worker absenteeism, and economic losses has made "Demon Rum" a perennial moral and political as well as health issue. It precipitated the most coercive intervention in America's habits: Prohibition. Given the continued controversy over public policies related to alcohol and illegal drugs, it may be useful to revisit the experiment of Prohibition.

[1]Annenberg School for Communication, University of Pennsylvania, 3624 Market St., Philadelphia, PA 19104

[2]For a similar review by the author, see Gerbner 1990.

PROHIBITION

Some claim that Prohibition had health benefits, but no one denies that it was a social disaster (Aaron and Musto 1981). In the light of new "wars on drugs," some interest groups propose banning alcohol advertising. However, the industry notes that their products are legal, and thus subject to First Amendment protections (Goodman 1986; McAvoy 1985). The experience of Prohibition may have lessons which inform the current debate.

The National Prohibition Act and the 18th Amendment to the U.S. Constitution (1919–1933) were adopted after many years of agitation and public discussion. Large majorities in Congress voted for it. More States ratified it than any other amendment—46 out of the 48 (Aaron and Musto 1981).

Giant industries, a booming international trade, and thousands of saloon keepers were outlawed without compensation. New enforcement agencies were created, and drastic police powers (including car searches without a warrant) were upheld in the courts. Treaties with other countries were signed to help prevent smuggling. Convictions for the illegal sale of alcohol rose from nearly 18,000 the first year to 53,000 in the last year (Gerbner 1990). Proponents of Prohibition claimed increased overall worker productivity and improved health status. The battle for morality, sobriety, and industry seemed to have been won (Aaron and Musto 1981).

As time went on, there were reports of more drinking by young people than before Prohibition. Stories of widespread smuggling, overcrowded jails, jammed courts, and the activities of underground empires flaunting the law grabbed the headlines. Moral issues were submerged in a storm of indignation and resentment directed against lawlessness and corruption. A review by the Federal Council of Churches (1925) of the research hinted at the absence of cultural supports for Prohibition when it concluded that "the illicit liquor traffic will be finally overcome when and where education in temperate living strongly reinforces the arm of the law" (p. 83).

Historian W.E. Woodward (1938) summed up Prohibition's "colossal failures" by observing that it simply turned the liquor business over to bootleggers.

> They sold liquor poor in quality and high in price, and they paid no taxes. The enormous revenue of the government from the excise tax in liquor vanished in a day. That meant an inevitable increase in the income tax and in the tariff. . . . Although thousands of enforcement officers were employed, the illicit liquor business continued to grow . . . . All the pre-Prohibition evils of liquor persisted, and were worse than ever, because they were beyond government control (p. 781).

When the Depression boosted demands for jobs and revenue, the 18th Amendment was repealed. All limitations—including controls on quality, marketing, price, and minimum legal drinking age—were passed on to a patchwork of liquor laws and regulations. Some former bootleggers emerged as leading industrialists (Haller 1985). And the profits and power of alcohol moved to take major control of a significant segment of media culture to advertise their products.

Prohibition, the last gasp of the Puritan ethic, was a largely moral and ultimately coercive attempt to assert values no longer salient to most Americans (Gusfield 1963). It showed that attempting to suppress behavior without also attending to its cultural roots drives production underground, finances criminal industries and fortunes, and pushes corruption deep into every community. The end of Prohibition marked the end of an era of illusions about laws regulating deeply ingrained and culturally supported behavior.

PREVENTION

Societies have three basic ways of dealing with risky and addictive substances endemic in a culture. The first is to prohibit their production and distribution. Foolproof in theory, prohibition is less effective against organized global marketing that caters to ubiquitous demands (Gerbner 1990).

The second is to impose controls on the weakest links in the chain. Consumers are urged to abstain from or limit consumption, to "Just Say No," even when the most attractive images of life around them say "Yes" (Gerbner 1990).

The third way is prevention. This approach aims to cut demand by addressing its cultural-environmental supports, especially the mass media (Gerbner 1990).

This third line of attack is the least corrupting and coercive. Prevention focuses on countering the daily cultivation of appeals and associations that render the use of alcohol and other addictive substances compelling and resistant to change. Yet health education by itself cannot match the mass appeal of alcohol promotion and its pervasive cultural influence.

The cultural preventive approach raises economic, legal, and political issues. Speech and the press, even if harmful or offensive, receive considerable protection under the First Amendment. That protection is not absolute; it is balanced with other constitutionally protected values. The courts have been defining and refining, sometimes inconsistently, the permissible limitations on commercial speech.

Ironically, although the Constitution forbids the abridgement of free speech, the power of global mass media conglomerates gives them the ability to strongly influence messages which, in turn, shape public opinion (Wallack 1981). This makes it necessary to consider new ways of realizing both the principles of the First Amendment and the interests of public health under changing cultural circumstances. It requires the development of mechanisms by which the public can participate in cultural policymaking and calls for greater diversity of health-related representations in the media. The complex regulatory and self-regulatory context in which media operate reflects the checkered history of such attempts.

Federal Alcohol Policies

Congress has given the Federal Trade Commission (FTC) general authority to regulate deceptive or unfair business practices. The responsibility is shared with the Department of the Treasury with regard to alcohol advertising. The U.S. Surgeon General and the Department of Health and Human Services develop goals and policy on public health and prevention.

The Federal Alcohol Administration Act of 1935 gives the Treasury Department's Bureau of Alcohol, Tobacco, and Firearms (BATF) specific responsibility for controlling false and misleading, as well as "obscene or indecent," statements in alcohol advertisements (27 USC 4). BATF regulations demand disclosure of alcoholic content and quality in distilled spirits and prohibit "disparaging of a competitor's products" (Gerbner 1990, p. 58). BATF regulations also govern advertising content, such as the use of athletes in ads.

BATF acts as a buffer between the industry and the public. When a proposed change in its advertising code evoked over 10,000 letters asking for tighter restrictions, the Bureau expressed concern about beer advertising at sports and entertainment events and about the number of brewery-sponsored activities on college campuses (Heath 1985; Mosher and Wallack 1981; Smith 1985). In 1986, BATF changed its policy to permit active athletes to appear in beer advertisements, as long as they were not shown drinking it.

Responding to strong, organized community efforts (Rothenberg 1988; Wallack et al. 1993) BATF banned PowerMaster, a malt liquor targeted at black communities and touted for its high alcohol content in violation of the law (Shapiro 1992; Wallack et al. 1993). The Bureau also revoked approval of the label for Black Death vodka for making a blatant and misleading appeal to the young (Kurtzman 1992; Marin Institute 1992). And BATF responded to groups protesting against Crazy Horse, another malt liquor (Center for Science in the Public Interest 1992*a*). But the G. Heileman Brewing Co., marketer of both PowerMaster and Crazy Horse, soon introduced the same product under a new name (*Multinational Monitor* 1992; Wallack et al. 1993).

The affected industries usually respond to BATF concerns. They promised to abide by the wishes of college administrations regarding easy availability and promotion of beer on campuses (Wallack et al. 1993). More recently, however, wineries were reported to have charged "censorship" when BATF opposed their therapeutic claims (Center for Science in the Public Interest 1992*b*; Jensen 1992). And the manufacturer of Black Death vodka took the agency to court rather than comply (Taylor et al. 1992).

The activism of the 1960's and early 1970's led to the adoption of such measures as the ban on broadcast cigarette advertising, warnings on ads for tobacco products, drug disclosure and labeling requirements, and the elimination of most hard liquor commercials from the airwaves. When the FTC proposed to regulate television advertising directed at children, the issue became moot when Congress acted to curtail the FTC's regulatory power to control unfair advertising practices on an industry-wide basis (Gerbner 1990; Wallack et al. 1993).

A consumer survey by the trade paper *Advertising Age* (Winski 1990) showed that 73.5 percent favor health warnings on beer, wine, and liquor advertising; 60 percent believe that warning labels will have some effect on alcoholic beverage consumption; and 42 percent even favor a ban on alcoholic beverage advertising. But the FTC ruled that there was no reliable basis on which to conclude that alcohol advertising significantly affects alcohol abuse (Associated Press 1990; Federal Trade Commission 1984, 1985; Gerbner 1990).

Consumer groups worry about weak regulations and policies (Mosher 1979; Syracuse Peace Council 1990), and even some industry voices warned that weakening regulatory oversight could reduce the government's power to protect them against measures by States and other agencies (Mosher 1979). Even *Advertising Age* warned that "consumer activists are increasingly taking their complaints against national advertisers to a few receptive state attorneys general" (Colford 1986, p. 82).

It took a relatively active Federal Communications Commission (FCC) and a court order to admit tobacco counteradvertising under the Fairness Doctrine (Wallack et al. 1993). But in the mid-1980's the FCC abandoned the implementation of the Fairness Doctrine, allowing many of its public interest provisions to lapse (Syracuse Peace Council 1990). The tactics that drove cigarette commercials from the air in 1971 proved to be virtually impossible to apply to alcohol advertising, especially in the deregulatory climate of the 1980's (Associated Press 1990; Gerbner 1990).

Broadcasters were "haunted by the memory of what happened with cigarettes and determined to protect their hefty beer and wine billings," according to *Advertising Age* columnist Maurine Christopher (1985, p. 46). With $750 million in television advertising to protect, the National Association of Broadcasters (NAB) joined with advertisers and the alcoholic beverage industry to block regulation. The NAB announced that saving beer and wine commercials would be the organization's "number-one priority" (Christopher 1985).

Concern about mass media as a source of health-related messages was evident in the 1972 Report of the Surgeon General's Advisory Committee on Television and Social Behavior (U.S. Congress 1972). An "update" 10 years later (National Institute of Mental Health 1982) also included studies on health and consumer behavior. A workshop convened by U.S. Surgeon General C. Everett Koop in 1988 recommended the elimination of alcohol advertising and promotion of events and publications that reach a high proportion of underage youth (U.S. Surgeon General 1989). His successor, Antonia Novello, stepped up the pressure on alcohol advertising to youth and complained about the lack of enforceable laws and codes (Taylor et al. 1992). "Brewers Fight Back" was the headline in an issue of *Advertising Age* announcing the industry's counterattack (Teinowitz and Colford 1991).

Congress

The 21st Amendment to the Constitution repealed Prohibition and left the re-legalized alcohol industry struggling under a patchwork of State regulations. Within 2 years Congress passed the Federal Alcohol Administration Act, which remains the basic Federal statute under which the alcoholic beverage industry operates (Gerbner 1990).

The Act is intended to control unfair competition and regulate the production, labeling, and advertising of alcoholic beverages. The industry opposes changes to the Act, because tampering with it will be likely to open a veritable Pandora's box of legal issues.

New bills emerge in each session of Congress, submitted by legislators sympathetic to consumer and health issues. Typical bills include measures to require public service time for antidrug messages; health and safety warnings on alcoholic beverage advertising; banning beer and wine commercials; eliminating the tax deductibility of alcohol advertising; supporting State educational programs; allowing State attorneys general to sue national advertisers when Federal agencies fail to act; and controlling or banning "lifestyle" advertising.

Industry and media opposition often has succeeded in delaying or diluting advertising control legislation. However, in 1984 Congress made highway funding contingent on States raising the minimum drinking age to 21. Although in 1989 it passed a law to include warnings on alcoholic beverage containers (but not in advertising and promotion), some beer cans still promote car racing while at the same time urging drinkers not to drive.

The Courts

Until 1975, commercial speech was outside the ambit of the First Amendment. That year the Supreme Court overturned a statute of the State of Virginia that prohibited the advertising of abortions (legal since 1973), because the specific information the ad conveyed was responding to a clear public need and thus was essential for the maintenance of democracy (*Bigelow v. Virginia*, 421 U.S. 809 1975).

The courts gradually expanded their protection of commercial speech, but this did not preclude specific restrictions that advanced substantial public interest. The Supreme Court also held that to be protected, commercial speech must concern lawful activity and must not be misleading (Taylor et al. 1992).

The statute that banned tobacco commercials on television and radio set legal precedents for the regulation of alcohol advertising. The Court upheld the constitutionality of the ban on grounds that (1) while printed messages require literacy and an affirmative act to be read, broadcast messages are "in the air" and virtually inescapable; (2) the public owns the airways, and broadcasting is a regulated and licensed activity in the public interest; and (3) the loss of advertising revenue per se does not deprive the broadcaster of First Amendment rights. A review by Schofield (1985) concluded that "should legislation be enacted banning alcoholic beverage advertising from radio and television, any First Amendment challenge to that law is most likely to fail" (p. 539).

Suing alcohol and other drug companies for failure to provide sufficient warnings about health hazards had been a longstanding and (except for tobacco) often fruitless practice. In a rare ruling, the widow of a brewery worker who became an alcoholic after taking advantage of free beer at work was held entitled to workers' compensation benefits (*The New York Times* 1990).

Changes in liability law after 1985 prompted several lawsuits that made judicial history. Hosts were held liable for the drunk-driving accidents of their guests. Sexist beer ads were held responsible for a repressive work environment. And in *Posadas de Puerto Rico Associates v. Tourism Company* (1986), the U.S. Supreme Court upheld a ban on advertising that, although not deceptive, promotes products or activities deemed harmful.

The *Posadas* ruling seemed to have far-reaching implications for the advertising of addictive substances. A legal analysis of the "Future of Alcoholic Beverage Advertising" (Hovland and Wilcox 1987) as a consequence of the *Posadas* decision concluded that "advertisers have good cause for concern." Another legal review by Trauth and Huffman (1988) pointed out that while the Court has so far refused to examine its First Amendment implications, "after *Posadas* there can be no question of the ability of the State to restrain such commercial speech" (p. 56).

But subsequently, the FTC interpreted *Posadas* as requiring empirical evidence that advertising alone causes significant harm. This is a difficult, if not impossible, task, as becomes evident when the problems of conducting research on communication effects are considered.

Industry Self-Regulation

Trade associations and media groups develop advertising codes to balance the competing demands of their client companies and to protect them from consumer pressure and public regulation. Advertisers also depend on broadcasting network censors for dealing with consumer and competitor challenges.

Another forum for complaints is the National Advertising Division (NAD) of the Council of Better Business Bureaus. If the NAD fails to resolve a controversy, appeal can be made to the advertising industry's National Advertising Review Board (NARB). Many of the claims seem to be petty competitive challenges, at least by outside standards.

The Distilled Spirits Council of the United States (DISCUS) approved a Code of Good Practice in 1983 that keeps its members from advertising liquor on radio and television, in comics or religious or youth publications, on movie screens, and "in any manner directed or primarily intended to appeal to persons below the legal drinking age" (Distilled Spirits Council of the United States 1983; Gerbner 1990, p. 63).

The Brewing Industry Advertising Guidelines adopted in 1984 similarly discourage appeals to minors; religious, scientific, or educational claims; the condoning of drunk driving or drunkenness in general; on-camera drinking; "improperly" disparaging comparisons to competing beers; and association with illegal or disreputable circumstances. The guidelines also recommend that "taverns or other places portrayed in beer advertisements should always be depicted as well-kept and respectable places" (Gerbner 1990, p. 63, citing the Beer Institute 1984).

The Wine Institute's Code of Advertising Standards, adopted in 1978 by California wine growers, stresses that "when subscribers to the code use wine advertising which visually depicts a scene or setting where wine is to be served, such advertising shall include foods . . ." (Gerbner 1990, p. 63). Excessive drinking, loss of control, feats of daring, underage models or appeals, medicinal values, the use of athletes, and demeaning portrayals of any group are to be avoided. Attuned to the more mature sensibilities of their markets, wine growers urge depictions of "wholesome persons enjoying their lives and illustrating the role of wine in a mature life style" (Wine Institute 1978; Gerbner 1990, p. 64). However, 40 percent of all wine sold in the United States is made by nonmember firms who are not bound even by these mild strictures (Gerbner 1990).

All of these codes are voluntary, and their application to trade association members is private. Any firm that does not wish to comply may leave the association. Compliance records are not public. Violations are evident to the casual observer and are occasionally exposed by public interest and community groups. A successful campaign in Philadelphia drove the malt liquor PowerMaster out of black neighborhoods. The Marin Institute for Alcohol and Other Drug Prevention publicized the targeting of low-income Latino neighborhoods with posters that violate the guidelines, including a billboard of two priests looking heavenward and holding large glasses of brandy, with the caption "Tomarlo no es pecado" ("To drink is not a sin") (Yanez 1992).

Complaints by business competitors are most likely to get a hearing from the Council of Better Business Bureaus' NAD. Marketing and promotional strategies that go beyond advertising (sponsoring sports teams and events, youth festivals, celebrity appearances, interviews, or contests) are out of reach of most advertising codes. The growing practice of product placement is another way to skirt industry codes. Messages and images embedded in entertainment and news often promote the forbidden themes in more credible and legally protected ways.

Faced with the results of its own private survey that showed wide public disapproval of alcohol advertising, the alcoholic beverage industry set up a new consortium, the Century Council, to launch a campaign to reduce drunk driving and underage drinking. It also unveiled a new Code of Responsible Marketing and Advertising Practices that prohibits the use of active athletes, models under 25, and appeals to minors. Member firms also agreed to obtain approval of college officials before marketing on campus or at college-sponsored events (Levin 1991).

Health advocates view the Council and the new code as attempts to avoid some of the political and public relations setbacks of the tobacco industry. They also point out that the three major U.S. brewers control two-thirds of the U.S. beer market and are most frequently cited for marketing to minors and promoting risk-taking behavior, but are not members of the Century Council (Advocacy Institute 1991*a*).

Media Codes

The old Motion Picture Production Code (in effect through 1968) advised that "The use of liquor in American life, when not required by the plot or for proper characterization, will not be shown" (Motion Picture Association of America, N.D.). It also proscribed the portrayal of illegal drug use in detail or "in such a way as to stimulate curiosity" (Gerbner 1990, p. 66). Ironically, a number of powerful antidrug films such as *The Lost Weekend* and *The Man with the Golden Arm* hastened the demise of the Code and its replacement in 1968 with the weaker voluntary Classification and Ratings Administration (Gerbner 1990; Tusher 1986).

Alcohol and drug use was not codified until 1986. At that time the Classification and Ratings Administration began to apply no less a rating than PG-13 ("may be inappropriate for children under 13") to films that show any use of drugs. However, it rejected demands for a new "SA" (substance abuse) rating to warn parents about features that "rationalize or glamorize the use of drugs" (Tusher 1986, p. 1).

The NAB Television Code that had included the "family viewing" policy was attacked in court, prompting NAB to abandon it. Code administration was left to the networks and stations. With deregulation, the dismantling of the code administrations, and layoffs of staff in the 1980's, the responsibility for program standards became dispersed and diluted.

The defunct NAB Television Code forbade the advertising of hard liquor and urged that beer and wine be "presented in the best of good taste and discretion" and not consumed on-camera. It cautioned against commercials that "convey the impression of, or appear to promote, excessive consumption of beer or wine" or "encourage use of these products by young people" or involve hazardous activities, athletic ability, or sexual attractiveness (Gerbner 1990, p. 65).

These strictures seem quaint by today's standards; and yet the network guidelines that are still in force, at least on paper, use similar language. The NBC code adds, for example, that the use of alcoholic beverages "should not be portrayed as being necessary to maintain social status, obtain personal achievement, relieve stress, or solve personal problems" (Gerbner 1990, p. 65). With respect to dramatic portrayals, the ABC guidelines urge avoidance of "glamorization" and suggest including the occasional refusal of an alcoholic beverage.

Network censors and other review boards pay most attention to competitive complaints and demands for advertising claim substantiation. Claims that promote the association of alcohol and other drugs with attractive living are rarely monitored or checked (Office of the Inspector General 1991, pp. 16–17). In fact, there is no authority, public or private, that systematically monitors compliance with or enforcement of codes or guidelines.

Furthermore, there is no reliable system of communication by which either public or private codes can reach those who actually produce the ads, commercials, and programs. A pilot study of the application of existing guidelines to the making of beer commercials (Meister 1987) found that the producers of the commercials, and even advertising agency account executives, had little specific knowledge about the laws and codes that presumably guide their work.

Citizen Action

In the 1960's the nascent consumer rights movement generated a media reform driven by concerns about juvenile delinquency, health, children's programming, violence on the air, and other issues around which large constituencies (and thus congressional leadership) could be mobilized. This movement did not survive the 1970's. Its momentum was blunted by a distracting and ultimately failed attempt to rewrite the Communications Act of 1934 and by an industry counterattack claiming, among other things, that new communication technologies are changing the structure of the industry anyway. (The movement is chronicled by Pertschuk [1982] and Rowland [1983].)

Since 1984, the Center for Science in the Public Interest (CSPI) has coordinated Project SMART (Stop Marketing Alcohol on Radio and Television), a coalition of some 25 citizen groups. This coalition supported legislation and petitioned the FTC to place warnings and other restrictions on alcohol advertising and to ban beer and wine commercials from the airwaves. The FTC rejected the petition and agreed with the advertisers and broadcasters that there was no convincing evidence that advertising by itself necessarily leads to abuse (Gerbner 1990). In 1992, CSPI headed up another coalition of 22 national organizations petitioning the FTC again to act on a broad range of alcohol marketing practices that "violate established public policies to minimize alcohol-related problems" (Taylor et al. 1992, p. 1).

Public health groups advocate reduction or elimination of subsidies for drug industries, higher alcohol excise taxes (which now amount to about $15 billion a year, a fraction of the damage), and the elimination of alcohol advertising as a tax-deductible business expense (this measure alone would raise $2 billion annually). They object to U.S. export supports such as the Agriculture Department's grant of $200 million to several distillers to promote sales abroad (Jacobson 1992). A grass-roots citizen action project of broader scope launched in the early 1990's is the Cultural Environment Movement (1993).

Industry Under Pressure

The alcoholic beverage industry spends $1.3 billion a year on advertising and pays 4 to 5 percent of the total cost of U.S. commercial media. More than half of these advertising expenditures are spent on television for beer and wine commercials; some 18 percent goes to magazines; 8 percent to newspapers; and the rest to outdoor, cable, and other media (Taylor et al. 1992).

Since the mid-1980's, the boom in the sale of distilled spirits has shifted into reverse. After growing at the rate of 3 to 4 percent a year in the 1960's (when the "baby boom" generation reached drinking age), the beer market went flat. And the "wine boom" of the 1970's and early 1980's, riding the crest of a demographic and lifestyle swell, also began to fade (Taylor et al. 1992).

Many pressures have contributed to this shift in drinking habits and sales. Health and calorie consciousness, the graying of the prime beer-drinking population, the substitution of wine for hard liquor, the raising of the drinking age in many States, the bans on "happy hours," the rising concern about drinking on campus and in the workplace, warning signs in many liquor stores, and lawsuits making the server legally responsible—all contributed to a change in the social climate regarding drinking. The Federal excise tax, which had previously been lowered to give industry a boost, rose by 19 percent in 1985. State taxes followed suit. The militant campaigns of MADD, the activism of SADD, and the petition by national organizations for a ban on all alcohol advertising directed at or reaching the young were additional manifestations of this shift (Gerbner 1990).

Despite the decline in overall sales, the numbers of adult alcoholics and students binge drinking were on the rise (Celis 1991; Shipp 1985). An increasing proportion of problem drinkers is made up of young people, women, and minorities. A National Association of Junior Leagues study found that more than half the women being treated for alcoholism in New York are 18 to 34 years old. The director of the study said that "We are seeing the first generation of women who report drinking for the purpose of getting drunk" (Collins 1987).

Alcohol remains a profitable business. The rising cost of advertising and the advantages of added marketing muscle encourage both conglomeration and concentration of ownership and control. The trend toward diversification and consolidation marks "a shift from weaker to stronger hands, a trend toward deeper pockets . . ." (Winters 1986, p. 28). Alcohol and other drug conglomerates now own television and other media, popular soft drinks and food products, theme parks, and many other enterprises. They sponsor sports events, art exhibits, concerts, and youth magazines. Philip Morris' acquisition of the beer giant Miller Brewing Co. and Coca Cola's acquisition of The Wine Spectrum represent further efforts to diversify and stabilize their markets, as well as to extend them into newer areas (Gerbner 1990).

Alcoholic beverage advertisers are exploring a variety of ways to protect and extend their reach. Brewers are the most vigorous in this effort. "Faced with similar problems," a marketing study reported, "many other industries would have pulled in their marketing horns long ago. . . . The brewing industry's response has been almost the opposite. . . . [It] is doing everything possible to attract new customers, and one brewing industry executive calls it a 'panic'" (Hume 1985, p. 16). While most advertising budgets shrank, the top three beer brands increased their advertising by more than 20 percent (Nutrition Action Health Letter 1992).

"Beer advertisers are calling in the heavy hitters in what could be an all-out battle to stop the National Collegiate Athletic Association (NCAA) from banning beer advertising on postseason tournament telecasts," reported *Advertising Age* (Teinowitz and Gordon 1988, p. 31). NCAA officials pointed out that the commercials clash with its own prevention efforts and public service messages. But the Anheuser-Busch Vice President for Marketing argued that "The sponsorship of beer companies is good not only for college athletics, but for the television industry because it gives the opportunity for millions of Americans to see these events on television" (Teinowitz and Gordon 1988, p. 31).

Some firms are promoting products with low alcohol content, offering more sobriety and fewer calories per glass. Other brewers make grants to safe driving campaigns. Still others, like some California wineries, are fighting regulation on the censorship front. One vintner accused BATF of suppressing therapeutic claims about wine as "inherently misleading and particularly deceptive" (Jensen 1992, p. 1). Another vintner accused BATF of "deliberately distorting information about the effects of alcohol so it can accomplish its goal of reducing consumption 25% by the year 2000" (Jensen 1992, p. 8).

In a publication of the National Beer Wholesalers Association (NBWA), *Beer Perspectives*, an editorial referred to a conference convened by the Office of Substance Abuse Prevention (OSAP) as "a direct assault on commercial free speech" and "a war against the American way of life" (National Beer Wholesalers Association 1991, p. 2). The NBWA mobilized 109 U.S. Representatives to co-sign a letter to the General Accounting Office requesting an investigation of OSAP's grass-roots prevention efforts as a use of taxpayer dollars for lobbying purposes (OSAP 1992). That investigation found no violations on the part of OSAP.

The response to the advertising–broadcasting alliance focuses mostly on bills before Congress requiring warnings on ads and commercials and restricting sports sponsorship or promotion. According to *Broadcasting*, a media newsletter, a major brewer hosts an all-industry luncheon at the annual convention of the National Association of Broadcasters. At the 1992 luncheon, ice buckets of a major brand beer were at every table, and logo key chains with the inscription "Friends Know When To Say When" were at every place setting. Furthermore, a featured speaker well known to the industry told his audience of 2,500 broadcasters that "Our industries must look out for each other. That's what friends do" (Sukow 1992, pp. 34–35).

STORIES THAT SELL: ADVERTISING AND MEDIA MARKETS

Ads are stories that sell. This involves the cultivation of identities and a sense that one is in need, even worthy, of what is being sold. It also involves avoidance or suppression, if possible, of information that may help the buyer rather than the seller.

Despite being surrounded with sales messages, or perhaps because of it, a Consumer Federation of America survey concluded that "Americans are not smart shoppers and their ignorance costs them billions, threatens their health and safety and undermines the economy" (Scanlan 1990).

Laws, codes, and regulations notwithstanding, no American can escape growing up and living with vivid images of daring, sexy, happy, and healthy drinkers. A young woman who got drunk and crashed her car told her psychologist, "I've been drinking beer since I was fourteen . . . . I just like the action." She said she had never seen an unhappy drinker on television and asked if she could ever be as happy as the "Beer Bunnies" (Moog 1990, pp. 48–49). Ten-year-olds responding to a survey could name more brands of beer than names of American presidents (*Harper's Magazine* 1988). The FTC once noted that funds spent promoting happy alcohol images are "several hundred times greater" than those spent alerting the public to their hazards (Federal Trade Commission 1981, pp. 2–3).

Holidays are promoted as special occasions for drinking. A major brewer pioneered itself as "The Official Beer of Halloween" in 1983. Despite warnings about increasingly rambunctious "fright nights" and alcoholic street parties, another major brewer led the way in 1990 by spending more than a million dollars on a Halloween campaign complete with displays, stickers, posters, sports paraphernalia, and commercials featuring such slogans as "I Vant To Drink Your Bud" and "What's Your Bud Type" (Advocacy Institute 1990, 1991*b*; Ryan and Mosher 1991).

A typical late fall newspaper supplement features a two-page spread of a misty Christmas scene. Seven young people are sitting in a festive living room, glasses in hand, roaring with laughter. Three open bottles are between them, and three unopened bottles are behind them. "Follow your instincts," the copy urges. "This year do it right." The advice is repeated on the bottom of the ad in large type beside another four bottles: "This year do it right." (*Philadelphia Inquirer* 1986).

MEDIA MARKETS

Advertising is also the principal form of media patronage. The marketing process that shapes the cultural mainstream is based on a hidden levy that is included in the price of advertised goods. The money consumers pay in higher prices is used by producers to support commercial media in exchange for exposing an audience to stories that sell the advertiser's goods, services, ideas, values, and policies. Media managers are, of course, free to ignore or reject all advertising—and to go broke. But no major medium can meet the cost of production and make a profit without an advertising subsidy or other promotional income unless they get a subsidy from the government, like the Corporation for Public Broadcasting. Thus, the income of the media comes largely from the hidden levy on consumer goods that some call taxation without representation. The consumer, as citizen, has little or no say about or control over the process and no choice but to pay the levy and play the role of consumer, irrespective of using or liking the media service. Citizens "pay when they wash, not when they watch." The money included in the cost of a bar of soap pays for the soap opera that sells it, along with its lifestyle and values (Lowery 1980). The system is shored up by legislation that makes advertising a tax-deductible business expense and thus fully available for media support.

A.C. Nielsen, the broadcast rating and market research company, provides point-of-sale information to brewers, distillers, importers, and vintners through its Alcoholic Beverage Service. Clients buying the service can assess the sales and marketing strategies of their own brands as well as those of their competitors (Nielsen Marketing Research 1985).

The heaviest concentration of alcohol ads is in such upscale magazines as *The New Yorker*, *Scientific American*, and *Psychology Today*, and in men's magazines. Minority-oriented magazines also have a higher-than-average concentration of alcohol ads. The use of celebrities is the most frequent device (one in four ads) in black adult-oriented magazines (Strickland and Finn 1984).

A study of lifestyle themes in a large sample of alcohol ads in 13 national magazines (Breed and De Foe 1979) observed that *Playboy* and *Ebony* devoted the most space to these ads, followed by *Harper's*, *The New Yorker*, and *Time*. The most frequent themes associated drinking with wealth, success, and luxury (28 percent); social approval and friendship (22 percent); relaxation (22 percent); and pleasure (22 percent). These were followed by exotic adventure, individualism, and sex (each more than 10 percent). The implied association between the beverage and the promised reward could stand a test of logic in only 7 percent of the ads. Appeals to moderation were made in only 10 of the 454 ads in the sample, but 28 seemed to encourage more than moderate drinking as implied by the number of glasses and bottles per person. Appeals to tradition, history, royalty, and military or literary success were made in more than one-third of the ads. The researchers questioned whether the ads supported heavy drinking (as well as distorted images of the "good life," past and present) by their glamorous associations and denial of problems. "Alcohol ads," they concluded, "show only the pleasant and relaxed face of alcohol while blacking out the ugly face" (Breed and De Foe 1979, p. 521).

Ethnic and Minority Markets

There is growing emphasis on extending the market into minority groups and ethnic communities that have not been prime advertising targets in the past (Milloy 1991). Targeting minorities requires a keen eye for the nuances of the culture.

Some marketers turn to minority advertising agencies to develop special campaigns. *Advertising Age* (McGeehan 1985) described how some of these agencies handled their alcohol accounts: Burrell Advertising of Chicago, a leading black-owned agency, was given the "black advertising account" by B-F Spirits Ltd., marketers of Canadian Mist. "The agency knew that the rugged outdoorsy general-market theme wouldn't play in a black consumer market. . . . Burrell's solution was to position drinking Canadian Mist as an event. . . . Each 'Misting' ad shows a smartly dressed couple. . . . against a vague background. . . . You didn't really know where they were. The 'Misting' campaign changed the face of liquor advertising . . . . Canadian Mist's share of sales to blacks has risen from about 7 percent to 25 percent" (McGeehan 1985, p. 5).

Jack Daniels Distillery, a Tennessee-based company with a "distinctly white, Southern image," also hired Burrell to launch a black-targeted effort. "The agency was careful to capture the history of Jack Daniels while skirting around its southernness," explains the manager of its liquor account, because blacks' memories of the "good ol' days in the South" tend to be negative (McGeehan 1985, p. 7).

Another African-American agency, Lockhart & Pettus of New York, was engaged by Hiram Walker's Canadian Club to create a "black version" of its "Be a Part of It" campaign prepared by the firm's general market agency. Lockhart reasoned that "'Being a part of it' is not always desirable or possible for blacks," and created an ad showing an African-American couple attending a fashion show and toasting each other. The caption in large type is "Forget About the Rest." "A copy change that suggests ignoring the rest of the world makes sense," Lockhart says. "It also supports a Hiram Walker program that pays tribute to black designers and the company's sponsorship of fund-raising fashion shows" (Schleier 1985, p. 19).

Advertising in Spanish may escape the scrutiny given to other campaigns. For example, Spanish-language television stations regularly advertised hard liquor until 1989, when activists called attention to the practice. And a survey in a New Jersey Latino community found 145 billboards and store ads, compared with seven in a nearby white neighborhood (Yanez 1992).

Relatively untapped market potentials also exist in countries where limited resources and cultural traditions have kept drinking within bounds and where advertising and marketing regulations are weak or nonexistent. Israel was such a market when a major brewer entered in 1984 with an aggressive campaign to promote "new American-style beer-drinking habits" (Weiss 1986, p. 3). The campaign highlighted the fact that the company's beer had an alcohol content higher than that of domestic beers, which is a practice illegal in the United States. This was first reported on the business page of the *St. Louis Post-Dispatch* by Howard Groller in 1985.

Youth Markets

Since 1975, the annual national survey of approximately 17,000 seniors conducted by the Institute for Social Research at the University of Michigan (known as the Monitoring the Future study) has provided information on trends in drug and alcohol use among adolescents (Johnston et al., in press). For every senior class in the past 19 years, alcohol is the drug of choice. In 1993, 76 percent of the seniors had used alcohol during the previous year and 50 percent had been drunk. Moreover, 28 percent responded that they had gone on a drinking binge (i.e., consumed 5 or more drinks consecutively on at least one occasion during the last 2 weeks). Nor is drinking limited to seniors. The same survey found that 42 percent of the 10th graders and 26 percent of the 8th graders had used alcohol at least once in the prior month and 20 and 8 percent, respectively, had been drunk during that period.

Johnston et al. (1991) also found that 64 percent of 8th graders and 83 percent of 10th graders stated that it was "fairly" or "very" easy to obtain alcohol. While some have older friends purchase it, almost two out of three youth between 7th and 12th grade reported buying it themselves (Office of the Inspector General 1991).

The Department of Health and Human Services reported that junior and senior high school students drink 1.1 billion cans of beer a year, 7th to 12th graders drink 35 percent of all wine coolers, and one-third of high school seniors had consumed five or more drinks at one sitting during the previous 2 weeks (Taylor et al. 1992). Surgeon General Antonia Novello announced the results of a survey that found that half of junior and senior high school students drink alcoholic beverages, and almost half a million go on weekly drinking sprees, many of whom "are already alcoholics and the rest may be on their way." Two out of three teenagers could not tell the difference between some alcoholic and nonalcoholic beverages because they looked so similar in color, labeling, and packaging (Associated Press 1991). A study of freshmen at 14 Massachusetts colleges also found that among those who drink at least once a week, 92 percent of the men and 82 percent of the women consume at least 5 drinks in a row. Half said they wanted to get drunk (Wechsler and Isaac 1992).

The alcoholic beverage industry continues to use cartoon characters and logos on toys and model trains, to hire youth-oriented entertainers, to sponsor family theme parks replete with beer displays, and to promote youth- and sports-oriented events, programs, and media. The industry pays about 20 percent of the cost of sports programming on television and radio (Wallack et al. 1990).

The National Association of Broadcasters engaged a prominent lawyer to help oppose a ban on beer and wine commercials during prime-time sports programs. The NAB President warned that the proposed ban would have "a major impact" on college and university revenues from such programs (*Broadcasting Magazine* 1984, p. 33). The ban did not materialize.

Although MADD and other groups expressed concern about alcohol-sponsored programming targeted at youth, and research findings showed that celebrity endorsements of alcohol products are highly effective with teenagers (Atkin and Block 1983), the BATF altered its interpretation to permit the use of active athletes in beer and wine commercials. But the broadcasting networks, mindful of the ever-present threat of further regulations, refused to take advantage of this new ruling. Athletes and their agents were also cautious. "For athletes, alcohol and substance abuse are such hot issues that a direct beer pitch might well lead to image meltdown," wrote *Advertising Age* columnist Robert Raissman (1986, p. 65).

No such restraint prevails in sponsoring racing (Buchanan and Lev 1990) and other sporting events. One major brewer paid nearly $1 million (not counting expensive television ad time) for the right to use its corporate logo at the 1987 Hagler-Leonard championship bout. "Once in a lifetime," the viewers heard over the loudspeaker, "legends meet in the ring." We are "proud to be the official sponsor of the Super Fight" (Gerbner 1990). A $25 million deal with NBC secured another brewer 3 years of major league baseball broadcasts as well as sponsorship of the 1988 Summer and Winter Olympics. Television viewers of the commercial-saturated Barcelona Olympics of 1992 saw two beer commercials during a typical hour of the games (Gerbner 1990).

The American Automobile Association's Foundation for Traffic Safety reported that beer companies are spending up to $50 million per year on promoting car races, power, and speed (Wallack et al. 1990). Alcohol ads and commercials feature thrilling scenes of fast boating, skiing, and surfing—despite the dangers of combining drinking with risky recreational activities. These ads thus encourage young people to violate all safety rules, codes, guidelines, as well as common sense.

Beer ads on banners, gate signs, athletes' uniforms, and other prominent places at frequently photographed and televised sports and other events circumvent many limitations on youth-oriented advertising. It was striking to see on the front pages of the sports sections of daily newspapers a news shot from the national collegiate track and field championship in which the words "Bud Light" appeared five times in one picture (Litsky 1989). At the same time, the era of "deregulation" has resulted in a 51-percent decrease in issue-oriented public affairs programs that may provide opportunities for education about alcohol (Donahue 1989).

The Busch Gardens and Sea World theme parks are owned and operated by Anheuser-Busch, which advertises its name in youth magazines such as those distributed by the Burger King Kids Club—at 3 million copies, Burger King claims to be the largest publisher of children's magazines in the United States (Hume 1993).

Drinking on Campus

Advertising continues to be directed at college campuses. Alcohol awareness campaigns and other administrative moves have dampened the "Spring Break" party promotions, but they have not fundamentally altered the culture of heavy drinking and sexual suggestiveness associated with alcohol advertising (Office of the Inspector General 1991; Ryan and Mosher 1991).

Magazine supplements folded into college newspapers relied heavily on alcohol (especially beer) advertising, at least until the late 1980's. Half of all national ads in a sample of 32 college papers were for alcoholic beverages (De Foe and Breed 1979). Typical beer ads showed likable rebels flouting the rules and having the time of their lives—with bottles in hand (Ryan and Mosher 1991).

A review of studies reported in the *Chronicle of Higher Education* (Hirschorn 1987, p. 32) concluded that "serious alcohol use among students remains at high levels." Most campus officials consider alcohol drinking by far the most damaging drug problem, promoted by the "glamorization of alcohol use in the media" (Hirschorn 1987, p. 34). An Alcohol Risk Survey of 325 campuses showed that many colleges have failed to back up their policies with adequate abuse prevention programs (Greene 1986). A followup study showed that despite efforts to reduce abuse, only 24 percent of administrators reported that the situation had improved (Magner 1988). Alcohol ads in college papers still accounted for over 10 times more column inches than ads for books and soft drinks combined (Breed et al. 1984).

Campus publishing guidelines have attempted to limit the most extreme forms of alcohol promotion, at least after 1989. But an FTC staff investigation found that about 32 percent of all college newspaper advertising revenue still comes from alcohol, that alcoholic beverage advertising is prevalent in student publications and radio programs, that the alcohol industry sponsors numerous college sports and social events in return for publicity, and that little or no effort is made to exclude the many students under age 21 from these events. Despite these findings, these conditions continue to exist.

Releasing a report on "Alcohol and Youth—Controlling Alcohol Advertising that Appeals to Youth" (Office of the Inspector General 1991) on November 4, 1991, Surgeon General Antonia Novello said that the Federal and State regulations are inadequate, the voluntary codes in industry and the media are unenforceable, and society is sending mixed messages to our children (Taylor et al. 1992). On June 7, 1994, a study was released reporting that an epidemic of binge drinking on college campuses was fueled partly by the fact that the percentage of college women who drink to get drunk has more than tripled over the last 15 years (Rios 1994).

Media Portrayals

Signorielli (1993) summarizes the research on portrayals of alcohol in the media. Males dominate in all portrayals, in addition to the bottle, which is centrally featured in about two-thirds of the commercials and half of the magazine ads. The most common lifestyle appeals are, in order of frequency: social camaraderie, masculinity/femininity, escape, elegance, romance, adventure, social acceptance, sexuality, social esteem, and success. Many ads (42 percent on television; 8 percent in magazines) imply that alcohol can be consumed in great quantities. Few suggest moderation (none on television; 8 percent in magazines), and no ads provide information about harmful consequences (Atkin and Block 1981; Atkin et al. 1983).

Magazine stories, fictional as well as factual, can be seen as "advising" readers on how to act or not to act. Breed et al. (1980), in a study of three popular magazines, found that the quality of advice to readers was uneven. In *Modern Romance*, readers get a picture of drinking as dangerous, while readers of *Playboy* discover that drinking is expected, and readers of *Cosmopolitan* receive mixed messages.

Similarly, in a study on "Comic Book Supercharacters and Their Role in Alcohol Education," Breed and De Foe (1981) found a mixed picture. Superman, of course, never drinks; other superheroes drink only ceremonially; and characters who drink to excess are either villains or derelicts. The Code of the Comic Book Association of America (1971) forbids scenes showing minors drinking alcohol. However, drawings of bottles, glasses, and goblets in the background of some frames suggest drinking, and the alcohol problem is ignored rather than given serious treatment, the researchers conclude (Breed and De Foe 1981).

The Motion Picture Code (in effect through 1968) cautioned against the use of liquor "when not required by the plot for proper characterization." Winick (1983) notes that during the 1960's, about 5 percent, and in 1972 about 9 percent, of films included significant portrayals of drinking. He describes lighter treatments, including the association with sex, in many plays, films, and television programs. He claims that British, French, and Italian films seldom show disinhibition resulting from alcohol; in those films drunks are more likely to fall asleep. He reports that jokes about drinking represent 6 to 8 percent of all jokes, and over half of these deal with the bizarre behavior of heavy drinkers (Winick 1983).

With the rise of television, movies became more specialized and sensational, with more frequent, casual, and explicit alcohol and drug use (Herd 1983). Drinking on television is inescapable. Dillin (1975) found it shown or mentioned in 80 percent of prime-time programs (not counting commercials). Futch and colleagues (1984) observed it on 12 of the 15 most popular prime-time programs, with an average of 2.2 drinking scenes and 5.3 verbal references to alcohol per program hour. The average duration of drinking scenes was 97 seconds, much longer than scenes where nonalcoholic beverages are consumed (40 seconds). Most such scenes took place in homes (42 percent) and bars (17 percent) (Futch et al. 1984). (For further summaries of program content see Brown and MacDonald, chapter 9, this volume.)

Despite the rising concern about alcohol, the frequency of drinking on television has not abated. De Foe et al. (1983) noted a steady increase in alcohol-related acts per hour, from less than five in 1976 to more than eight in 1982. Wallack (1984) reported that the frequency of alcohol use on television rose from 62 percent of all beverages to 74 percent during the 8-year period of the study. The University of Pennsylvania's Cultural Indicators data show that the frequency of references to or portrayals of alcohol has increased since 1969, reaching 70 percent of prime-time programs in the 1980's (Signorielli 1993). More than one-third of all characters in television dramas are shown actually drinking (something commercials are not allowed to do), but less then 2 percent suffer any ill effects (Signorielli 1987). Turow and Coe (1985) studied the incidence of illness in prime time and found that the frequency of an exotic disease like leprosy was the same as that of alcoholism.

Who are the drinkers on television? The Cultural Indicators data show that about 37 percent of major adult characters are seen drinking alcoholic beverages. Unlike in the real world, women on television are as likely to drink as men. Drinkers are as likely as nondrinkers to be good and successful, but more likely than nondrinkers to be serious, and to be married or romantically involved. They are also more likely to be wealthy (Signorielli 1987).

The most frequent reason given for drinking on television is a personal crisis. Drink is a means of dealing with a crisis or tension in 61 percent of significant incidents. Leading actors in prime-time series drink in a crisis 74 percent of the time. Lesser characters drink for social and other reasons. Only a few "bad" characters use alcohol to manipulate other people (Signorielli 1987).

Of 18 drinking and driving episodes analyzed, 4 involved accidents, 5 showed near misses, and 9 were problem free. Of the six "good" characters shown drinking and driving, only one met with an accident (Signorielli 1987).

Despite some memorable films and programs showing the consequences of alcoholism, perhaps the most conspicuously absent character, considering the high number of drinkers, is the problem drinker or alcoholic. Signorielli (1987) reports that the Cultural Indicators data show that an average of only 1 to 2 percent of major characters are depicted as problem drinkers.

CONSEQUENCES OF THE RISE OF TELEVISION

It is useful to distinguish between selectively used and relatively nonselectively used media. Selectively used media—print, film (in movie houses), audio and video recordings, and cable services—require some literacy, mobility, or special interest and buying ability to be chosen by the user. The choices reflect the tastes and predispositions cultivated by the stories told and habits acquired from parents, school, church, and other socializing institutions. These influences have traditionally distinguished different socioeconomic, ethnic, religious, political, and other groups.

Since the 1950's, however, a relatively nonselectively used medium that reached all groups began to erode some of these distinctions and absorb into its cultural mainstream many otherwise traditionally diverse perspectives. That medium is television.

Children are born into homes in which the television set is on for an average of 7 hours a day. Instead of acquiring tastes and values mainly from parents during the first 5 or 6 years of life, children are exposed to a consistent and repetitive symbolic environment of shows, news, and commercials designed to hold and sell the largest possible public at the least cost to the advertiser (Signorielli and Morgan 1990). Television tells its stories to children and parents at the same time and carries the information embedded in them to millions who otherwise may not select it (Gerbner 1990). It is, therefore, the only medium since preindustrial religion that can reach an entire community with a ritualistically used system of messages quickly, daily, and throughout life. The new technologies and proliferation of channels either substitute for more selectively used (mostly print) media or extend the most salable type of content even further into people's lives (Signorielli and Morgan 1990).

Television is the largest single source of information about drinking and other health-related behaviors. Regular exposure to its coherently composed and repetitively presented world of programs—news, commercials, and entertainment—has been found to cultivate a consistent conception about many aspects of life (e.g., Gerbner et al. 1986). For example, while television viewing seems to promote confidence in doctors, it also perpetuates poor nutrition and general complacency about health among heavy viewers (Gerbner et al. 1982*b*). Viewing is also associated with the erosion of religious prohibitions against drinking (Umble 1987).

Single programs and isolated messages or even campaigns may be submerged in the daily and weekly rhythms of the television ritual. But its recurrent patterns of images and messages that cut across most types of programs become parts of the inescapable cultural mainstream. They establish their own set of predispositions and affect preferences for other media. They blur the social, cultural, and political distinctions among otherwise diverse groups and publics (see Gerbner et al. 1981, 1982*a,b*, 1986).

IMPLICATIONS FOR PUBLIC HEALTH

These distinctions have far-reaching implications for analysis, research, and action. Selectively used media are obviously subject to selection by users. They are best used as targeted vehicles conveying specific types of information to those who seek it or to captive audiences.

Nonselectively used media in general, and television in particular, reach those who do not seek information or do not perceive a need or use for the information conveyed. For this audience, perhaps the majority of people, television entertainment is by far the most pervasive source of information. Cultivation analysis (Gerbner et al. 1986; Signorielli and Morgan 1990) has been developed to assess television's contributions, along with other factors, to the cultivation of people's conceptions of reality.

The daily flow of images and messages cultivates stable patterns of thinking and action. Most information campaigns fail to bring about change, but are simply absorbed into existing frameworks of knowledge. The Addiction Research Foundation (1981) concluded its wide-ranging review of the research literature by saying, "The overwhelming evidence. . . leads to the conclusion that health-oriented mass-persuasion programs have not succeeded in demonstrating lasting behavioral change" (p. 102). Behavior-change campaigns in an otherwise unchanging cultural environment face an uphill battle.

Writing about mass media campaigns in a hostile environment, Wallack (1983) noted several reasons for the failure of many prevention and information campaigns. They include inadequate models of behavior change, a narrow definition of the problem, a focus on the individual instead of culture as the target, and unrealistic expectations. Scare tactics, sources with obvious vested interests, and provocative arguments unwittingly running up against strongly held norms can all backfire.

Pervasive patterns of traditional behaviors deeply embedded in a culture and cultivated by a variety of images and stories cannot be expected to respond quickly to the withdrawal of one or a few of the many sources of cultivation. The lessons of advertising bans are mixed, and the lessons of prohibitions are generally negative. Effective prevention and control of the damage alcohol inflicts on people and society may require several strategies. These include reducing marketing imperatives over a wide sector of culture, including entertainment, drama, and news; producing freer and more diverse images and role models that challenge conventional patterns; and saturating the community with health information, but not criminalizing behavior attractive to many.

A broad attack on the problem of alcohol in American culture requires the development of mechanisms of effective public participation in cultural policymaking and financing. It requires a recognition that what has to be addressed is not just isolated messages or media, but the very structure of a seamless and coherent total cultural environment that has drifted out of democratic reach. Public health professionals have much to gain from participating in the leadership of such movements to improve and change our cultural environment.

REFERENCES

Aaron, P., and Musto, D. Temperance and prohibition in America: A historical overview. In: Moore, M.H., and Gerstein, D.R., eds. *Alcohol and Public Policy: Beyond the Shadow of Prohibition.* Washington, DC: National Academy Press, 1981. pp. 127–181.

Addiction Research Foundation. Task Force on Public Education and Social Policy. *Alcohol, Public Education and Social Policy: Report of the Task Force on Public Education and Social Policy.* Toronto, Ontario: Addiction Research Foundation, 1981.

Advocacy Institute. *Media Action Alert.* Washington, DC: the Institute, Oct. 24, 1990.

Advocacy Institute. *AARC Information Alert.* Washington, DC: the Institute, June 5, 1991*a*.

Advocacy Institute. *Media Action Alert.* Washington, DC: the Institute, Oct. 18, 1991*b*.

Associated Press. FTC won't push alcohol advertising. *The New York Times.* A10C3, July 20, 1990.

Associated Press. Survey says teen-age drinking is common. *The New York Times.* CXL(48,624):A18, June 7, 1991.

Atkin, C.K., and Block, M. *Content and Effects of Alcohol Advertising.* Pub. No. PB82-123142. Springfield, VA: National Technical Information Service, 1981.

Atkin, C.K., and Block, M. The effectiveness of celebrity endorsers. *J Advertising Res* 23:51–61, 1983.

Atkin, C.K.; Neuendorf, K.; and McDermott, S. The role of alcohol advertising in excessive and hazardous drinking. *J Drug Educ* 13(4):313–325, 1983.

Beer Institute. *Brewing Industry Advertising Guidelines.* Washington, DC: the Institute, 1984.

Breed, W.; Cruz, J.R.; and De Foe, J.R. "Shadings of Magazine 'Advice' on Drinking: Education and Miseducation." Unpublished report, Scientific Analysis Corporation, San Francisco, October 1980.

Breed, W., and De Foe, J.R. Themes in magazine alcohol advertisements: A critique. *J Drug Issues* 9(4):511–522, 1979.

Breed, L.A., and De Foe, J.R. Comic book supercharacters and their role in alcohol education. *J Alcohol Drug Educ* 27(1):1–13, 1981.

Breed, W.; De Foe, J.R.; and Wallack, L. Drinking in the mass media: A nine-year project. *J Drug Issues* 14(4):655-664, 1984.

Buchanan, D.R., and Lev, J. *Beer and Fast Cars: How Brewers Target Blue-Collar Youth Through Motor Sports Sponsorships.* Washington, DC: AAA Foundation for Traffic Safety, 1990.

Broadcasting Magazine. Another Round. July 16, 1984. p. 33.

Celis, W., 3rd. Fatal alcohol abuse persists on campus, but fewer drink. *The New York Times.* CXLI(48,831): A1, A14, Dec. 31, 1991.

Center for Science in the Public Interest. Malt Liquor: Congressional hearings on Crazy Horse. *Booze News* 4(3):1, 1992*a*.

Center for Science in the Public Interest. BATF approved deceptive "health claims" for wine. *Booze News* 4(6):3, 1992*b*.

Christopher, M. Nets Display Curious Double Standard on Sex. *Advertising Age.* Aug. 12, 1985. p. 46.

Colford, S.W. Push On for More State Control. *Advertising Age.* Dec. 15, 1986. p. 82.

Collins, G. Study contradicts stereotype of alcoholic women. *The New York Times.* CXXXVI(47,119):A16, Apr. 24, 1987.

Comic Book Association of America. *Code of the Comic Book Association of America.* New York: the Association, 1971.

Cultural Environment Movement. Pamphlet. P.O. Box 31847, Philadelphia, PA 19104, 1993.

De Foe, J.R., and Breed, W. The problem of alcohol advertisements in college newspapers. *J Am College Hlth Assoc* 27:195–199, 1979.

De Foe, J.R.; Breed, W.; and Breed, L.A. Drinking on television: A five-year study. *J Drug Educ* 13(1):25–37, 1983.

Dillin, J. TV Drinking: How Networks Pour Liquor Into Your Living Room. *Christian Science Monitor.* June 30, 1975. pp. 1–6.

Distilled Spirits Council of the United States. *Code of Good Practice.* Washington, DC: the Council, 1983.

Donohue, J. "Shortchanging the Viewers: Broadcasters' Neglect of Public Interest Programming." Washington, DC: Essential Information, P.O. Box 1945, Washington, DC, 1989.

Federal Council of Churches. "The Prohibition Situation." Research Bulletin No. 5. 1925.

Federal Trade Commission. Staff Report on the Cigarette Advertising Investigation (Public version), May 1981.

Federal Trade Commission. Recommendations of the Staff of the Federal Trade Commission, Docket No. 209-46. Washington, DC. Mar. 1984.

Federal Trade Commission. News release, Apr. 16, 1985.

Futch, E.J.; Lisman, S.A.; and Geller, M.I. An analysis of alcohol portrayal on prime-time television. *Int J Addict* 19(4):403–410, 1984.

Gerbner, G. Stories that hurt: Tobacco, alcohol, and other drugs in the mass media. In: Resnik, H., ed. *Youth and Drugs: Society's Mixed Messages.* Monograph No. 6. DHHS Pub. No. (ADM)90-1689. Washington, DC: Supt. of Docs., U.S. Govt. Print. Off., 1990. pp. 53–127.

Gerbner, G.; Gross, L.; Morgan, M.; and Signorielli, N. Special report: Health and medicine on television. *N Engl J Med* 305(15):901–904, 1981.

Gerbner, G.; Gross, L.; Morgan, M.; and Signorielli, N. Programming health portrayals: What viewers see, say and do. In: Pearl, D.; Bouthilet, L.; and Lazar, J., eds. *Television and Behavior: Ten Years of Scientific Progress and Implications for the 80's, Volume II, Technical Reviews.* DHHS Pub. No. (ADM)92-1196. Rockville, MD: National Institute of Mental Health, 1982*a*. pp. 291–307.

Gerbner, G.; Gross, L.; Morgan, M.; and Signorielli, N. What television teaches about physicians and health. *Mobius* 2(2):44–51, 1982*b*.

Gerbner, G.; Gross, L.; Morgan, M.; and Signorielli, N. Living with television: The dynamics of the cultivation process. In: Bryant, J., and Zillman, D., eds. *Perspectives in Media Effects.* Hillsdale, NJ: Lawrence Erlbaum Associates, 1986. pp. 17–40.

Goodman, W. Smoking policy debated. *The New York Times.* C18,C5, Nov. 11, 1986.

Greene, E. Students: Colleges Rebut Bennett on Drug Policies; Too Few Found Fighting Alcohol Abuse. *Chronicle of Higher Education.* Dec. 17, 1986. p. 29.

Groller, H. Alcohol content is focus of Budweiser campaign. *St. Louis Post Dispatch.* 107(335):1E, 3E, Dec. 1, 1985.

Gusfield, J.R. *Symbolic Crusade: Status Politics and the American Temperance Movement.* Urbana, IL: University of Illinois Press, 1963.

Haller, M.H. Bootleggers as businessmen: From city slums to city builders. In: D.E. Kyvig, ed. *Law, Alcohol and Order: Per-spectives on National Prohibition.* New York: Greenwood Press, 1985. pp. 139–157.

Harper's Magazine. Harper's Index. *Harper's Magazine.* 277(1662):14, 80, Nov. 1988.

Heath, D.B. In a dither about drinking. *The Wall Street Journal.* Feb. 25, 1985.

Herd, D. Images of drinking: Distortion or re-creation? In: Grant, M., and Ritson, B., eds. *Alcohol: The Prevention Debate.* London: Croom Helm, 1983. pp. 97–100.

Hirschorn, M.W. Alcohol Seen No. 1 Campus Abuse Problem, Despite Concerns About Students' Drug Use. *Chronicle of Higher Education.* Mar. 25, 1987, pp. 32, 34.

Hovland, R., and Wilcox, G.B. The future of alcoholic beverage advertising. *Commun Law* 9(2):5–14, 1987.

Hume, S. Brewers Enlist New Brands to Battle Problems. *Advertising Age.* Jan. 31, 1985. p.16.

Hume, S. Burger King Claims Crown in Magazines Aimed at Kids. *Advertising Age.* Mar. 8, 1993. p. 6.

Jacobson, M.F. Prevention's the Issue: Your Money or Your Life Style. *The Nation.* July 13, 1992. pp. 51–54.

Jensen, C. U.S. Bureau of Alcohol Censors Winery Info/Art. *America's CENSORED Newsletter.* Sept. 1992. pp. 1, 8.

Johnston, L.D.; O'Malley, P.M.; and Bachman, J.G. *Drug Use Among High School Seniors, College Students, and Young Adults, 1975–1990.* Pub. No. (ADM) 91–1813. Washington, DC: National Institute on Drug Abuse, 1991.

Johnston, L.D.; O'Malley, P.M.; and Bachman, J.G. *Monitoring the Future.* Ann Arbor, MI: Institute on Social Research, University of Michigan, in press.

Kurtzman, J. Business Diary/May 10–15. *The New York Times.* Sect. 3, p. 2, C3 (Financial Desk), May 17, 1992.

Litsky, F. Joyner-Kersee is finding obstacles in 400 hurdles. *The New York Times.* CXXXVIII(47,888):B9, June 1, 1989. [Photo which illustrates point was taken by David Weibtraub].

Levin, G. Alcohol Group Pushes Responsibility. *Advertising Age.* May 27, 1991. p. 34.

Lowery, S.A. Soap and booze in the afternoon: An analysis of the portrayal of alcohol use in daytime serials. *J Stud Alcohol* 41(9):829–838, 1980.

Magner, D.K. Alcohol-Related Problems Have Not Decreased on Most College Campuses, Survey Indicates. *Chronicle of Higher Education.* Nov. 9, 1988. p. A35.

Marin Institute. BATF takes action on Black Death Vodka, but is hampered by weak legislation. *Marin Institute: Media Action Alert.* Memorandum No. 2. Apr. 1992. p. 6.

McAvoy, K. Tide may have turned on beer–wine issue. *Brewers Digest* 60(2):18–22, 1985.

McGeehan, P. The Burrell Style: Building on a Solid Base on Michigan Avenue. *Advertising Age.* Dec. 19, 1985. pp. 5, 7.

Meister, J.W. "An Investigation Into the Application of Government Policies and Industry Codes and Guidelines to Television Beer Commercials." Unpublished paper, The Annenberg School of Communications, University of Pennsylvania, Philadelphia, Apr. 27, 1987.

Milloy, C. Selling of Black history. *The Washington Post.* Metro Section, p. 1, C3, Jan. 29, 1991.

Moog, C. *Are They Selling Her Lips? Advertising and Identity.* New York: William Morrow and Co., 1990.

Mosher, J.F. "Marketing Alcoholic Beverages in California." Presented at the International Study of Alcohol Control Experiences Conference, Asilomar, CA, Feb. 1979.

Mosher, J.F. and Wallack, L. Government regulation of alcohol advertising: Protecting industry profits versus promoting the public health. *J Public Health Policy* 2(4):333–353, 1981.

Motion Picture Association of America. *Motion Picture Production Code.* Los Angeles: the Association, N.D.

Multinational Monitor. BATF changes brand names. June 1992. p. 6.

National Beer Wholesalers Association. *Beer Perspectives.* July 25, 1991. p. 2.

National Highway Traffic Safety Administration. "Fact Sheet on Alcohol Impaired Driving." Prepared for the Surgeon General's Workshop on Drunk Driving press conference, Washington, DC, Mar. 1989.

National Institute on Alcohol Abuse and Alcoholism. *Sixth Special Report to the U.S. Congress on Alcohol and Health.* DHHS Publication No. (ADM) 87–1519. Washington, DC: Supt. of Docs., U.S. Govt. Print. Off. 1987. p. 3.

National Institute of Mental Health. *Television and Behavior—Ten Years of Scientific Progress and Implications for the Eighties.* Vol. I. DHHS Pub. No. (ADM)82-1195. Washington, DC: Supt. of Docs., U.S. Govt. Print. Off., 1982. *The New York Times.* Widow of alcoholic at brewery wins suit. CXL(48,405):A23, Oct. 31, 1990.

Nielsen Marketing Research. Nielsen Alcohol Beverage Service. *Advertising Age.* Jan. 31, 1985. p. 33.

Nutrition Action Health Letter. Center for Science in the Public Interest, Apr. 1992. p. 2.

Office for Substance Abuse Prevention. National Coalition to Prevent Impaired Driving. *Information Alert*, Rockville, MD. June 11, 1992.

Office of the Inspector General. *Alcohol and Youth: Controlling Alcohol Advertising That Appeals to Youth.* Washington, DC. DHHS Pub. No. (OIE)09-91-00654, 1991.

Pertschuk, M. *Revolt Against Regulation: The Rise and Pause of the Consumer Movement.* Berkeley: University of California Press, 1982.

Philadelphia Inquirer. Nov. 23, 1986.

Raissman, R. Beer Spots Expected to Remain Jockless. *Advertising Age.* May 26, 1986. p. 65.

Rios, B. Drinking Binges Grow on Campuses and Envelop Women. *Philadelphia Inquirer.* June 8, 1994. p. 1.

Rothenberg, R. The Media Business: Advertising & College Sports Commercials. *The New York Times.* D25, C4, Dec. 20, 1988.

Rowland, W.D. *The Politics of TV Violence: Policy Uses of Communication Research.* Beverly Hills: Sage, 1983.

Ryan, B.E., and Mosher, J.F. *Alcohol Promotion on Campus.* San Rafael, CA: The Marin Institute for the Prevention of Alcohol and Other Drug Problems, 1991.

Scanlan, C. Shoppers lack savvy, study finds. *Philadelphia Inquirer.* 322(87):1A, 4A, Sept. 25, 1990.

Schleier, C. Lockhart & Pettus: Some Things Haven't Changed. *Advertising Age.* Dec. 19, 1985. p. 19.

Schofield, L.B. First Amendment implications of banning alcoholic beverage ads on radio and TV. *Journalism Qtrly* 62(3):533–539, 1985.

Shapiro, E. Some old complaints arise over Heilman's new brew. *The New York Times.* D1C1, May 12, 1992.

Shipp, E.R. Alcohol abuse is becoming a public issue. *The New York Times.* CXXXV(46,549): A18, Oct. 1, 1985.

Signorielli, N. Drinking, sex, and violence on television: The Cultural Indicators Perspective. *J Drug Educ* 17(3):245–260, 1987.

Signorielli, N. *Mass Media Images and Impact on Health: A Sourcebook.* Westport, CT: Greenwood Press, 1993.

Signorielli, N., and Morgan, M.J., eds. *Cultivation Analysis: New Directions in Media Effects Research.* Newberry Park, CA: Sage, 1990.

Smith, S.B. Drive mounted to ban TV beer and wine ads. *The New York Times.* Jan. 15, 1985.

Sukow, R. Battling beer–wine labeling. *Broadcasting Magazine.* 122(17):34–35, Apr. 20, 1992.

Strickland, D.E., and Finn, A.T. Targeting of magazine alcohol beverage advertisements. *J Drug Issues* 3:449–467, 1984.

Syracuse Peace Council, to FCC Rcd 5043, 5057 thru 58 (1987), recon. denied, 3FCC Rcd 2035, 2035–36 (1988), aff'd sub nom. Syracuse Peace Council v. FCC 867 F.2.d 654 (D.C. Cir. 1989), cert. denied, 493 U.S. 1019 (1990).

Taylor, P.; Silverglade, B.; and Eskin, S.B. "In the Matter of Unfair Trade Practices in the Advertising and Promotion of Alcoholic Beverages." Petition to the Federal Trade Commission, Washington, DC, 1992.

Teinowitz, I., and Colford, S.W. Brewers Fight Back. *Advertising Age.* Nov. 11, 1991. p. 67.

Teinowitz, I., and Gordon, R.L. Brewers Belly Up To Battle NCAA. *Advertising Age.* Nov. 14, 1988. p. 31.

Trauth, D.M., and Huffman, J.L. The commercial speech doctrine: Posadas revisionism. *Commun Law* Feb. 1988.

Turow, J., and Coe, L. Curing television's ills: The portrayal of health care. *J Commun* 25(4):36-51, 1985.

Tusher, W. Majors draw up strong codes on drugs in films. *Variety* 321(13):1, 90, Jan. 22, 1986.

Umble, D. "The Consequences of Television Viewing for a Subculture: A Study of Mennonite Orientations." Paper presented at the American Association for Public Opinion Research annual conference, Hershey, PA, May 1987.

U.S. Code. Title 27. Intoxicating Liquors, Cumulative Annual Pocket Part, Section 29. St. Paul, MN: West Publishing Co., 1994.

U.S. Congress. Senate Committee on Commerce, Subcommittee on Communications. *Surgeon General's Report by the Scientific Advisory Committee on Television and Social Behavior.* Vol. 2, Appendix A. Serial No. 92-52. 92nd Congress, 2nd Session. Washington, DC: Supt. of Docs., U.S. Govt. Print. Off., 1972.

U.S. Surgeon General. *Surgeon General's Workshop on Drunk Driving: Proceedings.*

Washington, DC, Dec. 14–16, 1988. Report from Panel B, Advertising and Marketing, Recommendation B-3. Rockville, MD: U.S. Public Health Service, 1989. p. 28.

Wallack, L. Public health and the advertising of alcohol beverages. In: Holder, H., and Hallen, J., eds., *Control Issues in Alcohol Abuse Prevention: Local, State and National Designs for the '80's.* Charleston, SC: Prevention Research Center Proceedings, Sept. 27–29, 1981. pp. 95–107.

Wallack, L. Mass media campaigns in a hostile environment: Advertising as anti-health education. *J Drug Educ* 28(2):51–63, 1983.

Wallack, L. Public health and the advertising of alcoholic beverages. In: Holder, H., and Hallen, J., eds. *Control Issues in Alcohol Abuse Prevention: Local, State, and National Designs in the 80's.* Columbia, SC: Human Ecology Institute, 1984. pp. 95–107.

Wallack, L.; Cassady, D.; and Grube, J. *TV Beer Commercials and Children: Exposure, Attention, Beliefs, and Expectations about Drinking as an Adult.* Washington, DC: AAA Foundation for Traffic Safety, 1990.

Wallack, L.; Dorfman, L.; Jernigan, D.; and Themba, M. *Media Advocacy and Public Health: Power for Prevention.* Newbury Park, CA: Sage Publications, 1993.

Wechsler, H., and Isaac, N. 'Binge' drinkers at Massachusetts colleges. Prevalence, drinking style, time trends, and associated problems. *JAMA* 267(21):2929–2931, 1992.

Weiss, S. "Content Analysis of Hebrew Alcohol Advertisements in Israeli Magazines: Impact on Prevention." Unpublished research report, The Israel Society for the Prevention of Alcoholism, Ramat-Gan, Israel, 1986.

Wine Institute. *Code of Advertising Standards.* Washington, DC: the Institute, 1978.

Winick, C. Alcohol and disinhibition: Nature and meaning of the link. In: Room, R., and Collins, G., eds. *Proceedings of Conference.* Berkeley/Oakland, CA, Feb. 11–13, 1981. Rockville, MD: NIAAA, 1983. pp. 347–401.

Winski, J.M. Alcohol Warnings Favored. *Advertising Age.* Apr. 9, 1990. p. 1.

Winters, P. Marketers Lose Spirit for Alcohol. *Advertising Age.* Oct. 13, 1986. p. 28.

Woodward, W.E. *New American History.* Garden City, NY: Garden City Publishing, 1938.

Yanez, E. Ad and Alcohol Industries Target Latinos. *Extra!* July/Aug. 1992. pp. 24–25.

Chapter 2

A Meta-Analytic Perspective on "Alcohol in American Culture"

Joseph Gusfield[1]

Gerbner's chapter is a very useful compendium of material on the activities of commercial advertisers and mass media to increase consumption of alcohol. At the same time, it also suggests prevention strategies to decrease alcohol consumption in America. Rather than elaborating on what Gerbner has said about mass media and advertising, this chapter will use a meta-analytic approach to examine how it is that advertising and the media have become topics of interest in alcohol-use studies.

For many years, there have been doubts about the effectiveness of advertising and other mass media efforts in changing behavior related to alcohol. A number of conferences and books have addressed this issue. For example, Michael Schudson's (1984) *Advertising, the Uneasy Persuasion* asserted that the effectiveness of advertising has been greatly overestimated by Americans. A survey of the papers prepared for this monograph reveals a continued lack of consensus among social scientists on the effectiveness of alcohol advertising and mass media; the only agreement appears to be that there is no consensus.

In comparison with other Western societies, the United States can be categorized as a moderate user of alcohol, with a general use pattern that emphasizes episodic or binge drinking. As an example of this moderation, despite the great concern about alcohol use that developed in the late 1970's and early 1980's, automobile deaths over the last 10 to 15 years have decreased, perhaps by as much as 20 percent. This represents a significant number of lives saved, especially in light of the fact that the number of automobiles in the United States, the number of people who drive, and the total number of miles driven have greatly increased.

Furthermore, the United States restricts the use of alcohol to a much greater extent than many other countries do. We restrict the hours of sale; we

[1]Department of Sociology, University of California at San Diego, La Jolla, CA 92037

restrict sales to underage customers; we restrict public drunkenness. Even though we have been decriminalizing public drunkenness, there is still great concern with clearing the streets of public drunks. Indeed, as a society, we have less patience with public drunkenness than most other Western societies.

In addition, consumption of alcohol, especially hard liquor, has decreased in the last 15 years, despite the existence of television and other forms of advertising. Also, while decriminalizing public drunkenness, we have been criminalizing drinking–driving in the United States through stricter enforcement and longer sentences. Compared to other countries, it may be argued that we are not an alcohol culture, but rather a temperance culture.

As a temperance culture, the United States appears to be exceptional. There are aspects of our culture toward alcohol that are historically very deeply rooted in American life, in both the use and the condemnation of alcohol. In many respects, American society is less secular and more religious than many Western societies. For example, church attendance is higher than in most Western societies. This religiousness is frequently overlooked, although it lies very deep within American life. Not surprisingly, the impact of religious life on the use of alcohol in America has been enormous; however, at the same time, most religious institutions have ceased to address the problem and are no longer the major source of information about drinking.

If we turn to secular culture, the schools and other organizations have been tilted against the use of alcohol. We generally do not start drinking in the United States until after 5:00 p.m., and we do not allow drinking within work organizations, which is not true in many other countries. Thus, Americans are at least ambivalent about alcohol, if not condemnatory. Perhaps our interest in the effects of advertising and the mass media on alcohol use is itself suggestive of this attitude.

The implication of this concern with alcohol is illustrated by a United Nations (1974) report on automobile deaths which indicated that in Italy in 1972 there were only 750 deaths attributable to drinking and driving. According to the footnotes of the report, there had only been one study; the entire statistic was generated by a single study of a thousand people. In other words, the Italian picture of drinking and driving looked very innocuous because no one had looked at it closely. There was not a great deal of interest in it. In general, one finds that the more interest in an issue or problem, the greater it seems to become, because it is being more closely monitored and analyzed.

Complicating the picture of alcohol in America, we have to recognize that there is another, even conflicting, aspect of American popular culture, and that is the alcohol culture. This too is deeply seated, and it existed long before the development of television or the commercial advertising industry. This alcohol culture is evident in many of our television shows. For example, a recent episode of a show called *Law and Order* portrayed a man and woman in a bar, celebrating something by opening a bottle of champagne. They could have opened a bottle of Diet Pepsi, but that would not have been a true reflection of those characters in that situation. The association between alcohol and celebration is one reflection of the alcohol culture in American life. There is ambivalence and great cultural diversity in the United States about alcohol. This should not be glossed over.

Why are we so interested in advertising and mass media and their effects? Several reasons can be suggested. First, alcohol remains a big problem, or at least we see alcohol as a big problem in the United States. This is not to suggest that it is not really a problem, but to point out that we tend to see it as a bigger problem than do many other cultures. America is a society that has had, and still has, an active temperance and prohibition movement. In the past decade or so, there has even been an increase in the restrictions imposed on the use of alcohol. This increase is partly related to the health movement. It is also related to the rise of movements like Mothers Against Drunk Driving (MADD) and Rid Intoxicated Drivers (RID). It is also related to the active role of the Federal Government in alcohol policy, which is rather new in American history except for the Prohibition period. The creation of NIAAA in 1970 represented one of the first major efforts to organize a Federal policy toward alcohol, other than Prohibition.

A second reason for our interest in advertising and mass media is that we look for things that are manipulable, subject to legal regulation, or that seem to provide a "silver bullet" or simple solution to a problem. Advertising lends itself to regulation. A third reason for our focus on advertising is the American belief that whatever business does (especially big business) is somehow bad, and an associated perception that big business is all-powerful. We believe that business—including the news media and advertisers—must know what it is doing. Because there are profits to be made, business would not spend money on advertising unless it was effective and thus profitable. However, although it is likely that advertising can motivate people to shift from one brand to another, the crucial concern for alcohol researchers is not whether Miller or Budweiser is going to sell more beer, but what the total impact of their advertising campaigns will be.

A fourth reason to look at advertising in the mass media is that it fits our research paradigms, which include a dependent variable and an independent variable. Simply stated, research is designed to find the independent variable and correlate it with the dependent variable. Although it is beyond the scope of this paper, there are doubts about that model and how useful it is in our search for a manipulable villain.

Concerning the issue of mass media programming, Robin Room (1984) identified a concept called "problem inflation." This is when people magnify problems, as may arguably be the case with Gerbner's statements about the nature of television and information; at other times, people may tend to deflate problems.

From a sociological perspective, Americans' interest in the mass media may be related to what one might call "fun and profit." "Fun" in the sense that Americans have an interest in things that are perceived as immoral, sinful, or illegal. We are interested in crime; we are interested in violence; we are interested in sex. These things also happen to come across well on television. There is far more violence and probably more drinking on television than there is in real life. In brief, our fascination with violence, alcohol, and crime constitutes a dimension of entertainment.

Reflecting on some of the programs aired recently, one program directed against rape contained depictions and content that in some respects verged on the pornographic. Such a program sends a double message: On the one hand, it is condemnatory; on the other hand, it sends a sexual message that keeps the viewers' interest.

There is profit in deviance and the kinds of cultural releases that are implied in deviance. This leads our news media and other media to heighten what is dramatic. Gerbner points out that we live in a dramatic kind of culture where everything exciting gets heightened. The news on television seldom tells us, "There were no fires tonight." The media rarely monitors the good, the calm, and the positive.

The media has a great stake in heightening drama, which can be illustrated by several examples. Recently James Orcutt (1992) presented a paper in which he compared the results of the Institute of Social Research's surveys of drug use among youth over a long period of time with *Newsweek's* discussion and cover story on kids using cocaine. What *Newsweek* did was dramatize the increase from 1985 to 1986, which was very small, while the article failed to acknowledge a much larger increase that had occurred in the late 1970's. The second thing *Newsweek* did was to present lifetime prevalence data rather than incidence data for 1985 and 1986. Thus, what they reported was that the proportion of youth who responded that they had (ever) used cocaine rose from 16 to 17 percent. But the actual incidence of use in 1986 was only about 6.5 percent. The implication was that in the past year, adolescent use of cocaine had become much worse. Yet, when one looked at the whole picture, the increase was really quite small.

The news media appears to want viewers to think that what it reports is something to be really concerned about; therefore, it highlights the negative. Ironically, when viewers discover that things are not as bad as was reported, it increases their cynicism about reporting.

A second example of the media overdramatizing research was identified by Joel Best (1987), who studied missing children. We are faced daily with pictures of missing children on milk cartons and with stories in circulation about the evil people who prey on children. But in closely examining the data, Best found that most of these cases of missing children involved instances in which one parent kidnapped the child because they were involved in a custody battle with ex-spouse.

Studies of drinking–driving fatalities usually assert that 50 percent of these deaths are attributable to alcohol. Yet, there appears to be only one study that has examined specific cases to determine who was at fault or how frequently alcohol was actually a cause of the crash. That study reported that in crashes in which the drivers showed measurable blood alcohol levels, the drinking driver was at fault in only 60 percent of the cases. Thus the literature supports an assumption that wherever alcohol was present, its use was the determining factor.

The classic study on the risks associated with drinking and driving was conducted about 30 years ago in Grand Rapids, Michigan, by Borkenstein and his associates (1964) at Indiana University. They found that the greater the use of alcohol, the greater the possibility of a crash. However, they also found that between zero and 0.04 blood alcohol content (BAC), the use of alcohol was actually correlated with a decline in accidents. This came to be known as the Grand

Rapids dip. It created enormous consternation and generated vigorous debates over its explanation.

In our efforts to counter alcohol use, we may be paying too much attention to advertising and the mass media. It diverts our attention from the deeper policy issues. There are very real conflicts in our society between the alcohol culture and the temperance culture over where, how, and when alcohol is to be used; and these conflicts are related to broader kinds of concerns or issues.

Fetal alcohol syndrome is an example. There is a clear correlation between children displaying fetal alcohol syndrome and a lack of prenatal care. Perhaps trying to convince people not to drink with public service announcements and warning labels is less important than trying to improve access to prenatal care (which is also more costly).

As a closing observation, most Americans are cynical about advertising and, to some extent, about the mass media. It is a retreat from responsibility to try to make the news media and advertisers either the scapegoats for or the solution to our alcohol-use problems.

REFERENCES

Best, J. Rhetoric in claims-making. *Soc Prob* 34:101–121, 1987.

Borkenstein, R.F.; Crowther, R.F.; Shumate, R.P.; Ziel, W.B.; and Zylman, R. The Role of the Drinking Driver in Traffic Accidents. Bloomington, IN: Department of Police Administration, Indiana University, 1964.

Orcutt, J. "Shocking Numbers and Graphic Accounts: Quanitified Images of Drug Problems." Paper presented at the 1992 Annual Meeting of the Society for the Study of Social Problems, Pittsburgh, PA, August 1992.

Room, R. Alcohol and ethnography: A case of "problem deflation"? *Curr Anthropol* 25:169–191, 1984.

Schudson, M. *Advertising, the Uneasy Persuasion*. New York: Basic Books, Inc., 1984.

United Nations. *Statistics of Road Accidents in Europe, 1972.* New York: United Nations, 1974.

What We Really Know: Review of Research on Alcohol Advertising and Media Content

Chapter 3

Survey and Experimental Research on Effects of Alcohol Advertising

Charles K. Atkin[1]

This chapter reviews the controversial subject of alcohol advertising effects on alcohol use and misuse. The assessment is confined to two basic methods of investigation: experiments and surveys. The review focuses on the behavioral outcome of drinking patterns rather than cognitive or attitudinal responses, and emphasizes effects on teenagers and young adults rather than predrinkers or older adults.

Although theories of advertising effects are important in evaluating the appropriateness of research methodologies and interpreting the empirical evidence, there is insufficient space to adequately describe the complex and multifaceted processes by which alcohol advertisements influence audiences. For detailed overviews of key theoretical mechanisms, see Atkin (1987, 1989, 1990, 1993*a*) and Thorson (chapter 11, this volume).

This chapter is divided into three major segments. The first deals with experimental studies and the second covers field surveys; in each case, there are subsections that describe and critique the research literature, provide suggestions for promising approaches, and discuss barriers to implementation. The third segment offers a policy-relevant research agenda for future investigations of alcohol advertising.

EXPERIMENTAL STUDIES

Experimental Methods for Studying Alcohol Advertising

Advertising experiments feature manipulation of message stimuli and comparison of responses between randomly assigned audience subgroups who receive different treatments. Academic researchers usually perform experiments in the laboratory setting, where subjects are shown a few advertisements and immediate responses are measured; the relatively rare field

[1]Department of Communications, Michigan State University, Communication Arts Building, Room 472, East Lansing, MI 48824

experiments typically involve more extensive stimuli and realistic consumption behavior. The primary advantage of this basic method is investigator control over the independent variable, permitting both causal inference and isolation of the critical stimulus factors that produce effects.

However, there are a number of limitations that undermine the external validity of this method in the laboratory setting, including intrusive procedures, forced exposure, short-term responses, unrepresentative samples, weak stimulus, and unnatural consumption context. While artificiality is inherent in any lab experiment, certain aspects pose a particular problem when studying advertising or alcohol. These drawbacks will be discussed in the section entitled "Barriers to Implementation of Approaches."

Field experiments can overcome some of the limitations, depending on the degree to which the research features natural exposure and drinking conditions. Some small-scale field experimentation in advertising is carried out under fairly contrived conditions, in which exposure is brief or consumption is constrained; more elaborate experimental studies can potentially involve manipulation of extensive natural exposure to realistic advertising combined with unobtrusive measurement of consumption patterns (e.g., split-cable television messages and store purchase records).

The modest number of extant experimental investigations, mostly conducted in the 1980's under laboratory conditions, will be reviewed in the next two sections. The first set of experiments measure actual drinking behavior, and the subsequent set measure only intentions to consume alcohol.

Experimental Evidence on Advertising and Consumption

Six major published investigations measuring actual consumption of alcohol will be reviewed in detail. In each case, there is a description of the design and a summary of the findings, followed by a critique of the methodology and a conclusion.

Brown

The first experiment of its kind was carried out in New Zealand by Brown (1978). In this investigation, subjects were shown a series of 15 colored slides of magazine liquor advertisements and 15 comparison ads for cigarettes. In the counterbalanced design, subgroups first saw either the experimental or control ads and then participated in a "drink recognition test" featuring five vodka tonics varying in strength. The ostensible task for the subjects was to rate the relative amount of vodka and tonic in each drink while drinking as much as desired; the critical dependent variable was absolute quantity of alcohol consumed. In the liquor ad treatment, there was 28 percent greater consumption of vodka than in the control condition, a significant difference. The experimental data clearly show a positive effect of advertising.

Critique. There are numerous deficiencies that raise doubts about whether this experiment is a valid demonstration of advertising's role in stimulating drinking. The tasting task differs drastically from ordinary drinking behavior, and this unnatural aspect might have been more pronounced in the liquor advertising treatment due to sensitization. For example, the liquor ads might have heightened subjects' motivation to correctly detect the amount of vodka such that they sampled more of each glassful. Since vodka is a nonpreferred type of alcohol for these subjects, the taste test findings are even more remote from real-world drinking.

The series of 15 messages is far more concentrated than would normally be encountered in real life; while this massive saturation probably exaggerates the degree of positive impact, it could also undermine the effect by generating psychological reactance, stimulus satiation, or negative affect toward the messages. The persuasive quality of the advertising is restricted, because the print messages lack television's audiovisual channel capacity and broader range of lifestyle portrayals; a magazine ad that simply depicts a bottle or brand-related symbols is less likely to be influential in promoting absolute consumption. The stimulus potency is further restricted because only 1 of the 15 ads specifically featured vodka, the type of liquor used in the taste test.

The sample of 30 New Zealanders is small and atypical, which limits generalizability of the findings to wider populations. Finally, there is no theoretical rationale to predict and explain the results. The experiment is a crude comparison between advertising versus no advertising treatments, lacking an explicit examination of any mechanism by which influence processes might operate.

In summary, this study shows that intensive exposure to certain print liquor ads produces greater tasting of nonpreferred alcohol in an unusual sample of drinkers, but little is learned about why this happens and whether this impact would occur under natural conditions.

McCarty and Ewing

A similar experiment was conducted by McCarty and Ewing (1983). Subjects viewed a set of magazine ad slides for eight distilled spirit products or for nonalcohol products as part of a supposed evaluation of sexual stimuli in advertising messages. In the counterbalanced design, half saw the alcohol ads first and half saw them following the nonalcohol ads; a second manipulation involved access to a distilled-spirit mixed drink versus a soft drink before evaluating the slides. During a break between exposure sessions, all subjects fixed drinks with liquor and mixers at a private bar before viewing the opposite set of slides. Each ad was shown for 30 seconds initially and for 2.5 minutes during a later group discussion of sexual content. There was no significant main effect of advertising on amount of liquor poured, rate of consumption, or blood alcohol content (BAC) level on a breath-testing device at the end of the study. However, there was a significant interaction: Among subjects in the alcoholic predrink condition, those viewing alcohol ads in the second slide session following the break had higher BAC scores than subjects who viewed these slides first. The authors concluded that "the higher blood alcohol levels suggest that alcoholic advertising encouraged participants who had a prior drink to continue drinking during the second viewing session" (McCarty and Ewing 1983, p. 1017).

Critique. The procedures again pose a number of threats to external validity. First, the dependent measure of pouring offered liquor is not a sensitive indicator of transitory advertising effects, because the theoretical mechanisms suggest that ads should predominantly prompt immediate decisions to pour a drink or to continue drinking (which were not outcomes measured in this design) rather than influence the strength of the drink prepared (which is primarily based on habitual mixing patterns, utilizing one or two shots of liquor; this tendency may be affected by history of advertising exposure but not short-term stimulation in a time-constrained experiment). Since all subjects were told to fix drinks regardless of treatment, the nonsignificant main effect may simply reflect random individual differences in pouring practices.

Similarly, the dependent measure of consumption rate is dubious because the glasses were arbitrarily removed after 15 minutes, with some liquid remaining in most cases. While advertising might stimulate a higher cumulative quantity of alcohol consumed per occasion, there is no reason to believe that it would accelerate the rate within a single 15-minute period, especially when the drinking act is interrupted. Again, the null finding in this situation does not imply a lack of realistic advertising impact.

The sole positive finding on the third dependent variable (significantly higher BAC levels in the predrink/second-session alcohol advertising group) is also questionable because of unknown timing of the drinking behavior across the two sessions. The alcohol intake precipitating the elevated final BAC reading could have occurred primarily during first-session drinking.

Beyond these measurement deficiencies, a second weakness pertains to the nature of the advertising stimulus operationalization. On one hand, potential for impact was undermined by confining the messages to print ads and to liquor products unpopular with drinkers in the sampled 18-to-26 age range. On the other hand, there was an abnormally massive dosage of advertising, with forced exposure to eight ads for several minutes each.

Third, the evaluation task focusing attention on sexual stimuli in the ads might have detracted from the impact of the alcohol promotion aspect of the messages, or elicited negative cognitive responses such as counterarguing or source derogation. In combination with the group discussions dwelling on sexuality in advertising, these task-related components of the experimenter's diversionary probably served to diminish the consumption effects of the ads.

A final problem concerns the possibility that the alcohol ads increased the subjects' self-consciousness about their drinking, especially since the experiment was carried out at the Center for Alcohol Studies. This may have altered the natural patterns of processing messages, pouring drinks, and consuming the prepared drinks.

In conclusion, both the positive and null results reported in the McCarty and Ewing experiment provide scant evidence relevant to real-world effects of alcohol advertising, yielding a near-meaningless test of the natural advertising–consumption relationship.

Kohn, Smart, and Ogborne

A more externally valid and innovative attempt to study advertising effects under small-scale field experimental conditions was conducted by Kohn et al. (1984). In a Toronto shopping mall test site, they asked 19- to 45-year-old male passersby to evaluate either five "lifestyle" magazine ads for a little-advertised imported beer (portraying models enjoying the beer in attractive social contexts), five "tombstone" ads (simply picturing the same beer product and describing its intrinsic attributes such as flavor and quality), or no ads in a control condition.

The researchers monitored alcohol purchasing behavior in licensed mall restaurants later that day, and some subjects were also telephoned a couple of months later to measure longer-term effects. Differences between conditions were nonsignificant; those in the lifestyle treatment group were less likely to order alcohol in the restaurant, but reported more consumption in the ensuing months.

Critique. This field experiment represents a methodological advance over prior laboratory research, especially in the more realistic assessment of drinking responses. Furthermore, the head-to-head test of lifestyle versus tombstone message appeals is an appropriate application of the experimental technique. However, there are still some major flaws in the handling of these design features and other aspects of the investigation.

The first set of problems pertains to the dependent drinking variables. One key issue is the time lag between exposure to ads and subsequent drinking. Since an experiment is best suited for testing various transitory processes such as activation or disinhibition, the passage of several hours before the opportunity to drink may have allowed effects to dissipate. The delayed measurement is far more remote from the exposure, suggesting little possibility of impact.

In addition, monetary cost may have lessened the beer ad impact, because subjects were required to pay expensive restaurant rates for alcohol in order to score on the dependent variable. Several other extraneous factors may have deflected the advertising effect on restaurant alcohol consumption: the drinking behavior of nonparticipant dining companions, available drinking time, anticipation of postdinner shopping or driving activities, the type of food selected, the availability of various alcoholic and nonalcoholic beverages on the menu, and established food-drink habits.

A second array of problems concerns the degree of stimulus potency. Quantitatively, subjects saw just a handful of print ads, a minor input relative to the hundreds of alcohol ads seen in the months before the experiment and during the intervening period before the delayed measurement. Qualitatively, the themes presented in the ads were somewhat weak (the subjects gave mediocre ratings for the "perceived effectiveness" of the messages) and off-target (the appeal for this expensive imported beer was aimed at upper-middle-class segments of the market, while the subjects were predominantly blue-collar immigrants).

Further doubts about the adequacy of the experimental manipulation are raised by the near-zero impact on brand preferences. Only one subject in the lifestyle condition and two in the tombstone condition selected the advertised brand in the restaurant, and consumption of this brand in subsequent months was actually lower in the two experimental groups than in the unexposed control group. Since the brand-share influence of advertising is widely conceded and no such impact was detected in this experiment, there is little basis for expecting a more fundamental experimental effect on absolute consumption.

To summarize, this study is commendable in some respects, but the basic deficiencies identified in the critique suggest that the apparent null findings are attributable to methodological limitations rather than any lack of alcohol advertising effectiveness. Therefore, the authors' conclusion that the results "fail to justify strong public concern about undue impact of alcohol on aggregate consumption" (p. 40) is questionable, although the study certainly provides no evidence of special influence due to lifestyle themes.

Kohn and Smart

The first experimental test of television advertising effects was performed by Kohn and Smart (1984). Canadian college males viewed a 90-minute videotaped soccer match containing varying numbers and arrays of beer commercials: either nine beer ads (three per half-hour period), four beer ads (one at the end of the second half-hour and three in the final half-hour), or no beer ads. In a second manipulation, subjects either had immediate access to beer or experienced a half-hour delay.

The experiment was conducted in an informal lounge during the evening, where subjects were tested in small groups averaging six or seven persons. The dependent variable was the number of beers ordered from a research assistant, with an upper limit of four drinks imposed.

Advertising initially increased beer consumption; during the half-hour period when participants were first exposed to beer ads, they were far more likely than nonexposed groups to order beer. This finding can be seen most dramatically in the nine-ad condition with immediate access to alcohol, where 94 percent of the subjects ordered drinks in the first half-hour; that figure is double the rate for the other two immediate-access treatments. The proportions are also quite high for the initial drinking opportunity among delayed-access nine-ad subjects and for the postexposure period among four-ad subjects.

Over the full length of the experimental session, however, subjects in the control condition eventually consumed almost as much beer as those exposed to ads. In addition, there were low amounts of consumption during the late portions of the experiment, suggesting that multiple ads do not produce sustained drinking or excessive quantity of alcohol intake. The authors concluded that "limited exposure to televised beer commercials briefly stimulates consumption" but that "further exposure does not seem to contribute to further consumption" (Kohn and Smart 1984, p. 299).

Critique. The most plausible interpretation of this evidence is that the beer ads reduced inhibitions against ordering beer, such that subjects felt freer to ask for one or two drinks. An activation explanation is not tenable because the prompting function was neutralized by the repeated offering of drinks. Indeed, the frequent offers may have eventually played a disinhibitory role for the control subjects, who almost caught up with the exposed subjects.

The lack of sustained impact of ads in the later stages of the experiment is not surprising, because there is no compelling theoretical reason to expect that subjects seeing their sixth or eighth beer ad would drink an incrementally greater amount than those seeing fewer ads. After a couple of exposures, there is little new in the way of benefit reinstatement from subsequent ads, and little potential for additional disinhibition. In fact, the higher quantity of ads might be sensitizing in the experimental context, such that subjects become suspicious or at least self-conscious about the amount they are consuming and decide to discontinue drinking.

Another major methodological problem involves the social situation in which drinking occurred. Consumption by individual subjects may have been unduly influenced by the norms in each tested subgroup, since ordering and drinking by others was readily observable. In particular, the procedure of publicly requesting each drink from an experimental assistant could be a socially constraining factor after the first couple of drinks, especially if other subjects were not maintaining that pace; this may partially account for the lack of sustained impact in the exposure conditions.

In sum, this is an elaborate and carefully conducted study that overcomes many of the technical shortcomings of other experiments. Strengths include the use of television commercials, the realistic embedding of the messages in a lengthy program, the relaxed evening party setting, the immediate and ready access to alcohol, and the unobtrusive measurement of the dependent variable.

The central shortcoming is conceptual; the absence of a guiding theoretical rationale restricts the applicability of the study to real-life advertising effect processes. The design does not provide for a clear-cut test of any specific effect mechanism, and both the positive findings (the initially increased drinking) and the null findings (the lack of sustained drinking) are subject to alternative explanations. While these two results are suggestive, this study provides no definitive evidence on the key issue of whether natural exposure increases consumption.

Kohn and Smart II

In a followup experiment featuring wine commercials interspersed in a lengthy television program, female college subjects were either heavily exposed (nine ads), lightly exposed (three ads), or exposed to no ads in a control condition (Kohn and Smart 1987). At four points during the experiment, the women were given an opportunity to order either soft drinks or small servings of white wine.

Although absolute consumption levels were very low overall, women in the nine-ad condition drank significantly more than those exposed to little or no advertising. The heavily exposed subjects consumed an average of 2.6 ounces of wine, compared with 0.7 ounces in the three-ad treatment and 1.6 ounces in the control condition. The authors concluded that "women in the present study responded positively to a large number of wine commercials but negatively to a few" and that "concurrent heavy exposure increases consumption of on-hand alcohol by college women, whereas concurrent light exposure decreases their consumption" (Kohn and Smart 1987, pp. 164, 166).

Critique. Since this research closely follows the basic design of the earlier experiment, the same criticisms apply. The problem of drinking constraints associated with the settings and procedures of other laboratory experiments seems to particularly plague this investigation. Even with four drinking opportunities presented to each subject, less than half of the overall sample ordered any wine, and few had more than one glass (the most glaring example of the repressed response occurred in the light exposure group, where 92 chances to drink resulted in just 5 glasses being ordered).

The low mean level of consumption combined with the small sample size produces unstable results; for example, if one woman in the light exposure condition had consumed three additional drinks, and one woman in the control condition had consumed three fewer drinks, the difference between these conditions would disappear. The instability is especially problematic because subjects were tested in small subgroups susceptible to normative standards of drink ordering; this may partially account for the finding that lightly exposed subjects drank so little alcohol.

Another explanation for the lack of advertising influence on lightly exposed subjects is that the manipulation was simply insufficient to produce a meaningful disinhibitory impact; in this condition, only one ad had been presented by the time most drink orders occurred.

The apparently positive finding for the heavily exposed group cannot be readily discounted. Although the amount consumed is rather modest, it is significantly higher than for those less exposed to advertising. Thus, this experiment provides tentative evidence that advertising can cause increased drinking. Due to weaknesses in the design of the study, however, the real-life implications are far from compelling.

Sobell, Sobell, Riley, Klajner, Leo, Pavan, and Cancilla

These seven researchers conducted a laboratory experiment examining the impact of both beer commercials and entertainment drinking portrayals upon quantity of beer consumed in a taste test. In the advertising manipulation, the hour-long videotaped program contained either four beer ads or four control ads for nonalcoholic beverages or food products. Afterwards, subjects were provided with three mugs of light beer in an ostensibly unrelated taste-rating task. Quantity of beer tasted did not differ significantly between the two advertising treatments (exposed and nonexposed groups consumed an average of 5 ounces from each mug) or between the two program treatments. The authors concluded that "neither drinking scenes in television programs nor beer commercials precipitated increased drinking by viewers" (Sobell et al. 1986, p. 339).

Critique. Many conceptual shortcomings and methodological limitations undermine the validity of this investigation. Most fundamentally, there was no theoretical rationale advanced to explain why the commercials were expected to significantly influence the amount of beer tasted (aside from an implicit notion that ads "precipitate" increased drinking). The reliance on a postviewing taste-test dependent measure does not permit examination of the pertinent activation and reinforcement mechanisms that might produce such transitory effects. Theoretically, this tasting of a medium versus a small number of ounces should not be expected to vary according to advertising exposure.

The experimental procedures also minimize the potential for ascertaining any meaningful impact of advertising on amount of alcohol consumption. First, the drinking opportunity was relatively remote from the precipitating cue, because it occurred in a task context designed to be distinctly separate from the viewing situation after a considerable elapse of time following exposure to the ads. Second, subjects were given only light beers to test, while the commercials promoted regular full-strength beer. Third, the subjects tasted the drinks in isolation rather than in the social context featured prominently in beer commercials as the appropriate setting and reward for drinking. Fourth, procedural constraints in the tasting task artificially limited variance on the dependent variable; a ceiling on amount consumed was induced by instructions to drink just the quantity necessary to make an adequate tasting judgment, and a minimum amount was induced by the repeated retasting needed to judge the beer on the separate rating scales measured in the prolonged test.

Finally, the overall staging of the experiment was inhibiting and sensitizing. All subjects were given a preliminary breath test to ensure they were alcohol-free and were told they must score low on an alcoholism screening test to be eligible; some were also administered several batteries of drinking-pattern tests, until this procedure was discontinued halfway through the data collection because of undue sensitization. The experiment was conducted at the Addiction Research Foundation laboratories, rather than at a neutral site or a more comfortable drinking environment. The viewing and tasting occurred in late morning and early afternoon, a time when few males normally drink beer and when few beer commercials are aired, primarily because of the low probability of triggering drinking. These factors are likely to make subjects highly self-conscious and constrained in displaying natural drinking tendencies in response to advertising cues.

In conclusion, major design flaws in this experiment can readily explain the null effects findings and negate the applicability of the findings to the natural drinking behavior that advertising seeks to influence.

Other Advertising Experiments

Several other lab experiments measured intention to consume alcohol, and one field experiment examined sales figures. These studies will be briefly described and critiqued.

Atkin and Block (1981) carried out a series of experiments to compare the impact of different versions of print alcohol advertisements on affective reactions to the messages and the products. In one test, randomly assigned subgroups of individuals were exposed to ads that showed either older or younger characters posed with the product; all other aspects of the content remained the same in each stimulus ad. Younger subjects (under age 21) gave significantly higher ratings to ads with youthful characters and felt more favorable toward the advertised brand; character age made little difference to adult subjects. The second experiment manipulated the sexual suggestiveness of the models posed in beer ads; the sexy version was more highly rated and the product attitude was more favorable among the younger subjects, while the adults were more positive toward the nonsuggestively posed models. In a third experiment reported by Atkin and Block (1983), ads featuring a product endorsement by a celebrity produced higher ratings than ads promoted by a noncelebrity character in both age groupings.

Friedman et al. (1977) conducted an earlier experiment comparing the effectiveness of celebrity versus noncelebrity models in a magazine advertisement. College subjects indicated a significantly greater intention to purchase the wine product in the version in which a famous movie actor provided the testimonial.

• The effects of a magazine liquor ad containing subtly embedded visual sexual stimuli were examined by Kilbourne et al. (1985). In the experimental treatment, college subjects were shown an ad containing the image of a nude female appearing as a reflection on the bottle; control subjects were exposed to the same basic message modified to remove the embed. The sexual embed produced significantly higher ratings on all dependent variables: message evaluations (e.g., trustworthy, attractive), sexual imagery (e.g., sensual, erotic), sexual arousal (GSR responses), and behavioral intentions (e.g., try product, buy product).

Critique

All five experiments employed similar design and measurement approaches. On the positive side, these lab investigations appropriately utilized the main strength of advertising experimentation by examining qualitative differences in message content in order to identify influential features. However, each suffers from a lack of overt behavioral measures such as purchasing or drinking alcohol; verbal reports of intention to act may not be a valid predictor of actual consumption. Furthermore, this type of experiment only demonstrates the relative effectiveness of various themes, revealing little about the absolute impact. The generalization problems of previously reviewed experiments also apply to these studies.

Despite certain limitations, the evidence from these lab experiments suggests that two thematic strategies widely employed in alcohol advertising are effective for drinkers of high school or college age. Two studies indicate that sexual imagery enhances the impact of alcohol ads, and another pair of studies indicate that celebrity endorsements are influential.

One provocative field experiment deserves a brief mention. Ackoff and Emshoff (1975) sketchily cited findings from large-scale manipulations of Budweiser advertising budgets in several dozen test markets throughout the 1960's. Actual sales figures showed increases when advertising expenditures increased, but even larger increases were evident when spending for advertising was decreased over various time periods. Unfortunately, the published report of these proprietary data does not describe the methodology in sufficient detail to adequately assess the validity of the study or the meaning of the seemingly inexplicable sales increases following reduction of advertising. The results are of dubious relevance to the issue of advertising and absolute consumption levels, because market-share implications were the focus of this single-brand field testing.

Conclusion Based on Experimental Literature

The body of research utilizing experimental methodology is the most well-developed domain of the alcohol advertising literature. Unfortunately, the diligent efforts of these investigators have not produced a conclusive answer to the basic question of whether alcohol ads increase consumption. This is partially due to the equivocal mixture of null and positive findings, which fails to provide a consistent picture across studies. However, the more basic sources of ambiguity are due to methodological deficiencies, compounded by the lack of conceptualization underlying the design of most experiments.

Thus, apparent findings of no impact can be readily explained away or even reinterpreted as indicating positive effects, while the data showing significant influence of advertising can also be dismissed. The conclusions of null effects drawn by some reviewers and researchers are clearly unjustified, based upon the experimental evidence amassed to this point. The section below and the closing segment of this chapter discuss future research directions.

Promising Experimental Designs

This section will suggest some promising methods for laboratory and field experimental research involving alcohol advertising. Artificiality problems create considerable doubt about whether the lab experimental method is appropriate for generating definitive proof concerning effects of real-world advertising on absolute consumption levels. It would be more illuminating if future laboratory experimentation attempted to identify how people respond to some theoretically relevant qualitative variations in advertising messages, rather than seeking to demonstrate the mere existence or absence of impact under contrived conditions.

Advertising lab experiments are best suited for testing the relative influence of key message elements (e.g., characteristics of human models, type of persuasive appeal, style of presentation) rather than varying quantities of ads. The manipulation of advertisement qualities permits isolation of critical content dimensions and serves to neutralize many of the methodological shortcomings. In addition, new lab investigations should broaden the array of dependent measures to include perceptions, beliefs, and attitudes, as well as overt behavior, because these "intermediate" variables are more sensitive to the manipulations and are likely to illuminate the processes by which behavioral effects operate.

Field experiments that attempt to approximate more natural exposure and drinking conditions are preferable to laboratory experimentation because of increased generalizability to real-world settings. Several basic types of large-scale designs are most promising.

First, the tightest control in studying television advertising can be achieved in tests carried out in split-cable television communities. Over a period of many months, the quantity and quality of beer commercials and television public service spots can be manipulated so that randomly assigned sets of households receive different combinations of available messages. The dependent variables can be measured in terms of alcohol purchasing patterns (based on computer records of sales to household members in local stores) or survey interviews about consumption behavior in households.

Second, the effects of magazine ads (especially for distilled spirits) can be examined in field experimental manipulations of advertising volume using the split-run technique. Households subscribing to certain magazines can be randomly assigned into treatment conditions that receive issues carrying increased or decreased quantities of liquor ads; survey research would be needed to measure differences in liquor consumption.

Third, multiple test markets could be used to compare the effects of variations in volume or channel placement of advertising; in these locales, experimental manipulations might involve increases or decreases in the quantity of advertising disseminated for a period of several months via television, newspapers, and billboards. The unit of analysis would be the total community, so a relatively large number of sites is desirable. The primary dependent variable would be community-wide sales figures compiled at the aggregate level from alcohol outlets; fluctuations in certain indicators of alcohol misuse (such as drunk driving arrests) might also be examined.

Barriers to Implementation of Experimental Approaches

The key limitations of lab experiments revolve around the artificiality of the laboratory situation. While this is not a major problem in many social psychological studies of persuasion processes, the contrived nature of the experimental procedures becomes highly problematic in research examining mass media effects, particularly the impact of advertising. The following external validity drawbacks render laboratory testing dissimilar to real-life alcohol advertising influence:

- Procedures are intrusive (participants realize they are being scrutinized);
- Exposure is enforced (in reality, people pay varying attention to ads);
- Responses are usually measured almost immediately (before effects wear off);
- Samples are unrepresentative (demographically skewed toward younger ages and higher social classes, and composed of those willing to devote the substantial effort to participate);
- The dependent variable of consumption is either constrained, facilitated, or measured indirectly (the access to alcohol, social drinking context, length of consumption period, time of day, type of beverage served, and physical environment differ from natural drinking conditions; some studies measure intentions to consume or attitudes toward drinking as indicators of consumption);
- The independent variable manipulation is severely truncated (only a single message or series of ads can be shown, which does not permit tracing of cumulative effects of high-frequency exposure over long time periods); and
- The potency of the experimental stimulus is weak relative to prior messages that have been seen (after experiencing thousands of alcohol ads, exposure to a few more in an experiment is unlikely to provide a meaningful incremental impact).

As a result of these last three factors, lab studies are likely to underestimate advertising effects on consumption. In order to address these methodological problems, researchers need to use more innovative lab designs, acknowledge the limitations of this basic method, and focus on those issues for which lab experimentation is most appropriate.

Although field experiments seem to be an attractive solution, there are major monetary, cooperation, and design barriers that restrict the potential of this method. For example, a long-term field test in a split-cable community or across multiple comparable markets would involve huge expenses and require involvement of the major alcohol producers. There are several fundamental design limitations. First, the manipulation may not be strong enough to produce a measurable difference, due to limited timeframe, limited control over nonmanipulated alcohol messages reaching the audiences, and limited increase or decrease in the flow of treatment messages; in the case of split-cable or split-run experiments, the manipulation is limited to a single medium. Second, split-cable or split-run consumption variables may not be measured precisely enough to isolate individual responses to the stimuli (due to gross indicators such as household-level purchases), or comprehensively enough to encompass all types of alcohol purchases (supermarket optical scanning records do not include liquor store purchases or bar/restaurant drinking). Finally, measures of misuse such as drunk driving arrests or fatalities may not be sensitive enough to gauge the effects of the relatively weak manipulation.

FIELD SURVEY STUDIES

Survey Methods for Studying Alcohol Advertising

The second major approach is survey research, in which a large and more representative sample of people are asked questions about real-life advertising. Investigators seek to determine whether there is a link between individuals' advertising exposure and consumption patterns; cognitive and attitudinal variables are also examined.

The most widely used technique in the mass media research field is the correlational survey. The relationship between separately measured indices of exposure and behavior is calculated to ascertain if heavily exposed persons drink more alcohol (a more primitive "subjective impact" technique directly asks respondents to report whether the messages they have seen produce certain effects on their behavior).

The key advantage of the correlational survey method is the measurement of natural behavior uncontaminated by artificial laboratory procedures and settings. Furthermore, cumulative effects of long-term exposure can be assessed. A disadvantage of mass media field surveys is the lack of a true control group. Because of the pervasiveness of advertising in our society, there is no substantial portion of the population that is unexposed to alcohol ads. Instead, the researcher must compare people who experience greater-than-average exposure with those having relatively lower levels of exposure, even though the latter still see a large number of messages.

Researchers represent the relationship between the exposure level and the consumption level with a correlation coefficient; a positive correlation indicates that the heavily exposed persons consume more alcohol than the lightly exposed persons. In media effects research, a coefficient around +.10 is considered slight, a coefficient in the +.20 range is modest, a +.30 coefficient is moderate, and any association higher than +.40 or +.50 is interpreted as strongly positive.

There are two major drawbacks to correlational survey research. First, the investigator is unable to definitively infer causality in the typical static survey design, because the relationship might be spuriously inflated by the contribution of third variables, or it might be partially attributable to reverse causal flow from consumption to exposure. Second, most survey studies rely on respondent self-reports of their exposure patterns and drinking behavior; these measures may lack validity because individuals are unable or unwilling to provide accurate responses.

The subjective impact method can be used for introspective assessment of the degree and direction of advertising effects upon respondents' attitudes and behaviors, based on self-report measures in survey questionnaires (e.g., impact on images of drinkers or on quantity consumed). A parallel estimated impact technique measures perceptual judgment about impact on others. Both variations are sensitive but superficial approaches to measuring the effects of advertising. Respondent inability or unwillingness to accurately answer impact questions is especially problematic.

Correlational Survey Evidence

There are three key studies in the alcohol advertising literature using the correlational survey technique. Two investigations test adolescents and one deals with adults.

Strickland

In a survey focusing on television advertising, Strickland (1983) administered questionnaires to 772 adolescent drinkers drawn from 7th-, 9th-, and 11th-grade classrooms in a midwestern city. The consumption variable was indexed by respondent reports of usual quantity and frequency of drinking beer, wine, and liquor. The index of advertising exposure was not based on directly measured viewing of commercials, but instead was extrapolated from reported television program viewing during the prior month (weighted for the number of beer and wine ads carried during those particular shows).

The partial correlation between the indicator of television advertising exposure and overall alcohol consumption was +.12, controlling for age, sex, race, and total television viewing time. The standardized regression coefficient in a path model showed a total causal effect of +.18. Although the coefficient is significantly positive, Strickland concluded that "advertising was shown to have meager effects on the level of consumption" (p. 221).

In another analysis based on this data set, Strickland (1982) found that two intervening message-processing variables interacted with exposure to enhance advertising effects. There is a stronger exposure–consumption relationship in the subset of adolescents who identify most closely with role models portrayed in commercials, and in the subset who are above-average in motivation to watch commercials for social comparison purposes (to learn about the latest fashionable products and to observe which kinds of people are users of the advertised products).

Critique. Although Strickland's survey is basically sound in design and analysis, several methodological problems must be taken into account in evaluating the findings. The first issue concerns the method of measuring exposure simply based on program viewing with minor adjustments for embedded commercial ads. This reflects only the potential access to commercials rather than actual contact with the ads or degree of attention paid to the messages. Attention is a critical factor determining behavioral effects, since many viewers may mentally tune out the encountered ads or passively glance at the content. Thus, the indirect measurement approach probably results in a weaker relationship between exposure and consumption.

On the other hand, there is less chance that the exposure variable is subject to a reverse causal linkage; sheer program viewing is unlikely to be influenced by drinking behavior since it is not sensitive to selective attention processes. Therefore, the weaker coefficient that is obtained reflects a predominantly exposure-to-consumption sequence of causality.

Second, Strickland's scope of purview is limited to television commercials, and to only those commercials aired during certain programs in the month prior to the study. Television is just one of several media carrying alcohol advertising, and television viewing is lower during the teenage years than in any other period in the lifecycle. The exclusion of the print media in this survey ignores the impact of distilled liquor advertising, which has been shown to be influential in other studies. Since exposure is measured only for the previous month, the study misses cumulative effects and possible delayed effects. In addition, the focus on regular weekly series and daily programs overlooks the large numbers of beer commercials presented in sports broadcasts.

A related deficiency in the analysis is the lack of correspondence between the types of alcohol advertised and the type of alcohol consumed; even though liquor advertising was omitted from the exposure index, liquor drinking constituted a major portion of the consumption index. Beer and wine advertising effects should be reflected primarily in beer and wine drinking rather than in the overall consumption of a broader array of alcoholic beverages. These scope and correspondence problems serve to understate the degree of relationship obtained in the survey analysis.

Third, the sampling of respondents is biased in two respects. More than 2,500 students in the selected schools were eligible for participation, but only 1,650 were actually administered the questionnaire due to absenteeism and lack of parental permission to participate, and only 988 were analyzed because parental questionnaires were not returned. This huge attrition rate is problematic because absent students might be more likely to have drinking problems, and those with noncooperating parents might come from homes where alcohol is a special concern.

More troublesome is the further exclusion of more than 200 respondents who were nondrinkers and predrinkers, as only students with past drinking experience were included in the final analysis. The drinker-only criterion artificially restricts the range of variance in the consumption variable and probably suppresses the correlation; for example, if the light viewers tend to be nondrinkers, the coefficient based on the full sample would be more strongly positive. The exclusion also overlooks the possible recruitment influence of advertising in creating a predisposition to experiment with alcohol.

In summary, the Strickland survey shows that alcohol advertising has a significant but modest positive relationship with adolescent drinking, and it appears that the predominant causal flow is in the direction of advertising influencing consumption. Although several major methodological deficiencies are identified in this review, each shortcoming probably serves to diminish the potential for discovering a connection between exposure and drinking. Thus, it is likely that the actual impact of advertising is stronger than evidenced in the obtained findings, lending support to the interpretation that alcohol advertising stimulates drinking by teenagers.

Atkin, Hocking, and Block

Another correlational survey of adolescents was performed by Atkin et al. (1984). A sample of 665 respondents in the 12-to-17 age range from diverse geographic and demographic backgrounds was administered a detailed instrument measuring alcohol consumption patterns and level of exposure. The survey was operationalized in terms of the number of magazines read and television programs watched that frequently carry alcohol ads, the frequency of exposure to advertising for certain brands and to specimen messages pictured in the questionnaire, and the degree of attention given to advertising for product categories and to specimen ads.

This technique permitted construction of an elaborate index of actual exposure to advertising messages. Based on these measures, the researchers estimated that the typical adolescent encounters more than 2,000 beer, wine, and liquor ads in magazines, newspapers, television, radio, and billboards each year, and pays attention to more than half of the television commercials and one-third of the print ads.

A subindex of exposure to liquor advertising is correlated +.41 with liquor consumption. To illustrate this relationship, the sample can be divided at the midpoint of the exposure index. Consumption of at least one drink per week was reported by 45 percent of the heavily exposed subgroup, compared with 27 percent of the lightly exposed subgroup; of 11 liquor brands listed in the questionnaire, an average of 31 percent of the heavily exposed subgroup versus 15 percent of the lightly exposed subgroup said they had tried each one.

Since this raw association is partly spurious, regression analyses were performed to control for demographic factors (age, sex, race, community size, socioeconomic status, and church attendance), social influences (parent and peer consumption patterns and approval of the respondent's drinking), and exposure to other media content (alcohol public service messages and televised entertainment portrayals of drinking). With these contaminating variables eliminated, the standardized regression coefficient between liquor advertising exposure and liquor drinking is +.34.

The subindex of beer-wine advertising exposure is correlated +.24 with beer drinking, and +.12 with wine drinking. For six listed brands of beer, an average of 52 percent of the heavily exposed versus 37 percent of the lightly exposed respondents indicated that they had tried each one. Regarding consumption in a typical week, 46 percent versus 29 percent reported drinking at least one beer per week (16 percent versus 10 percent said they drank five or more beers). Controlling for the demographic, social, and other media exposure variables, the standardized regression coefficient for beer remains modestly positive at +.20, while the wine relationship becomes nonsignificant.

Critique. There are several weaknesses in this investigation that must be taken into account. A detailed critique by Strickland (1984) raises measurement, sampling, and causal inference issues that are addressed in a response by Atkin (1984). The first two problems are relatively minor, but the question of causality remains a legitimate concern.

First, the construction of the exposure indices involved summation of a number of components representing different types of measures: opportunity for contact versus frequency of exposure versus degree of attention, general categories of ads versus concrete specimen ads, and magazine versus television advertising. While this has the advantage of "surrounding" the exposure construct with a comprehensive array of measures taken from various angles (unlike the Strickland survey, which relied on the single indicator of mere opportunity for television commercial contact), the technique is subject to an "apples and oranges" criticism because of the combination of disparate items and scales.

Second, the sample does not constitute a representative cross-section of all U.S. teenagers; respondents were drawn from a small set of classrooms in only four locales across the country. While this suggests caution in extrapolating population figures in the case of individual variables (e.g., number of beer ads viewed, or frequency of wine drinking), it is unlikely to produce a significant bias in estimating the more fundamental nature of the relationship between variables.

The major issue concerns causal inference of advertising effects. The multivariate analyses controlled for the spurious contribution of the most likely antecedent variables, but it is possible that certain unmeasured personality characteristics, attitudinal predispositions, or media exposure preferences might still account for part of the relationship. For example, psychological dissatisfactions might simultaneously produce dependence on alcohol and heavier exposure to television programs that happen to carry beer ads. The question of causal direction cannot be definitively resolved, especially in the case of this survey, because attention levels constituted an important part of the exposure index; any tendencies toward selective attention to alcohol messages by pro-alcohol teenagers would imply that reverse causation also accounts for a portion of the association.

In conclusion, potential problems with spuriousness and reverse causality suggest that the obtained coefficients probably inflate the causal influence of beer and liquor advertising to a slight degree. Nevertheless, the most reasonable interpretation of these data is that liquor ads have a substantial impact on liquor drinking, and that beer advertising makes a significant but mild positive contribution to beer drinking among teenagers. Regarding wine advertising, the effect might actually be underestimated due to measurement limitations; furthermore, changes in the nature of wine products and commercials in subsequent years might have rendered these latter findings obsolete.

Atkin and Block

Using the same design, instrument, and analysis as the teenage survey, Atkin and Block (1984) also sampled 562 adults; since the greatest concern has been expressed about drinking-related problems in young adults, respondents were disproportionately drawn from the 18-to-22 age segment. Exposure to liquor advertising is modestly related to the liquor consumption index, with a standardized regression coefficient of +.21. For exposure to beer and wine advertising, the regression coefficient is +.28 with beer consumption and +.14 with wine consumption. Adding together all brands of beer, the high-exposure subgroup reported drinking an average of 30 beers over the previous month; by comparison, the low-exposure subgroup said they drank 15 beers. Consumption of at least five beers per typical week was reported by 32 percent of heavily exposed respondents versus 19 percent of those with lower than average exposure.

Critique. The Atkin and Block survey of adults suffers from the same limitations as their parallel survey of the teenage sample. In addition, the findings cannot be broadly applied to all adult age segments because of the purposive oversampling of younger adults.

In summary, this investigation shows that advertising exposure is modestly related to liquor consumption and moderately related to beer drinking in the early adult years. While inferences of causality must be drawn tentatively, it appears that a substantial portion of the obtained association is due to the influence of advertising upon consumption. Thus, the data indicate that advertising increases beer and liquor drinking to a mild extent.

Drinking Attitudes. In addition to the examination of the exposure–consumption relationship, both the teenager and adult samples were asked a series of questions to measure attitudes toward drinking and images of drinkers. Across all age groups, the 50-item attitudinal index was moderately associated with overall exposure to beer, wine, and liquor advertising, with a coefficient of +.27. For instance, one-third of the high-exposure subgroup versus one-fifth of the low-exposure subgroup agreed that it was acceptable for teenagers to get drunk; the high-exposure subgroup were also 12 percent more likely to feel that alcohol provides relaxation. Averaging across a list of 12 possible drinking situations (e.g., after playing sports, at the beach, after work), an average of 51 percent of the high-exposure subgroup versus 38 percent of the low-exposure subgroup considered each setting to be appropriate.

By contrast, the low-exposure subgroup was almost twice as likely to agree that a party without alcohol is more fun than a party where people are drinking. Amount of advertising exposure is also modestly related to holding flattering images of the typical beer or whiskey drinker; heavily exposed respondents more often cited attributes such as friendly, fun-loving, happy, successful, and sophisticated in characterizing drinkers. These affective orientations may have important indirect impact on consumption by enhancing predispositions to drink alcohol.

Subjective Impact Survey Evidence

Atkin and Block (1981) conducted a self-perceived effects survey to obtain individuals' introspective assessment of how advertising influences their drinking behavior. A questionnaire was administered to 535 adults, primarily in the 18-to-22 age range; straightforward items asked how often various acts were affected by beer, wine, and liquor advertising. Instead of inferring impact from differences between experimental groups or correlations between exposure and behavior, respondents simply reported whether they perceived a connection between exposure to ads and subsequent consumption.

To measure consumption stimulation, participants were asked, "When you see an ad for beer while watching television, how often do you decide to go to the refrigerator to get a beer?" or, "When you see an ad for liquor while reading through magazines, how often do you decide to fix yourself a drink?" Averaging across the three types of alcohol, 4 percent indicated "once a week," 11 percent "once a month," 16 percent "a couple times a year," and 11 percent "once a year." The frequency of reported prompting was highest for beer, as 28 percent reported this effect occurring at least once per month. A parallel question asking if drinking of a preferred brand of alcohol was stimulated by an ad for another brand yielded almost the same distribution of answers, suggesting a response generalization effect.

Another item asked how often an ad "reminds you to go out and buy" some beer/wine/liquor at the store; 3 percent said this happens weekly, 10 percent monthly, 21 percent a couple times per year, and 16 percent yearly, with beer purchasing cited most frequently. Similar proportions of the sample reported that newspaper ads telling about special discount prices motivated them to go out and buy alcohol, indicating that learning about reduced cost also augments advertising effects.

To explore the impact of advertising on trial purchases of new kinds of alcohol on the market, respondents were presented with a listing of 18 recently introduced brands and instructed to "mark the ones you have tried, and circle all the reasons why you decided to try each one: because you saw ads for it, because family or friends told you about it, because you saw it in the store." Among those who had tried a brand, an average of 22 percent reported that it was due to advertising; this compares to 26 percent for store observation and 67 percent for interpersonal influence. In addition, in response to a more general question, "How often do you decide to try the new brand after encountering an ad for it?" 26 percent reported that this happens about once a year, and 29 percent reported a trial purchase two or more times per year.

Critique

These subjective impact data are flawed in both measurement and sampling. The validity of direct questioning about the influence of advertising is suspect, because respondents may misattribute to advertising a portion of consumption behavior that is actually internally or socially motivated, and because they may be unaware of subtle or cumulative advertising impact that actually does occur. While these two tendencies may cancel each other out, there remains substantial doubt about the ability of drinkers to recognize and report their behavioral responses to alcohol advertising.

The nonrepresentative sampling is a special concern in this survey, because estimates are being projected for individual variables rather than relationships. There is a bias toward drinkers in the sample, as the proportion who report consumption of beer, wine, and liquor is slightly higher than for the general population in this age range. Thus, the percentages obtained in this survey are probably inflated.

In conclusion, the evidence suggests that individuals are occasionally prompted by advertising to purchase and consume alcohol, particularly beer and newly introduced brands. This does not occur on a very frequent basis, and the overall increase in the volume of drinking seems to be rather limited. This method is fraught with methodological deficiencies, so the findings should be interpreted with caution.

Conclusion Based on Survey Literature

Based on the correlational surveys of teenagers and adults, several overall conclusions can be drawn. First, all three studies suggest that television beer ads mildly increase the consumption of beer. Despite divergent measurement techniques, the two surveys of teenagers are consistent in indicating a correlation in the +.15 to +.20 range; the relationship is somewhat stronger for young adults. Second, magazine-oriented liquor advertising appears to have a modest positive influence on liquor drinking in both surveys that examined this type of advertising. Third, the effect of wine advertising is rather weak, although the sole study was conducted before the era of heavily promoted wine coolers. Due to inherent limitations of the correlational design, the degree to which advertising acts as a causal agent in these relationships cannot be definitively specified. In addition, the tentative evidence from the subjective impact survey suggests a slightly higher frequency of drinking due to advertising.

Correlational Surveys Examining Alcohol Misuse

Beyond the effects on basic consumption, alcohol advertising might also influence problematic forms of drinking in either a positive or negative direction. The relevant alcohol abuse dimensions include excessive quantity of consumption, intoxication, deficit motivations for drinking, and harmful consequences of drinking. These outcomes can be considered in terms of direct effects of ads, and as indirect effects via advertising-stimulated increases in consumption levels.

Direct Effects

Based on the content of alcohol advertising, there is little theoretical potential for most ads to directly increase the degree of alcohol misuse. While ads may sell drinking, advertising themes seldom sell problem drinking (see Atkin 1990, 1993*a*).

Although few messages promise that alcohol is intoxicating and few explicitly advocate excessive drinking, the many ads implying that the product should be consumed heavily may be interpreted by some viewers as supporting this practice. Furthermore, advertising does not disclose information about potential adverse consequences or warn the audience about the risks of improper drinking practices; indeed, the implicit message that alcohol is harmless may actually be reassuring to some abusers.

Indirect Effects

There is much greater potential for advertising to contribute to misuse through indirect processes, as certain effects on consumption may serve to facilitate excessive drinking. First, advertising promotes greater frequency of consumption on a wider variety of occasions; thus, there are more opportunities for drinkers to exceed proper quantity limits. Second, many television viewers, radio listeners, and magazine readers are already drinking at the time of exposure; the sheer volume of advertising increases the chances that they will encounter an ad that stimulates them to continue consumption, perhaps beyond a moderate level. Third, advertising reinforces pro-drinking attitudes, which may be generalized by the individual to apply to excessive drinking levels; if advertising leads a drinker to hold a much more liberal view of normal drinking, this may carry over to a slightly more permissive view toward excessiveness.

Empirical evidence examining the impact of alcohol advertising on drinking problems is minimal. It is almost impossible to study such effects in controlled experiments due to ethical and pragmatic considerations. The most appropriate method is survey research, but only a handful of studies have assessed these relationships. The primary data come from Strickland's correlational survey described earlier in this report; there are also some fragmentary data from the Atkin and Block project.

Strickland

In his survey of adolescent drinkers, Strickland (1983) measured advertising exposure, overall consumption, and five alcohol misuse variables: frequency of intoxication, symptomatic consumption (e.g., drinking alone, sneaking drinks, rapid drinking, skipping meals), negative consequences (e.g., specific drinking-related problems with family, friends, legal authorities, task performance and schoolwork, and general belligerence), psychological involvement (e.g., drinking for reasons of tension relief, anxiety, and feelings of inadequacy), and self-reported seriousness of the respondent's drinking problem.

There is one significant coefficient in the path model, a +.12 relationship between advertising exposure and negative consequences (especially the belligerence dimension). The standardized regression coefficients are +.08 for both symptomatic consumption and psychological involvement, and +.03 for both intoxication frequency and self-reported problems. The causal connection is almost exclusively indirect, primarily operating via the impact of advertising on overall consumption, which in turn contributes to the abuse variables.

Critique. The strongest feature of this investigation is the comprehensive and precise measurement and scaling of the alcohol misuse variables. In evaluating these findings, however, the methodological shortcomings identified in the earlier discussion of this study must be considered. The measurement of advertising exposure is restricted to television commercials and does not gauge attention to the ads, and the attrition in the sampling may have excluded many problem drinkers and constrained variance. Thus, the obtained relationships may underrepresent the actual degree of association.

In sum, the data provide little indication of any direct impact of alcohol advertising on problem drinking among adolescents. The indirect effects via increased consumption appear to be slightly positive, but it is clear that advertising does not exert a major influence on the forms of alcohol abuse examined by Strickland.

Atkin, Neuendorf, and McDermott

Several alcohol misuse variables from the previously described samples in the Atkin and Block project were analyzed by Atkin et al. (1983). Their alcohol advertising index combined both beer/wine and liquor exposure components because of the focus on problem drinking regardless of alcohol type. A two-item index of excessive consumption reflected number of drinks typically consumed and frequency of consuming "at least five or six drinks in a single day or night." Two other items measured each respondent's reported concern about drinking habits and trouble experienced at school or work due to drinking.

Overall advertising exposure correlates +.30 with the excessive drinking index; those above the median in exposure reported consuming an average of 4.5 drinks during a typical evening at a party or bar, compared with 2.9 for those with lower exposure. In the high-exposure subgroup, 33 percent said they consume 5 or more drinks at least once per month, compared with 16 percent of the less exposed respondents. Regression analyses controlling for demographic, social, and other media influences reduce this raw relationship to a standardized regression coefficient of +.22; when the general consumption index was also controlled, the direct-effect coefficient drops to +.10.

In addition, highly exposed respondents are more likely to report worrying that they drink too much (18 percent of the high-exposure group versus 12 percent of the light-exposure group said they were "very" or "slightly" concerned) and to report getting into trouble because of drinking (8 percent versus 3 percent experiencing "much" or "slight" trouble).

Critique. This study is subject to the same limitations of the correlational surveys described earlier, particularly the reverse causation explanation. Moreover, the specific items measuring excessive and problem drinking represent a superficial attempt to measure these variables; a more elaborate and well-validated instrument is needed to provide precise data.

Although interpretations must be advanced tentatively, the Atkin et al. findings suggest that advertising influences problem drinking to a modest degree. Most of the impact operates indirectly via increased consumption, which in turn leads to heavy or problematic drinking. There appears to be a small positive direct effect as well.

Drunk Driving. The Atkin et al. (1983) investigation also attempted to provide a preliminary exploration of whether advertising might indirectly increase the likelihood of drunk driving. Many ads promote bar drinking and consumption in outdoor locations; to the extent that drinkers are influenced to consume more alcohol in these nonhome settings, there is a greater chance of driving after drinking. Furthermore, the impact of advertising in stimulating greater frequency and quantity of drinking increases the odds of drunk driving. There is even a slight potential for direct effects of advertising, based on the occasional ads juxtaposing moving cars with scenes of beer drinking, the associations between alcohol and racing cars, and the more subtle linkage between alcohol and the challenge and excitement of speed and risk-taking.

In the same sample of adolescents and younger adults, these researchers found that advertising exposure was significantly related (r=+.26) to an index of drinking and driving (encompassing drunk driving, driving after drinking, drinking while riding, drinking while parked, and estimated drink limit for safe driving). For example, 39 percent of heavily exposed individuals reported having driven "when you were really too drunk to drive," compared with 28 percent of lightly exposed respondents; 47 percent versus 31 percent reported drinking while riding in the previous month.

The regression analysis indicates that the relationship is partly spurious, as the coefficient drops to +.18 when interpersonal, demographic, and other media exposure variables are controlled. Only a portion of the effect appears to be direct; when consumption is also controlled, the coefficient decreases to +.09.

Critique. These findings are open to challenge, because the self-reported measures of drinking/driving may lack validity due to the sensitive subject matter, and the correlational data may be partially explained by reverse causation. This exploratory study does not provide a sophisticated, indepth examination commensurate with the social significance of the issue.

In conclusion, the evidence from this single investigation must be regarded as highly tentative. It appears that advertising exerts a weak direct effect on drinking/driving behavior; when the indirect effect operating via increased consumption is also considered, the data suggest that the overall influence is mildly positive.

Promising Survey Designs

The correlational survey method offers considerable potential for providing valuable evidence regarding real-life influences of advertising. In order to take best advantage of this technique, there is a need to refine measurement of both the independent and dependent variables, to more comprehensively measure the full array of third variables, to employ more sophisticated multivariate statistical analyses that reveal the nature of the advertising–drinking relationship, to conduct multiwave panel studies that permit time-lagged analyses, and to select more representative and diverse samples.

The independent variable of exposure to advertising is surprisingly complex and multifaceted. Researchers must measure both the frequency of viewing or reading ads that individuals encounter in the mass media, and the degree of attention given to these messages. Because audience members are not highly conscious of exposure patterns, elaborate measurement efforts are needed to aid their recall (e.g., still photos of key scenes from television commercials). In measuring the drinking variables, media researchers should borrow some standard items from the alcohol consumption literature. To broaden the scope of the research, studies can add cognitive and affective dependent variables (e.g., knowledge about alcohol, images of drinkers, beliefs about the consequences of various consumption patterns, attitudes toward drinking, and perceived social norms). Some of the measurement problems associated with respondent self-reports can be addressed through "single source" studies that rely on unobtrusive electronic measures of television viewing and optical scanning records of purchases.

Aside from the basic exposure and drinking variables, there are a variety of "third" variables that are relevant to the relationship. The survey instrument should include measures of exposure to nonadvertising media messages that may influence drinking (e.g., viewing of drinking depictions in entertainment programming, and attention to pro-health and safety messages), and personal characteristics that jointly predispose persons to advertising exposure and to drinking orientations (e.g., gender, age, socioeconomic status, religiousness, values, and lifestyles). In addition to these antecedent and concomitant factors, survey researchers should include measures of intervening message-processing variables (e.g., identification with characters and situations in ads, perception of the meaning of depictions, and counter-arguing).

Multivariate analyses of data collected in static survey designs should serve two primary purposes: isolating the functional relationship between advertising and drinking by statistically controlling the contaminating influences of demographic, personal, social, and media variables, and specifying the contingent conditions under which the bivariate association is stronger or weaker.

The causal ordering issue can be addressed by employing panel designs that measure the respondent on two or more occasions; due to the long-term cumulative nature of advertising effects, a time lag of at least 1 year is preferable. In a one-shot survey, researchers might attempt retrospective measurement of earlier exposure and drinking patterns to provide a crude indicator of time order.

Finally, it is crucial that researchers carefully sample a representative cross-section from the defined population, because convenience samples are too readily dismissed by critics. In addition, surveys should draw samples from special populations that might be especially susceptible to certain types of advertising influence, such as chronic abusers, young teenage males, and disadvantaged minorities.

Aside from correlational designs, the subjective impact and estimated impact surveys are an efficient and sensitive method for collecting evidence. In the subjective impact technique, respondents introspectively assess the degree and direction of advertising effects upon their own attitudes and behaviors, based on self-report measures in questionnaires. To assess long-term effects, audience members attempt to characterize the extent to which their mental images or attitudinal feelings have been formed or changed as a result of cumulative exposure to ads (e.g., greater perceived prevalence of drinking in society, or more favorable opinions toward alcohol companies). This technique can be most effectively applied when respondents are asked for reactions to specimen messages displayed by the researcher, because individuals are in a better position to judge whether they are being influenced when a specific message stimulates an immediate behavioral response or intention.

Rather than posing global questions, these surveys should present a series of items that identify specific types of advertising (such as television beer commercials featuring athletes, or liquor billboards in low-income neighborhoods) and then identify specific dependent variables (such as trial purchase of newly advertised brands, or advertising-prompted beer drinking while viewing televised sports events). To attain greater precision, the response categories should offer fine gradations in quantity and frequency of drinking; for balance, the array of alternative outcomes should include options of "no effects" and a continuum of reductions as well as increases in consumption.

The estimated impact technique measures respondents' perceptual judgment about the degree and net direction of message effects on other people. Heretofore, this method has been applied rather superficially in public opinion polls that ask questions such as "Do you think that alcohol advertising increases the amount of drinking in society?" This type of survey item should feature the same precision and balance refinements, and might also identify specific audience segments as referents (e.g., teenagers or alcoholics) and facilitate audience judgments by identifying potential mechanisms of influence (e.g., modeling or disinhibition).

Barriers to Implementation of Survey Approaches

The primary barrier to the effective implementation of correlational survey findings centers on the issue of causal inference. If two variables such as exposure and consumption are positively correlated in a static survey design, it does not necessarily mean that one variable causes the other. Two primary alternative explanations must be considered: the bivariate relation might be spurious (produced by contaminating third variables that jointly affect exposure and consumption), or it may be due to reverse causality (where drinking patterns stimulate individuals to selectively seek out ads). Indeed, the relationship might reflect reciprocal causation, such that drinking produces exposure and exposure contributes to drinking in an upward spiral.

In order to guard against spuriousness, survey researchers attempt to measure the extraneous variables most likely to inflate the raw correlation; through multivariate analysis, these contaminating influences can be controlled to provide a more meaningful indicator of the functional relationship between the two focal variables.

The issue of causal direction cannot be definitively resolved in media surveys because audiences tend to be selectively exposed to messages, but it can be addressed by discussing rationales regarding the logical time-ordering between the pair of variables and for the relative potency of the forward and reverse causal processes. Several considerations suggest that advertising is the more active prior force in the relationship with drinking, especially for adolescent audiences. Exposure is antecedent in the lifecycle because most people see numerous ads before the time of initial experimentation and the development of a regular drinking habit. In addition, exposure to advertising is seldom a highly motivated form of selective information-seeking, unlike exposure to partisan political newspaper items or violent television programming. Typically, people are indiscriminantly exposed to whatever ads they encounter while watching television or reading magazines; the entertaining style of the advertising is more likely to attract attention than is the substantive nature of the product in most cases. Selectivity is especially unlikely for youth, who have not yet developed the attitudinal predispositions that would motivate seeking or avoidance of ads. These issues demonstrate the importance of focusing greater attention on theoretical considerations that would indicate whether advertising is the more active prior force in the relationship with drinking for various segments of the audience.

Although panel survey designs provide a sounder methodological basis for inferring causality, there are numerous technical problems associated with multiwave surveying, such as respondent attrition, sensitization to subsequent messages, tendency to maintain consistent responses, preservation of anonymity, and complex practical arrangements.

A minor drawback of the survey method is the reliance on respondent self-reports of their exposure and drinking patterns. Although there are problems of accurate recall and truthfulness, thousands of survey investigations have successfully measured advertising exposure or alcohol consumption using standard questionnaire items, and further measurement refinements can help overcome these problems. A more significant doubt associated with estimated impact survey measurement concerns the respondent's adequacy of knowledge about a particular audience segment; instead of an informed judgment, the answer may be a rough guess or reflect personal biases.

POLICY-RELEVANT RESEARCH AGENDA

Government agencies, public interest associations, and the alcohol industry have discussed regulatory and self-regulatory policies concerning alcohol advertising for almost two decades. Researchers can provide valuable input to the decisionmaking process if their empirical evidence is relevant and credible. Based on the current literature showing relatively modest degrees of harmful effects, and the pragmatic political barriers to fundamental change, imposition of broad-scale restrictions on advertising does not appear to be a promising solution; nevertheless, debates about a partial or full ban would be better informed by additional research (see Atkin 1993*b*). It is more likely that future initiatives will focus on narrower policy options: eliminating a small array of the most problematic practices, inserting disclaimers and positive role modeling in ads, restricting the placement of advertisements, and increasing the number of public service ads that promote moderation or warn against drunk driving. Thus, new research on the subject of alcohol advertising effects should attempt to provide the following five types of information.

1. Definitive determination of the degree of advertising contribution to alcohol use and misuse (primarily via field experimental and survey research methods). These specific questions should be addressed:

- How strong is the causal impact that can be traced to advertising, directly and indirectly?
- What are the other independent and intervening variables that amplify or attenuate the influence of advertising?
- Is the advertising impact reflected primarily in increased frequency or increased quantity of consumption patterns?
- Is there is a direct or indirect connection between advertising and drunk driving behavior, particularly among young drivers?
- What role does advertising play in children's learning about alcohol and their predispositions to initiate drinking?

2. Specification of the differential effects on various audience segments due to general-audience and targeted advertising (via survey and lab experiment methods):

- What is the relative impact for age groupings (children, early teens, late teens, young adults, mature adults)?
- Are effects different for males versus females and for different socioeconomic segments (low-income, blue collar, middle class)?
- How do the effects differ across racial/ethnic groups (Caucasian, African-American, Hispanic, Asian-American) and according to degree of acculturation among recent immigrants?
- Are there differential effects according to drinking habits (light versus moderate versus heavy drinkers)?

- Does advertising in specialty media channels contribute to alcohol consumption and drinking problems, especially among underage and minority audiences (e.g., inner-city billboards, display ads in campus newspapers, cinema ads)?
- Would restrictions on placement of ads in certain broadcast time-slots reduce the impact on young people?

3. Isolation of influential message content and stylistic factors in ads, both in terms of generic product demand and brand preferences (via lab experiment stimulus manipulations):

- Which types of advertising sources are most influential (e.g., celebrities, youthful characters, physically attractive models)?
- How much impact is due to the nature of lifestyle portrayals (e.g., social setting, recreational activities, elegance)?
- Which persuasive appeals are most effective (e.g., camaraderie, escape, relaxation, refreshment, sexuality)?
- Do certain styles of presentation attract high-risk audiences (e.g., rock or rap music, fast-paced shots, fantasy scenes)?
- Are there forms of brand imagery and symbolism that can influence brand switching and loyalty without increasing overall consumption (e.g., jingles, slogans, trade characters, distinctive settings, text-only tombstone ads)?
- What changes in the nature of advertising practices would reduce hazardous drinking practices (e.g., elimination of scenes depicting driving, boating, climbing)?
- Would the audience learn responsible behaviors if commercial advertisements incorporated depictions of positive role modeling (e.g., drivers refusing drinks, companions intervening to discourage excessive drinking or to prevent drunk driving)?
- How do these message variables differentially influence segments of the audience (e.g., according to gender, age, ethnicity, or drinking habits)?

4. Comparison of the relative impact of varying quantities of ads versus public service messages dealing with alcohol (via surveys and field experiments):

- Can drinking problems be more effectively reduced by decreasing the quantity of advertising or by increasing the quantity of responsible drinking and drunk driving messages?
- What is the optimum ratio of ads versus public service announcements in reducing problems while maintaining brand-share goals?
- What is the relative effectiveness of responsible drinking and impaired driving messages that are sponsored by alcohol companies versus nonindustry organizations?

5. Examination of inoculation strategies for educational messages designed to directly counteract alcohol advertisements (via lab experiments):

- Are counter-messages effective in reducing the deleterious influences of commercial advertising?
- Which message appeals are most effective in inoculating the audience (e.g., parody, counter-arguments, factual challenges)?
- How effective are advertisement warnings that disclose health and safety risks involved in consuming their products (especially in a driving context)?

CONCLUSION

The array of evidence from field surveys and experiments is suggestive but not yet definitive. Despite the substantial accumulation of empirical data, there remains considerable ambiguity regarding the nature and extent of advertising's influence on consumption. Part of this uncertainty is due to certain inconsistencies in the pattern of findings across various investigations, and part is due to methodological limitations in the techniques available to researchers and deficiencies in the execution of specific studies.

Nevertheless, the preponderance of the evidence indicates that alcohol advertising stimulates higher consumption of alcohol by both adults and adolescents; the net effect of advertising is in a positive direction. The key question is no longer whether advertising influences drinking, but what degree of impact occurs. The conclusion of null effects is not tenable in the face of numerous findings of positive effects in all types of investigations. In rejecting the null hypothesis, this review differs from several earlier examinations of the literature (e.g., Smart 1988); one reason is that this reviewer has applied critical evaluative criteria to studies purporting to show null effects as well as to the positive-effect studies that have been targeted for critiques in the past.

On the other hand, the evidence clearly does not support the interpretation that advertising exerts a powerful influence on drinking behavior. It appears that advertising is a contributing factor that increases drinking to a modest degree, rather than a major determinant. Additional research is needed to pinpoint the precise extent of impact and to identify the theoretical processes that account for this outcome (see Atkin 1990, 1993*a*). Other priorities for future studies include specifying differential effects on audience segments, isolating influential message factors, comparing the relative impact of ads versus public service announcements and examining inoculation strategies.

In general, conclusive evidence on advertising effects requires longitudinal research with multiple data points, particularly over the formative teenage years during and following the onset of drinking. Long-term field experiments and panel surveys are best suited for assessing the basic impact of advertising, supplemented by more theoretically driven studies using the lab experiment and static survey designs that characterize the present literature.

REFERENCES

Ackoff, R.L., and Emshoff, J.R. Advertising research at Anheuser-Busch, Inc. (1963–1968). *Sloan Manage Rev* 16:1–15, 1975.

Atkin, C.K. A reply to Strickland. *J Stud Alcohol* 45:93–100, 1984.

Atkin, C.K. Alcoholic-beverage advertising: Its content and impact. *Adv Subst Abuse* (Suppl. 1)267–287, 1987.

Atkin, C.K. Mass communication effects on drinking and driving. In: *Surgeon General's Workshop on Drunk Driving*. Washington, DC: U.S. Department of Health and Human Services, 1989. pp. 15–34.

Atkin, C.K. Effects of televised alcohol messages on teenage drinking patterns. *J Adolesc Health Care* 11:10–24, 1990.

Atkin, C.K. Effects of media alcohol messages on adolescent audiences. In: Strassburger, G., and Comstock, G., eds. *Adolescents and the Media*, Adolescent Medicine: State of the Art Reviews, 12:71–88, 1993*a*.

Atkin, C.K. On regulating broadcast alcohol advertising. *J Broadcast Electr Media* 37:107–113, 1993*b*.

Atkin, C.K., and Block, M. Content and effects of alcohol advertising. Prepared for the Bureau of Alcohol, Tobacco, and Firearms. Pub. No. PB82-123142. Springfield, VA: National Technical Information Service, 1981.

Atkin, C.K., and Block, M. Effectiveness of celebrity endorsers. *J Advert Res* 23:57–61, 1983.

Atkin, C.K., and Block, M. The effects of alcohol advertising. In: Kinnear, T.C., ed. *Advances in Consumer Research*. Vol. 11. Provo, UT: Association for Consumer Research, 1984. pp. 688–693.

Atkin, C.K.; Hocking, J.; and Block, M. Teenage drinking: Does advertising make a difference? *J Commun* 34:157–167, 1984.

Atkin, C.K.; Neuendorf, K.; and McDermott, S. The role of alcohol advertising in excessive and hazardous drinking. *J Drug Educ* 13:313–325, 1983.

Brown, R.A. Educating young people about alcohol use in New Zealand: Whose side are we on? *Br J Alcohol Alcohol* 13:199–204, 1978.

Friedman, H.; Termini, S.; and Washington, R. The effectiveness of advertisements utilizing four types of endorsers. *J Advert* 6:22–24, 1977.

Kilbourne, W.E.; Painton, S.; and Ridley, D. The effect of sexual embedding on responses to magazine advertisements. *J Advert* 14:48–56, 1985.

Kohn, P.M., and Smart, R.G. The impact of television advertising on alcohol consumption: An experiment. *J Stud Alcohol* 45:295–301, 1984.

Kohn, P.M., and Smart, R.G. Wine, women, suspiciousness and advertising. *J Stud Alcohol* 48:161–166, 1987.

Kohn, P.M.; Smart, R.G.; and Ogborne, A.C. Effects of two kinds of alcohol advertising on subsequent consumption. *J Advert* 13:34–41, 1984.

McCarty, D., and Ewing, J.A. Alcohol consumption while viewing alcoholic beverage advertising. *Int J Addict* 18:1011–1018, 1983.

Smart, R.J. Does alcohol advertising affect overall consumption? A review of empirical studies. *J Stud Alcohol* 49:314–323, 1988.

Sobell, L.C.; Sobell, M.B.; Riley, D.M.; Klajner, F.; Leo, G.I.; Pavan, D.C.; and Cancilla, A. Effect of television programming and advertising on alcohol consumption in normal drinkers. *J Stud Alcohol* 47:333–340, 1986.

Strickland, D.E. Alcohol advertising: Orientations and influence. *Int J Advert* 1:307–319, 1982.

Strickland, D.E. Advertising exposure, alcohol consumption and misuse of alcohol. In: Grant, M.; Plant, M.; and Williams, A., eds. *Economics and Alcohol: Consumption and Controls.* New York: Gardner Press, Inc., 1983. pp. 201–222.

Strickland, D.E. Content and effects of alcohol advertising: Comments on NTIS publication No. PB82-123142. *J Stud Alcohol* 45:87–93, 1984.

Chapter 4

A Methodological Interpretation of the Experimental and Survey Research Evidence Concerning Alcohol Advertising Effects

John L. Lastovicka[1]

INTRODUCTION

This commentary on the literature and Atkin's review (chapter 3, this volume) takes a methodological perspective and proceeds in three basic steps. First, attention will be paid to the kinds of research designs found in the extant literature concerning advertising's effect on alcohol use and abuse. Second, prescriptions for the kinds of designs that *should* be used to study advertising effects will be examined. Finally, one additional advertising–alcohol-abuse study, which uses an appropriate methodology but was unpublished at the time Atkin prepared his review, will be briefly reviewed.

THE RESEARCH DESIGNS

When reviewing the literature on advertising effects, it is paramount to evaluate the kinds of research designs used in the different investigations. This is because when empirically evaluating a causal proposition like "Does advertising influence alcohol use and abuse?" the design used in any given study can limit the ability to produce a clear-cut inference about the proposition under investigation. With an emphasis on research design, Atkin's review examines six laboratory experiments concerned with advertising effects on drinking behavior, five other lab experiments that look at behavioral intention, four cross-sectional sample surveys (or correlational surveys, to use Atkin's term) that contain measures of advertising exposure and alcohol-related behaviors, and finally one field experiment that examines an advertising campaign's impact on a beer brand's sales.

LABORATORY EXPERIMENTS

The overwhelming majority (11 of 16) of the studies reviewed by Atkin rely on laboratory experimentation. Although these studies offer high "internal" validity via

[1]Department of Marketing, College of Business, Arizona State University, Box 874106, Tempe, AZ 85287

experimental control and, hence, the ability to make clear-cut causal conclusions, these studies are unfortunately weak in terms of "external" validity, or the degree to which generalizations can be made about advertising's influence on alcohol use outside of the laboratory, in the real world.[1]

To illustrate, in the typical laboratory-based television advertising experiment, the independent variable usually includes a manipulation of randomly selected groups that are exposed to a few ads (or not, in the control group) as part of all experimental subjects' forced viewing of a taped hour- or half-hour-long television program. This allows the investigator to be rather precise in making conclusions about the effect of those few ad exposures on experimental subjects' behaviors or behavioral intentions. Unfortunately, government agencies, public interest associations, and others interested in the effects of advertising on alcohol use and abuse are rarely interested in the effects of just a few ads. Instead, by "advertising," many users of this research are more likely thinking in a less limited and much more modal basis. They are concerned about the broader institution of advertising, or the advertising of a particular industry (e.g., brewers), or the advertising campaign of a particular company (e.g., the Anheuser-Busch "Know when to say when" campaign). These more modal concerns properly consider advertising's aggregate effect over months or years; over many brands' ads in multimedia campaigns; in real-world viewing, listening, and reading environments; and in real-world alcohol consumption environments.

This concern over the external validity of the 11 lab studies should not result in totally dismissing their results. In fact, when one considers the econometric/time series evidence that advertising is a cumulative force that works gradually over time (e.g., Moriarty and Lastovicka 1985) or the theoretical work suggesting that advertising influences purchasing by gradually moving a consumer (over advertising exposures) through a hierarchical series of psychological stages to behavioral change (Preston and Thorson 1984), then this means that these short-lived lab-based experiments—that *at most* use a few ads and only take an hour or so of their subjects' time—are methodologically biased in favor of the null hypothesis. Stated simply, lab experiments are biased against finding advertising effects on behavior.

Consequently, when method bias is taken into account, lab experiments reporting even some rather modest positive findings are consistent with the proposition that advertising does influence alcohol use and abuse. In and of themselves, however, these lab study findings are only suggestive—and not definitive—evidence for a positive effect.

Sample Surveys

Another set of studies reviewed by Atkin are based in the survey research tradition of analyzing data from large, representative cross-sectional samples. Here the methodological problem is the reverse of laboratory experiments: sample surveys have high external validity but offer poor

[1] See the classic Campbell and Stanley (1966) work on "internal" and "external" validity for generic definitions of these two ways of evaluating the integrity of a research study.

internal validity. Stated simply, making strong causal inferences from cross-sectional sample survey data is not possible.

To illustrate, a typical sample survey has measures of alcohol-related activities and measures of media or advertising exposure taken from a representative sample of some population of interest. These sample survey data—relative to the simulated ad exposures and contrived behaviors measured in lab experiments—have considerable external validity, as survey measures assess real media exposure and real alcohol use/abuse behaviors. Positive partial correlations revealing that higher exposure to alcohol ads (after accounting for the effects of other independent variables) covaries with higher alcohol consumption have been obtained in several studies. It is tempting to conclude as Strickland (1983) did from his survey data that "advertising was shown to have meager effects on the level of consumption" (p. 221). Here is where the problem with internal validity emerges.

The well-known problem with claiming any kind of independent variable effect—meager or otherwise—using correlational evidence is that correlational evidence is only a necessary, but not sufficient, condition for demonstrating causality. That the variables AD (for advertising) and AL (for alcohol use) are found empirically correlated is consistent with several alternative explanations; namely, AD influencing AL, *or* AL influencing AD, *or* AD and AL being simultaneously influenced by some third causal variable. Atkin supports the AD→AL conclusion in the Strickland study by logically arguing against the plausibility of AL→AD, stating that "sheer program viewing is unlikely to be influenced by drinking behavior since it is not sensitive to selective attention processes" (Atkin, chapter 3, p. 53, this volume). However, a third logical alternative explanation is ignored by Atkin. These correlational data are also very consistent with numerous third possibilities that take the form AD←X→AL. For example, the X variable could be something like the personality trait of "lethargy." The more lethargic spend more time around the house drinking beer and watching ball games (that are full of beer ads); in contrast, the less lethargic spend their time out of the house actually playing ball (and see fewer ads) and drink nonalcoholic beverages like Gatorade, consistent with their more active lifestyle.

Although there are other problems in the sample survey research that have limited these surveys' ability to study advertising–alcohol use/abuse relationships—like the precision of the independent or dependent variable measurement or the representativeness of the samples—these are really minor issues that can be easily fixed in comparison to the difficulty of making causal inferences from cross-sectional sample survey data.

This concern over the internal validity of the sample survey evidence does not mean their results should be totally dismissed. Much survey research data are consistent with the AD→AL hypothesis; unfortunately, these survey data are also consistent with other alternative explanations. Therefore, like the laboratory experiment results, the sample survey findings are only suggestive—and not definitive—evidence for a positive effect.

Field Experimentation

Atkin briefly discusses the results of a single series of related field experiments.

This was Ackoff and Emshoff's (1975) description of Anheuser-Busch's advertising budgeting experiments for Budweiser beer in the 1960's. In this research, demographically matched cities were assigned different levels of brand advertising budgets, and the results in brand share were tracked over time. Results showed a multimodal, "M-shaped" response curve between advertising expenditure and market share; this was explained as being caused by two different market segments with different response curves. These results were replicated in two studies; the first field experiment used 18 markets, while the second used 38 markets. In the advertising budgeting literature (e.g., Aaker and Carman 1982), this series of studies is used as an example of overadvertising, or advertising beyond the level of saturation.

Relative to lab experiments or sample surveys, this research speaks with a rather clear voice. The external validity is high: the results are based on changes from a real advertising campaign and were assessed with real marketplace behaviors over a series of months. The internal validity is also rather high: the results were replicated, and reasonable efforts were made to equalize or match the cities assigned to the different treatments.

From this series of field experiments, the following was learned about the advertising–beer-brand-share relationship: (1) increasing the level of a brand's advertising expenditure—up to a point—positively influences the brand's market share, and (2) if the current level of advertising is beyond a saturation level, then decreasing advertising can result in increased sales.

What is most unfortunate about this series of field studies for the current interest is that (1) Atkin's search revealed *only one* field experiment examining advertising and alcohol consumption, and (2) the dependent variable used in this research—Budweiser market share—is somewhat far afield from the alcohol-related behaviors of interest to NIAAA.

The relative scarcity of relevant field experiments only serves to reinforce the fact that quality field experimentation is very costly, both in terms of dollars and intra-organizational cooperation. Furthermore, the research conducted to understand one phenomenon (e.g., some brand's share) may not be very useful for understanding another (e.g., initial usage behavior among adolescents of some product category, like beer).

A RESEARCH DESIGN PRESCRIPTION: MORE FIELD EXPERIMENTS

To have better knowledge about whether advertising influences alcohol initiation, consumption, or abuse levels, there is a limited need for more lab experiments and sample surveys. The results of such studies are mired in problems of either external or internal validity and have, so far, produced only circumstantial evidence. Additional lab studies and sample surveys will most likely be similarly limited.

Field experimentation, however, that is specifically focused on advertising's direct effects on alcohol use and abuse seems to be very much in order. The circumstantial evidence from less definitive research designs puts the scientific alcohol literature at the stage where studies based on large-scale field experimentation are justified. Given the suggestive evidence offered by the less costly, but more limited, lab studies and surveys, it makes good sense to pay the steep price of implementing field experiments at this stage of knowledge development. Only carefully controlled field studies offer the promise of results with both high external and internal validity.

Split-Cable Television Advertising Experimentation

Atkin suggests that alcohol researchers' field experiments can be carried out in split-cable television communities. Although split-cable facilities are routinely used by marketers of packaged goods like cake mix or yogurt to conduct television advertising experiments or to test-market new products, it is unlikely that these facilities would be very useful for research questions of interest to NIAAA.

The limitations of commercial split-cable facilities for alcohol researchers become obvious once the procedures used are spelled out. In brief, several large marketing research firms (e.g., Nielsen, Information Resources, Inc., etc.) operate panels of some 3,000 households per city in dozens of medium sized cities around the country (e.g., Midland, TX, Springfield, MO) that are dependent upon cable for television reception. Households in these cities' panels are assigned to split-cable cells of advertising manipulations, and matched cells of households are exposed, according to some experimental design, to different television advertising treatments. Panelists know their television signals are being manipulated, but do not know which ads are "test" ads. Panelists identify themselves as panel members at the checkout stand when making purchases in grocery or drug stores. The purchases of panel households are recorded at checkout via optical scanning of UPC codes contained on the packages of their purchases. Consequently, the purchasing behavior of panelists assigned different advertising treatments can be examined.

For alcohol researchers, an important limitation of these split-cable facilities concerns the dependent variables. First, note that *household* purchasing—not *individual* usage, consumption, or abuse—is being measured. Second, only grocery or drug store purchases of packaged goods are being tracked. Totally missed are purchases for off-premise consumption at liquor stores, convenience stores, etc., and purchases for on-premise consumption at bars, restaurants, etc. Third, there is little opportunity for survey research measurements of panelists' beliefs, attitudes, behaviors, and so on. The research firms operating these split-cable panels typically are simultaneously managing multiple experiments for their packaged-goods clients in every panel. If every client had their way, panelists' purchasing would not only be unobtrusively measured via optical scanning, but panelists' beliefs, attitudes, and usage behaviors would be constantly and obtrusively measured via written diaries or repeated phone or face-to-face surveys. This, of course, would sensitize and wear out the panel and thus seriously compromise all split-cable data for everyone. Consequently, these research firms seek to protect panelists from obtrusive measures, and thus survey research is typically limited to one or two combined (or omnibus-type) questionnaires for all clients per panel per year.

Split-cable facilities have been developed as an off-the-shelf research product to meet the needs of the packaged-goods marketer who relies on television advertising and whose goods are sold in grocery and drug outlets. Because of problems with dependent variable measurement, these facilities are not directly applicable in their present form to the needs of alcohol researchers.

By augmenting these off-the-shelf, split-cable laboratories, however, some inventive researchers in public health fields related to alcohol research have been able to ameliorate dependent variable measurement problems. An example is the Robertson et al. (1974) split-cable experiment studying advertising effects on seat-belt usage. This study succeeded due to an unobtrusive measure of wearing belts, as researchers peered down on drivers' laps and shoulders from high step-ladders placed at major street intersections and then recorded seat-belt behavior and the license tag number (to establish panelist identification). Perhaps inventive alcohol researchers can be just as creative in solving their dependent variable measurement problems.

Multicity Field Experiments

Given the obstacles associated with commercial split-cable facilities for alcohol research, it makes sense to reconsider the precursor of split-cable—the multicity field experiment. In addition to the obvious benefit of high external validity compared with lab experiments, multicity field experiments offer two key advantages over split-cable: (1) freedom to assess beliefs, attitudes, behaviors, etc., via conventional surveys or panel diaries and thus do a better job of measuring dependent variables other than grocery-store purchasing, and (2) ability to manipulate all advertising media (i.e., not just television, as in split-cable).

The internal validity of multicity field experiments can be limited if there are insufficient replications per treatment. In these field studies, different experimental treatments may be assigned between sites or cities. Therefore, differences observed between sites may be due to inherent differences in the sites rather than differences between treatments. However, with careful matching of sites, multiple sites per treatment, and monitoring of other non-advertising activities at the site, this problem can be adequately addressed.

Another Multicity Field Experiment

To help make Atkin's review of advertising effects on alcohol abuse more complete, a brief discussion follows of a field experiment reported by Murry et al. (1993, 1994) that was not published at the time Atkin completed his review. Moreover, some discussion of this additional study will help to illustrate the advantages and disadvantages of multicity field experiments.

Overview

This research examined the effect of a *paid* media advertising campaign on youth drinking-driving behavior. Although previous media efforts to combat drinking and driving have been largely unsuccessful, these efforts have relied primarily upon *donated* media campaigns using public service announcements (PSAs) (Salmon 1990). In contrast, this research examined if a well-funded anti–drinking-and-driving advertising campaign targeted at youth could be successful.

Campaign Planning

The campaign relied upon lifestyle research discussed in Lastovicka et al. (1987, 1990) to guide its development.

The primary target for these messages was 18- to 24-year-old males, although it was anticipated that the campaign would have a spillover effect on a secondary target segment, namely, the more general 15- to 24-year-old male *and* female population.

Experimental Design

This field experiment relied upon a multiple time series quasi-experimental design that included an "advertising" site and a "control" site. Campbell and Stanley (1966) deem such a design to be one of the strongest of quasi-experimental designs. Thus, this design evaluated the effects of a real advertising campaign on two different, but comparable, geographic markets.

Dependent variables relied on two independent measurement systems: (1) pretest and posttest surveys of self-reported drinking-driving behavior, and (2) counts of fatal and incapacitating highway accidents at each site.

Site Selection

The two demographically comparable cities portrayed in table 1 were used as sites. These sites—both from the same "Great Plains" section of the country—are sufficiently separated geographically so that broadcast signals from one do not leak to the other.

Experimental Treatment

In the advertising site (Wichita, KS), a paid media campaign was implemented from March through August 1986. In total, some $90,000 worth of media time and space was purchased over five media (television, radio, newspapers, outdoor, and theater trailers), with about two-thirds

Table 1. Wichita and Omaha Demography (1980 Census).

	Wichita	Omaha
Total population	411,313	483,053
Percentage of the population aged 15 to 24	19.2	19.5
Racial composition (percentage)		
White	88	89
Black	8	9
Hispanic	4	2
Other	3	2
Percentage of 18-year-old and older population that are high school graduates	75.4	79.9
Private car ownership	184,641	198,723

Note: Totals do not equal 100 percent as Hispanics are often counted as "others."

Reprinted with permission from Murry et al. 1993.

of this spent on television. If the broadcast campaign were scaled up to a national level, this would be comparable to a $22 million effort.

The control site (Omaha, NE) received no campaign treatment during the same time period.

Results of Sample Survey Data

Independent preintervention and postintervention telephone sample surveys of 18- to 24-year-old males were conducted at each site in September 1985 and September 1986. These surveys included measures of self-reported drinking-driving behavior, the major results of which are summarized in table 2. As these self-report data reveal, the percentage of respondents reporting to have driven during the previous month after consuming either four or six drinks decreased in the advertising site. In contrast, respondents at the control site indicated an increased propensity to drink and drive between the pretest and posttest periods.

Results From Vehicle Accident Data

Since nearly half of fatal and incapacitating accidents—especially single-vehicle accidents and nighttime accidents—result from drinking-driving, such accident counts are frequently used as proxies for alcohol-related accidents (Arnold 1985; Williams 1986). The six accident count variables (described in detail in table 3) were analyzed for 57 months, which included the 38 months before the intervention, the 6-month campaign intervention period, and the 13 months following the campaigns.

As with the self-reports from the sample surveys, initial examination of accident counts in table 4 suggests that the ad campaign reduced targeted drinking-driving behaviors. Table 4 compares the average monthly accident count for the period of the campaign (spring and summer 1986) relative to the prior spring and summer. Like the survey data findings, accident rates in the experimental site declined, and rates increased in the control site.

Table 2. Preintervention and Postintervention Sample Survey Estimates of Drinking-Driving.

	Wichita (Media Campaign)		Omaha (Control)	
	Preintervention	Postintervention	Preintervention	Postintervention
Sample size	205	221	203	157
Percentage who drove after 4 drinks in previous month	34.6	27.6	37.9	43.9
Percentage who drove after 6 drinks in previous month	20.5	16.7	22.2	24.2

Reprinted with permission from Murry et al. 1993.

Table 3. Definitions of Variables Used in Time Series Analysis.

Targeted Population	Variable	Definition
18- to 24-year-old males (M)	TOTAL-M	Total fatal and incapacitating accidents for 18- to 24-year-old males
	SINGLE-M	Single-vehicle fatal and incapacitating accidents for 18- to 24-year-old males
	NIGHT-M	Nighttime (8 p.m.–8 a.m.) fatal and incapacitating accidents for 18- to 24-year-old males
15- to 24-year-old males and females (MF)	TOTAL-MF	Total fatal and incapacitating accidents for 15- to 24-year-old males and females
	SINGLE-MF	Single-vehicle fatal and incapacitating accidents for 15- to 24-year-old males and females
	NIGHT-MF	Nighttime (8 p.m.–8 a.m.) fatal and incapacitating accidents for 15- to 24-year-old males and females

Reprinted with permission from Murry et al. 1993.

Such a rudimentary analysis of these accident statistics does not take into account long-term trends and autocorrelations that also could be responsible for the over-time differences in accident rates between sites in table 4. Therefore, the accident data were analyzed with the intervention method developed by Box and Tiao (1975). This method develops a statistical model of the time-series data prior to the campaign (termed a "preintervention model"), as well as a model of the data during the campaign (termed an "intervention model"). In five of the six series examined, there were statistically significant differences between the experimental site's intervention model predictions and the control site data, thus providing evidence of a campaign effect.

To help make this abbreviated discussion of a complicated time-series intervention analysis more concrete, a graphical illustration is offered. Figure 1 contains the preintervention model's prediction (the dotted line) of the proportion of single-vehicle incapacitating and fatal accidents involving 15- to 24-year-olds relative to the actual data (the solid line) versus the intervention model's prediction (the dashed line). As is shown, the actual accident rate—starting 2 months after the campaign began and continuing 2 months after the campaign ended—was less than the preintervention model's predictions. Such a gradual and lagged effect is consistent with how advertising is thought to influence behavior. Further, and also consistent with how advertising is thought to

Table 4. Average Number of Monthly Fatal and Incapacitating Accidents During Two Spring–Summer Periods.

Time Period	TOTAL-M	SINGLE-M	NIGHT-M	TOTAL-MF	SINGLE-MF	NIGHT-MF
			Wichita (Media Campaign)			
Spring–Summer 1985	11.33	2.17	6.00	19.50	3.67	9.33
Spring–Summer 1986	9.17	2.17	5.83	16.17	2.83	8.67
Percentage change	-19.12	0	-2.75	-17.09	-22.73	-7.14
			Omaha (Control)			
Spring–Summer 1985	6.83	2.17	4.17	9.83	2.67	5.67
Spring–Summer 1985	6.67	2.33	4.33	9.50	3.33	6.33
Percentage change	-2.44	+7.69	+4.00	-3.39	+25.00	+11.76

Reprinted with permission from Murry et al. 1993.

work, note that the campaign effects were temporary and the series returned to a preintervention forecast level less than 6 months after the campaign ended.

Discussion

This field experiment provides several types of evidence for the positive effect of an advertising campaign on one type of alcohol abuse behavior. Two important kinds of evidence stem from the diverse measurements. First are the sample survey results. Although these data are certainly plagued by under-reporting, which is characteristic of the measurement biases encountered with self-reports of undesirable behaviors (Sudman and Bradburn 1974), these are *direct* measures of the behavior the advertising was designed to influence, namely, drinking-driving behavior. Second are the accident data. Although these measures are only *indirect* measures of an *outcome* of drinking-driving behavior, these data do provide impressive collaborative evidence for the results suggested by the self-report data. Together, these two independent sources of dependent variable measures speak with an unambiguous voice. This research should clearly illustrate the virtues of constructing field experiments with multiple dependent variables, based in independent measurement systems possessing different forms of measurement bias.

These results must be tempered by internal validity concerns: Are the detected effects really due to advertising or to something else? For example, MacKinnon (1994) notes the major changes in Kansas legislation in July of 1985—changing the legal drinking age from 18 to 21 years of age and making seat-belt use compulsory—and then suggests these legal changes were responsible for the drinking-driving decreases observed in Wichita.

Due to the richness of this experiment's dependent variables, strong arguments support the position that the effects detected in this field experiment were due to a short-lived, but intense, advertising campaign (Murry et al. 1994) and not to State laws enacted 8 months before the start of the campaign. In particular, the mathematical time-series intervention model detects an experimental effect that was delayed (by 2 months after the campaign's start) and temporary (the accident rates return to baseline 2 months after the campaign's end). That advertising works step-by-step (i.e., *delayed* effects) and that advertising effects dissipate (i.e., *temporary* effects) in the absence of the reinforcement of a continuing campaign (due to the failings of human memory and the claims of competing campaigns) are well-accepted tenets of our understanding of how advertising works. In contrast, changes in legislation have more ***immediate*** and ***permanent*** effects. Furthermore, seat-belt laws should have no effect on self-reports of drinking-driving behavior; belt use and drinking-driving are two distinct behaviors.

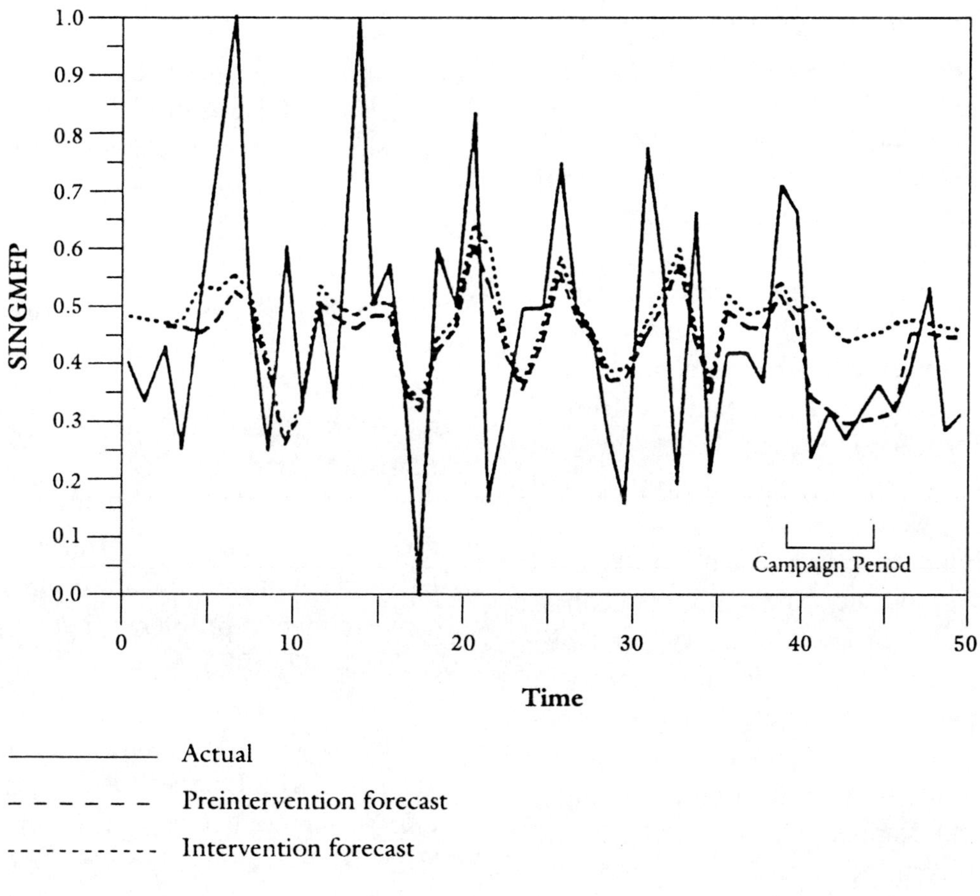

Figure 1. Time series plots of actual data (solid line), preintervention forecast (dotted line), and intervention forecast (dashed line).

Reprinted with permission from Murry et al. 1993.

CONCLUSIONS

The extant literature examining advertising effects on alcohol use and abuse relies too much on sample surveys and laboratory experiments. These research designs are ill-suited to provide strong causal evidence. The result is that although there are circumstantial data about the effects of advertising on alcohol use and abuse, there is very little direct evidence. Although advertising's influence on attention, perceptions, and attitudes can be effectively studied in surveys and lab studies, more field experiments are needed to study advertising's behavioral effects. Although costly and cumbersome to implement, field experiments offer the best promise of reasonable internal validity and high external validity.

Furthermore, future research needs to be precise in examining what kind of advertising is influencing what kind of alcohol-related behaviors. The extant literature is too heterogeneous; virtually all kinds of alcohol advertising and alcohol-related behaviors were discussed in the review. Data about the effect of any one kind of advertising on any one kind of alcohol-related behavior are scarce. Without distinctly identifying priorities in independent and dependent variables, future research results are doomed, when aggregated together, to continue to produce ambiguous, circumstantial results favoring a "no strong advertising effects" conclusion.

More crispness and focus is needed, as there are a variety of important and distinct questions that need answers, and it is unlikely that the answer to any one research question adequately addresses another. For example, the following questions are all worthy issues (to some), and all require distinct programs of research: Does branded alcoholic beverage advertising encourage underage drinking? Do the PSA-like campaigns run by brewers reduce drinking-driving? Do beer brands' television campaigns influence brand choice behavior? Do a brand's anti–drinking-driving PSAs encourage consumer switching behavior to the advertiser's brand or away from it?

REFERENCES

Aaker, D.A., and Carman, J.M. Are you overadvertising? *J Advert Res* 22(Aug./Sep.):57–70, 1982.
Ackoff, R.L., and Emshoff, J.R. Advertising research at Anheuser-Busch, Inc. (1963-68). *Sloan Manage Rev* 16(Winter–Spring):1–15, 1975.

Arnold, R. *Effect of Raising the Legal Drinking Age on Driver Involvement in Fatal Crashes: The Experience of Thirteen States.* Washington, DC: National Center for Statistical Analysis, 1985.

Box, G.E.P., and Tiao, G.C. Intervention analysis with applications to economic and environmental problems. *J Am Stat Assoc* 70:70–92, 1975.

Campbell, D.T., and Stanley, J.C. *Experimental and Quasi-Experimental Designs for Research.* Chicago: Rand McNally & Company, 1966.

Lastovicka, J.L.; Murry, J.P., Jr.; and Joachimsthaler, E.A. Evaluating the measurement validity of lifestyle typologies with qualitative measures and multiplicative factoring. *J Market Res* 27(Feb.):11–23, 1990.

Lastovicka, J.L.; Murry, J.P., Jr.; Joachimsthaler, E.A.; Bhalla, G.; and Scheurich, J. A lifestyle typology to model youthful male drinking driving. *J Consum Res* 14(Fall):257–263, 1987.

MacKinnon, D.P. Comment on Murry, Stam and Lastovicka. *J Am Stat Assoc* 89(426):724, 1994.

Moriarty, M.M., and Lastovicka, J.L. Time interval bias: Its impact on advertising budgeting. *Curr Issues Res Advert* 8(1):115–128, 1985.

Murry, J.P., Jr.; Stam, A.; and Lastovicka, J.L. Evaluating an anti-drinking and driving campaign with a sample survey and time series intervention analysis. *J Am Stat Assoc* 88(Mar.):50–56, 1993.

Murry, J.P., Jr.; Stam, A.; and Lastovicka, J.L. A reply to MacKinnon. *J Am Stat Assoc* 89(426):724–725, 1994.

Preston, I.L., and Thorson, E. The expanded association model: Keeping the hierarchy concept alive. *J Advert Res* 24(Feb./Mar.):59–65, 1984.

Robertson, L.S.; Kelly, A.B.; O'Neil, B.; Wixom, C.W.; Eisworth, R.; and Haddon W. A controlled study of the effect of television messages on safety belt use. *Am J Pub Health* 64:1071–1080, 1974.

Salmon, C.T. Information campaigns: Balancing social values and social change. *Sage Ann Rev Commun Res* 18:19–53, 1990.

Strickland, D.E. Advertising exposure, alcohol consumption and misuse of alcohol. In: Grant, M.; Plant, M.; and Williams, A., eds. *Economics and Alcohol: Consumption and Controls.* New York: Gardner Press, 1983. pp. 201–222.

Sudman, S., and Bradburn, N.H. *Response Effects in Surveys: A Review and Synthesis.* Chicago: Aldine Press, 1974.

Williams, A.F. Raising the legal purchase age in the United States: Its effects on fatal motor vehicle crashes. *Alcohol Drugs Driv* 2(2):1–12, 1986.

Chapter 5

Alcohol Advertising and Alcohol Consumption: Econometric Studies

Henry Saffer[1]

INTRODUCTION

Alcohol advertising is a public health issue if it increases total alcohol consumption.[2] The *Economist* estimates that the alcoholic beverage industry spends about $2.3 billion a year on all forms of promotion. The industry uses television, radio, print, and billboards to present consumers with favorable information about their products. In addition, the industry creates visibility and positive associations for their products with point-of-purchase advertising, consumer novelties, and sponsored events. Portrayals of alcohol consumption are also found in television programs, films, books, and music. These additional sources of information are usually unpaid but often portray alcohol consumption in a positive fashion. While both paid and unpaid media portrayals generally reflect social norms regarding alcohol consumption, the public health concern is that these messages may also affect social norms and ultimately result in increased alcohol consumption.

A number of studies have been conducted that examine the effects of alcohol advertising on public health. These econometric studies of alcohol consumption are based on demand theory, which hypothesizes that consumption is related to price, income, taste, and other factors. To estimate this demand function, the theoretical constructs must be represented by measurable empirical variables. This has directed econometric work on alcohol in the media to studies of paid advertising.

[1]National Bureau of Economic Research, 269 Mercer St., New York, NY 10003

[2]The public health issue is alcohol abuse rather than alcohol consumption. However, many researchers assume that in an alcohol consumption distribution function there is a proportionate relationship between the mean and the upper tail. If this assumption is true, then per capita consumption is a good proxy for alcohol abuse.

An econometric model of alcohol advertising typically specifies a function such as

$$C = \beta_0 + \beta_1 X_1 + \beta_2 X_2 + \ldots + \beta_n X_n + u$$

where C = alcohol consumption, and the X_i variables include alcohol advertising, alcohol price, income, demographic variables, and variables relating to the specific data set. The β_i values are estimated by regression and measure the effect of a small change in an X_i variable on C.

The purpose of this chapter is to review prior econometric work on alcohol advertising and to provide some recommendations for future work in this area and suggest some possible methodological approaches. Prior studies of alcohol advertising expenditures, alcohol advertising bans, and alcohol counteradvertising are reviewed, as are similar studies of cigarette advertising. A novel feature of this review is a simple economic model of how advertising affects demand, which shows why certain methodological approaches are more appropriate than others. This model is discussed in the next section of this chapter.

AN ECONOMIC MODEL OF ALCOHOL ADVERTISING AND ALCOHOL CONSUMPTION

Research on the effects of alcohol advertising has found a place in a varied academic literature. The communications and marketing literature (Atkin 1987) tends to focus on the cognitive processes that describe how alcohol advertising may change an individual's perceptions of a product. The economics literature (Schmalensee 1972) assumes that advertising contains persuasive information and focuses on the effects of advertising on industry demand, industry concentration, and profitability. A simple economic model of alcohol advertising is outlined in this section. This economic model of alcohol advertising is important because it provides some insights into how econometric studies of alcohol advertising should be conducted.

Advertising response functions show the marginal effect of a change in advertising at various levels of advertising. Economic theory suggests that due to diminishing marginal product, advertising response functions flatten out at some point.[3] Brand-level empirical work on the advertising response function clearly supports the diminishing marginal product assumption (Rao and Miller 1975; Ackoff and Emshoff 1975). The same theory that describes the brand-level advertising response function could be applied to the industry-level (i.e., alcohol) response function. An alcohol advertising response function is different from the brand-level response function in that advertising-induced sales must come at the expense of sales of nonalcohol products. Lambin (1976) provides some empirical support for the assumption of diminishing marginal product on the industry level.

There are a number of sources of both positive and negative information about alcohol available to consumers. Positive sources include sports and cultural event sponsorships, consumer novelties, in-store displays, clothing with brand names,

[3]The theory that continuous increments of an input to a production process will, at some point, begin to yield ever smaller increments of output is known as diminishing marginal product.

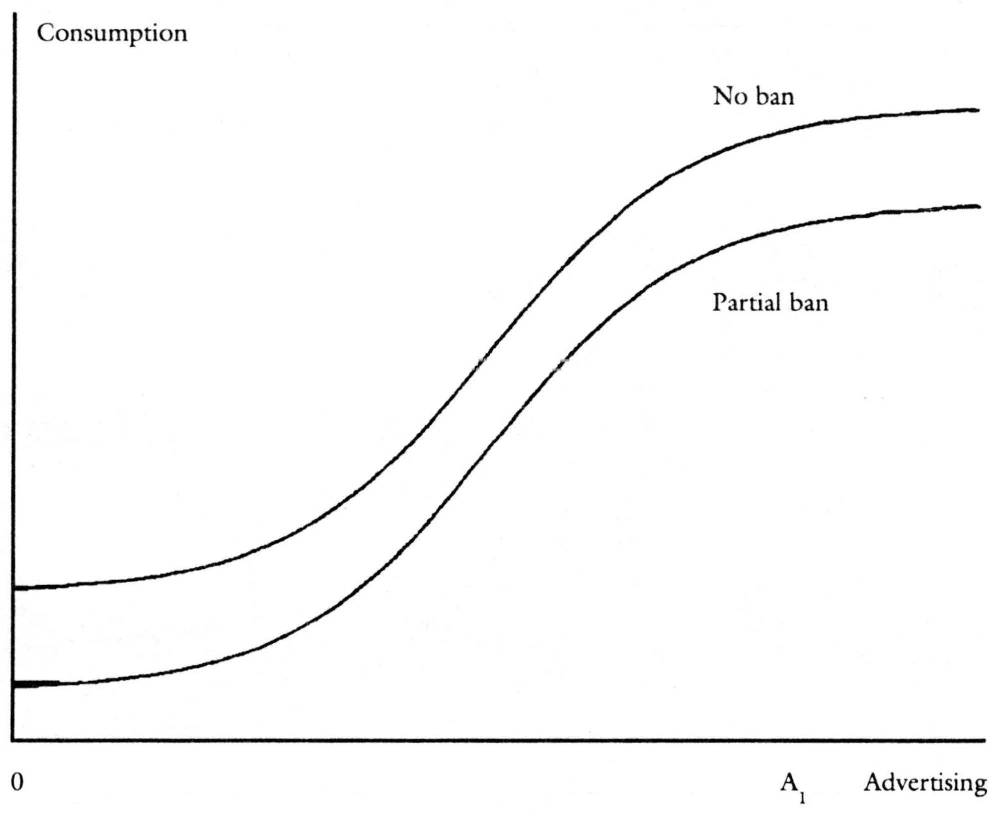

Figure 1. Alcohol advertising response function.

closed-circuit television in public places, product placements, direct marketing, and unpaid media portrayals. Negative information about alcohol comes from counteradvertising, health news reported in the mass media, other health education, and warning labels. Counteradvertising is defined as the use of the mass media to promote healthy behaviors. All of these additional sources of information are also subject to diminishing marginal product.

The alcohol advertising response function is graphed in figure 1. The vertical axis measures alcohol consumption, and the horizontal axis measures alcohol advertising. In figure 1, alcohol advertising increases consumption, but its effect is subject to diminishing marginal product. The counteradvertising response function is graphed in figure 2. Counteradvertising reduces consumption, and its effect is also subject to diminishing marginal product.

In figures 1 and 2 the imposition of an advertising ban on one or more media is shown as shifting the response function downward. The imposition of a ban on the use of one or more media can result in substitution of other media and other forms of marketing. However, since the marginal product of advertising in each specific media declines, the concentration of a given advertising budget into fewer media will result in a lower average product of advertising. A ban could also re-

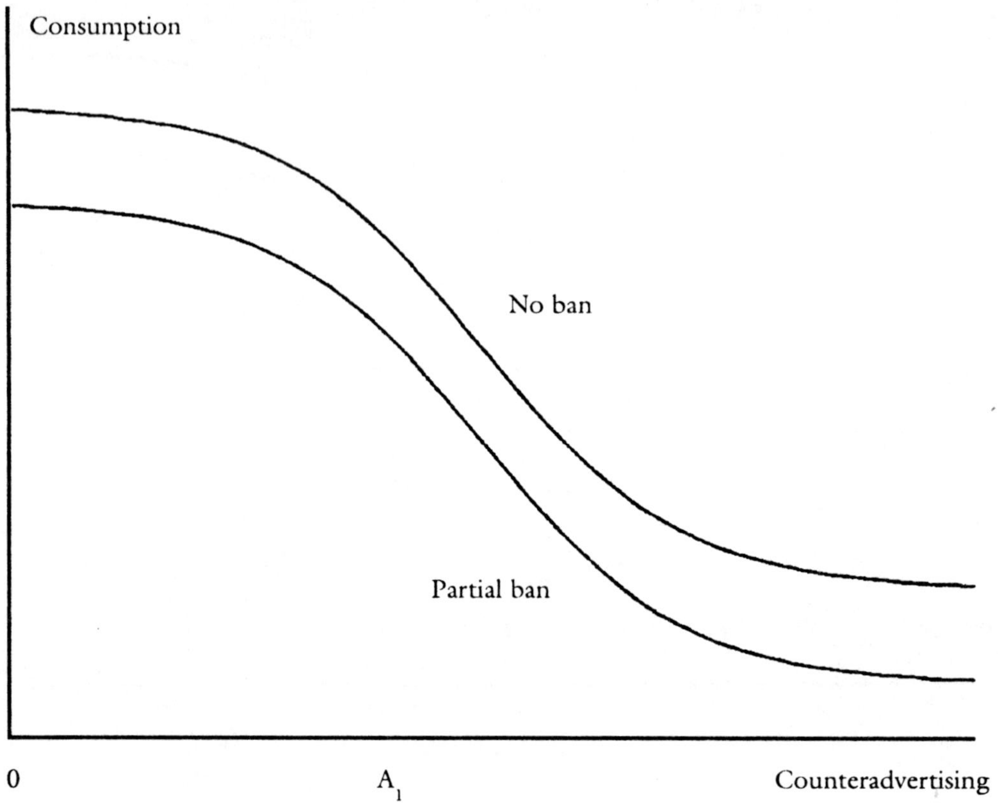

Figure 2. Alcohol counteradvertising response function.

duce consumption by signaling the collective perception that alcohol has potentially adverse health consequences. Changes in the level of other information about alcohol will also shift the function vertically as shown in figures 1 and 2.

Whether the response functions depicted in figures 1 and 2 accurately characterize the relationship between consumption, advertising, counteradvertising, and advertising bans is an empirical question. A more complete case for the industry-level response function can be made if the discussion is extended to include cigarette advertising. Econometric studies using highly aggregated measures such as annual national advertising expenditures do not find any effect of alcohol or cigarette advertising. Highly aggregated measures of advertising are likely to be in the range of marginal product near zero and to have little variation within the data set. In figure 1, this would be measuring advertising in a narrow range around A_1. The level of counteradvertising has been relatively low, so that empirical measurement occurs in a range where marginal returns are significant. Studies of counteradvertising measure advertising in a range around A_1 in figure 2. In this range the function has a measurable slope. Counteradvertising studies find that counteradvertising is effective in reducing consumption. Advertising ban studies find that bans reduce consumption. This supports the theory that bans shift the response function downward.

In future empirical studies, data sets should be constructed so that the measures of alcohol advertising cover a large variation in advertising. For example, a large variation in advertising would be from 0–A_1 in figure 1. This variation in alcohol advertising is more likely to be associated with a significant variation in consumption. One empirical strategy is to use short time aggregates such as quarters and to include as much cross-sectional variation as possible. The advertising must originate on the local level. Short time aggregates and cross-sectional variation are likely to have a larger variance in alcohol advertising due to local variation in the determinants of alcohol advertising demand, pulsing schedules, seasonal alcohol advertising patterns, and market targeting.[4] Another empirical strategy is to construct a data set that includes places or time periods in which alcohol advertising occurs and places or time periods in which alcohol advertising has been banned.

In summary, there are two key assumptions made in this section. The first assumption is that there is an industry-level advertising response function that is subject to diminishing marginal product. The second assumption is that when advertising expenditures are aggregated to the industry level, this level of spending is in the range of zero marginal product. These assumptions suggest that if marginal advertising effects are measured at a high level of advertising, these effects will be small or zero. This does not mean that the total effect of advertising is zero. The total effect of advertising can be large, while in certain ranges the marginal effect of advertising can be small or zero. These assumptions also suggest that extrapolating the results from studies that use a limited data range can lead to erroneous conclusions.

SPECIFICATION ISSUES IN ECONOMETRIC MODELS OF ADVERTISING

In addition to the data set requirements suggested above, four specification issues are worth noting[5]: (1) the nonlinear relationship between consumption and advertising, (2) simultaneity between consumption and advertising, (3) controlling for cumulative effects of advertising, and (4) the measurement of advertising.

The first econometric issue is specification of the functional relationship between advertising and consumption. The arguments presented in the previous section suggest that this relationship is nonlinear. There are several methods of allowing for a nonlinear specification. These include a logarithmic transformation of the dependent variable and the use of linear, squared, and cubed advertising terms.

The second econometric issue is simultaneity between advertising and con-

[4]Advertisers have developed a technique known as pulsing to avoid the problem of diminishing marginal product of advertising. Pulsing is the use of comparatively short bursts of advertising in a few markets at a time rather than running a steady, but weaker, schedule of advertising simultaneously in many markets.

[5]These are discussed in more detail in Saffer (1993) and Berndt (1991).

sumption. Some economists argue that advertising budgets are adjusted so that advertising expenditure is a fixed percentage of consumption. Alternatively, advertising may increase consumption. These assumptions imply that advertising and consumption are jointly determined. If this is the case, ordinary least squares estimation will be biased, and a two-stage least squares estimation model is needed. A two-stage estimation model must have a structural consumption equation and a structural advertising equation. The structural advertising equation is a demand-for-advertising equation. Both structural equations must be identified by at least one exogenous variable that does not appear in the other equation.

The third econometric issue in estimating the effects of alcohol advertising on alcohol consumption is controlling for the possible cumulative effects of advertising. Advertising will have cumulative effects if, as assumed in the previous section, consumption is a function of prior levels of advertising. One way to estimate this type of model is to include current advertising and lagged consumption as dependent variables. The coefficient of the advertising variable measures the contemporaneous effect of advertising on consumption. The coefficient of the lagged consumption variable measures the carryover effect of the prior period's advertising and other past determinants of consumption.

The last econometric issue involves the measurement of advertising. In estimating a demand curve using aggregate data and a per capita dependent variable, the advertising variable should measure the number of advertising messages presented in the aggregation group. If the dependent variable is not per capita, then the advertising variable should measure the number of advertising messages viewed.

REVIEW OF ECONOMETRIC STUDIES

Introduction

A summary of the methods suggested above for econometric studies of alcohol advertising may be useful before going on to the studies themselves. I have suggested that the type of data used for the analysis be chosen to maximize the variance in alcohol advertising. This can be achieved by including aggregates that ban advertising and aggregates that allow advertising. These aggregates should have had their advertising policy in place for some time to insure that consumers have adjusted to the policy. A second method of insuring sufficient variation in the advertising data is to include a considerable cross-sectional dimension in the data set. This must include advertising that originates in the cross-sectional observation. I have also suggested four specification issues that should be addressed. The possibility of implementing or testing these specification issues varies with the type of data employed. The first issue, testing nonlinear specifications, is relatively straightforward and should be possible with all data sets. The second issue, testing for simultaneous equations bias, is dependent on identifying an advertising demand curve. However, variables that could be used for this purpose are not always available. The third issue, cumulative effects of advertising, may not be testable if there is no lagged data for the dependent variable. The fourth issue is empirical proxies for effective advertising messages. It may not be possible to compute advertising messages in many data sets; however, advertising expenditure data are a reasonable alternative.

Since the type of data used in a study is likely to have considerable influence on the results, the studies of alcohol advertising that are reviewed in this chapter are grouped into three general categories based on the type of advertising data used in the study: (1) studies of alcohol advertising expenditure on alcohol consumption, (2) studies of alcohol advertising bans on various alcohol consumption measures, and (3) studies of alcohol counter-advertising on alcohol consumption.

Advertising Expenditure Studies

The most common type of expenditure study relies on a short time series of annual data from one country. This type of data measures advertising in the A_1 range in figure 1. As mentioned above, this type of study is likely to find no effect of advertising. Advertising is measured by expenditures, and control variables such as price and income are generally included. The studies by Grabowski (1976), McGuiness (1980), Duffy (1987), and Selvanathan (1989) are representative of this group.[6]

Grabowski (1976) studies the effect of advertising on consumer expenditure on alcohol. He uses a sample that includes 17 observations of annual data over the time period from 1956 to 1972. Logarithmic specifications are tested. He uses both a simultaneous model to account for endogeneity and lagged expenditure to account for the stock aspect of advertising. Grabowski thus accounts for nonlinearities, simultaneity, and cumulative effects. Annual data as well as the very small sample size are a problem. He finds that advertising has no effect on alcohol expenditures but that expenditure has a positive effect on alcohol advertising.

McGuiness (1980) examines the effect of print and television advertising on alcohol consumption. The time period includes 20 annual observations from 1956 to 1975 for the United Kingdom, and separate measures for beer, wine, and spirits advertising are used. Logarithmic models are tested, and a simultaneous model of consumption and advertising is estimated. McGuiness thus accounts for nonlinearities and simultaneity. Annual data and cumulative effects as well as the very small sample size are problems. He finds that spirits advertising has an effect on total alcohol consumption.

Duffy (1987) uses a nonlinear specification to examine the effect of television and print advertising on alcohol expenditures.[7] The data include 21 annual observations from 1963 to 1983 for the United Kingdom. Simultaneity, cumulative effects, and temporal aggregation bias are problems. He finds that beer advertising has an effect on alcohol expenditures.

[6]See also Comanor and Wilson (1974), Walsh (1982), McGuiness (1983), Duffy (1983), Johnson (1985), and Lee and Tremblay (1992). The results and methods used in these studies are not reviewed since they do not provide any additional information about expenditure studies.

[7]The specification is called a Rotterdam model. This specification is nonlinear but imposes additional constraints on the estimation parameters.

Selvanathan (1989) uses a systemwide analysis of the effects of advertising on the demand for beer, wine, and spirits in the United Kingdom for the period 1955 to 1975. He accounts for nonlinearities, simultaneity, and cumulative effects. The results show that beer advertising increases beer consumption and decreases wine and spirits consumption. Moreover, both wine and spirits advertising decrease the consumption of beer. The analysis is extended by considering advertising as a stock rather than a flow. It is found that advertising of alcoholic beverages fully depreciates in consumers' minds in 1 year. These results are somewhat surprising since annual data are employed in the estimation models.

Three additional studies improve upon the data problems somewhat. A study by Duffy (1991) and a study by Franke and Wilcox (1987) use quarterly data. Another study by Bourgeois and Barnes (1979) adds some novelty with cross-sectional data. The results in all three studies, however, provide no support for the hypothesis that advertising increases total demand.

Duffy (1991) extends his earlier work to include four aggregate categories of consumer nondurables. One of the included categories is alcoholic drink and tobacco. Duffy argues that better estimates of the effect of advertising on the interproduct distribution of demand are found with a set of product demand curves. The data are quarterly observations for the United Kingdom for 1963 to 1985. Nonlinearities and temporal aggregation bias are addressed, although simultaneity and cumulative effects are not considered. He concludes that advertising has no effect on total demand.

Franke and Wilcox (1987) examine the relationship between total advertising expenditures and per capita consumption of beer, wine, and distilled spirits in the United States. Advertising expenditures were analyzed for six different media: network and spot television, network radio, magazines, newspaper supplements, and billboards. Nonlinearities, simultaneity, and cumulative effects were not considered. The results show no evidence of a significant relationship between total advertising and consumption of beer. However, positive significant relationships were found between advertising and the consumption of wine and distilled spirits.

Bourgeois and Barnes (1979) use data for 10 Canadian provinces for the period 1951 to 1974. However, advertising data were available for only 5 of the years in the data set. In 4 of these 5 years, the data were limited to five regions. This apparently leaves only 30 observations. Nonlinearity, simultaneity, and cumulative effects were not considered. Temporal aggregation bias is also a problem because annual data were used. They find that neither print nor broadcast advertising has any effect on total alcohol consumption.

These studies provided little evidence that alcohol advertising increases the total demand for alcohol. The reason these studies do not find any effect of advertising is that they measure advertising at a high level with relatively little variance. In figure 1, these studies measure advertising around the range of A_1. Since the function is relatively flat in this range, a regression will appropriately generate slope coefficients that are not significantly different than zero.

Another type of study by Saffer (1994) uses market-level data to test the effects of alcohol advertising on highway fatality rates. The unit of observation in this data set is an area of dominant influence (ADI), as defined by the Arbitron Company. The ADI consists of an aggregation of counties within the reach of a group of television transmitters. The ADI is similar to, but somewhat larger than, a metropolitan statistical area. The data set consists of quarterly observations from 1986 to 1989 for the top 75 ADIs in the United States. These 75 television markets account for more than 75 percent of the total population. The advertising data used in this study is of local origin and is called spot advertising. The dependent variables in this study consist of a series of highway fatality rates computed with data from the Fatal Accident Reporting System. A logistic transformation of the dependent variables is used. The independent variables consist of alcohol advertising expenditures on television, radio, and billboards. Other independent variables on the ADI level include alcohol prices, personal income, and demographic information. Regional dummies are also included in the regressions. Results from regression models that account for endogeneity of advertising expenditure show that advertising increases highway fatalities.

In this study the use of 75 cross-sectional observational aggregates, observed on a quarterly basis, with locally originating advertising builds in considerable variation in the advertising data. In figure 1, advertising is measured over a range between 0 and A_1. Since the data fall in a range where the function is upward-sloping, a regression will likely generate a positive slope coefficient.

Advertising Ban Studies

As detailed above, the problem with most studies of alcohol advertising expenditures is the use of data measuring relatively small variations in alcohol advertising. Since advertising bans represent large variations in advertising expenditure, cross-sectional or time-series studies of advertising bans are more appropriate empirical strategies for testing the effect of alcohol advertising on alcohol consumption.

Prior studies of alcohol advertising bans include Smart and Cutler (1976) and Ogborne and Smart (1980). These studies examine the effect of advertising bans in British Columbia and Manitoba, respectively. The ban in British Columbia included all alcohol advertising but lasted only 1 year. The ban in Manitoba included only beer advertising and was analyzed using an 8-year time series. Both studies concluded that these advertising bans had no effect on alcohol consumption. These studies were done using interrupted time series, which cannot account for other factors such as cross-border alcohol advertising coming from the United States. These results may indicate that in a single province or country study, a long time period is necessary before there is any observable change in alcohol consumption.

Another study of advertising bans was conducted by Saffer (1991). The data set used in this study is a time series of cross-sections consisting of 17 countries for the years 1970 through 1983. The independent variables include measures that indicate whether alcohol advertising is allowed or banned. An international data set is the best way to measure the effect of a ban on alcohol advertising. Data from one country is not adequate since changes in alcohol advertising bans within countries are rare, and the imposition of a ban requires an extended period for consumption to adjust. There is, however, considerable variation in the use of advertising bans across countries. The outcome measures used in this study are mean alcohol consumption, liver cirrhosis mortality rate, and motor vehicle fatality rate. Two dichotomous alcohol advertising ban variables were defined. One variable measures bans on spirits broadcast advertising and the other measures bans on beer and wine broadcast advertising. Every country that bans beer and wine advertising also bans spirits advertisements. Other variables included in the regressions were alcohol price, real income, tourism, and road kilometers. Several methods were used to control for cultural differences across countries that may affect alcohol consumption. The empirical results show that countries with bans on alcohol advertising generally have lower levels of alcohol abuse.

Counteradvertising

Counteradvertising is subject to the same increasing and diminishing marginal returns as advertising. However, the level of counteradvertising is relatively low, so that empirical measurement occurs in a range where marginal returns are significant. Studies of counteradvertising are likely to measure advertising in a range around A_1 in figure 2. Empirical studies are thus likely to show that counteradvertising reduces alcohol consumption. Defining counteradvertising is complicated by the fact that many moderation-oriented advertisements are sponsored by alcohol producers. Since these messages always prominently display the company's brand name, it is not clear how this type of advertising should be classified.[8] Counteradvertising messages are often aimed at young consumers and are designed to reduce drunk driving.

Most studies of alcohol counteradvertising are not econometric and are based on social learning theory. However, a recent econometric study by McCarthy and Ziliak (1990) suggests the possible effects of counteradvertising. The purpose of this study was to evaluate the effect that Mothers Against Drunk Driving (MADD) chapters have on alcohol-related accidents. One of MADD's functions is to educate people about the dangers of drunk driving. The observational units are incorporated cities in the State of California during the period from 1982 to 1985. Drunk driving is measured by the number of per capita alcohol-related accidents in a city. MADD activities are measured by a dummy variable that is equal to 1 if the county in which the city is located has a MADD chapter. An initial look at the data reveals that counties with more serious drunk-driving problems were more likely to establish MADD chapters. A simultaneous estimation model is used to account for the endogenous nature of MADD chapters and drunk driving. The results indicate that drunk driving increases the probability of a MADD chapter and that MADD had a significant effect on reducing the number of DUI accidents.

Cigarette Advertising

Since there have not been many alcohol advertising ban studies or many alcohol

[8]An example from non-alcohol-producer sponsorship illustrates the complications this type of advertising creates. Freeman and Walley (1988) report that a General Foods Corporation campaign raised $100,000 for MADD and increased sales of a product associated with the campaign by 13 percent.

counteradvertising studies, an examination of the econometric results from cigarette advertising studies may provide some additional empirical support for the economic model presented earlier. Cigarette consumption in the United States has been affected by two important information events and two important changes in policy governing the use of broadcast media by cigarette advertisers. First, in 1953, a highly publicized report was released by the American Cancer Society warning about the dangers of smoking. In 1964, in another highly publicized report, the Surgeon General of the United States concluded that cigarette smoking caused cancer. This was followed by mandatory cigarette counteradvertising from mid-1967 to 1970. Finally, in 1971, broadcast advertising of cigarettes was banned. Econometric studies of cigarette advertising must account for the impact of these events as well as advertising, price, and other factors. While this requires more variables in cigarette advertising studies that cover this time period, these events also provide more opportunity for econometric models to demonstrate their relevance.

There are four cigarette advertising expenditure studies that are representative of this type of study. These studies use U.S. annual advertising expenditure, although for different time intervals, and all of them find that advertising has no effect on cigarette consumption. These studies are Hamilton (1972; data period 1925–70); Schmalensee (1972; 1955–67); Schneider et al. (1981; 1930–78); Baltagi and Levin (1986; 1963–80).

There are two studies of cigarette advertising per capita that use aggregate time-series data and find a positive effect of per capita advertising on consumption. The first study is McGuiness and Cowling (1980), who used U.K. quarterly advertising messages from the second quarter 1957 to the fourth quarter 1968. The second study is Seldon and Doroodian (1989), who used U.S. annual advertising expenditures from 1952 to 1984.[9] The results of these studies are hard to interpret since per capita advertising, whether expenditures or messages, is not an appropriate method of measuring advertising. This is because an advertising message is a type of public good that is not depleted in any way when seen by one individual.

Another study, by Lewitt et al. (1981), used a data set of 6,768 youths observed from March 1966 to March 1970. This time period includes the period of the Fairness Doctrine. The data set included the month of interview, cigarette consumption, and time spent watching television. Using national-level data on advertising and counteradvertising and individual data on hours spent watching television, they constructed variables measuring individual exposure to advertising and counteradvertising. Since these youths are distributed across the country, these variables proxy for advertising and counteradvertising originating both locally and nationally. The local advertising component increases the variance in advertising, which increases the probability of observing advertising in a range where the marginal product is significantly greater than zero. Their results showed that when consumption was

[9] Hamilton (1972) used both per capita advertising and aggregate advertising. Advertising was insignificant in both cases.

regressed on a nonlinear specification of these advertising variables, advertising had a positive effect on consumption, while counteradvertising was found to have a negative effect on consumption.

Two studies of cigarette advertising bans using international data have also been published. Hamilton (1975) used data on 11 countries over the period from 1948 to 1973. He presents country-specific regressions that include a ban dummy if the country enacted a ban during the period covered by the data set. These regressions do not find any significant effect of a ban. This lack of any effect may simply indicate that in a single cross-section, a long period is necessary before the effect of a ban can be observed. Hamilton also presents a set of regressions using pooled data. The three pools include countries with bans and countries without bans. The three pools include two, four, and nine countries, respectively. These regressions also find no effect of a ban.

A second study of cigarette advertising bans using international data was done by Laugesen and Meads (1991). They used data from 22 Organization for Economic Cooperation and Development countries for the period 1960 to 1986. Like Hamilton, they also find that prior to 1973, cigarette advertising bans had no effect on consumption. However, they find that after 1973, cigarette advertising bans have had a significant negative effect on consumption. Laugesen and Meads argue that prior to 1973, manufacturers were able to increase alternative marketing efforts in response to broadcast advertising restrictions. This is unmeasured in the data set and offsets the effect of the broadcast bans. However, after 1972, more comprehensive antismoking legislation was enacted, which restricted advertising efforts to a greater degree and resulted in lower cigarette consumption.

All of the U.S. studies described above include various types of variables that measure the antismoking publicity events in 1953 and 1964 and during the Fairness Doctrine period. The studies conclude that counteradvertising was effective in reducing cigarette consumption. A comprehensive review by Flay (1987) of 56 counteradvertising campaigns also concludes that counteradvertising is effective in reducing cigarette consumption.

RECONCILING THE MODEL AND THE ECONOMETRIC STUDIES

The econometric studies of alcohol advertising reviewed above have been grouped into three categories. The first category included studies of alcohol advertising expenditures on alcohol consumption. Although most econometric studies fall in this category, these studies do not provide any consistent evidence that alcohol advertising affects alcohol use. The second category included studies of alcohol advertising bans on various aggregate alcohol use measures. Studies of this type using international data provide evidence that advertising bans reduce alcohol abuse. The third category included studies of alcohol counteradvertising on alcohol use. Although there is only one study that can be classified as a counteradvertising study, it suggests that counteradvertising may reduce abuse.

When econometric studies of cigarette advertising are grouped by expenditure studies, ban studies, and counteradvertising studies, the results parallel the corresponding alcohol advertising studies. That is, cigarette advertising expenditure studies show no effect on consumption. International cigarette advertising ban studies find that bans reduce consumption. There have been a number of econometric studies that estimate the effects of cigarette counteradvertising, and these studies consistently find that counteradvertising is an effective method of reducing cigarette consumption.

The results from all of these alcohol and cigarette studies support the economic model of advertising presented earlier in this chapter. This model is summarized in figure 1, which has consumption on the vertical axis and advertising on the horizontal axis. The relationship between consumption and advertising is nonlinear with decreasing marginal product at high levels of advertising. Studies of alcohol and cigarette advertising expenditures are likely to measure advertising near A_1 in figure 1. This is in the range where the marginal returns to advertising are near zero. Since the function is relatively flat in this range, there will be no clear relationship between advertising and consumption found in the econometric results. Studies using cross-sectional data and local advertising measure advertising in a range such as $0–A_1$. Since the function is relatively steep in this range, econometric studies of this type are more likely to find significant effects. Studies of advertising bans compare aggregation units with and without advertising. Studies of counteradvertising are likely to measure advertising in a range around A_1 in figure 2. Again, this type of study is likely to find a significant relationship.

FUTURE RESEARCH

There are three interesting topic areas for future econometric research on alcohol advertising: (1) studies using data sets that maximize the variance in the advertising data, including new studies on international advertising bans that use cross-sectional data and include advertising originating in the cross-sectional units; (2) studies on counteradvertising; and (3) studies on the effects of targeted advertising and targeted counteradvertising.

In the first topic area, the international study of advertising bans by Saffer (1991) could be extended with a data set that has more independent variables, more countries, and more recent data. The study of advertising bans is important because the large variation in expenditure that bans represent is more likely to result in measurable variations in consumption than studies using expenditures. The study of advertising bans is also important since they are a likely policy choice for regulation of alcohol advertising. New studies of this type should also consider endogeneity between alcohol use and advertising bans, as well as the effects of serial correlation. Additional studies using extensive cross-sectional data such as Saffer (1994) could also be useful.

The second topic area is counteradvertising. Econometric work on alcohol counteradvertising is very limited. One approach to studying the effects of counteradvertising is based on the ADI-level data described above. ADI-level alcohol sales data and other ADI-level indicators of alcohol abuse can be used as dependent variables, and alcohol counteradvertising expenditures could be used as additional independent variables. Since this type of data is not routinely collected by Arbitron and LNA (Leading National Advertisers), a first step in this type of work would be data collection.

The third area of study for future research is targeted advertising and counteradvertising. Targeting refers to tailoring advertising content to appeal to specific demographic groups and choosing a media designed to reach specific demographic groups. For targeting to be a public health issue, the level of exposure must be higher than in nontargeted groups. Targeting can also be a public health issue if the targeted groups are more vulnerable to advertising imagery and have less access to health education than the population in general.

Several public interest groups and the Surgeon General of the United States have criticized alcohol producers for targeting advertising at blacks, Hispanics, and young people. The alcohol producers contend that their advertising has no causal influence on the level of alcohol abuse. They also contend that there is no targeting of individuals under the legal drinking age, since the industry has adopted voluntary advertising guidelines that prohibit such advertising.

Econometric research on targeted advertising is very limited. One econometric approach to this problem is addressed in the study by Saffer (1994) described earlier in this chapter. A demand-for-advertising equation is estimated as a part of this study. The demand for advertising is a function of the price of advertising and other factors that vary systematically across ADIs. Since there is variation in the percentage of each ADI that is black, Hispanic, and underage, these percentages can be included as independent variables in the regression models.

Some preliminary regressions show that ADIs with larger minority populations and underage populations have more alcohol advertising. These regressions provide some initial evidence that minorities, and particularly youth, are targeted. Additional work in this area would be very useful.

Another approach to targeting is to study selective media such as billboards, magazines, and non-English-language newspapers and broadcasting. Magazine data offer the best possibility of measuring targeted advertising; alcohol advertising by specific magazine, by month, and by region are available. Annual demographic profiles for all major magazines are also available.[10] A data set could be constructed, using the magazine as the unit of observation, to include alcohol advertising expenditures and demographic characteristics. This data set could be used to test for disproportionate advertising expenditures by demographic category.

The final issue is targeted counteradvertising. If the cost of health information is higher for certain demographic groups than for the population in general, then these groups will consume less health information. If this is the case, then targeted counteradvertising would be appropriate. Targeted counteradvertising is counteradvertising that uses appropriate media and content to reach the designated demographic groups. There is relatively little known about health knowledge differentials across demographic groups and how these differentials are affected by counteradvertising. Casual empiricism

[10]The magazine data are available from the Publishers Information Bureau of Leading National Advertisers. The demographic data on magazine readership are available from Simmons Market Research Bureau. See Warner et al. (1992) for an interesting application of these data to cigarette advertising.

suggests, however, that there are significant differences in health knowledge across demographic groups. Future research on the determinants of these differentials, if they exist, and on whether targeted counteradvertising can affect these differentials, would be very useful.

ACKNOWLEDGMENTS

I would like to thank Michael Grossman, Frank Chaloupka, Robert Kaestner, Victor Tremblay, Susan Martin, the participants at the NIAAA Working Group on Mass Media, and two anonymous referees for their helpful comments on this chapter.

REFERENCES

Ackoff, R., and Emshoff, J. Advertising research at Anheuser-Busch, Inc. (1963–68). *Sloan Manage Rev* 16(2) 1–15, 1975.

Atkin, C. Alcoholic-beverage advertising: Its content and impact. In: Holder, H., ed. *Control Issues in Alcohol Abuse Prevention: Strategies for States and Communities*. Greenwich, CT: JAI Press, 1987. pp. 267–287.

Baltagi, B., and Levin, D. Estimating dynamic demand for cigarettes using panel data: The effects of bootlegging, taxation and advertising reconsidered. *Rev Econ Stat* 68:148–55, 1986.

Berndt, E. *The Practice of Econometrics: Classic and Contemporary*. Reading, MA: Addison-Wesley, 1991.

Bourgeois, J., and Barnes, J. Does advertising increase alcohol consumption? *J Advert Res* 19(4):19–29, 1979.

Comanor, W., and Wilson, T. *Advertising and Market Power*. Cambridge: Harvard University Press, 1974.

Duffy, M. The demand for alcoholic drink in the United Kingdom, 1963–78. *Appl Econ* 15(1):125–140, 1983.

Duffy, M. Advertising and the inter-product distribution of demand. *Eur Econ Rev* 31:1051–1070, 1987.

Duffy, M. Advertising in demand systems: Testing a Galbraithian hypothesis. *Appl Econ* 23:485–496, 1991.

Flay, B. *Selling the Smokeless Society*. Washington, DC: American Public Health Association, 1987.

Franke, G., and Wilcox, G. Alcoholic beverage advertising and consumption in the United States, 1964–1984. *J Advert* 16(3):22–30, 1987.

Freeman, L., and Walley, W. Marketing With a Cause Takes Hold. *Advertising Age*. May 16, 1988. pp. 30–32.

Grabowski, H. The effects of advertising on the interindustry distribution of demand. *Explor Econ Res* 3(1):21–75, 1976.

Hamilton, J. The demand for cigarettes: Advertising, the health scare, and the cigarette ban. *Rev Econ Stat* 54:401–11, 1972.

Hamilton, J. The effect of cigarette advertising bans on cigarette consumption. In: *Proceedings of the Third World Conference on Smoking and Health*. Washington, DC: U.S. Dept. of Health, Education, and Welfare, 1975. pp. 735–740.

Johnson, L. Alternative econometric estimates of the effects of advertising on the demand for alcoholic beverages in the United Kingdom. *Int J Advert* 4(1):19–25, 1985.

Lambin, J. *Advertising, Competition and Market Conduct in Oligopoly Over Time.* Amsterdam: North-Holland, 1976.

Laugesen M., and Meads, C. Tobacco advertising restrictions, price, income and tobacco consumption in OECD countries, 1960–1986. *Br J Addict* 86:1343–1354, 1991.

Lee, B., and Tremblay, V. Advertising and the US market demand for beer. *Appl Econ* 24:69–76, 1992.

Lewitt, E.; Coate, D.; and Grossman, M. The effects of government regulation on teenage smoking. *J Law Econ* 24:545–569, 1981.

McCarthy, P., and Ziliak, J. The effect of MADD on drinking-driving activities: An empirical study. *Appl Econ* 22:1215–27, 1990.

McGuiness, T. An econometric analysis of total demand for alcoholic beverages in the U.K. 1956–1975. *J Ind Econ* 29(1):85–105, 1980.

McGuiness, T. The demand for beer, spirits and wine in the UK, 1956–1979. In: Grant, M.; Plant, M.; and Williams, A., eds. *Economics and Alcohol.* New York: Gardner Press, 1983. pp. 238–242.

McGuiness, T., and Cowling, K. Advertising and the aggregate demand for cigarettes. *Eur Econ Rev* 14:127–30, 1980.

Ogborne, A., and Smart, R. Will restrictions on alcohol advertising reduce alcohol consumption? *Br J Addict* 75:293–296, 1980.

Rao, R., and Miller, P. Advertising/sales response functions. *J Advert Res* 15(Apr.):7–15, 1975.

Saffer, H. Alcohol advertising bans and alcohol abuse: An international perspective. *J Health Econ* 10:65–79, 1991.

Saffer, H. Advertising under the influence. In: Hilton, M. E., and Bloss, G., eds. *Economics and the Prevention of Alcohol-Related Problems.* NIAAA Research Monograph No. 25. NIH Pub. No. 93–3513. Washington, DC: Supt. of Docs., U.S. Govt. Print. Off., 1993.

Saffer, H. "Alcohol Advertising and Highway Fatalities." Unpublished manuscript. National Bureau of Economic Research, New York, 1994.

Schmalensee, R. *The Economics of Advertising.* Amsterdam: North-Holland, 1972.

Schneider, L.; Klein B.; and Murphy, K. Governmental regulation of cigarette health information. *J Law Econ* XXIV:575–612, 1981.

Seldon, B., and Doroodian, K. A simultaneous model of cigarette advertising: Effects on demand and industry response to public policy. *Rev Econ Stat* 71(4):673–677, 1989.

Selvanathan, E. Advertising and alcohol demand in the UK: Further results. *Int J Advert* 8:181–188, 1989.

Smart, R., and Cutler, R. The alcohol advertising ban in British Columbia: Problems and effects on beverage consumption. *Br J Addict* 71:13–21, 1976.

Walsh, B. The demand for alcohol in the UK: A comment. *J Ind Econ* 30(4):439–446, 1982.

Warner, K.; Goldenhar, L.M.; and McLaughlin, C. G. Cigarette advertising and magazine coverage of the hazards of smoking. *N Engl J Med* 326(5):305–309, 1992.

Chapter 6

"Alcohol Advertising and Alcohol Consumption: Econometric Studies"—Comments

Victor J. Tremblay[1]

Saffer provides a useful discussion of the potential effects of alcohol advertising on alcohol consumption (see chapter 5, this volume). He provides an excellent review of the empirical work done in this area, examining international and U.S. studies and summarizing the major econometric problems associated with advertising. Most importantly, he develops the concept of a "nonlinear advertising response function," which helps to justify the seemingly contradictory empirical evidence regarding the effects of alcohol advertising, advertising bans, and counteradvertising on alcohol consumption. He also describes new empirical evidence on the demand for advertising, which shows that there is more advertising in regions with larger minority and underage populations. Finally, he provides recommendations for future research.

Although Saffer's chapter provides an accurate assessment of the econometric evidence regarding the relationship between alcohol advertising and consumption, I have several comments. First, even though the focus of this monograph is on the effects of the mass media on alcohol consumption, policies other than advertising constraints may be more effective in reducing alcohol consumption. For example, if society's goal is to reduce alcohol consumption, a more direct and effective route may be to simply increase prices by raising alcohol taxes. Note, however, that the opposite has occurred in the brewing industry, where the real (or effective) tax rate per 31-gallon barrel (in 1982–84 dollars) fell from about $36 in 1951 to just $13 in 1991.[2] In addition, a closer look at the empirical work on cigarette and egg demand suggests that a stronger economic case could be made for the positive social effects of public education, which includes more than just narrowly defined counter-

[1]Department of Economics, Oregon State University, Ballard Extension Hall 303, Corvallis, OR 97331-3612

[2]According to Brewers Almanac (1993), the actual rate was $9 per barrel from 1951 through 1990 and was raised to $18 per barrel in 1991. Average State taxes per barrel also fell in real terms, although less dramatically.

advertising (see Wallack and DeJong chapter 16, this volume). Recent evidence indicates that consumer information regarding the health risks associated with cigarette smoking reduced cigarette demand by 10 to 12 percent (Porter 1986; Kao and Tremblay 1988), and information regarding the health risks associated with cholesterol consumption reduced egg demand by 16 to 25 percent (Brown and Schrader 1990). Because alcohol consumption is less addictive than cigarette smoking, one would expect that information about the health risks associated with alcohol consumption, however disseminated, would have a substantial impact on the abuse of alcohol.

Second, Saffer's discussion of the nonlinear advertising response function fails to determine why advertising has little or no effect on alcohol consumption at the market level but has a significant positive effect on alcohol consumption at the brand or firm level. In the brewing industry, for example, Lee and Tremblay (1992) found that beer advertising has no significant effect on the market demand for beer, while Tremblay (1985) found that beer advertising has a large, significant positive effect on the firm demand for beer. Perhaps the industry operates at point A_3 and firms operate at point A_1, as Saffer's figure 1 suggests. Alternatively, advertising may simply increase the market share of a particular brand and have no effect on total alcohol consumption.

Third, because consumer knowledge about the health risks of alcohol consumption is likely to vary over time (with changes in marketing technology and consumer sophistication) and across countries (with different cultures), the slope and not just the intercept parameters may vary over time when time-series data sets are used, and among countries when cross-country data sets are used. This variation could be especially important to this discussion, because as consumers become more knowledgeable about the health risks associated with alcohol use, advertising may become less influential. It this is true, then some type of varying coefficients model is in order.[3]

Fourth, the surveyed econometric studies that have used aggregate data sets can only address the important public policy question concerning the impact of advertising on alcohol abuse if one assumes that per capita alcohol consumption and alcohol abuse are highly correlated. An alternative approach that would avoid this assumption is to combine market advertising data with detailed survey information about the drinking patterns of individual consumers. Unfortunately, respondents are unlikely to provide honest answers to direct questions about sensitive issues such as alcohol abuse. In order to avoid this problem, one could use a randomized response technique, which allows individuals to provide honest answers to sensitive questions without revealing their true status regarding the sensitive issue.[4] Answers to such questions, along with other information, could then be used to generate an estimate of the probability that an individual is engaging in the sensitive behavior (Warner 1965; Maddala 1983). This information could then be combined with market advertising data to directly analyze the effect of advertising on individual alcohol use and abuse.[5]

[3] See Maddala (1977) for a discussion of varying parameter models.

Finally, although Saffer finds that alcohol producers advertise more intensively to minority and underage consumers, these results should be interpreted with caution. The fact that alcohol producers target minorities and teenagers does not prove that such advertising targets vulnerable groups and leads to greater consumption or abuse. For example, even if the decision to drink alcoholic beverages is unrelated to advertising, the producer of brand X may still target these groups if they have low brand loyalties[6] and if advertising influences brand choice. In this setting, advertising could induce a current consumer with low brand loyalty to try a new brand and still have no effect on the consumer's total alcohol consumption.

In summary, Saffer identifies the important issues and provides a very good summary of the current econometric evidence on the relationship between advertising and alcohol consumption. Unfortunately, most of this work suffers from one or more flaws, leaving many of the important questions unanswered. Further research is needed to help answer them, and Saffer provides a number of helpful suggestions to direct future research.

ACKNOWLEDGMENT

I would like to thank Susan Martin and Carol Horton Tremblay for their helpful comments on an earlier version of this comment.

REFERENCES

Brewers Almanac. Washington DC: Beer Institute, 1993.

Brown, D.J., and Schrader, L.F. Cholesterol information and shell egg consumption. *Am J Agricult Econ* 72:548–555, 1990.

Duffy, J.C., and Waterton, J.J. Randomized response vs. direct questioning: Estimating the prevalence of alcohol related problems in a field study. *Aust J Stat* 30:1–14, 1988.

[4] For example, one might ask the following question:

Please circle yes if one or both of the following statements are true. If both statements are false, circle no.

(1) You are an alcohol abuser (however defined).

(2) The last digit of your social security number is 9.

As one might expect, use rates are generally higher in randomized response surveys. In his analysis of cocaine use, Kerkvliet (in press) found that these two techniques generated significantly different use rates. The direct survey technique indicated an 8-percent cocaine use rate, while the randomized response survey technique indicated a 48-percent use rate. Regarding alcohol abuse, Duffy and Waterton (1988) found that the direct survey technique indicated a 4.7-percent abuse rate, while the randomized response survey technique indicated a 5.8-percent abuse rate. These rates are not significantly different, however.

[5] The only application of this technique has been done by Kerkvliet (1994), who used it to analyze the determinants of the demand for cocaine.

[6] Because of their lack of experience in the world and their generally exploratory behavior, reflected in the maxim "don't knock it until you've tried it," teenagers and young adults are likely to have lower brand loyalties than more experienced consumers.

Kao, K., and Tremblay, V.J. Cigarette "Health Scare," excise taxes, and advertising ban: Comment. *South Econ J* 54:770–776, 1988.

Kerkvliet, J.R. Estimating a logit model with randomized data: The case of cocaine use. *Aust J Stat* 36:9–20, 1994.

Lee, B., and Tremblay, V.J. Advertising and the U.S. market demand for beer. *Appl Econ* 24:69–76, 1992.

Maddala, G.S. *Econometrics.* New York: McGraw-Hill, 1977.

Maddala, G.S. *Limited-Dependent and Qualitative Variables in Econometrics.* Cambridge: Cambridge University Press, 1983.

Porter, R.H. The impact of government policy on the U.S. cigarette industry. In: Ippolito, P.M., and Scheffman, D.T., eds. *Empirical Approaches to Consumer Protection Economics.* Washington DC: Bureau of Economics, Federal Trade Commission, Mar. 1986. pp. 447–482.

Tremblay, V.J. Strategic groups and the demand for beer. *J Ind Econ* 34:183–198, 1985.

Warner, S. Randomized responses: A survey technique for eliminating evasive answer bias. *J Am Stat Assoc* 60:63–69, 1965.

Chapter 7

Television Alcohol Portrayals, Alcohol Advertising, and Alcohol Expectancies Among Children and Adolescents

Joel W. Grube[1]

Does exposure to televised alcohol portrayals and advertisements influence children's and adolescents' alcohol expectancies and consequently their intentions to drink and their drinking behaviors? This question arises from a concern about the frequency and content of these portrayals and advertisements and the extent to which young people are exposed to them. The research evidence relevant to this question is considered here and critically evaluated. A model of the relationships among exposure to alcohol in the media, alcohol beliefs, and drinking behaviors is developed, and data are presented that test this model as it relates to exposure to television and to television beer advertisements.

ALCOHOL EXPECTANCIES

Alcohol expectancies are beliefs about the social, psychological, and physical consequences of drinking (Christiansen et al. 1987; Critchlow 1987; Leigh 1989). Broadly defined, they subsume a number of variables that have been considered important for understanding drinking behaviors, such as reasons for drinking, expected utilities, images of drinkers, and related concepts. More generally, expectancy beliefs are central to social learning theories of behavior (e.g., Bandura 1977, 1986) and to contemporary attitude theories (e.g., Ajzen and Fishbein 1980). These theories propose that individuals abstract information from their personal experiences and from observations of social models into symbolic representations of the anticipated reinforcements and punishments associated with a given behavior. Social learning theories maintain that it is these expectations, and not direct reinforcement contingencies, that serve as guides to behavior and control its expression.

Alcohol expectancies are important beliefs for understanding how drinking behaviors develop and how they are main-

[1]Prevention Research Center, 2150 Shattuck Avenue, Suite 900, Berkeley, CA 94704

tained. They have been found to predict drinking among children and adolescents (e.g., Bauman and Bryan 1980; Bauman et al. 1985; Christiansen and Goldman 1983) as well as among adults (e.g., Brown et al. 1985). Furthermore, differences in alcohol expectancies may underlie drinking problems and problem drinking among youth and adults (Christiansen et al. 1985; Connors et al. 1986). Beyond their immediate effects on drinking behaviors, alcohol expectancies may be important because of their predisposing effects on the future expression of behaviors: Children and adolescents who hold favorable beliefs about drinking are more likely to say they intend to drink in the future and are more likely to show increases in drinking over time (e.g., Grube and Morgan 1986). Although direct experience with drinking, and the influence of parents, peers, and other immediate social models are important for the development of alcohol expectancies, a social learning perspective suggests that alcohol portrayals in the media and alcohol advertising may also play a role in shaping these beliefs among young people.

FREQUENCY AND CONTENT OF ALCOHOL PORTRAYALS ON TELEVISION

Drinking is a regular feature of fictional television programming. Our ongoing content analyses of prime-time fictional television programming (e.g., Wallack et al. 1990), based on random samples of dramas and situation comedies, indicate a steady increase in drinking portrayals on television, from just under 5 drinking acts per hour in 1976 to more than 10 drinking acts per hour in 1984 (figure 1). Although alcohol portrayals have declined since then, more than 6 drinking acts occurred during each hour of prime-time fictional programming in the most recent television season for which we have analyzed data (1990–91). Overall, 55 percent of the 168 program episodes in the 1990–91 sample portrayed at least one character drinking alcohol, and 81 percent of these episodes contained some visual or verbal reference to alcohol. Analyses from earlier seasons indicate that approximately 16 percent of prime-time fictional characters are drinkers (Wallack et al. 1990). Moreover, these drinking characters tend to be high status and familiar (i.e., wealthy, upper class, regular players). These attributes are likely to enhance the modeling potential of television drinkers. Only rarely is drinking associated with consequences in prime-time portrayals. Thus, for example, just over 13 percent of programs depicting drinking during the 1990 season showed negative consequences and only 1 percent showed positive consequences. The fact that the great majority of televised alcohol portrayals show no overt consequences of drinking is significant. Research shows that social modeling is nearly as effective when the behavior is unaccompanied by consequences as when it is rewarded (Bandura 1977). This especially appears to be the case when the model is powerful or of high status. In such cases, the observer appears to assume that the behavior is socially approved or likely to lead to valued outcomes.

Importantly, drinking by underage youth is rare on television. Analyses of 10 years of prime-time television programming indicate that underage drinking accounts for fewer than 2 percent of alcohol portrayals (DeFoe and Breed 1988).

However, the few portrayals that do occur may present an inappropriate message about drinking. In particular, underage drinking is often treated humorously and its seriousness diminished. Furthermore, although televised portrayals of actual drinking by youth are infrequent, portrayals of youth expressing a desire to drink

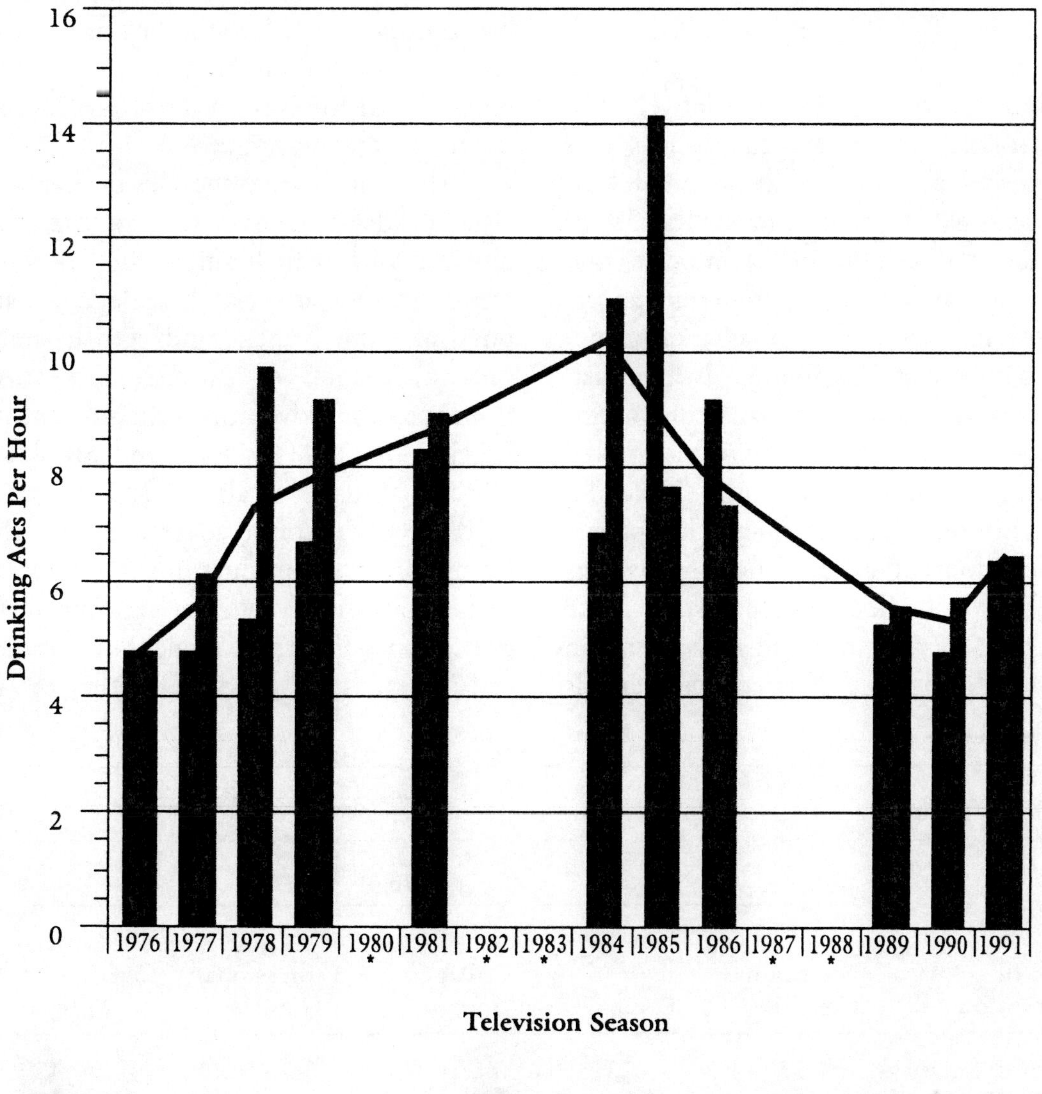

Figure 1. Frequency of drinking on television: 1976–1991.

are more common. When it occurs, underage drinking or expression of a desire to drink is often presented as a means of appearing grownup.

FREQUENCY AND CONTENT OF TELEVISION ALCOHOL ADVERTISING

Alcohol advertising also is relatively frequent on television, particularly in sports programming. Analyses of recent television seasons (Madden and Grube 1991; Madden and Grube 1994) indicate that about one alcohol advertisement appears every 4 hours, on the average, in prime-time fictional programming. In contrast, an average of more than two alcohol commercials appear in each hour of major professional sports programming (table 1), and about one alcohol commercial appears in each hour of college sports programming. Overall, alcohol commercials make up about 7 percent of all advertisements in sports television, and beer commercials comprise over 90 percent of all alcohol commercials in these programs. Nonstandard advertisements such as stadium signs, brief product sponsorships, and other onsite promotions that are broadcast to the television viewing audience constitute another form of advertising for alcohol products. Although they are rare in college sports, about three such advertisements occur for every hour of professional sports programming.

More qualitative analyses of television alcohol advertisements suggest that they link drinking with highly valued personal attributes such as sociability, elegance, and physical attractiveness, and with desirable outcomes such as success, relaxation, romance, and adventure (e.g., Atkin and Block 1981, 1984*a*; Finn and Strickland 1982; Strickland et al. 1982; Postman et al. 1988). Alcohol advertisements that strictly promote product quality, tradition, or taste are relatively rare, accounting for only about 10 percent of alcohol commercials (Madden and Grube 1994).

Table 1. Hourly Rates of Alcohol Advertising on Television: 1990–1991.

	Type of Program				
Type of Promotion	**Situation Comedies**	**Dramas**	**College Sports**	**Major Professional Sports**	**Other Professional Sports**
Beer Commercials	.13	.23	1.16	2.20	.43
Wine/Wine Cooler Commercials	.09	.06	.06	.18	.16
Stadium Signs	—	—	.00	2.08	1.75
On-Site Promotions	—	—	.00	.00	.98
Brief Sponsorships	—	—	.26	1.22	.28
Total	.22	.29	1.48	5.68	3.60

Note: The prime-time data are from Fall 1990, and the sports data are from Fall 1990 through Summer 1991.

Celebrity endorsers, usually sports or entertainment figures, appear in about 15 percent of alcohol advertisements (Madden and Grube 1994).

Although younger adolescents and children may be unaware of the more subtle messages contained in alcohol commercials, these messages are perceived quite accurately beginning in mid-adolescence at about 14 years of age (Aitken et al. 1988). Alcohol advertisements become increasingly attractive and salient to adolescents between the ages of 10 and 14 years. By age 16, adolescents routinely list alcohol commercials among their favorite advertisements. Young people appear to find lifestyle advertising and advertising with celebrity endorsers to be particularly appealing (Atkin and Block 1983; Covell et al. 1991).

Our own monitoring research shows that television alcohol advertisements often depict situations that are potentially hazardous if combined with alcohol, such as driving and water activities: 33 percent of the unique[2] television beer advertisements in our Fall 1990 through Summer 1991 sample contained such images (Madden and Grube 1991). Importantly, viewers may interpret these advertisements as implying that drinking took place ***during*** the hazardous activity, even though actual consumption is not shown (e.g., Atkin et al. 1983). Moderation messages and warnings about excessive or hazardous drinking appear in very few television alcohol advertisements. Fewer than 1 percent of the alcohol commercials in our sample contained such messages.

EFFECTS OF ALCOHOL PORTRAYALS

The available published research does not provide a definitive answer to the question of whether exposure to alcohol portrayals in television programming influences young people. Only a handful of correlational and experimental studies have addressed this issue. Generally speaking, the correlational studies have found small but significant relationships between television viewing and alcohol-related beliefs and behavior among young people. Thus, Tucker (1985) found that high school boys who were heavy television viewers drank more than light viewers. This relationship was maintained when important background and demographic variables were controlled. Similarly, Neuendorf (1985) reported that television viewing was related to more favorable beliefs about drinking among 10- to 14-year-old adolescents: Heavy viewers were more likely than light viewers to agree that "people who drink are happy" and "you have to drink to have fun at a sporting event."

Unfortunately, both of these studies are problematic. Tucker provides only limited information about his sample and how it was obtained. He does not provide data on response rates. Moreover, the effects he reported were quite modest, accounting for only about 4 percent of the variance in drinking status, on the average. Neuendorf (1985) provides no information about her sampling frame, response rates, or other important methodological aspects of her study. In the published arti-

[2]Unique advertisements include all nonduplicated commercials captured in the sample, ignoring the frequency with which they were aired.

cle, she only generally describes her findings, and the differences she reports are not accompanied by significance tests. As a result, the validity of her findings cannot be evaluated. In addition, neither of these studies actually addressed the influence of *exposure* to televised alcohol portrayals on youth. Rather, both of them relied on measures of hours of overall television viewing. Although some approaches to media influence (most notably cultivation theory) maintain that total exposure to television is the important variable, recent research indicates that measures of specific viewing patterns are better predictors of differences in beliefs (Potter and Chang 1990). Moreover, our own media studies indicate that children generally do not view programs that have high alcohol content; these programs apparently do not appeal to younger adolescents. Thus, using overall viewing measures may not capture young people's exposure to alcohol on television. Using overall measures of viewing also confounds the effects of exposure to alcohol portrayals and exposure to alcohol advertising. Finally, because simple correlational analyses were used, these studies do not provide evidence for the causal effects of exposure to television on drinking beliefs and behaviors. It is possible that some unconsidered third variable may influence both television viewing and drinking, or that predisposition to drinking influences television viewing rather than the converse.

In addition to the two survey studies, the influence of televised alcohol portrayals on young people has been addressed in two experimental studies. In one of these (Kotch et al. 1986), children were shown a videotape composite from several episodes of a popular television series. In one condition the tape contained drinking scenes, while in the control condition the drinking scenes were excluded. Boys exposed to the tape with the drinking scenes were more likely to report on a followup questionnaire that the good things about alcohol were more important than the bad things. No effects were found for girls or for other measures of alcohol beliefs and expectancies. Although this study is suggestive, it was based on a small and potentially biased sample (only 43 of 237 students recruited for the study actually participated). Moreover, a significant effect was found for only one item out of a longer series, and then only when the item response categories were arbitrarily collapsed. Finally, there appear to be serious measurement problems. Measures of alcohol beliefs were constructed based on factor analyses that accounted for only about 12 percent of the variance in the survey items. Thus, the scales that were used in the analyses do not adequately reflect the underlying structure of these items.

In a second experimental study (Rychtarik et al. 1983), children between the ages of 8 and 11 were randomly assigned to one of three conditions. In the experimental condition they viewed a videotaped episode of the television program *M.A.S.H.* that contained a brief drinking scene. In one control condition, they viewed the same episode with the drinking scene edited out. In a second control condition, they were not exposed to the video. In an immediate posttest, the children were asked to choose a drink of whiskey or water to offer to pictured adults and children. The experimental and control respondents did not differ in the drinks they chose for the pictured children. However, the respondents in the experimental condition offered whiskey to significantly more of the pictured adults (74 percent) than did the children in the two control conditions (54 percent and 52 percent, respectively). Although expectancies were not directly assessed, this study does suggest that exposure to drinking portrayals can influence children's beliefs about the appropriateness and normativeness of drinking. However, as with the previous study, this one suffers from some shortcomings. First, the possibility that the results are due to demand characteristics cannot be discounted. That is, the children may have perceived the drinking in the video as representing the experimenter's expectations regarding their task in the experimental situation. Thus, they may have been responding to what they believed the experimenter wanted them to do, rather than the drinking scenes per se. Second, as with the first study, the adequacy of the sample can be questioned. The participants in the study were selected among children in a waiting room at a university pediatrics clinic. How specific children were selected to take part in the study is not discussed, and neither the sociodemographic makeup of the sample nor the refusal rate is mentioned.

In addition to the individual shortcomings in each of these studies, both of them suffer from a lack of ecological validity. That is, the experimental situation in both cases is highly artificial. Self-selection and other factors that operate in the natural viewing situation are not present. Moreover, exposure to the drinking portrayals in these studies is very brief, and the issue of long-term exposure cannot be addressed. Finally, in both cases the posttest occurred immediately after the experimental intervention. Thus, the possibility of the findings being the result of experimental demand and other artifacts of the situation cannot be discounted. In sum, although these studies are suggestive, they do not provide strong evidence that exposure to alcohol portrayals on television influences young people.

EFFECTS OF ALCOHOL ADVERTISING

Perhaps the best known studies of the effects of alcohol advertising on young people are those by Atkin and his colleagues. Their results showed that adolescents who were heavily exposed to advertising were more likely to believe that drinkers possess valued characteristics such as being attractive, athletic, or successful (Atkin and Block 1981). They also held more favorable beliefs about drinking (e.g., drinking is relaxing) and were more likely to believe that it is acceptable for teenagers to get drunk. In addition, adolescents heavily exposed to alcohol advertising were more likely to drink, drink heavily, and drink in hazardous situations such as while driving (Atkin et al. 1983; Atkin et al. 1984). These relationships were maintained when peer and parent influences, religiousness, sex, and age were controlled. More recently, other researchers have found that young drinkers are more likely to be exposed to alcohol advertisements, are more accurate in identifying brands of beer from edited alcohol advertisements, and are more favorably disposed toward these advertisements than are nondrinkers (e.g., Aitken et al. 1988).

In contrast, other studies have found little support for substantively meaningful effects of advertising on drinking beliefs and behaviors among young people.

Thus, Strickland (1983) found only a very small relationship between exposure to advertising and consumption of alcohol by young people when significant demographic and personal variables were controlled. There was no significant association in this study between exposure to advertising and abusive or hazardous drinking. Strickland also found that beliefs about drinking and approval of drinking by parents and peers were considerably more important as predictors of drinking than was exposure to advertising. A reanalysis of Strickland's data using structural equation modeling techniques confirmed these findings (Adlaf and Kohn 1989). In another study (Strickland 1982) no effect was found for advertising on adolescent drinking, although there was an indication that young people who believed they gained positive vicarious social benefits from viewing alcohol commercials were somewhat more likely to drink. Unfortunately, in neither of these studies were intervening beliefs about drinking directly addressed.

All of the previous studies can be criticized on methodological or conceptual grounds. First, the analyses of the data from the Strickland studies (Strickland 1982, 1983; Adlaf and Kohn 1989) excluded nondrinkers. Thus, the variability in the dependent measures was unnecessarily restricted, and moreover, the effects of exposure to alcohol advertising on initiation to drinking were ignored (Atkin 1990). As a result, it is possible that these studies underestimate the effects of alcohol advertising. Second, the Strickland studies constructed measures of advertising exposure by summing the frequency with which respondents viewed specific television programs, where each program was weighted by the number of minutes of alcohol advertising it contained. Using such a measure assumes that simple exposure to alcohol advertising is sufficient to bring about change. Moreover, this measure only represents *potential* exposure. It does not take into account the fact that some children and adolescents may pay little attention to advertisements and are thus not actually exposed to them, even if they view programs in which they are imbedded. Although the Atkin studies included measures of awareness of advertising, these apparently were combined with simple exposure measures, and it is unclear what these combined scales represent. Other issues, including the use of nonrandom samples, have been raised for some of the studies (i.e., Atkin and Block 1981). These criticisms, however, do not appear to apply to the aspects of these studies that focus on youth (Atkin and Block 1984*b*).

The greatest problem with these studies is their failure to address the causal nature of the relationship between exposure to alcohol advertising and beliefs and behaviors among youth. All of the relevant research has relied on essentially correlational analyses. As a result, there is no evidence regarding the *direction* of the relationship between alcohol advertising and drinking beliefs and behaviors (Strickland 1984). Although exposure to advertising may influence drinking beliefs and behaviors, it is possible that young people who are predisposed to drink seek out information about alcohol and are more attentive to advertising. This latter possibility has been dismissed by some researchers as unlikely (e.g., Atkin 1990) because it is assumed that exposure to advertising generally precedes the development of drinking and because there is little evidence that youth are motivated to seek out advertising as a source of information. Nonetheless, the causal relationships among advertising, drinking beliefs, and drinking behaviors remain to be established, and the evidence for advertising effects based on these studies should be considered circumstantial.

Experimental research on the effects of television alcohol advertising on children is rare.[3] Apparently only a single recently published study has addressed this issue (Lipsitz et al. 1993). In this study, fifth- and eighth-grade schoolchildren were shown videotapes of 40 television advertisements and asked a brief series of questions about them. In the experimental condition, five beer commercials were embedded within the tape. All of the participants in the experiment were then taken to another room and asked to complete an alcohol expectancies questionnaire. Exposure to the five alcohol advertisements was found to have no effect on the children's alcohol expectancies in this study.

Unfortunately, interpretation of these findings is problematic. Although such experimental studies may be appropriate for investigating immediate facilitative or disinhibitory effects of alcohol advertising, it is not clear that they are a reasonable methodology for ascertaining if exposure to advertising has effects on beliefs or behaviors. In general, experimental studies of this type lack ecological or external validity. As with similar studies of exposure to alcohol portrayals in television programming, the experiment constitutes a highly artificial situation, and important factors contained in the natural viewing context (e.g., selective attention and exposure, interactions and discussion with peers) are absent. Moreover, the experimental manipulation consists of only a single relatively brief exposure to the advertising materials that is not analogous to the real-world situation, in which children and adolescents are exposed to television advertisements repeatedly over long periods of time. Finally, it should be recognized that experiments of this type are not really a test of whether advertising influences young people. Rather, they can only address the question of whether a single brief exposure to alcohol commercials has an ***additional*** effect over and above any that may result from cumulative long-term exposure to similar advertisements over many years.[4]

Our own ongoing research program on the influence of television on youth has attempted to address some of the methodological and conceptual issues raised by the existing survey and experimental studies (Grube and Wallack 1994). We have attempted to go beyond previous studies by using an information processing model

[3]Some experimental studies have addressed this issue with college students and other adults (e.g., Kohn and Smart 1984, 1987; Kohn et al. 1984) with mixed results. These studies are not reviewed here because they do not address beliefs or behaviors among adolescents and children.

[4]It should be kept in mind that the children in both the experimental and control conditions had probably been exposed to many hundreds of similar alcohol advertisements in the course of their normal television viewing outside the experimental context.

of media effects. In contrast to a simple exposure model, an information processing approach suggests that advertisements have significant effects on knowledge, beliefs, intentions, and behaviors only when they are attended to, processed, and remembered (McGuire 1985; Klitzner et al. 1991). It is *awareness* of advertising, not simple exposure to it, that is important. Finally, we have attempted to address the issue of directionality of media effects by using nonrecursive modeling techniques. The advantage of nonrecursive modeling over the analyses used in previous survey studies is that it allows for the estimation of the effects of awareness of advertising on drinking knowledge, beliefs, and intentions and the simultaneous effects of those variables on awareness. That is, this type of modeling provides evidence concerning the direction of the relationships observed among variables.

The data used for the modeling were obtained during the first phase of a 3-year panel survey conducted in a suburban city in northern California. The purpose of the study is to examine the influence of parents, peers, and the media on children's alcohol-related beliefs and behaviors. The data were obtained from an ethnically diverse random sample of 468 fifth- and sixth-grade schoolchildren drawn at random from a complete roster for the participating school district. Potentially sensitive information (e.g., drinking intentions) was ascertained using a self-administered questionnaire, and less sensitive questions (e.g., television viewing) were asked directly in structured interviews.

A wide range of variables were included in the study. The children were asked about their usual television viewing habits, and particularly about their frequency of viewing sports and other weekend programming. Awareness of beer advertising was ascertained by having them view still photographs of television beer commercials with all references to product and brand blocked out. They were asked to indicate for each photograph whether they had seen the depicted advertisement and, if so, to name the product and brand being advertised. Measures of knowledge about alcohol products were obtained by asking the children to name as many brands of beer as they could and to match brands with their respective advertising slogans. The children's beliefs about alcohol were measured with a series of items asking them about positive and negative aspects of drinking. The positive items were designed to reflect the themes of beer advertisements (sociability, relaxation, reward for work) as determined from previous studies (e.g., Postman et al. 1988). The negative belief items targeted health effects and drinking and driving. Because very few of the children had consumed more than just a sip of alcohol, a primary outcome variable was their intention to drink as an adult. Finally, measures of perceptions of peer and parental drinking and attitudes toward drinking, and indicators of a number of background characteristics were obtained.

The reciprocal relationships among exposure to alcohol in fiction television, awareness of advertising, and drinking intentions, beliefs, and knowledge were examined through a series of hierarchical simultaneous equations analyses using a generalized least squares procedure (Bentler 1989). Latent variables (factors) were derived for awareness of beer advertising, drinking intentions, beliefs about the positive aspects of drinking, and beliefs about the negative aspects of drinking. Measures of frequency of television viewing, frequency of sports program viewing, perceived parental and peer drinking, perceived parental and peer attitudes toward drinking, and personal and family characteristics (sex, age, ethnicity, family income, parent's education) were initially included in the modeling. However, those background variables that were not significantly related to advertising awareness, knowledge of alcohol products, alcohol beliefs, or drinking intentions were subsequently dropped from the analysis.

Figure 2 depicts the final model that was obtained. Solid arrows in this figure represent statistically significant ($p<.05$) effects, and broken arrows represent nonsignificant effects ($p>.05$).[5] The numbers adjacent to the arrows are standardized regression (path) coefficients. This model provided a good fit to the data, scaled chi^2 ($330, n = 458$) = 369.88, $p<.07$, indicating that it adequately reproduced the observed covariances among the variables.

The most important findings shown in figure 2 are that awareness of alcohol advertising significantly ($p<.05$) increased knowledge of beer brands and slogans and led to more positive beliefs about drinking. Awareness also had a significant effect on intentions to drink as an adult, primarily mediated through positive beliefs ($\beta = .19$). These effects were maintained even though the reciprocal effects of beliefs, intentions, and knowledge on advertising awareness were controlled. That is, the results suggest that alcohol advertising may influence young people to be more favorably predisposed toward drinking. Interestingly, awareness of television beer advertising was not significantly related to beliefs about the negative aspects of drinking.

The children's awareness of advertising appears to result primarily from exposure to sports and other weekend afternoon and evening programming. Those who watched more television sports and weekend afternoon and evening television, in general, were more aware of beer advertisements. This pattern is consistent with the data from content analyses indicating that television alcohol advertisements are largely concentrated in these areas of programming.

CONCLUSION

Alcohol advertising and alcohol portrayals are frequent occurrences on television. They present drinking in a manner that is often glamorized and associated with desirable outcomes and attributes. The frequency and nature of these alcohol portrayals has led to a concern that they may influence young people's drinking beliefs and expectancies. Studies of the influence of exposure to alcohol portrayals in fictional television on young people are rare. Survey studies investigating natural exposure to such portrayals have been inadequately described and cannot be evaluated or have serious methodological flaws that limit their value. In addition, these studies have focused on overall exposure to television

[5]The nonsignificant relationships among intentions, beliefs, and advertising awareness were retained in the model in order to control for the reciprocal influences of these variables on one another and thus allow for inferences about the direction of the effects.

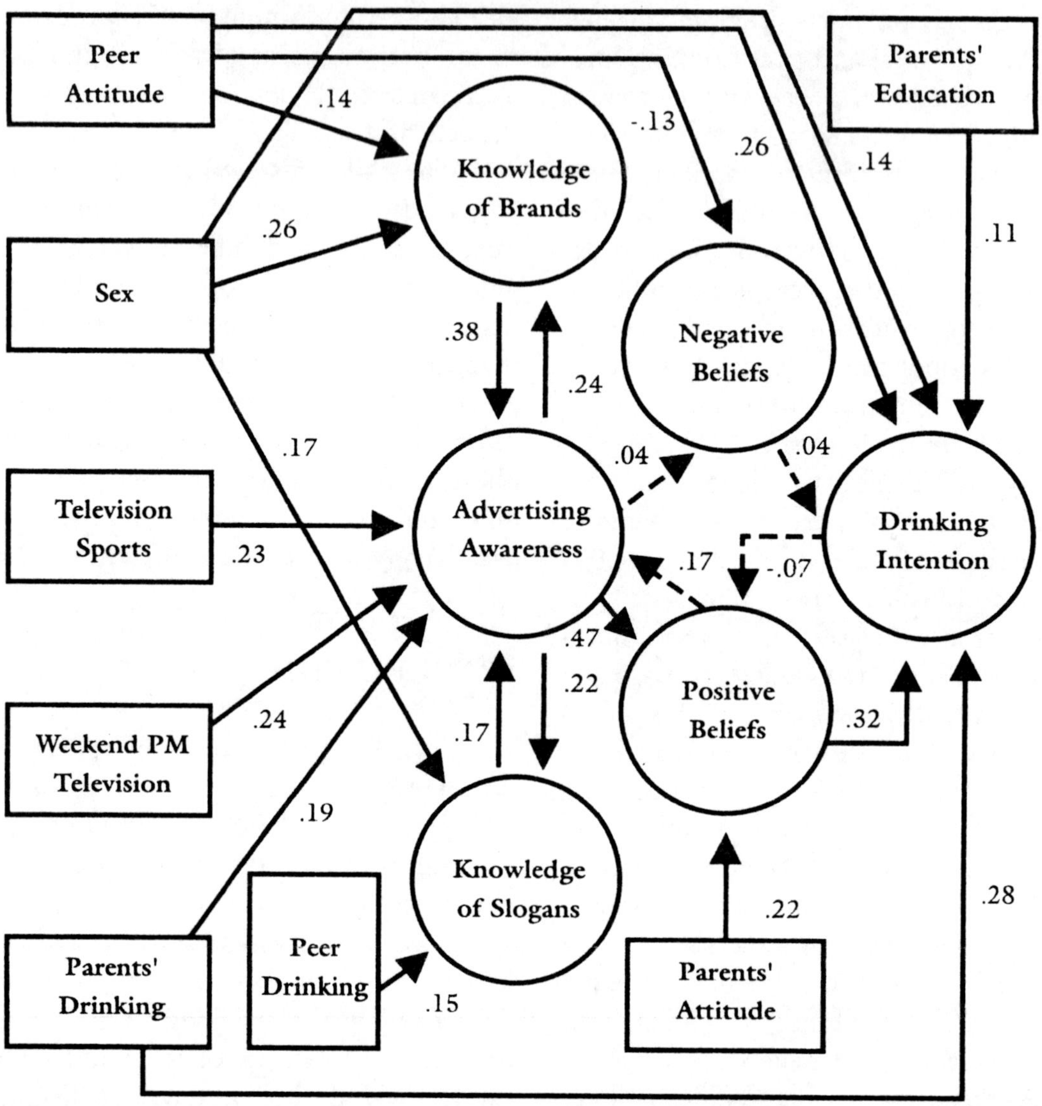

Figure 2. Model of alcohol advertising, knowledge, beliefs, and intentions. Solid lines represent statistically significant effects. Broken lines represent nonsignificant effects. Numbers adjacent to arrows are standardized path coefficients.

and not specifically on exposure to alcohol on television. Experimental studies on exposure to alcohol portrayals are problematic also. They have suffered from inadequate sampling and are susceptible to alternative interpretations. Experimenter demand in particular is a possible problem in these studies. They also lack ecological validity. As a result, there is limited evidence that exposure to alcohol portrayals on television influences young people. Additional research on this question is necessary.

Somewhat more research has investigated the potential effects of alcohol advertising on young people. Survey studies generally indicate that there are small but significant correlations between exposure to and awareness of alcohol advertising and drinking beliefs and behaviors among youth. These correlations tend to be larger when measures of awareness or attention to advertising are used rather than simple exposure measures. However, most of the available studies on alcohol advertising effects on young people's beliefs and behaviors do not adequately address issues regarding the direction of the relationship between these variables. They thus allow for the possibility that this relationship is spurious or that the direction of causality is the opposite of that assumed by most researchers. The only available experimental study does not provide support for the influence of alcohol advertising on children's beliefs about drinking. Furthermore, this study lacks ecological validity, and the experimental paradigm generally may not be appropriate for addressing this question.

Our own ongoing research has attempted to build upon previous studies of alcohol advertising and youth, and to address some of the issues raised by these studies. Our research indicates that children who are more aware of television beer advertisements hold more favorable beliefs about drinking and intend to drink more frequently as adults. They also have greater knowledge of beer brands and slogans. Importantly, these effects are maintained even when the reciprocal effects of knowledge and beliefs on awareness of advertising are controlled. Thus, this research provides evidence that awareness of advertising may influence beliefs about drinking, drinking knowledge, and drinking intentions. Interestingly, we found that awareness of advertising was unrelated to beliefs about the negative aspects of drinking. This finding probably results from the fact that alcohol advertisements generally ignore problems such as drinking and driving, birth defects, and alcoholism. Rather, they portray drinking as a normative activity and one that is consistently associated with positively valued activities and consequences such as romance, sociability, and relaxation. We also found evidence for reciprocal effects. Specifically, knowledge about beer brands and slogans increased awareness of television beer commercials. Most likely, these effects represent the fact that children who are curious about drinking seek out information about alcohol. Beer advertisements may represent one source of such information.

Taken as a whole, the findings reported in the available studies indicate that alcohol advertising may have small but significant effects on the beliefs, intentions, and possibly behaviors of young people. These findings suggest that efforts to prevent drinking and alcohol problems among youth should give some attention to alcohol advertising. In particular, efforts should be made to reduce the extent to which such advertising appeals to children and also reduce their exposure to it.

One strategy to achieve these goals is to restrict television alcohol advertising during prime viewing hours for children (e.g., during weekend mornings, early prime-time, and sports programs); limiting alcohol sponsorship of concerts and similar events that are attended by underage youth might also be considered. Such actions, however, are controversial and are certain to meet considerable resistance from alcohol advertisers. They also may be counterproductive. It has been suggested, for example, that banning tobacco advertising from television may have actually hindered public health efforts to reduce smoking because it restricted equal-time access to the medium for counter messages.

Another possible approach to bringing about changes in advertising—assuming that advertisers do not intentionally set out to influence underage youth—is through cooperative consultation. Cooperative consultation is a method originally developed for working with producers and writers of prime-time fictional television programs to reduce the presence of inappropriate drinking on television (Breed and DeFoe 1982). Using this method, producers and writers are provided with empirically based feedback about alcohol portrayals in their programs, along with suggestions designed to help them avoid potential problems. Apparently, these efforts have resulted in some reductions in inappropriate drinking on television programs. Similar efforts with alcohol advertisers to address advertising content that appeals to youth may be useful. Although it is known that lifestyle themes and celebrity endorsers make some alcohol advertisements appealing to young people, further research should focus on identifying what aspects of alcohol advertisements make them more or less attractive to and influential for youth.

Counteradvertising also may be a reasonable strategy. However, for counteradvertising to be effective, it must compete with commercial alcohol advertisements in terms of quality, interest, and frequency of exposure during prime viewing hours. Equal-time requirements for public health messages about alcohol, or alcohol tax monies dedicated to this purpose might help achieve these goals. The recent California antismoking campaign funded by tobacco taxes might provide a model for an intervention of this type. Similarly, including health warning labels on alcohol advertisements may also help counteract their overwhelmingly positive messages, although the evidence for the effectiveness of such messages on young people is equivocal at best (MacKinnon et al. 1993).

Educational efforts also may be important as one part of an overall public health strategy to help children develop and improve their critical skills regarding alcohol advertisements. Many school-based programs, for example, include media components that are designed to teach young people to understand the intent of alcohol advertising and develop counter-arguments to it. Some of these media education efforts appear to have met with limited success in delaying the onset of drinking among underage youth, especially when they are combined with normative education or resistance skills training (e.g., Botvin 1986; Botvin and Tortu 1988).

In the final analysis, however, it must be recognized that alcohol advertising and alcohol portrayals in the media are only two of many factors that influence drinking beliefs and behaviors among young people. Removing all alcohol advertising and all alcohol portrayals from the media would not, in and of itself, eliminate drinking among underage youth. Rather, efforts to reduce media influences must be embedded within a broader approach that targets a wide range of personal, social, and environmental factors.

REFERENCES

Adlaf, E.M., and Kohn, P.M. Alcohol advertising, consumption and abuse: A covariance-structural modeling look at Strickland's data. *Br J Addict* 84:749–757, 1989.

Aitken, P.P.; Eadie, D.R.; Leathar, D.S.; McNeill, R.E.J.; and Scott, A.C. Television advertisements for alcoholic drinks do reinforce under-age drinking. *Br J Addict* 83:1399–1419, 1988.

Ajzen, I., and Fishbein, M. *Understanding Attitudes and Predicting Social Behavior.* Englewood Cliffs, NJ: Prentice-Hall, 1980.

Atkin, C.K. Effects of televised alcohol messages on teenage drinking patterns. *J Adolesc Health Care* 11:10–24, 1990.

Atkin, C.K., and Block, M. *Content and Effects of Alcohol Advertising.* Report No. PB-82-123142. Washington, DC: Bureau of Tobacco, Alcohol, and Firearms, 1981.

Atkin, C.K., and Block, M. Effectiveness of celebrity endorsers. *J Advert Res* 23:57–61, 1983.

Atkin, C.K., and Block, M. The effects of alcohol advertising. *Adv Consum Res* 11:688–693, 1984*a*.

Atkin, C.K., and Block, M. A reply to Strickland. *J Stud Alcohol* 45:93–100, 1984*b*.

Atkin, C.K.; Hocking, J.; and Block, M. Teenage drinking: Does advertising make a difference? *J Commun* (Spring) 157–167, 1984.

Atkin, C.K.; Neuendorf, K.; and McDermott, S. The role of alcohol advertising in excessive and hazardous drinking. *J Drug Educ* 13:313–325, 1983.

Bandura, A. *Social Learning Theory.* Englewood Cliffs, NJ: Prentice-Hall, 1977.

Bandura, A. *Social Foundations of Thought and Action: A Social Cognitive Theory.* Englewood Cliffs, NJ: Prentice-Hall, 1986.

Bauman, K.E., and Bryan, E.S. Subjective expected utility and children's drinking. *J Stud Alcohol* 41:952–958, 1980.

Bauman, K.E.; Fisher, L.A.; Bryan, E.S.; and Chenoweth, R.L. Relationship between subjective expected utility and behavior: A longitudinal study of adolescent drinking. *J Stud Alcohol* 46:32–38, 1985.

Bentler, P.M. *EQS Structural Equations Manual.* Los Angeles, CA: BMDP Statistical Software, 1989.

Botvin, G.J. Substance abuse prevention research: Recent developments and future directions. *J School Health* 56:369–374, 1986.

Botvin, G.J., and Tortu, S. Preventing adolescent substance abuse through life skills training. In: Price, R.H., and Cowen, E.L., eds. *Fourteen Ounces of Prevention.* Washington, DC: American Psychological Association, 1988. pp. 98–110.

Breed, W., and DeFoe, J. Effecting media change: The role of cooperative consultation on alcohol topics. *J Commun* 32:88–99, 1982.

Brown, S.A.; Goldman, M.S.; and Christiansen, B.A. Do alcohol expectancies mediate drinking patterns of adults? *J Consult Clin Psychol* 53:512–519, 1985.

Christiansen, B.A., and Goldman, M.S. Alcohol related expectancies vs. demographic/background variables in the prediction of adolescent drinking. *J Consult Clin Psychol* 51:249–257, 1983.

Christiansen, B.A.; Goldman, M.S.; and Brown, S.A. The differential development of adolescent alcohol expectancies may predict adult alcoholism. *Addict Behav* 10:299–306, 1985.

Christiansen, B.A.; Goldman, M.S.; and Brown, S.A. Expectancy theory: Thinking about drinking. In: Blane, H.T., and Leonard, K.E., eds. *Psychological Theories of Drinking and Alcoholism.* New York: Guilford, 1987. pp. 181–226.

Connors, G.J.; O'Farrell, T.J.; Cutter, H.S.G.; and Thompson, D.L. Alcohol expectancies among alcoholics, problem drinkers, and nonproblem drinkers. *Alcohol Clin Exp Res* 10:667–671, 1986.

Covell, K.; Dion, K.L.; and Dion, K.K. "The Appeal of Lifestyle Advertisements for Tobacco and Alcohol." Paper presented at the annual meeting of the American Psychological Association, San Francisco, Aug. 1991.

Critchlow, B. A utility analysis of drinking. *Addict Behav* 12:269–273, 1987.

DeFoe, J.R., and Breed, W. Youth and alcohol in television stories, with suggestions to the industry for alternative portrayals. *Adolescence* 23:533–550, 1988.

Finn, T.A., and Strickland, D.E. A content analysis of beverage alcohol advertising. II. Television advertising. *J Stud Alcohol* 43:964–989, 1982.

Grube, J.G., and Morgan, M. *Smoking, Drinking, and Other Drug Use Among Dublin Post-Primary Pupils.* Dublin, Ireland: The Economic and Social Research Institute, 1986.

Grube, J.G., and Wallack, L. Television beer advertising and drinking knowledge, beliefs, and intentions among school children. *Am J Pub Health* 84:254–259, 1994.

Klitzner, M.; Gruenewald, P.; and Bamberger, E. Cigarette advertising and adolescent experimentation with smoking. *Br J Addict* 86:287–298, 1991.

Kohn, P.M., and Smart, R.G. The impact of television advertising on alcohol consumption: An experiment. *J Stud Alcohol* 45:205–213, 1984.

Kohn, P.M., and Smart, R.G. Wine, women, suspiciousness and advertising. *J Stud Alcohol* 48:161–166, 1987.

Kohn, P.M.; Smart, R.G.; and Ogborne, A.C. The effects of two kinds of alcohol advertising on subsequent consumption. *J Advert* 13:34–40, 48, 1984.

Kotch, J.B.; Coulter, M.L.; and Lipsitz, A. Does televised drinking influence children's attitudes toward alcohol? *Addict Behav* 11:67–70, 1986.

Leigh, B.C. In search of the seven dwarves: Issues of measurement and meaning in alcohol expectancy research. *Psychol Bull* 105:361–373, 1989.

Lipsitz, A.; Brake, G.; Vincent, E.J.; and Winters, M. Another round for the liquor industry: Television ads and children's alcohol expectancies. *J Appl Soc Psychol* 23:439–450, 1993.

Madden, P.A., and Grube, J.W. "Alcohol Advertising in Sports and Prime-Time Television." Paper presented at the annual meeting of the American Public Health Association, Atlanta, GA, Nov. 1991.

Madden, P.A., and Grube, J.W. Alcohol and tobacco advertising in sports television. *Am J Pub Health* 84:297–299, 1994.

MacKinnon, D.P.; Pentz, M.A.; and Stacy, A.W. The alcohol warning label and adolescents: The first year. *Am J Pub Health* 83:585–587, 1993.

McGuire, W.J. Attitudes and attitude change. In: Lindsey, G., and Aronson, E., eds. *Handbook of Social Psychology.* Vol. II. New York: Random House, 1985. pp. 233–346.

Neuendorf, K.A. Alcohol advertising and media portrayals. *J Inst Socioeconomic Stud* 10:67–78, 1985.

Postman, N.; Nystrom, C.; Strate, L.; and Weingartner, C. *Myths, Men, and Beer: An Analysis of Beer Commercials on Broadcast Television, 1987.* Falls Church, VA: AAA Foundation for Traffic Safety, 1988.

Potter, W.J., and Chang, I.C. Television exposure measures and the cultivation hypothesis. *J Broadcast Elect Media* 34:313–333, 1990.

Rychtarik, R.G.; Fairbank, J.A.; Allen, C.M.; Foy, D.W.; and Drabman, R.S. Alcohol use in television programming: Effects on children's behavior. *Addict Behav* 8:19–22, 1983.

Strickland, D.E. Alcohol advertising: Orientations and influence. *J Advert* 1:307–319, 1982.

Strickland, D.E. Advertising exposure, alcohol consumption and misuse of alcohol. In: Grant, M.; Plant, M.; and Williams, A., eds. *Economics and Alcohol: Consumption and Controls.* New York: Gardner Press, 1983. pp. 201–222.

Strickland, D.E. Content and effects of alcohol advertising: Comments on NTIS Pub. No. PB82-123142. *J Stud Alcohol* 45:87–93, 1984.

Strickland, D.E.; Finn, T.A.; and Lambert, M.D. A content analysis of beverage alcohol advertising. I. Magazine advertising. *J Stud Alcohol* 43:655–682, 1982.

Tucker, L.A. Television's role regarding alcohol use among teenagers. *Adolescence* 20:593–598, 1985.

Wallack, L.; Grube, J.W.; Madden, P.A.; and Breed, W. Portrayals of alcohol on prime-time television. *J Stud Alcohol* 51:428–437, 1990.

Chapter 8

Prevention as Skills Training: An Approach to Lessening the Impact of Alcohol Advertising

R. Lorraine Collins[1]

Grube presents a study of the relationships among exposure to televised advertisements for alcohol, awareness of alcohol, alcohol expectancies, knowledge of alcohol, and intentions to drink (see chapter 7, this volume). This model was tested in a sample of 468 students (median age 11.9 years) composed of males (49 percent) and females (51 percent) from a variety of ethnic backgrounds.

The results suggest what we would expect: (1) males reported that they were more likely to drink as adults, particularly to drink beer; (2) students who intended to drink more frequently as adults had more positive expectancies, believed their peers were approving of drinking, and believed that their parents drank more frequently; (3) students who saw more peer approval for drinking believed alcohol was less likely to have negative consequences; and (4) awareness of beer advertising was predicted by watching television sports and watching more weekend and evening television, as well as by the belief that parents drank frequently.

Based on these findings, Grube concluded that "awareness of advertising may influence beliefs about drinking, drinking knowledge, and drinking intentions" (p. 117). These results are said to have implications for prevention, namely that prevention efforts should include reduction of the appeal of such advertising to children and reduction of children's exposure to alcohol advertisements. The present commentary on Grube's research will include a discussion of some of the limitations of the study as well as a presentation of a skills training approach to the primary prevention of alcohol problems.

LIMITATIONS OF THE STUDY

The results are based on cross-sectional data and therefore do not directly address causality. Even though the use of

[1]Research Institute on Addictions, 1021 Main Street, Buffalo, NY 14203

structural equation modeling allows the relationships among the variables to be examined in the same context, it does not provide us with information about causal relationships per se. It is only with longitudinal or experimental data that the truly causal nature of these relationships can be determined. Thus, future research in this area should include longitudinal or experimental designs that exhibit an awareness of children's developmental changes. For example, the ages 14 through 17 years represent an important transition period in adolescents' use of alcohol. Therefore, these ages may represent a time when exposure to alcohol advertising could be particularly salient. In addition, children's attitudes toward alcohol vary with age, usually becoming more positive as they grow older. It may be important to identify the environmental changes (including the salience of advertising) that correspond to this shift in attitude. Laboratory studies could provide converging evidence for the results of surveys. Whatever the specific design, longitudinal and experimental data will expand our knowledge and understanding of the impact of exposure to alcohol advertising.

A related issue is **the use of drinking intentions as the outcome variable**. True, such a variable is the only viable outcome given the age of the sample. However, one has to wonder to what extent the findings for intentions would generalize to actual drinking behavior. There is evidence of a strong correlation between intentions and behavior, but this typically occurs when both are measured proximal in time. As stated by Ajzen (1988), the "accuracy of prediction will usually decline with the amount of time that intervenes between measurement of intentions and observation of behavior" (p. 115). Therefore, it does not seem likely that these results will generalize to the time (possibly years later) at which this sample of 12-year-olds actually begins drinking. Even if the findings generalize, there is an implicit notion that children's intention to drink (as an adult) represents a harmful/bad outcome. This is not the case; statistics suggest that most adults are social drinkers who experience little or no harm from drinking. The intention to drink as an adult could represent children's anticipation that they will engage in normal adult activities (such as drinking or getting married) when they reach adulthood. Since we live in a society where social drinking is a legal and common activity, the intention to drink as an adult seems very reasonable.

Another limitation is **the age of the sample**. To the extent that we want to have a meaningful test of the relationships among alcohol advertising, expectancies, and actual drinking behavior, then an age cohort in which some drinking was actually occurring would be more useful. For example, as mentioned earlier, the ages of 14 to 17 years represent an important transition; therefore, high school students or even college freshmen would be a more appropriate sample. The sample of 12-year-old students could be responding to demand characteristics or other aspects of the situation in completing the questionnaire. Data on actual drinking behavior would provide a more meaningful context in which to examine the implications of these findings.

ALCOHOL PREVENTION EFFORTS AND YOUTH

The general focus of Grube's study is the prevention of alcohol use/abuse among youth. His research seeks to address the concern that alcohol advertising makes alcohol attractive, thereby encouraging alcohol use among young people, and that such use will ultimately lead to the development of alcohol-related problems. This commentary will focus on some of the prevention-related issues raised by this study, with the general thesis that our culture's ambivalence about alcohol contributes to the mixed messages that youth receive about alcohol.

A case in point is the following quotation taken from Grube's chapter. He refers to the fact that "alcohol advertisements generally ignore problems such as drinking and driving, birth defects, and alcoholism. Rather, they portray drinking as a normative activity and one that is consistently associated with positively valued activities and consequences such as romance, sociability, and relaxation." This quotation is representative of the beliefs of many prevention experts who are concerned about the effects of advertising. However, when examined carefully, it is clear that rather than being an indictment of alcohol advertisements, this quotation (1) portrays alcohol advertisements as being comparable to other advertisements in their focus on the positive aspects of using the product, and (2) suggests that alcohol advertisements are relatively accurate in their representation of the social situations in which most people drink.

Generally, the advertising for most products tends to associate the product with positively valued activities and to present the use of the product as a normative activity. The quotation suggests that alcohol advertisers should do what no other advertiser does; that is, present the negative impact of their product. This suggestion holds alcohol advertisers to a standard that is different from that of any other producer of a potentially harmful product. For example, the auto industry does not advertise cars by pointing out that their use can cause injury or death or by highlighting their generally poor safety record in high-speed crashes. Instead, advertisements for cars often portray attractive yet risky driving situations likely to appeal to the young. The dairy industry does not advertise its products by talking about cholesterol and the potential for heart attacks. However, the cholesterol in dairy products contributes to heart disease, and heart disease is a major cause of death as well as a contributor to the high cost of health care. Learning to eat lots of dairy products in youth may directly contribute to the development of heart disease at a later age. Although there are many potentially harmful products whose use begins in youth, manufacturers and advertisers rarely if ever highlight the problems caused by these products. The advertisements for products such as automobiles and dairy products are not expected to contain a balanced picture, so why would we expect this of alcohol advertisements?

Alcohol advertisements are somewhat accurate in their portrayal of alcohol-related activities because they tend to represent the social situations in which most people drink (parties, bars, and other leisure activities). In addition, alcohol use is a normative activity. Recent statistics from the National Institute on Alcohol Abuse and Alcoholism (NIAAA) (1990) suggest that approximately 34 percent of adults over 18 years of age abstain from using alcohol, while 66 percent consume alcohol and most of these do not have problems with alcohol. Approximately 10 percent of adult drinkers have alcohol problems (NIAAA 1990). Thus, the majority of American adults consume alcohol socially in a variety of contexts and situations that represent positive activities such as celebrations (weddings, promotions), special social occasions (parties), and meals. These are positively valued activities that our society has deemed appropriate for the use of alcohol, and for the most part the members of society conform to such use without experiencing any negative consequences. Therefore, we should not be afraid to portray alcohol as associated with such activities.

The negative effects of alcohol usually are related to excessive drinking or alcohol *abuse*. Although there is individual variation and controversy as to the exact number of drinks that constitutes excessive or abusive consumption, research suggests some general guidelines. For example, Sanchez-Craig and Israel (1985) have suggested that "an average consumption of four drinks (54 g/ethanol), on average of three days/week" (p. 178) constituted the point where drinking became hazardous. Descriptions of drinking patterns in the general population also have suggested that 12 drinks per week represents the cutoff for "heavy drinking" (Cahalan et al. 1969), and most social drinkers consume alcohol at lower levels.

Alcohol is a substance that is legally available and is used in a variety of social contexts; therefore, it is incumbent on our society to be open and honest in our dealings with adolescents about its use as well as its positive and negative effects. It may be true that alcohol advertising paints an overly positive picture of the consequences of drinking, but all too often, our approach to youth is to paint an overly negative picture of the consequences of drinking. For example, three of the five items on the negative beliefs measure used in Grube's study contain simple messages that do not reflect the true picture of the effects of alcohol.

Item: "Drinking can harm health." It is true that the abuse of alcohol can be harmful to one's health, but it is also true that light to moderate drinking has been shown to reduce the risk of heart attack in men and in women (Gordon and Kannel 1983; LaVecchia et al. 1987; Moore and Pearson 1986; Stampfer et al. 1988). Thus, an honest portrayal of alcohol's impact on health would need to include both aspects of our present knowledge and should make a clear distinction between alcohol use and alcohol abuse. A better message would be, "Drinking small amounts of alcohol (e.g., 1 to 2 drinks per day) does not harm health, but drinking excessively (e.g., 4 or more drinks per day) on many occasions can harm health."

Items: "Mother's drinking can harm unborn child" and "Mother's drinking can cause birth defects." This statement simplifies the many complex issues related to alcohol consumption during pregnancy. Fetal alcohol syndrome (FAS) involves a variety of birth defects (e.g., growth retardation, intellectual impairment). However, "FAS has been identified only in children born to mothers who drank heavily while pregnant" (NIAAA 1994, p. 204). Further, "... not all women who drink excessively during pregnancy give birth to children with FAS" (NIAAA 1994, p. 204). Research to date suggests that there is much variability in outcomes related to mother's drinking (Roman et al. 1988). Some of the factors related to pregnancy outcome include the topography of the drinking behavior, use of other harmful substances including illicit drugs, period of gestation, and preexisting physiological state (e.g., nutrition). Thus, these factors could be better stated to reflect what we know about the effects of mothers' excessive drinking, rather than the overly broad generalization to consuming any amount (however small) of alcohol.

We undermine our credibility by confusing the effects of drinking any amount of alcohol (no matter how small) with the effects of drinking excessive amounts of alcohol, or alcohol abuse. We lose further credibility by portraying alcohol in uniformly negative terms while continuing to legalize the selling of alcoholic beverages and to condone social drinking. This loss of credibility vis-a-vis alcohol use is a disservice to ourselves and our adolescents.

Another conclusion reached by Grube concerns the finding of reciprocal effects in which knowledge about beer brands increased awareness of beer commercials. It was suggested that this probably represents the fact that beer advertising represents a source of information for children who are curious about drinking. However, since the majority of adults in the population consume alcohol, why would we not expect children to show some curiosity about alcohol? Also, why do we leave it to children to learn about alcohol from beer commercials?

A SKILLS TRAINING APPROACH TO PRIMARY PREVENTION

The prevention of alcohol use among youth is a highly complex undertaking that encompasses a wide variety of theories and strategies. There is an abundance of research on primary prevention of substance use among adolescents in the general population, particularly programs implemented in schools. Reviews of this literature have been uniformly negative in their assessment of the efficacy of school-based programs (Bangert-Drowns 1988; Moskowitz 1989). Such reviews find support for changes in knowledge and attitudes, but few changes in behavior. Some studies report short-term success, but not long-term maintenance of behavior change (Ellickson et al. 1993; Pentz et al. 1989) or report changes in drug use but no changes in drinking behavior (e.g., Ellickson and Bell 1990).

In a similar fashion, many studies on the impact of alcohol advertising have reported negative findings (Adlaf and Kohn 1989; Makowsky and Whitehead 1991; Smart 1988). For example, while citing the methodological limitations of existing studies, Smart (1988) concluded that "advertising bans do not reduce alcohol sales, total advertising expenditures have no reliable correlation to sales of alcoholic beverages, and that experimental studies typically show no effect of advertising on actual consumption" (p. 314). Research to date suggests that legislative strategies, such as increased taxes on alcohol and restrictions on the density of outlets selling alcohol, are highly effective in reducing underage drinking (Klitzner et al. 1993). Moskowitz (1989) also has suggested that changing social norms regarding alcohol may be effective in preventing alcohol use by youth. Despite evidence indicating the promise of these approaches to reducing alcohol consumption among adolescents, they are rarely implemented, and traditional prevention efforts continue to focus on changing individual behavior.

Social learning theory is one of the conceptual frameworks used in prevention research. Social learning theorists view alcohol use as a learned behavior. Vicarious and direct learning experiences contribute to the development of a particular behavioral repertoire. As such, prevention efforts should focus on not just acquiring knowledge about alcohol's positive and negative effects, but also on learning about appropriate ways to use alcohol. This approach provides an alternative to prevention efforts that seek to demonize alcohol use among youth.

Social learning approaches can take many guises and may involve a variety of prevention strategies. One potentially useful approach based on social learning principles is to provide training in the appropriate use of alcohol. This may seem like a radical notion, but we already have programs that train adolescents in how to handle other potentially harmful situations. A good example of such an approach is teaching adolescents how to drive. Most people agree that giving an automobile to someone who does not know how to drive is very risky. We handle the potential risk by providing lessons in which the new driver learns how to handle the car under controlled circumstances, often in the form of lessons provided by a school or certified program. New drivers practice until they reach an adequate level of proficiency, at which time their knowledge and skills are tested. Those who pass the test are given a license to drive. Those who do not pass the test are expected to go back to school and/or get more practice until they can pass the test. Those who do not take and pass the driving test cannot receive a license to drive. It is a relatively simple system and it seems to work.

Driver training does not guarantee that each licensed driver is an excellent driver, but it does seem to assure a modicum of safety on the roads, and thereby has probably reduced some of the harm related to the use of automobiles. Even with the provision of training and the testing of driving proficiency, the age and experience of the driver has an impact on driving-related harm. Thus, the evidence suggests that driving skills training and testing, placing limitations on those who have little driving experience, and increasing the minimum age for receiving a driver's license are the best methods for decreasing driving-related harm (Klitzner et al. 1993).

During the 1980's, the legal drinking age was raised to 21 years as a way of decreasing the number of drunk-driving fatalities in the United States. This strategy has resulted in some decreases in alcohol-related fatalities among drivers overall as well as among younger drivers (Hingson 1993; O'Malley and Wagenaar 1991). Interestingly, increasing the legal driving age also reduces the number of driving fatalities (Klitzner et al. 1993), but this strategy has not yet been tried in the United States. Raising the minimum legal drinking age has also been linked to reductions in alcohol consumption among high school seniors and has carried over into cohorts in their early 20's (Johnston et al. 1992; O'Malley and Wagenaar 1991). However, it is difficult to disentangle the contributions of a legal minimum drinking age of 21 years from the general trend of decreases in a variety of addictive behaviors, including smoking and use of illicit drugs, which could also be reflected in decreased alcohol use.

At present, the only license to drink that one needs is to reach the age of 21 years. This means that an individual who may have never touched an alcoholic beverage until reaching 21 can legally buy and consume whatever quantity of alcohol he or she chooses based on the attainment of a certain chronological age. The logic of choosing 21 years of age as the time when drinking is legal and appropriate is difficult to articulate. Why not 23 years, 25 years, or even 30 years? There is no evidence to suggest that someone who does not know how to handle alcohol at the age of 20 will magically be able to handle alcohol at the age of 21. Knowledge of alcohol's effects does not automatically increase at age 21, nor do cognitive and motor skills, as a function of alcohol use, change at age 21. Thus, the current approach of legalizing alcohol use based only on chronological age is arbitrary and somewhat foolhardy given the potential harm (to self and others) posed by excessive consumption of alcohol.

Some people who subscribe to a social learning approach have proposed that alcohol use be regarded as a skill, for which individuals might receive training and testing. Using the analogy of driver education, one might consider some of the benefits and problems in implementing drinker education and testing. Although we know that many adolescents under 21 drink alcohol (Johnston et al. 1992), the minimum legal drinking age limits such skill training to those 21 and older. For those of legal age, the skills involved in the use of alcohol must be geared to allowing the individual to experience its positive effects (e.g., relaxation, sociability, cardiovascular health) without experiencing its negative effects (e.g., nausea, loss of psychomotor coordination, addiction). The components of existing "skills training" typically include providing knowledge of the psychological and pharmacological properties of alcohol, training in how to estimate blood alcohol levels, setting and maintaining limits on alcohol consumption, training in relaxation, providing alternatives to alcohol use, and so on (see also Kivlahan et al. 1990). Thus, a skills training prevention program could include both knowledge and practice components. Trainees of legal drinking age could learn about topics such as types of alcoholic beverages, alcohol metabolism, and the impact of beliefs about alcohol effects. They could also practice how to use alcohol under controlled circumstances. Such practice could occur via homework assignments with parents and/or other licensed drinkers. After completion of the program, trainees would take tests (both written and practice) where their level of skill would be assessed. Only when the individual had reached a level of proficiency deemed appropriate by the larger society would she or he become a licensed drinker.

One example of the efficacy of this type of approach was conducted at the University of Washington (Kivlahan et al. 1990). In this study, college students at high risk for problem drinking were randomly assigned to either skills training, alcohol information, or an assessment-only condition. The results at a 1-year followup suggested that although all subjects showed reductions in self-reported alcohol intake, the skills training approach was consistently best. Although this study involved secondary prevention (i.e., it was implemented *after* the college students were already engaging in relatively high levels of alcohol use), it provides a useful starting point for a skills training approach to primary prevention.

Although a skills training approach to primary prevention might be most effective in reducing harm related to drinking during adolescence, the practice aspects of such training cannot be implemented. However, expanded efforts to provide a balanced presentation of information as well as some behavioral training in skills directly relevant to the use of alcohol might have a more direct impact on alcohol abuse than would efforts to shape the behavior of alcohol advertisers. By providing young people with appropriate skills and knowledge, it also is likely that we could reduce the impact of alcohol advertising in developing unreasonably positive expectations for the effects of alcohol.

This approach to primary prevention comes to the heart of concerns about the effects of alcohol advertising on adolescents. We do not want advertising to present too positive a picture of alcohol use and its effects because we are aware of the potential harmfulness of alcohol abuse. Even so, we must be clear and honest in our portrayal of harm. For most drinkers the harm is not in consuming low to moderate amounts of alcohol, the harm is in consuming excessive amounts of alcohol. Media portrayals of alcohol, whomever the target audience, may promote use. However, these portrayals can only succeed to the extent that we maintain our ambivalence toward alcohol and fail to deal honestly with adolescents who are the future consumers of alcohol. Some controls on alcohol advertising, particularly limiting the targeting of underage drinkers, may reduce the incentives to begin drinking. However, in the current system, adolescents are essentially passive consumers of alcohol advertising. As such, they are likely to be more susceptible to media influences. A skills training approach to primary prevention could make adolescents better informed and more critical, assist in enhancing their skepticism concerning media (including advertising) portrayals of the positive effects of alcohol, and provide them with the appropriate tools to help them regulate their use of alcohol.

REFERENCES

Adlaf, E.M., and Kohn, P.M. Alcohol advertising, consumption and abuse: A covariance-structural modelling look at Strickland's data. *Br J Addict* 84:749–757, 1989.

Ajzen, I. *Attitudes, Personality, and Behavior.* Chicago: Dorsey, 1988.

Bangert-Drowns, R.L. The effects of school-based substance abuse education: A meta-analysis. *J Drug Educ* 18:243–264, 1988.

Cahalan, D.; Cisin, I.; and Crossley, H. *American Drinking Practices.* New Brunswick, NJ: Rutgers Center of Alcohol Studies, 1969.

Ellickson, P.L., and Bell, R.M. Drug prevention in junior high: A multi-site longitudinal test. *Science* 247:1299–1305, 1990.

Ellickson, P.L.; Bell, R.M.; and McGuigan, K. Preventing adolescent drug use: Long-term results of a junior high program. *Am J Pub Health* 83:856–861, 1993.

Gordon, T., and Kannel, W.B. Drinking habits and cardiovascular disease: The

Framingham study. *Am Heart J* 105:667–673, 1983.

Hingson, R. Prevention of alcohol-impaired driving. *Alcohol Health Res World* 17:28–34, 1993.

Johnston, L.D.; O'Malley, P.M.; and Bachman, J.G. *Smoking, Drinking and Illicit Drug Use Among American Secondary School Students, College Students, and Young Adults, 1975-1991.* Vol. 1: Secondary school students. NIH Pub. No. 93-3480. Washington, DC: Supt. of Docs., U.S. Govt. Print. Off., 1992.

Kivlahan, D.R.; Marlatt, G.A.; Fromme, K.; Coppel, D.B.; and Williams, E. Secondary prevention with college drinkers: Evaluation of an alcohol skills training program. *J Consult Clin Psychol* 58:805–810, 1990.

Klitzner, M.; Stewart, K.; and Fisher, D. Reducing underage drinking and its consequences. *Alcohol Health Res World* 17:12–18, 1993.

LaVecchia, C.; Franceschi, S.; Decarli, A.; Pampollona, S.; and Tognoni, G. Risk factors for myocardial infarction in young women. *Am J Epidemiol* 125:832–843, 1987.

Makowsky, C.R., and Whitehead, P.C. Advertising and alcohol sales: A legal impact study. *J Stud Alcohol* 52:555–567, 1991.

Moore, R.D., and Pearson, T.A. Moderate alcohol consumption and coronary artery disease. *Medicine* 65:242–267, 1986.

Moskowitz, J.M. The primary prevention of alcohol problems: A critical review of the research literature. *J Stud Alcohol* 50:54–88, 1989.

National Institute on Alcohol Abuse and Alcoholism. *Seventh Special Report to the U.S. Congress on Alcohol and Health.* DHHS Pub. No. (ADM)90-1656. Washington, DC: Supt. of Docs., U.S. Govt. Print. Off., 1990.

National Institute on Alcohol Abuse and Alcoholism. *Eighth Special Report to the U.S. Congress on Alcohol and Health.* NIH Pub. No. 94-3699. Washington, DC: Supt. of Docs., U.S. Govt. Print. Off., 1994.

O'Malley, P.M., and Wagenaar, A.C. Effects of minimum drinking age laws on alcohol use, related behaviors and traffic crash involvement among American youth: 1976–1987. *J Stud Alcohol* 52:478–491, 1991.

Pentz, M.A.; MacKinnon, D.P.; Dwyer, J.H., Wang, E.Y.I.; Hansen, W.B.; Flay, B.R.; and Johnson, C.A. Longitudinal effects of the Midwestern Prevention Project on regular and experimental smoking in adolescents. *Prev Med* 18:304–321, 1989.

Roman, E.; Beral, V.; and Zuckerman, B. The relation between alcohol consumption and pregnancy outcome in humans. *Issues Rev Teratol* 4:205–235, 1988.

Sanchez-Craig, M., and Israel, Y. Pattern of alcohol use associated with self-identified problem drinking. *Am J Pub Health* 75:178–180, 1985.

Smart, R.G. Does alcohol advertising affect overall consumption? A review of empirical studies. *J Stud Alcohol* 49:314–323, 1988.

Stampfer, M.J.; Colditz, G.A.; Willett, W.C.; Speizer, F.E.; and Hennekens, C.H. A prospective study of moderate alcohol consumption and the risk of coronary heart disease and stroke in women. *N Engl J Med* 319:267–273, 1988.

Chapter 9

Portrayals and Effects of Alcohol in Television Entertainment Programming

Jane D. Brown and Trevy McDonald[1]

ALCOHOL IN TELEVISION ENTERTAINMENT PROGRAMMING

The use of alcohol has been depicted in visual entertainment media since their invention. As film analysts put it, "from the earliest peep-show slapstick of Carry Nation doused in beer, through the champagne-drenched courtship in *Casablanca* and the drunken cackles of *Arthur*," drinking and drunkenness have played significant roles in American cinema (Herd and Room 1982; Room 1988*a*). As the newest visual medium, television continues the pattern. Alcohol is inescapable, appearing in more than 70 percent of prime-time shows.

Health advocates are concerned not only because alcohol is drunk more frequently than any other beverage on television, but also because drinking is rarely presented as a problem or foregrounded as an issue in the television world. The rare occurrences of drunkenness are laughed at, and almost no one dies in car accidents caused by drunk drivers. The few alcoholics who appear are portrayed as despicable or pathetic characters who are alcoholic because they lack the willpower to quit drinking. Paradoxically, if an alcoholic is on a show long enough to be rehabilitated, the recovery is quick and permanent.

Does this televised view of normative and relatively trouble-free drinking affect the drinking patterns of television viewers? It certainly seems reasonable to expect that such pervasive portrayals on such a pervasive medium would have an impact both on the young who have not yet established their beliefs about drinking and on adults who use television as a window on cultural norms (Tudor 1979). However, as communication researchers have learned over the past couple of decades, establishing the effects of television content is not an easy

[1]School of Journalism and Mass Communication, Howell Hall CB3365, University of North Carolina, Chapel Hill, Chapel Hill, NC 27599-3365

task. This chapter reviews what is known about the portrayal and effects of alcohol on entertainment programming on television[2] from content studies and the few existing surveys and experiments, and then considers how alternative research and theoretical approaches may be fruitful in learning more.

CONTENT AND EFFECTS

Two theories have guided much of the research on the potential effects of televised portrayals of alcohol. Cultivation analysis, as formulated by Gerbner and his colleagues (Gerbner et al. 1986), predicts that people who view television frequently are more likely than lighter viewers to adopt the world view offered by television. Tests of the cultivation model typically begin with analyses of the manifest content of television programs, and then use surveys to assess the extent to which people who report viewing more television than others concur with the conceptions of social reality presented in the programs. Given the frequent incidence of problem-free drinking on television, cultivation analysis predicts that heavy viewers will be more likely than light viewers to believe that most people drink and that drinking is not a problem, and thus, may be more likely to drink themselves.

Social learning theory (Bandura 1977, 1986) is derived from classic learning theory and posits that humans learn by watching others and will engage in behaviors they see rewarded (or not punished). In the case of alcohol, the theory predicts that viewers who see glamorous characters on television drinking and not suffering serious consequences will model or imitate the drinking.

From the perspective of both theories, then, analyses of portrayals are important first steps in establishing the effects of television viewing. Cultivation theory focuses content analyses primarily on the sheer frequency of specific drinking behaviors, while social learning theory focuses on both the frequency and the positive or negative attributes of models and their drinking behavior. What do these content analyses show?

Frequency of References to Alcohol

Between 1969 and 1986, the number of programs on American television making reference to alcohol increased steadily, from a low of 10 percent of prime-time network dramatic programs in 1969 to more than 70 percent since 1983 (Signorielli 1987*b*; Wallack et al. 1990). An analysis of 24 hours of British television programs in 1988 found similar frequencies, with nearly three-fourths of the programs containing visual or verbal references to alcohol (Pendleton et al. 1991).

The proportion of drinks consumed that contain alcohol has increased since the beginning of television and is a dramatic distortion of the frequency of drinking in the real world. From 1950 to 1963, alcohol comprised less than half (48 percent) of all beverage use. By 1982, however, 62 percent of television drinks were alcoholic, and by 1984 almost three-fourths (74 percent) of all beverages depicted contained alcohol. In the real world, alcohol accounts for only 16 per-

[2]The concentration on entertainment programming on television thus excludes advertising or news content.

cent of total beverage use, but on television, alcohol is drunk almost three times as often as the combined total for coffee/tea, soft drinks, and water (Breed and De Foe 1981, 1984; Wallack et al. 1987).

The number of alcohol acts per hour more than doubled from a low of 4.8 per hour in 1976 to a high of 10.2 per hour in 1984, but the most recent figures show that frequency dropped to 9.1 in 1985 and 7.9 in 1986 (Wallack et al. 1990). This pattern is paralleled on British television, where in 1988 a reference to alcohol occurred on the average of every 6.5 minutes of programming, but this frequency also appeared to be decreasing as compared to 1986 levels (Pendleton et al. 1991).

Thus, even though the use of alcohol on entertainment programming is decreasing, alcohol still appears in more programs now than in the past, and is consumed more frequently than any other beverage on television.

Tests of the Cultivation Hypothesis

Given such content patterns, the cultivation hypothesis as typically tested would predict that heavy television viewers are more likely than light viewers to believe that most people drink and that alcohol is the preferred beverage. Surprisingly, the three existing studies of the cultivation hypothesis regarding alcohol have skipped the perceptual test and have gone directly to assess the behavioral implications of accepting television's view of drinking. The results of the three studies are contradictory.

Signorielli (1987*a*), using National Opinion Research Corporation (NORC) General Social Survey data, examined whether heavier television viewers were more likely than lighter television viewers to be drinkers. She found little evidence for the cultivation effect, although she claimed to find a mainstreaming effect, i.e., the "difference between college and non-college respondents and white and non-white respondents who say they drink is smaller among heavy viewers than among light viewers" (p. 256). But the coefficients are tiny, e.g., the Pearson *r* between television viewing and use of alcohol, after controlling for sex, age, education, and income, is .028; before controls, the *r* is –.051, suggesting that heavier viewers are less likely to drink than lighter viewers, which is counter-hypothetical.

In a test of the hypothesis among high school males, Tucker (1985, 1987) did find that heavy viewers reported consuming alcohol significantly more often than light or moderate viewers, even after controls for demographics were introduced. Among a sample of 14- to 16-year-olds, Klein et al. (1993) found that adolescents who had engaged in more risky health behaviors (such as drinking) watched music videos more frequently than those who had engaged in fewer risky behaviors, regardless of their race, gender, or parents' education. The direction of effect is not clear in such cross-sectional data, however, and there is a reasonable possibility that selection confounds the findings. As Tucker notes, it is possible that boys who drink frequently also select television as a primary form of entertainment more frequently than boys who drink less.

Similarly, a relationship between music video viewing and alcohol consumption may be more a function of the social situation of the teenager than evidence of the effects of television. Studies of both Swedish and Canadian youth suggest that when adolescents are not doing well in school, they turn to non-normative peer groups as an alternative source of self-esteem. Such peer groups typically prefer non-mainstream forms of music and may also model and reinforce deviant or unhealthy behaviors, such as heavy drinking (Roe 1989; Tanner 1981).

Another study of teenagers suggests that correlations between television viewing and alcohol consumption might be due more to the effect of the alcohol advertising surrounding the programming than the content of the programs. Atkin et al. (1984) concluded from a survey of male and female teenagers that exposure to alcohol advertising was more strongly related to both beer and liquor drinking than a number of other variables, including demographics and the frequency of viewing alcohol in entertainment programming. They, too, raised the question of direction of causality and the possibility of a spurious relationship, and suggested that other factors, such as dissatisfaction with life, could motivate viewing of television shows that attract heavy beer advertising, and could also produce reliance on alcohol.

Wober (1987, p. 180) found that adult heavier viewers of soap operas were more likely than lighter viewers to perceive a greater risk of being affected by a disease caused by drinking alcohol. Wober also suggested that the relationship could be spurious and might better be explained by an antecedent perception of a risky world that leads to both the perception of alcohol use as risky and the frequent viewing of soap operas that provide a "reassuring atmosphere" in general.

Thus, the results of correlational studies testing the basic cultivation hypothesis are inconclusive. The evidence is stronger for specific program types, such as soap operas and music videos, rather than for overall television viewing, but the relationships typically have been small or counter-hypothetical and could be attributed to other factors. Since data have not been collected over time, it is impossible to determine whether the television viewing or drinking behavior came first.

Characteristics of Portrayals and Effects

Another explanation for the contradictory findings of the cultivation tests is that alcohol is portrayed differently on different kinds of entertainment programs, and although most drinking is sanctioned or not even noticed, alcoholism is most often portrayed negatively. Classic cultivation theory assumes that portrayals are consistent across television programs, but this assumption is not borne out by content studies.

Genre Differences

The context and frequency of drinking differs by genre (e.g., situation comedies, dramas, soap operas, music videos) and even among programs within a genre. In the top-rated television series of the 1979 season, for example, alcohol drinking rates varied from a high of 16.5 per hour on *Archie's Place* and 13.3 on *Dallas*, to 3.0 per hour on *Alice* and *Three's Company* (Greenberg 1981). Made-for-television movies and movies seen first in theatres (and then on pay movie channels and videotapes) have significantly higher frequencies of alcohol use than situation comedies (Wallack et al. 1987) and also have the highest proportion of drinking characters (20.6 percent as compared to

8.9 percent in situation comedies) (Wallack et al. 1990).

Soap operas. Soap opera viewers see fewer drinking acts per hour than prime-time viewers (3 to 6 alcohol acts per hour on soaps as compared to 5 to 8 on prime-time) and see more realistic portrayals of the negative consequences of heavy drinking (Garlington 1977; Greenberg 1981; Lowery 1980; Wallack et al. 1985).

Children's television. Children who watch television mostly on Saturday morning and in early evening see fewer drinking scenes than if they watch more adult-oriented programming (Cafiso et al. 1982; Greenberg et al. 1979).

Music videos. Although no systematic analyses of the frequency of references to alcohol in music videos have been conducted, analyses of music lyrics, and reports of the frequent alcohol consumption of rock musicians, suggest that heavy-metal music video fans especially may be exposing themselves to a norm of heavy alcohol use (Gore 1987). Music videos may be an especially important genre to study since adolescents are the primary and perhaps most vulnerable audience.

Of 26 offensive songs released in 1986–87 according to the Parents' Music Resource Center, 7 included some reference to alcohol use, some more obviously than others. For example, in "Shake Your Foundations," the heavy-metal group AC/DC sings, "See me leaning on the bar, I got my head in a whiskey jar. Feelin' good 'cos the city's alive, I'm gettin' ready to rock and jive . . ." Another group with a telling name, Waysted, sings in "Wild Night," "Crawling back for more, pounding on the floor, bottle breakin', walls are shakin', making one helluva noise." A member of the heavy-metal band Van Halen has appeared at concerts playing a guitar shaped like a Jack Daniels whiskey bottle; Motley Crüe band members and singer David Lee Roth have drunk Jack Daniels on stage (Gore 1987). Frequently, such concert performances are used as parts of music videos shown on television.

In the mid-1970's, a study of the lyrics of the most popular rock and country music songs found that about 17 percent of the rock songs and 11 percent of the country music songs contained alcohol or other drug-related references or themes (Beckley and Chalfant 1979). Alcohol was almost the only drug mentioned in country music songs and was presented as an unfortunately effective way of forgetting problems. Rock music, in contrast, included references to a number of other drugs and portrayed the use of drugs as contributing to self-expression and transcendence from the mundane.

But not all recent rock songs with references to alcohol are positive. For example, a band called Junkyard (1990, p. 94) sings in the song "Blooze":

> I'm talking about drinkin'
> Talkin' 'bout when you get home
> at three
> But you don't make it 'til four
> 'cause you can't find the door
> Went home, went straight to bed
> I didn't make it that far, fell flat
> on my head

Adolescents' Media Use

Such inconsistencies in portrayals within and across genres call into question one of the basic assumptions of the cultivation hypothesis. Most television viewers today can choose from a wide array of programming at any given moment, courtesy of cable, satellite dishes, and video cassette recorders. The content analyses suggest that different television diets may expose viewers to different levels of alcohol use. Some tests of the cultivation hypothesis with other issues such as sex role stereotypes and faith in others (Rubin et al. 1988; Walsh-Childers and Brown 1993) have found that television effects are linked to content selectivity and individual audience members' beliefs and activities, and not simply to high levels of exposure to television.

Today's adolescents are an especially selective and active media audience. They have grown up with viewing flexibility. Few parents impose viewing rules, and children learn early how to find the kind of programming they want. Furthermore, adolescents use a number of other media besides television. Music is adolescents' preferred medium, and a majority also read a wide variety of magazines. They also often do a variety of other things while watching television. In one study, early adolescents reported watching an average of 6 hours of television a day and listening to the radio 6 hours a day (during the school year!). Subsequent in-depth interviews revealed that youth often are attending to more than one medium simultaneously—the television is on, they are listening to music on their headsets, and they are reading a magazine or doing their homework (Klein et al. 1993). At this point, we do not know to what extent such selectivity and/or divided attention affects exposure to or understanding of media messages. Such viewing patterns, however, certainly call into question conclusions based on an assumption of uniform portrayals across media.

Characteristics of Portrayals

Drink preference. Over the past decade, the preferred alcoholic beverage on prime-time has shifted from distilled spirits to beer and wine, reflecting consumption trends toward "softer" alcoholic beverages in the general population. Increased beer drinking also may be due to more frequent portrayals of working-class characters, who traditionally are more frequent beer drinkers, and to specific shows such as *Archie's Place* and *Cheers* that have been set in working-class bars. Men on television are more likely than women to drink beer; women are more likely to drink wine (Lowry 1981; Wallack et al. 1990). As Heilbronn (1988) has pointed out, alcohol is often used on television both to provide a context for action (e.g., a bar) and to provide information about a character (e.g., the man is working-class because he drinks a beer rather than a cocktail).

Age of drinkers. Historically, most criticism of television has been motivated by a desire to protect children from learning or imitating undesirable values and behavior (Wartella and Reeves 1987). Social learning theory suggests that modeling occurs more readily when a viewer perceives a model as similar to themselves, and thus, we would expect concern if television presents young people drinking.

Content analyses, however, have found that young people are rarely shown drinking in entertainment television programs (Breed and De Foe 1984; Signorielli 1987*a,b*; Wallack et al. 1990), but young characters sometimes do express "pro-alcohol orientations" (De Foe et al. 1983). In a 5-year study of prime-time situation comedies and dramas, De Foe et al. (1983) calculated only one drinking act every 12.5 hours for characters under 18 years old, and most of the underage drinking was portrayed as a problem. A few young characters, however, were shown wanting to drink when they were older, and approving of drinking by others.

Character regularity and attributes. Examination of regular versus nonregular and "good" versus "bad" characters also has important implications for modeling, given that we would expect more modeling of regular, good characters. Content analyses show that regular characters on television series are more likely to be drinkers, and drinking characters (except alcoholics) tend to be upper-class, attractive, and glamorous (Wallack et al. 1990). Good characters drink five times as much as bad characters (De Foe et al. 1983).

Gender. An analysis of 1986 prime-time shows found that the percentage of women who drank (18.5 percent) was slightly higher than the percentage of men who drank (14.5 percent) (Wallack et al. 1990). But women suffered more severe sanctions for drinking than men, and were also more likely to disapprove of others drinking (Breed and De Foe 1981; Greenberg et al. 1979). In movies, women were less likely than men to be depicted as alcoholics, but when they were, the cause of the alcoholism was typically a lack of personal control and was associated with "abuse of her sexuality" (Harwin and Otto 1979, p. 48). Thus, we might expect viewers who identify with female characters to get a more negative view of drinking than viewers who identify with male characters.

Consequences of drinking. Only a few studies have taken on the difficult task of assessing what happens to television characters who drink, but this is a question of fundamental importance, especially from a social learning perspective that predicts that characters who experience positive consequences will be modeled more readily than those who suffer negative consequences.

The most comprehensive look at consequences, Signorielli's (1987*b*) analysis of 1,215 programs broadcast between 1969 and 1985, found that the harmful effects of alcohol were mentioned in only 5 to 25 percent of the shows and were more often mentioned in action-adventure programs and dramas than in situation comedies. A thorough analysis of the top shows in 1976–77 found that humor was used much more frequently in situation comedies than in dramas to portray the heavy drinker "as a lovable human despite the inebriety" (Breed and De Foe 1981, p. 66). The latest analysis of prime-time series found that in the majority (62 percent) of episodes, alcohol was portrayed neutrally; in only 12 percent of the episodes was alcohol presented in a clearly unattractive manner (Wallack et al. 1990).

Soap operas may present the most realistic picture of alcohol use on television. Analysis of 4.5 years of one of the most popular soap operas on television, *All My Children*, showed that alcohol was used primarily as an adjunct to other activities, and heavy drinking was frowned on. Characters who drank inappropriately suffered negative consequences ranging from social sanctions to loss of life (Wallack et al. 1985).

An earlier analysis of all 14 soap operas on the networks in 1977, however, identified three patterns of alcohol use: drinking ritualistically or to reduce tension in social situations (47 percent of the 520 drinking incidents observed), drinking to escape reality (30 percent of the incidents), and drinking to manage a crisis (23 percent). In 86 percent of all the cases of crisis-management drinking portrayed in soap operas, there were either no consequences or reinforcing consequences. Lowery (1980) concluded:

> The message conveyed is that alcohol can enhance the enjoyment of social interaction and reduce tension, allowing people to deal more effectively with unpleasant situations. The soap operas suggest that drinking for the purpose of social facilitation (the most frequently portrayed drinking pattern) is common and even proper in everyday life (p. 835).

As Lowery pointed out, tests of the social learning model have found that subjects who see characters experience no consequences of their behavior or avoid anticipated negative outcomes are just as likely to imitate the modeled behavior as those who see the behavior reinforced (Bandura 1965). The lack of negative consequences for social facilitation drinking or crisis-management drinking may also reduce inhibitions among viewers who come to the portrayals thinking alcohol use is undesirable.

Refusing drink offers. One hopeful trend is that recent studies of prime-time shows have found that the few drink offers made were as likely to be turned down as accepted (Wallack et al. 1987, 1990). Such portrayals could be important modeling events, especially for teenagers who may be learning the rituals of drinking.

Alcoholics. Despite the frequent portrayals of alcohol, very few problem drinkers appear on television or in the movies, and when they do, they typically are unattractive characters. As Denzin (1991) concludes from his historical analysis of alcoholics in American films, "while Americans want to drink, they do not want alcoholics" (p. 237).

Between 1978 and 1985 the proportion of alcoholics on American prime-time television remained steady at about 1 to 2 percent of the major characters in each yearly sample (about 38 alcoholics over 17 years). Only one-third of the alcoholics were presented as "good," as compared to 60 percent of nonalcoholic characters. Thirty percent were unsuccessful, in contrast to 20 percent of nonalcoholic characters. Alcoholics were much more likely than other characters to be involved in lethal violence and to be portrayed as physically or mentally ill, and they were judged by viewers as less fair, strong, rational, and happy than nonalcoholics (Signorielli 1987*a*).

However, Wallack et al. (1985) and others (Buscombe 1979) have expressed concern that the few portrayals of people with severe alcohol problems on television are inadequate in that problems typically are relatively easily taken care of and are seen as the individual's and not the community's concern.

Effects From a Social Learning Perspective

Thus, according to television, alcohol preferences differ by class and gender, women should be more careful with alcohol than men, and drinking helps good people interact with other people, but bad people may become alcoholics. How do such distinctions about the use of alcohol affect viewers? Only three small studies have addressed the question.

Kotch et al. (1986) tested the hypothesis that a lack of negative consequences would increase positive beliefs about drinking among young viewers. They found that boys who viewed a videotape of television programs that contained drinking scenes in which no negative consequences occurred were more likely than boys who saw a tape in which the drinking scenes had been edited out to believe that the good effects of alcohol are more important than the bad. No significant results were apparent for girls.

In another study, children who were shown the television program *M*A*S*H* were subsequently more likely to choose an alcoholic beverage over water as the beverage most appropriate for serving to adults than were children who viewed the same program with the drinking scenes deleted or children who did not watch the television program (Rychtarik et al. 1983). Among college males, however, no difference in drinking behavior was found immediately after viewing an episode of *Dallas* that either included or did not include drinking scenes (Sobell et al. 1986).

These few studies suggest that we might expect greater effects among children, that a lack of negative consequences may increase positive beliefs about alcohol, and that television may be teaching our children that adults prefer to drink alcohol. But these are tentative conclusions from limited studies that should be replicated and expanded.

COOPERATING WITH THE MEDIA

Despite the rather inconclusive evidence that television portrayals of alcohol have an effect on viewers, at least two groups have worked with the television industry in the interest of creating more socially responsible portrayals of alcohol in entertainment television. In 1979, Warren Breed and James De Foe opened an office in Hollywood and began lobbying industry professionals. They proceeded with a philosophy that "research is a start-up factor" (De Foe and Breed 1986, p. 39), and over the next decade they continued policy and content analyses that kept the television entertainment industry aware of what it was doing well and what could bear improvement (Breed and De Foe 1980, 1982, 1984; De Foe and Breed 1980, 1988*a,b*; Wallack et al. 1985). In 1982 the Caucus for Producers, Writers and Directors called for formal adoption of the 10 guidelines for portrayal of alcohol that Breed and De Foe had been promoting.[3] The most recent content analyses suggest that their work has had some impact, at least in terms of less gratuitous drinking as measured by drinking acts per hour (Wallack et al. 1990).

In 1987 the Center for Health Communication of the Harvard School of Public Health launched the Harvard Alcohol Project, which was designed to encourage the use of designated drivers and "promote a fundamental shift in U.S. social norms related to driving after drinking" (DeJong and Winsten 1990, p. 33). The Harvard staff met with more than 160 television producers, writers, and studio executives and won endorsements from the Writers Guild of America and the Screen Actors Guild. In the 1988–90 television seasons, more than 80 television episodes included dialog that the Project considered "consonant" with their goals. The three major networks also produced and ran a corollary blitz of public service announcements. National surveys collected by Gallup between September 1988 and June 1989 showed that awareness and use of designated drivers had increased significantly, especially among males (DeJong and Winsten 1990).

Both of these projects are important models of how research can be used to work with the industry in promoting more responsible portrayals of alcohol use. Despite the current lack of hard evidence that portrayals of alcohol on entertainment television affect viewers, continued communication and consultation with television producers is a worthwhile tactic.

Producers are hungry for relevant story lines. Breed and De Foe (1984) appropriately acknowledge that alcohol has properties that appeal to writers and producers. As Heilbronn (1988) also has pointed out, alcohol is often used by television writers as an indication of a character's personality, background, and/or current emotional state, which partly explains why alcohol is so prevalent but so rarely foregrounded as the theme or topic of a show. Health educators, guided by relevant research, could contribute to more responsible portrayals of alcohol by suggesting alternative dialog, stories, plot lines, and cues for establishing a character.

However, such interventions are not a panacea. The editorial content of magazines is often influenced by the magazine's most important advertisers (Warner and Goldenhar 1989). Magazines that carry more alcohol advertising also include more favorable editorial content about alcohol (Tankard and Pierce 1982). Although we have only anecdotal evidence that similar pressures are sometimes exerted on the producers of television programs (Silverman 1991), producers of programs that attract alcohol advertising are probably also less comfortable embedding anti-alcohol messages in their programs than producers of programs that attract other kinds of audiences and advertising.

Part of the reason that these two "cooperative consultations" have been so successful is that the television industry realizes it is under fire regarding alcohol. The industry has used examples of cooper-

[3]The "Ten Suggestions for the Portrayal of Alcohol in the Media" are (reprinted in Montgomery 1989):

(1) Do not glamorize the drinking or serving of alcohol as an especially sophisticated or adult pursuit.

(2) Do not show the use of alcohol gratuitously—in those cases where another beverage might easily and fittingly be substituted.

(3) Do not omit the grim consequences of alcohol misuse or alcoholism.

(4) Do not deny characters a chance to refuse an alcoholic drink by statements such as, "What will you have?" or "Do you want a drink with the rest of the guys?"

(5) Do not show drinking alcohol as an activity which is so "normal" that everyone must indulge; allow for decisionmaking on the part of every character.

(6) Do not show excessive drinking without consequences or with only pleasant consequences.

(7) Do not show miraculous recoveries from alcoholism; normally it is a most difficult task.

(8) Do not show children "lusting after" alcohol and the time when they are adult enough to drink it.

(9) Do not associate drinking alcohol with macho pursuits in such a way that heavy drinking is a requirement for proving oneself as a man.

(10) Do not omit the reaction of others to heavy alcoholic drinking, especially when it may be criticism.

ation with anti-alcohol activists as evidence that they are socially responsible and as justification for fighting a ban on alcohol advertising (Montgomery 1989). The industry has been willing to insert only specific kinds of messages, especially those like the designated driver that focus on the individual as the source of the problem and the solution. Given this history and the difficulty of reframing issues in a more structural way, it is unlikely that we will see discussions or portrayals that address the bigger issues of why drinking is so prevalent and what might be done at the community or policy levels to address the problem.

Reliance on strategies such as the designated driver campaigns may also distract public health advocates and policymakers from other, more effective strategies, such as stricter enforcement of laws against sales to minors and higher excise taxes (DeJong and Wallack, in press).

RESEARCH RECOMMENDATIONS

Content Analyses

Simple frequency counts are not as important as assessing the context and consequences of portrayals of alcohol (Atkin and Arkin 1990). But counts are important for establishing trends, for suggesting the kind and range of possible effects, and to see whether producers are responding to comment and criticism (Wallack et al. 1990).

In the future, content analyses could be helpful in two ways. First, in the interest of monitoring trends, something like Gerbner's Violence Index would be useful so that the industry and activists can continue to have some indication of whether television norms are changing. It may be difficult to create such an index now, however, given the increasing fragmentation of television viewing. The most extensive content analyses have previously focused on situation comedies and dramas, which constituted almost one-half of prime-time shows during the periods studied (De Foe et al. 1983), but it is more appropriate now to look at a broader array of available content and to consider alternative sampling strategies that take the spectrum of audience viewing patterns into account.

One possibility is to sample shows based on modal viewing patterns, say for early adolescent boys and girls, who probably are of most concern. Greenberg and his colleagues have adopted such a strategy in studying sexual content on television and movies and have achieved a better understanding of what a typical teenager may be learning about sex from television (Greenberg et al. 1993).

Second, both quantitative and qualitative analyses could help establish parameters for what we might expect to find in experimental studies of effects. Quantitative analyses could point researchers to which kinds of portrayals are most frequent and thus most likely to affect a viewer's perceptions of appropriate drinking behavior. Qualitative analyses or "readings" of specific episodes or segments of shows, such as the ones De Foe and Breed (1986) conducted on two made-for-television movies about alcohol issues, could help establish which interpretations are most likely. For example, the three patterns of drinking in soap operas (social facilitation, crisis management, and escape from reality) that Lowery (1980) identified could be norms that viewers may be acquiring. Some of the earliest work by Breed and De Foe (1981) and their more recent interpretative analyses of significant alcohol episodes and "enablers" on prime-time provide other models of productive qualitative work on content (DeFoe and Breed 1988*a,b*). Heilbronn's (1988) analysis of how alcohol is used as cultural codes of attributes such as class and personality is especially provocative and potentially useful in understanding how audiences learn about the role of alcohol in everyday life.

Studies of Effects

At this point we can only conjecture about the effect the frequent portrayal of alcohol on entertainment television has on the viewer. The numerous content analyses have established trends and parameters for possible effects, but only a few have considered the consequences of portrayals. Even fewer studies have taken the audience's perception of these portrayals into consideration. The few studies conducted that directly test either the cultivation hypothesis or hypotheses generated by social learning theory are contradictory and inconclusive.

Establishing the effects of television is difficult, but communication researchers have learned a great deal about how television works, and this knowledge can be applied to the question of alcohol. One of the most promising recent trends in television effects research is a return to looking more closely at the audience rather than primarily at content. Building on theories developed by cognitive psychologists as well as recent work in cultural studies, communication researchers have begun to expand their definition of effects to consider not only viewers' beliefs and behavior but also selection and interpretation. How does the audience choose what to pay attention to and how does the audience make sense of what they see? (Biocca 1991; Hansen 1988; Shapiro and Lang 1991)

From this perspective, a television viewer is a complex information processor who makes choices about what to watch and comes to the viewing moment with existing beliefs and stores of knowledge. What sense viewers make of a given image depends on a number of factors, including whether they are paying attention, what emotional state they are in at the time, and how they "frame" the images to which they pay attention. As viewers pay attention to television images, they construct personal mental models that answer such questions as "What is the topic?" "Is it relevant?" and "How does it fit with what I already know?" The viewer constructs an early model, based on previous memory structures (schemata), that is used to handle subsequent information (Biocca 1991).

One way to think about this perspective is to consider some models of media effects. The simplest model is S–R, where S is the stimulus (the alcohol portrayal) and R is the response to the portrayal. This is the model that the cultivation hypothesis assumes; no selection or interpretation is taken into account. The social learning model is an elaboration of the simplest model because it does assume some processing of the stimulus, and thus could be depicted as S–O–R, with the O representing the organism (person) processing what is seen. But social learning theory, at least as typically applied, also does not take into account the viewer's selection of content, as attention to the stimulus is assumed. A more appropriate model, then, would include another O in the beginning to depict selection of the stimulus. This O–S–O–R model emphasizes the cognitive processes involved as the person comes to view television and as he or she tries to make sense of what is viewed (McLeod et al. 1991).

Such an elaborated perspective helps explain the results of the few tests already conducted on the effects of alcohol portrayals. We might conclude from the three experimental studies discussed earlier that boys are more likely to be affected by drinking scenes than girls and that children are more affected than adult males. From an information processing point of view (O–S–O–R), such results fit with the idea that males and females and children and adults would have different existing schemata with which they process television depictions of alcohol. Girls may already have learned that drinking is more problematic for females than males in this culture. Similarly, heavy drinking on a television show may not stimulate college males to drink more because their drinking script (a behavioral schema) already includes such behavior.

Thus, we should expect different effects of similar portrayals among different segments of the audience. Only a very few studies have examined how portrayals of alcohol have been perceived and interpreted by different audiences (MacDonald 1983; Hansen 1988), but these suggest that viewers' previous experiences with alcohol influence their interest in and understanding of the television images. MacDonald, for example, found that regular soap opera viewers remembered the few soap stories about alcoholics. Hansen (1988) suggests that the viewers' inexperience with problematic drinking patterns might result in their paying greater attention to such portrayals.

Studies of the audience's use and interpretation of alcohol portrayals could be especially helpful in considering when and how to address alternative messages about alcohol. We may find, for example, that as adolescents get closer to using alcohol themselves, depictions of alcohol on television become more relevant and are more quickly assimilated into their developing schemata about alcohol. In studying how young adolescent girls learn about sex from the media, we have found that some girls simply are not paying attention to sexual messages, while others are actively seeking and interpreting whatever they can find from a variety of sources, including television, magazines, movies, and music (Brown et al. 1993). This is the moment when health educators should be prepared to offer alternative scripts of healthier drinking behavior or refusal.

CONCLUSIONS

Television programs are suffused with alcohol. Alcohol is drunk more frequently than any other beverage on television, yet characters rarely get drunk or suffer negative consequences from their drinking. The rare alcoholic is ridiculed or quickly rehabilitated. Although television entertainment programming does not pretend to be a reflection of the real world, it offers the illusion of reality, and health educators are rightly concerned that such unrealistic pictures of alcohol use and abuse may affect young television viewers' perceptions of appropriate drinking behavior and perhaps their own use of alcohol.

However, most of what is currently known about the effects of entertainment programming on viewers is based on extrapolations from content analyses. Such extrapolations are speculative and inadequate because one cannot know without observing the audience whether the content was attended to, understood, and acted on. The few studies that have considered the audience in testing the link between viewing and beliefs and behavior are contradictory and inconclusive. At this point, one could conclude that further research is not necessary because many studies have documented effects for a range of other behaviors, such as aggression, sex roles, and altruism (Pearl et al. 1982). But such studies may not be directly transferable to the issue of alcohol, and there is still much to learn about how television affects its audiences.

Three recommendations for future research are as follows:

(1) **Conduct studies that include the audience**. Current studies of media effects typically are based on a more complicated model than either the cultivation hypothesis or social learning theory assume. Sometimes called the "active audience perspective," this model asks researchers to take into account the fact that audiences have a great deal of freedom in selecting media and media messages and that audiences bring existing beliefs about how the world works to the viewing moment. From this perspective, research should focus on how audiences make choices about which shows to watch and which characters to pay attention to. We also would want to know, for example, whether audiences notice drinking when it so often occurs only in the background, whether children understand the symbolic uses of alcohol (e.g., do they know that drinking wine connotes upper class?), and whether children interpret the sometimes obscure references to drinking in music and music videos the same way adults do.

Including the audience is, of course, a more difficult proposition than simply studying content (Room 1988*b*), and the traditional experimental and survey tools may need to be supplemented with or informed by more qualitative approaches. But this is a necessary step if researchers want to be able to say how and to what extent television portrayals of alcohol affect viewers.

(2) **Continue limited content analyses**. Both quantitative and qualitative content analyses can be useful in assessing whether the industry has responded to calls for more responsible portrayals. Content analyses can also be used to predict possible interpretations of portrayals. How might one expect audiences to respond? What might they be learning other than the idea that everyone drinks? Other, more difficult, kinds of measures such as motivations, consequences, and symbolic meaning could predict effects. Content analyses should also be conducted on a broader range of content and should be tied to the prototypical media diets of particular target audiences, such as young adolescents, rather than restricted to prime-time situation comedies and dramas. Today's television audiences are no longer limited to network fare.

(3) **Continue sharing research and recommendations with the television programming industry**. The two cooperative consultations discussed here apparently have been effective in raising the consciousness of television writers and producers. Continued dialog between researchers and the industry is probably worthwhile, if researchers keep in mind

that the industry's collaboration may be used to impede other, less individually focused, strategies, such as a ban on alcohol advertising.

REFERENCES

Atkin, C., and Arkin, E.B. Issues and initiatives in communicating health information to the public. In: Atkin, C., and Wallack, L., eds. *Mass Communication and Public Health: Complexities and Conflicts.* Newbury Park, CA: Sage, 1990. pp. 13–40.

Atkin, C.; Hocking, J.; and Block, M. Teenage drinking: Does advertising make a difference? *J Commun* 34(2):157–167, 1984.

Bandura, A. Influence of models' reinforcement contingencies on the acquisition of imitative responses. *J Pers Soc Psychol* 1:589–595, 1965.

Bandura, A. *Social Learning Theory.* Englewood Cliffs, NJ: Prentice Hall, 1977.

Bandura, A. *Social Foundations of Thought and Action: A Social Cognitive Perspective.* Englewood Cliffs, NJ: Prentice Hall, 1986.

Beckley, R.E., and Chalfant, H.P. Contrasting images of alcohol and drug use in country and rock music. *J Alcohol Drug Educ* 25(1):44–51, 1979.

Biocca, F. Viewers' mental models of political messages: Toward a theory of the semantic processing of television. In: Biocca, F., ed. *Television and Political Advertising: Psychological Processes.* Vol. 1. Hillsdale, NJ: Lawrence Erlbaum Associates, 1991.

Breed, W., and De Foe, J. Mass media, alcohol and drugs. *J Drug Educ* 10(2):135–143, 1980.

Breed, W., and De Foe, J. The portrayal of the drinking process on prime time television. *J Commun* 31:58–67, 1981.

Breed, W., and De Foe, J. Effecting media change: The role of cooperative consultation on alcohol topics. *J Commun* 32:88–99, 1982.

Breed, W., and De Foe, J. Drinking and smoking on television, 1950-1982. *J Public Health Policy* Jun.:257–270, 1984.

Brown, J.D.; White, A.B.; and Nikopoulou, L. Disinterest, intrigue, resistance: Early adolescent girls' use of sexual media content. In: Greenberg, B.; Brown, J.D.; and Buerkel-Rothfuss, N., eds. *Media, Sex, and the Adolescent.* Cresskill, NJ: Hampton Press, 1993. pp.-176–177.

Buscombe, E. The representation of alcoholism on television. In: Cook, J., and Lewington, M., eds. *Images of Alcoholism.* London: Educational Advisory Service and British Film Institute, 1979. pp. 57–62.

Cafiso, J.; Goodstadt, M.S.; Garlington, W.K.; and Sheppard, M.A. Television portrayal of alcohol and other beverages. *J Stud Alcohol* 43(11):1232–1243, 1982.

De Foe, J., and Breed, W. The mass media and alcohol education: A new direction. *J Drug Alcohol Educ* 25(3):48–58, 1980.

De Foe, J., and Breed, W. The family, research and prime time television in alcohol education. *Int Qtrly Commun Health Educ* 7(1):33–40, 1986.

De Foe, J., and Breed, W. Youth and alcohol in television stories, with suggestions to the industry for alternative portrayals. *Adolescence* 23(91):533–550, 1988*a*.

De Foe, J., and Breed, W. Response to the alcoholic by 'the other' on prime time television. *Contemp Drug Prob* 15(2):205–228, 1988*b*.

De Foe, J.; Breed, W.; and Breed, L. Drinking on TV: A five year study. *J Drug Educ* 13(1):25–38, 1983.

DeJong, W., and Wallack, L. The role of designated driver programs in the prevention of alcohol-impaired driving: A critical reassessment. *Health Educ Qtrly*, in press.

DeJong, W., and Winsten, J.A. The use of mass media in substance abuse prevention. *Health Affairs*, Summer: 30–46, 1990.

Denzin, N. *Hollywood Shot by Shot: Alcoholism in American Cinema*. New York: De Gruyter, 1991.

Garlington, W.K. Drinking on television: A preliminary study with emphasis on method. *J Stud Alcohol* 38(11):2199–2205, 1977.

Gerbner, G.; Gross, L.; Morgan, M.; and Signorielli, N. Living with television: The dynamics of the television cultivation process. In: Bryant, J., and Zillmann, D., eds. *Perspectives on Media Effects*. Hillsdale, NJ: Lawrence Erlbaum Associates, 1986.

Gore, T. *Raising PG Kids in an X-Rated Society*. Nashville: Abingdon Press, 1987.

Greenberg, B.S. Smoking, drugging and drinking in top rated TV series. *J Drug Educ* 11(3):227–233, 1981.

Greenberg, B.S.; Brown, J.D.; and Buerkel-Rothfuss, N., eds. *Media, Sex, and the Adolescent*. Cresskill, NJ: Hampton Press, 1993.

Greenberg, B.S.; Fernandez-Collado, C.; Graef, D.; Korzenny, F.; and Atkin, C.K. Trends in use of alcohol and other substances on television. *J Drug Educ* 9(3):243–253, 1979.

Hansen, A. The contents and effects of television images of alcohol: Towards a framework of analysis. *Contemp Drug Prob* 15(2):249–279, 1988.

Harwin, J., and Otto, S. Women, alcohol and the screen. In: Cook, J., and Lewington, M., eds. *Images of Alcoholism*. London: Educational Advisory Service and British Film Institute, 1979. pp. 37–56.

Heilbronn, L.M. What does alcohol mean? Alcohol's use as a symbolic code. *Contemp Drug Prob* 15(2):229–248, 1988.

Herd, D., and Room, R. Alcohol images in American film 1909-1960. *Drinking Drug Pract Surv* 18:24–35, 1982.

Junkyard. "Blooze." *Hit Parader Magazine*, Jun. 1990. p. 94.

Klein, J.D.; Brown, J.D.; Childers, K.W.; Oliveri, J.; Porter, C.; and Dykers, C. Adolescents' risky behavior and mass media use. *Pediatrics* 92(1):24–31, 1993.

Kotch, J.B.; Coulter, M.L.; and Lipsitz, A. Does televised drinking influence children's attitudes toward alcohol? *Addict Behav* 11:67–70, 1986.

Lowery, S. Soap and booze in the afternoon. *J Stud Alcohol* 41(9):829–838, 1980.

Lowry, D.T. Alcohol consumption patterns and consequences on prime time network TV. *Journalism Qtrly* 58:3–8, 1981.

MacDonald, P.T. The "dope" on soaps. *J Drug Educ* 13(4):359–369, 1983.

McLeod, J.M.; Kosicki, G.M.; and Pan, Z. On understanding and misunderstanding media effects. In: Curran, J., and Gurevitch, M., eds. *Mass Media and Society*. New York: Edward Arnold, 1991. pp. 235–266.

Montgomery, K.C. *Target: Prime Time. Advocacy Groups and the Struggle Over Entertainment Television*. New York: Oxford University Press, 1989.

Pearl, D.; Bouthilet, L; and Lazar, J. *Television and Behavior: Ten Years of Scientific Progress and Implications for the Eighties*. Washington, DC: National Institute of Mental Health, 1982.

Pendleton, L.L.; Smith, C.; and Roberts, J.L. Drinking on television: A content analysis of recent alcohol portrayal. *Br J Addict* 86:769–774, 1991.

Roe, K. The school and music in adolescent socialization. In: Lull, J., ed. *Popular Music and Communication*. Newbury Park, CA: Sage, 1989. pp. 212–230.

Room, R. The movies and the wettening of America: The media as amplifiers of cultural change. *Br J Addict* 83:11–18, 1988*a*.

Room, R. Shifting perspectives in studies of alcohol in the media. *Contemp Drug Prob* 15(2):139–148, 1988*b*.

Rubin, A.M.; Perse, E.M.; and Taylor, D.S. A methodological examination of cultivation. *Commun Res* 15(2):107–134, 1988.

Rychtarik, R.G.; Fairbank, J.A.; Allen, C.M.; Foy, D.W.; and Drabman, R.S. Alcohol use in television programming: Effects on children's behaviors. *Addict Behav* 8:19–22, 1983.

Shapiro, M.A., and Lang, A. Making television reality: Unconscious processes in the construction of social reality. *Commun Res* 18(3):685–705, 1991.

Signorielli, N. Drinking, sex, and violence on television: The cultural indicators perspective. *J Drug Educ* 17(3):245–60, 1987*a*.

Signorielli, N. Children and adolescents on television: A consistent pattern of devaluation. *J Early Adolesc* 17(3):255–268, 1987*b*.

Silverman, J. TV's Creators Face a New Caution. *The New York Times*, Dec. 8, 1991. pp. H1, H31.

Sobell, L.C.; Sobell, M.B.; Riley, D.M.; Klajner, F.; Leo, G.; Pavan, D.; and Cancilla, A. Effect of television programming and advertising on alcohol consumption in normal drinkers. *J Stud Alcohol* 47(4):333–340, 1986.

Tankard, J.W., and Pierce, K. Alcohol advertising and magazine editorial content. *Journalism Qtrly* 59(2):302–304, 1982.

Tanner, J. Pop music and peer groups: A study of Canadian high school students' responses to pop music. *Can Rev Sociol Anthropol* 18(1):1–13, 1981.

Tucker, L.A. Television's role regarding alcohol use among teenagers. *Adolescence* 20(79):593–598, 1985.

Tucker, L.A. Television health and teenagers. *J Youth Adolesc* 16:415–25, 1987.

Tudor, A. On alcohol and the mystique of media effects. In: Cook, J., and Lewington, M., eds. *Images of Alcoholism.* London: Educational Advisory Service and British Film Institute, 1979. pp. 6–14.

Wallack, L.; Breed, W.; and Cruz, J. Alcohol on prime-time television. *J Stud Alcohol* 48(1):33–38, 1987.

Wallack, L.; Breed, W.; and De Foe, J.R. Alcohol and soap operas: Drinking in the light of day. *J Drug Educ* 15(4):365–79, 1985.

Wallack, L.; Grube, J.W.; Madden, P.A.; and Breed, W. Portrayals of alcohol on prime-time television. *J Stud Alcohol* 51(5):428–37, 1990.

Walsh-Childers, K., and Brown, J.D. Adolescents' acceptance of sex-role stereotypes and television viewing. In: Greenberg, B.; Brown, J.D.; and Buerkel-Rothfuss, N., eds. *Media, Sex, and the Adolescent.* Cresskill, NJ: Hampton Press, 1993. pp. 117–133.

Warner, K., and Goldenhar, L. The cigarette advertising ban and magazine coverage of smoking and health. *J Public Health Policy*, Spring:32–42, 1989.

Wartella, E., and Reeves, B. Historical trends in research on children and the media 1900-1960. In: Gurevitch, M., and Levy, M., eds. *Mass Communications Review Yearbook, 6.* Newbury Park, CA: Sage, 1987. pp. 160–75.

Wober, M. Perceived risk of disease from alcohol, asbestos and AIDS: Links with television viewing? *Health Educ Res* 2(3):175–84, 1987.

Chapter 10

Viewers' Interpretation of Television Images of Alcohol

Anders Hansen[1]

Brown's chapter provides an excellent review of research on television entertainment portrayals of alcohol and does an admirable job of examining the key literature in this field (see Brown and McDonald, chapter 9, this volume).

The central theme of Brown's chapter is an argument for greater differentiation and more sensitive models, both in the study of television content and in the study of audiences and influence. It seems right and proper that as audiences grow more selective in what they choose to watch, analyses of television portrayals must distinguish more clearly between the images or messages that are available to viewers in different program types and genres.

I agree with Brown's point that if we want to understand the symbolic environment created by television, we need to go much further than entertainment programs; we also need to look at factual portrayals in news, documentaries, and current affairs programs. The major problem for any critique of portrayals of alcohol and drinking in entertainment television is that our cultural values associated with drinking are themselves highly ambiguous (as was also pointed out by Collins [chapter 8, this volume]) and saturated with double standards.

Paradoxically, fictional depictions of serious alcohol consumption and associated outcomes often convey a much more clear-cut message about alcohol than do factual accounts in news programs, such as reports on automobile accidents, crime, and court cases. The images of alcohol and drinking in factual television programming are frequently ambiguous and contradictory, as they reflect the wider social, legal, and cultural double standards associated with alcohol consumption.

Turning to the evidence from studies of media influence, Brown rightly points to the inconclusive and sometimes confus-

[1]Centre for Mass Communication Research, University of Leicester, 104 Regent Rd., Leicester LE1 7LT England

ing evidence from both experimental research and cultivation studies. However, rather than arguing for further replication and expansion of experimental studies as Brown does, I would argue that laboratory experiments are seriously limited in terms of what they can contribute to our understanding of media influence. The reason for this is their focus on direct, immediate, quantifiable effects. As one of the founding fathers of mass communication research, Paul Lazarsfeld, put it so well nearly 40 years ago, "The real problem is the cumulative effect of television, what it does to children six years, not six minutes, later" (Lazarsfeld 1955, p. 246).

A further problem with experimental studies is that whatever effects are found (and this is not always clear) cannot be generalized beyond the walls of the laboratory. A laboratory experiment is an artificially created viewing situation that has little resemblance to how viewers normally encounter media messages.

Perhaps the most crucial problem with examining media influence in terms of direct effects on individual behavior and attitudes is a political one. For well over 30 years, the advertising and alcohol industries have been successful in focusing public debate about the rights and wrongs of alcohol advertising, and about the regulation of advertising, on the single question of proving direct causal effects. One suspects that as long as this remains the central terrain for research and debate, the industry will have little cause for concern: for every study that finds some causal effects, there will be another one that calls these effects into question.

The cultivation approach—which was born out of a reaction against the decontextualized search for immediate effects perceived as changes of attitudes and behavior—represents a major step forward. However, this approach also runs into considerable problems, more so, in fact, when it comes to looking at alcohol and television than at some of the other issues that cultivation studies have examined.

Gerbner's chapter describes how cultivation studies have shown that heavy viewers of television are less concerned about their health than light viewers, and how at the same time, television cultivates in them a belief in the magical powers of the medical profession. In the case of alcohol and drinking, however, it has proved to be far more difficult to demonstrate any cultivation effects. This is perhaps partly due to the fact that such studies—quite uncharacteristically for cultivation research—have looked at drinking *behavior* rather than at alcohol-related beliefs (see Gerbner et al. 1982).

The cultivation approach to the study of media influence has other problems too. It does not work very well in countries such as Britain, where viewers on the whole spend far less time watching television than they do in the United States. Consequently, it is more difficult to divide people into heavy and light viewers. In a study that we carried out at Leicester University, drawing on the cultivation approach, we found no significant differences between heavy and light viewers (Hansen 1988*a*).

There was one exception to this finding: Heavy viewers were considerably more likely to believe that people in the United States tend to drink spirits rather than beer or wine. This finding was not entirely unexpected, as our content analyses of television portrayals of alcohol had shown the consumption of spirits to be far more frequent in American serials shown on British television than in British serials. This finding simply confirmed what has been known for several decades in mass communications effects research: in matters where viewers can draw on their own experiences or on widely available sources of information *other* than the mass media, television has relatively little influence; but in matters that are not readily observable in viewers' social environment (in this case, the drinking habits of Americans), television steps in as a supplier of information, images, and messages and has a stronger influence on viewers' beliefs.

Brown suggests that the use of more qualitative approaches to the study of television audiences may offer a way out of the often confusing and contradictory findings of experimental and survey-based approaches. This is a suggestion that I fully agree with. If we wish to begin to understand what role television images of alcohol play in people's everyday lives, then we must move away from the search for immediate, short-term effects. We must begin to examine instead how viewers interact with television images, and to examine the dynamic process through which viewers draw on television images for making sense of their own lives, and equally, how viewers draw on their personal experiences, knowledge, and skills for making sense of television.

Viewers bring different interpretative frameworks to bear on alcohol images in television programs. At a very general level, it is useful to distinguish between at least two different ways in which viewers might approach the interpretation of television images of alcohol. One approach might be called a "real life frame," meaning that viewers perceive television images primarily in terms of how well those images represent reality as it is known to them. The other approach is what might be called a "conventions of television frame," meaning that television images are perceived primarily in terms of the format, narrative, and genre requirements of television (Hansen 1988*b*). In other words, viewers invoke their knowledge of the genre and aesthetic conventions of television as a framework for assessing the images portrayed.

This can be illustrated by a few examples from a study of British 12- to 16-year-olds and their interpretations of alcohol images in their favorite television serials. At the time of the study, the favorite programs for this age group included a British serial called *EastEnders*, set in a working-class area in the East End of London, and American serials such as *Dallas*, *Dynasty*, *Falcon Crest*, and *The Colbys*.

The quotes below, taken from study participants, clearly indicate a refined familiarity on the part of the viewers with how television uses alcohol as a way of telling us about the nature of the characters and their mental states.

> If someone's had an accident or something, then you see them all like with their shirts undone, and, you know, worrying, with a drink in their hand.

> They always show you that whenever they're drinking—it's 'cos they're worried or something or they're afraid or something, and they're trying to get rid of the problems.

> They only get on drink [i.e., drink excessively] . . . I don't know . . .

> if they've got a problem or something, like Miles did in *The Colbys* when Fallon went off.
>
> Deb [*EastEnders*] drinks white wine . . . she's always drinking white wine . . . cos she's supposed to be educated . . . high class. Well, she's always been a bit upper class from the rest of them . . . snob.
>
> [In *Dallas* or *Dynasty*] well, they'll drink champagne or something; you don't exactly see Alexis [key character in *Dynasty*] sitting there, you know, with a glass of lager in front of her, do you?

The extent to which viewers draw on both their personal experience and their knowledge of television conventions was perhaps even more pronounced in relation to their interpretation of alcoholism on television. At the time of the study, both *EastEnders* and *Dallas* featured central characters with alcohol problems. Without going into detail about the portrayals, what essentially became clear was that while the viewers did, to some extent, draw on a "real life" framework in their assessment of the portrayal of problem drinking, they also, and perhaps more significantly, invoked television stereotypes. Thus, the portrayal of alcoholism in *Dallas*, with its emphasis on the physical manifestations of alcohol addiction and on a medical model of cure, was seen by viewers as being the more authentic of the two portrayals—"authentic" in the sense that it conformed to the viewers' perception of what alcoholism is "supposed to look like" on television. This interpretative practice, of course, indicates the power of deep-seated cultural images and the difficulties that programs come up against in terms of credibility when attempting to break with such stereotypes.

These very brief examples indicate some of the complexity of how viewers make sense of television images of alcohol; but they also indicate some of the productive avenues of inquiry that open up when we abandon the search for immediate, short-term effects and instead turn our attention to questions about how viewers make sense of television and how they use television images for making sense of their own lives.

Brown does an admirable job of reviewing the many content analysis studies of television entertainment portrayal of alcohol. I would like to emphasize one or two of the major limitations of content analysis. The most serious problem with content analysis is the fragmentation of meaning that inevitably takes place when we attempt to describe complex narratives in terms of counts of single attributes and dimensions. Viewers, of course, do not watch programs as a series of disjointed images or attributes; they watch programs as stories, narratives, and moral lessons.

A second problem is the way that content analyses tend to reduce very complex narrative and thematic patterns into a small number of neat categories. A classic example is the often-quoted study by Sharon Lowery (1980), in which images of alcohol were classified into just three dimensions: drinking for *social facilitation*, *crisis management*, and *escape from reality*. Although such classification is neat and convenient, it inevitably glosses over the complexity and variation of television images of drinking.

In the final section of her chapter, Brown points—with some enthusiasm—to the cooperative consultation work of Breed and DeFoe and others as "important models of how research can be used to work with the industry in promoting more responsible portrayals of alcohol use" (p. 142).

What is meant by "responsible portrayals" is, however, clearly problematic and potentially very contentious. What is a responsible portrayal for a mature adult audience may well not be for a child or teenage audience; what counts as a responsible portrayal for one racial, ethnic, or religious group may not count as "responsible" in the eyes of another audience with different cultural values regarding alcohol and drinking.

Prescriptive guidelines about the appropriate portrayal of alcohol in television entertainment programs would be no different from the statutory and/or voluntary guidelines that govern broadcast and press advertising for alcoholic beverages in many European countries. These guidelines and codes, incidentally, are a central battleground in the ongoing attempts to homogenize the regulation of advertising in the European Community. Such guidelines are based, not on scientific evidence that certain portrayals adversely influence drinking and alcohol-related behavior, but on common-sense assumptions; for example, that portraying heavy drinking and automobile racing as activities that go well together is not a good idea.

It is difficult not to be enthusiastic about the "cooperative consultation" work of Breed and DeFoe, but it is nevertheless important to be absolutely clear that guidelines about how alcohol, drinking, and alcohol-related phenomena should be portrayed on television are essentially based on notions of balance; they are not, nor are they ever likely to be, based on hard scientific evidence about the effects of particular types of portrayals on people's beliefs, attitudes, or behavior.

Brown suggests two future uses of content analyses: (1) to monitor trends (and by implication, to inform programming policies), and (2) to inform experimental studies of effects. For the reasons outlined earlier in this chapter, I would argue that the successful and productive use of content analysis is far more likely in the former than in the latter.

The attractiveness of the cooperative consultation model stems mostly from a fear of the one-sidedness that would result from a laissez-faire approach in which market forces were allowed to run freely. It is in this respect that there is a great difference between intervening in the works of, say, William Shakespeare by suggesting to the author that his portrayals of drinking are not socially responsible, and on the other hand, intervening in modern day television portrayals of alcohol. The difference, of course, is that powerful commercial interests, rather than artistic enterprise, govern the production of television programs. Thus, the primary justification for content analyses aimed at cooperative consultation-type intervention stems, not from scientific evidence of adverse effects, but from what we might call an "informed citizen's" or "citizen's right-to-know" perspective. The cornerstone of such a perspective is essentially that in an informed democracy, citizens should have ready access to images, portrayals, and information on the full range of pleasures *and* problems associated with alcohol use, as opposed to the largely pleasure-oriented images of alcohol and drinking that currently predominate in television entertainment and advertising content.

REFERENCES

Gerbner, G.; Morgan, M.; and Signorielli, N. Programming health portrayals: What viewers see, say and do. In: Pearl, D.; Bouthilet, L.; and Lazar, J., eds. *Television and Behavior: Ten Years of Scientific Progress and Implications for the Eighties*. Vol. 2. Washington, DC: Supt. of Docs., U.S. Govt. Print. Off., 1982. pp. 291–307.

Hansen, A. *Young People, Television and Alcohol*. Leicester: Centre for Mass Communication Research, University of Leicester, 1988*a*.

Hansen, A. The contents and effects of television images of alcohol: Towards a framework of analysis. *Contemp Drug Prob* 15(2):249–279, 1988*b*.

Lazarsfeld, P.F. Why is so little known about the effects of TV and what can be done? *Pub Opinion Qtrly* 19:243–251, 1955.

Lowery, S.A. Soap and booze in the afternoon: An analysis of the portrayal of alcohol use in daytime serials. *J Stud Alcohol* 41(9):829–838, 1980.

Advertising and Marketing: Applying the Principles, Practices, and Outcomes to Alcoholic Beverages

Chapter 11

Studies of the Effects of Alcohol Advertising: Two Underexplored Aspects

Esther Thorson[1]

INTRODUCTION AND OVERVIEW

Although a small number of studies purport to show that alcohol advertising influences the drinking-related cognition or behaviors of youth (e.g., Kohn and Smart 1984; Atkin et al. 1984), reviews of the impact of alcohol advertising often conclude that there exists no strong or unequivocal evidence of a relationship between alcohol advertising and any response (e.g., Atkin, in press; Saffer, chapter 5, this volume).

Research on the issue has taken several different approaches. Experiments have been employed in which alcohol advertising is directly manipulated and the impact on individuals is examined (Kohn and Smart 1984). Surveys have been employed to explore the correlation between alcohol and media (Atkin et al. 1984). Finally, econometric studies have been employed to examine the relationships between alcohol advertising expenditures and consumption, the influences of alcohol advertising bans on aggregate alcohol use, and the effects of alcohol counteradvertising (see Saffer, chapter 5, this volume). Many of these studies have looked for effects in adults and a few have studied minors. But whether at the individual or aggregate level, and whether for adults or minors, few unarguable relationships have been found.

A tempting response to this pattern in the research literature is to conclude that alcohol advertising has no major effects on drinking-related behavior. Before this conclusion should be accepted, however, it seems important to compare the approaches used in the alcohol advertising literature with those in the more general literature concerned with how advertising creates its effects. This chapter will focus on two areas of possible contributions the general literature on advertising research could make to research on alcohol advertising and its effects.

[1]School of Journalism, P.O. Box 838, University of Missouri, Columbia, MO 65205

One aspect of advertising research that alcohol research has not taken advantage of concerns the roles of the strategic advertising planning and execution that underlie alcohol ads and commercials. Unless researchers know how alcohol ad campaigns are strategized and executed, it seems likely they will fail to know where exactly to look for advertising effects on alcohol-related human activity. To help remedy this lack, an outline of a commonly used strategic planning system is examined. A series of print alcohol ads is then used to illustrate how the strategic planning links with those particular ads or ad campaigns. Examination of alcohol ads in terms of strategic planning makes it possible to suggest changes in how experiments and surveys are designed to examine possible alcohol advertising effects.

A second aspect of advertising research that alcohol research has not been sufficiently concerned with is the analysis of alcohol ads in terms of their cultural meanings and the impact of those cultural meanings. There have been a number of large-scale and thorough content analyses of alcohol ads in magazines and television (e.g., Breed and DeFoe 1979; DeFoe and Breed 1979; Finn and Strickland 1982, 1983). But none of these articles analyze alcohol messages in terms of the variables that cultural researchers argue to be important to our understanding of how these messages affect us (e.g., Postman et al. 1987; Strate 1991). Unfortunately, none of the cultural researchers have tried to measure the impact of the alcohol message types they identify, although one can argue that this could be done quite straightforwardly.

With these introductory remarks and their rationales in place, this chapter turns first to a discussion of how an understanding of advertising strategy can inform and help increase the sophistication of studies of alcohol advertising and its possible effects.

STRATEGIC PLANNING AND EXECUTION: ITS ROLE IN ADVERTISING EFFECTS

An aspect of advertising research that is missing from alcohol advertising research is recognition of the role of strategic advertising planning and execution. Ads are designed with highly specific marketing objectives and strategies in mind, and consideration of these objectives and strategies is important for researchers when they are searching for various kinds of effects that ads or ad campaigns can have.

Every approach to strategic planning involves some assumptions about how advertising works. The most common model of advertising effects used in creating advertising strategies is the hierarchy of effects. Although every large ad agency and every introductory text on advertising has its own planning model, most of them contain similar elements of a hierarchy of different effects that an ad can have. The one used as illustrative here is the R.O.I. strategic planning model (Wells 1989), which was developed at the DDB Needham advertising agency during the 1980s.

The R.O.I. (which stands for relevance, originality, and impact) strategic planning model posits a seven-stage hierarchy of advertising effects. These stages are awareness, acceptance, preference, search, selection, use, and satisfaction. These stages suggest the specific behaviors advertising can focus on and the major barriers there are to use of the brand.

There are two critical strategic questions to answer in advertising planning: What is the purpose of the advertising? and Who is its target? Both the purpose and target of an ad must be explicit and clear. For example, a purpose statement for Michelob that said, "To get people to drink more Michelob," would be useless for developing an ad plan. It fails to specify which people are being referred to, when they would drink Michelob, or how much they would drink. A preferable alternative would be the statement, "The purpose of the advertising is to convince *drinkers of regular premium beers* that Michelob need not be consumed only on culturally defined special occasions (e.g., a night on the town, a party, after a getting a raise), but during any event that is personally important." This definition of campaign purpose clearly refers to drinkers of regular premium beers who already think Michelob is for special occasions. Very importantly, marketers have extensive data on who these people are, what other attitudes they hold, and what lifestyles they conform to, as well as other information that enables marketers to talk directly and relevantly to them.

Extensive knowledge of a target group opens further opportunities for selling the brand. For example, if a message can teach the target group that even something as mundane as successfully assembling a child's bicycle is a special event deserving a Michelob, then there will be more occasions when purchasing the brand is appropriate. Even those who generally drink less expensive beers most of the time will come to have more willingness to spend the extra money for Michelob. The bottom line in this example is that when a clearly defined target and a clearly defined purpose for the advertising message exists, the message creates more motivation, and greater sales can be the result.

It is also important to note in this example that advertisers would never expect this campaign to affect underage drinkers. A typical ad that might appear in this campaign is shown in figure 1, which shows yuppie sisters having a reunion. Ads like this one are not likely to appear in programs or magazines that underage drinkers consume. Furthermore, ads in this kind of campaign are unlikely to contain stories, actors, situations, music, or other attributes that are particularly appealing to minors (12- to 20-year-olds). Therefore, using commercials from this campaign to test the impact of alcohol advertising on minors would be unlikely to produce any results of interest.

In contrast, however, we examine a possible strategic statement for Bud Light: "To convince young college grads that drinking Bud makes any party more fun." This strategic statement is likely to lead to the kind of ad in figure 2, which appeared in *Rolling Stone.* We would expect that this ad would be far more likely than the Michelob ad to influence underage drinkers, and its incorporation into a study of the effects of advertising on minors would be far more appropriate.

In looking at the experimental literature on advertising and alcohol behavior, attention to strategy aspects of ads appears to be consistently lacking. For example, in studies by Brown (1978) and McCarty and Ewing (1983), there is simply no description of the ads that were employed. In the Kohn et al. (1984) study, we know only that half of the ads were of the "tombstone" type (showing only the product and listing its attributes) and the other half were "lifestyle" ads. But obviously what the product's attributes are and whose lifestyle is being depicted in the ad are critical for predicting the amount and type of impact the ads will have. Indicative of some recognition of this problem, Atkin (in press) points out that he thinks the beer brand in the study was not a brand that would appeal to the age group tested. It is also likely that the ad executions themselves were not structured to appeal to the youthful participants in the study.

Commercials are never created without being strategically targeted. For that reason, to test the impact of any ad, it is necessary to verify that the execution was aimed specifically at those who will serve as participants in the study. Furthermore, it is necessary to ensure that the dependent measure employed in the study is appropriate to the impact that the ad was designed to create. For example, if the strategic goal underlying a commercial is to increase the likelihood of purchase, then purchase behavior would be the appropriate dependent variable to employ. But if the strategic goal was to change the perception of the brand from being a very special, limited-occasion drink to one that consumers could justify drinking on many occasions, expecting an observable impact on purchase behavior is at best naive. Unfortunately, attention to the strategic planning and intended target of alcohol commercials does not appear in the alcohol advertising literature.

To emphasize further the significance of using appropriately targeted ads, it is helpful to explore some additional examples. Figures 3–5 show beer ads aimed at women. Of course, the Michelob Light ads are for college-age women, or those just slightly older or younger. These women are heavy consumers of women's fashion magazines, and ads like these are common in such publications. The Tia Maria ad aims at the older woman who can or at least desires to seek exotic adventure and travel. The ad provides a glamorous but clearly independent female role model. This ad would not be expected to have much influence on a 15-year-old, much less on a male of any age. (The ad appeared in *Elle*.)

It is also instructive to examine some illustrations of the principle of advertising purpose. Figures 6–8 show alcohol ads with three very different purposes. The Bacardi ad is designed to bring thoughts of summer fun—lounging on a hot beach and wanting a sip of lemonade—"Why not add a cool refreshing splash of Bacardi?" The Hennessy ad is designed to inform the consumer that this cognac has a gentle, exciting, delicious taste—and that it is very special, like a kiss in the middle of a European square. The Coors Light ad is designed to tell young women that when working or socializing together, a Coors facilitates interpersonal interactions, as well as the work that needs to be accomplished. One would not expect these three ads to increase consumption in a laboratory test situation peopled with male college students. They would also be inappropriate in a study where the participants were blue-collar workers—again, because the targeting would be inappropriate.

The next step in R.O.I. strategizing is to identify the target. Here again, careful attention should be given to the selection of ads. Ads that are not targeted to a particular group should not be expected to have much influence on members of that group. On the other hand, ads correctly and effectively targeted toward a particular group would be expected to have major influence.

Good target definitions are specific and vivid. "Rumple Minze Schnapps is for the blue-collar man who drinks schnapps to verify his masculinity and his ability to stand up to a considerable alcohol kick." The Rumple Minze ad in figure 9 would be consistent with such a targeting statement. DeKuyper Butterscotch Schnapps is for the female schnapps drinker who likes to have a number of differently flavored after-dinner drinks available for guests. The DeKuyper ad in figure 10 would be consistent with this targeting statement.

The most significant aspect of these examples is their demonstration that every alcohol ad is designed to appeal to and influence a target. If the researcher wants to find the influence of alcohol ads, careful attention to targeting aspects of the ads used in the study is crucial. As can be seen, both Rumple Minze and DeKuyper are selling schnapps, but to entirely different targets.

The next step in strategy development is the *promise* the ad makes and the *support* it provides to back up that promise. The promise is the competitive benefit that the campaign intends to emphasize. Promises often refer to the subjective experience the consumer can expect to have. The support is everything that lends credibility in the consumer's mind to the promise that is made. Of course, promises and supports are designed for specific targets.

Sometimes intrinsic product attributes provide the promise and support in an ad. For example, the DeKuyper ad (figure 10) tells the consumer that the liquors come in 40 different flavors. The Grolsch ad (figure 11) tells the consumer that Grolsch is nonpasteurized, is triple cold-filtered, has all natural ingredients, is Holland's number-one selling premium beer, and is made by a company with four centuries of brewing experience.

Occasionally, promise–support combinations are dramatic. In figure 12, for example, the Monte Alban ad promises that "this Mezcal is not for the wine-and-cheese, salad bar, or bloody Mary man." This is a drink for a tough guy who goes for male activities and refuses to conform to social customs (i.e., celery in the drink) if they do not suit him. The promise in this ad is that drinking Monte Alban puts you in the same class with the "real men." The J&B ad (figure 13) promises that J&B is so closely associated with baseball that when you purchase the alcohol, you might instantly win a baseball experience. The detachable ticket is the support for this promise.

The ads in figures 14–16 promise the consumer that drinking their products will verify that the drinker is sophisticated and not vulnerable to superficial or juvenile messages. The guy who drinks Heineken does it for taste. Drinking Cutty Sark informs others that the drinker is wise enough to know a quality drink. In both campaigns, the target is flattered for being in on the promise of the brand and not being swayed by the silliness and excesses of advertising for other alcohol brands.

Again, it should be noted that the promise and supports that an ad offers to the target are critical for creating its effect. Therefore, promises and supports present in alcohol ads must be appropriately linked with the audiences who will serve as participants in the study. Otherwise the responses of those audiences fail to reveal the true impact of the promises and supports the ads offer.

Inappropriate selection or combinations of ads in studies would be expected to create confusion in the consumers. It is probably important in an alcohol advertising study to place consumers in a situation relevant to what the promises are in the ads. It might also be best to employ ads that make the same promise or consistent ones in a single viewing experience. Clearly, if a study presents participants with a group of ads that make different promises and provide different supports, there is no reason to expect the combined impact of these ads to produce a single result such as an increase in consumption.

Although this problem generally has not been recognized in any extant studies of alcohol advertising, one study did use an approach that appeared to take into account these aspects of strategic targeting. Kohn and Smart (1984) showed beer ads embedded in a soccer program. The article does not indicate what ads were employed, but if the ads were somewhat homogeneous in their promises and supports, this may explain why relatively strong results were reported in the study.

The last area of strategic planning to be discussed here concerns the media that are used to convey the message—which media and when they are used. The question of media selection must be focused on "when, where, and under what circumstances will the target be most receptive to the promise of the message" (Wells 1989, p. 37). Choosing media so as to maximize target receptivity is referred to as "aperture" in the R.O.I. system. Aperture involves three aspects: time (e.g., of day or of year), place, and circumstances. It is important to examine each of these aspects in some detail.

Breakfast is aperture for cereals, pancake mixes, and coffee (for those over 30) or soda (for those under 30). Most alcohol is consumed after 5 p.m., except during holidays or during sports events, so any study that examines consumption during the day is, of course, likely to show diminished effects. More distilled alcohol is consumed during certain holidays, which helps to explain the "time of year" aperture exhibited in the ads of figures 17 (J&B and Christmas), 18 (Grand Marnier and Christmas), 19 (Beefeater and summer days), and 20 (Bacardi Black and summer nights).

Place and circumstances are also important aspects of determining aperture. The Southern Comfort ad (figure 21) suggests the brand is for a night out in the big city. Budweiser (figure 22) is for times of active partying.

Of course, television commercials are more specifically apertured than magazine ads in terms of when and during what kind of programming they are shown. Prime-time news is considered the time when people are in a "learning mode," so one can be didactic rather than dramatic in the presentation of a commercial. Early evening is also considered to be the time when people are feeling most tired, achy, beat-up, and generally in poor health. This explains why the most frequently advertised products during prime-time news are headache remedies, constipation and diarrhea remedies, antacids, and life insurance.

The concept of aperture is another critical attribute to attend to in looking for the impact of alcohol advertising. As has been seen, ads are often designed for particular times, places, and circumstances. These aspects of aperture are carefully coordinated with the associations, habits, and lifestyles of the targeted group. When people are presented with ads at times, places, and in circumstances that are inconsistent with the aperture represented in the ads, the impact is likely to be reduced or even eliminated. Thus, for example, the best place to test certain beer executions would be in a bar during a baseball or football game. The participants in the study should be a group of males who know and are comfortable with one another. Certainly the formal environment of a social science laboratory is unlikely to match the drinking aperture represented in any ad, or to match any other aspect of the aperture that people have for alcohol. In general, any study wherein the goal is to observe an immediate impact of alcohol advertising on consumption must deal carefully and accurately with aperture in all of its dimensions.

As can be seen then, most research on alcohol advertising effects has ignored the strategic aspects of the ads that were tested. Given the popularity of strategic positioning as an approach to advertising, attention to the strategic implications of alcohol ads would seem critical. It is therefore important to consider ads as part of a carefully constructed strategy for creating specific effects in specific consumers at specific times. If these aspects are not considered, it seems likely that researchers will continue to observe little or no interesting impact of alcohol advertising.

This discussion would be incomplete, however, if we did not acknowledge that paying attention to strategy in ads assumes that the *intended effects* are what are important. Alcohol advertising researchers (Strate 1991) as well as advertising researchers in general (Pollay 1986), however, tell us that often ads targeted to one group affect another. For example, beer commercials may be targeted toward an adult audience, but their actual audience also includes many children and youth. And just as the sports hero in the beer commercial may be a role model for 35-year-old junior executives, he may also be a role model for 15-year-olds. Likewise, the influence of alcohol ads on youth may not be a function of a single ad or a handful of them, but rather may result from the presentation of alcohol products right along with, and therefore the "same as," toothpaste, Levi's, and Chevy trucks (Strate 1991). Certainly then, the impact of alcohol advertising on nontargeted groups is important to consider. The suggestion here, however, is that the first step in any investigation of the impact of alcohol ads is to look carefully at their strategic aspects and then plan the examination of their impact within the constraints of those aspects.

Unintended effects of alcohol advertising are certainly worthy of investigation and may prove to be the real culprits in such problems as underage drinking, drunk driving, and alcohol dependency. But the possible significance of unintended effects does not negate the importance of alcohol researchers paying attention to the strategy aspects of alcohol advertising. The promises, purposes, and aperture strategies reflected in ads can certainly influence their impact on unintended audiences. Having examined the potential importance of strategy as a factor in the impact of alcohol advertising, this chapter now turns to the issue of what ads mean as messages within cultural symbols and meanings.

CULTURAL INTERPRETATION OF ALCOHOL ADS

A second aspect of advertising research that is missing from the alcohol advertising literature is the analysis of alcohol ads in terms of their cultural meanings—and tests of the impact of those cultural meanings. As noted earlier, there have been many large-scale and thorough content analyses of alcohol ads in magazines and television. These studies were characterized by extensive sampling of television or magazines or both. Unfortunately, however, the categories used in the content analyses often had little to do with strategy variables that are critically important for understanding the impact of the ads. For example, alcohol ads have been distinguished by whether they were broadcast or print, whether they had human models or not, and whether they used celebrities. They were also segmented by what type of "benefits" they linked to alcohol—benefits such as flavor, social camaraderie, masculinity, escape, refreshment, relaxation, elegance, romance, and adventure.

Unfortunately, a problem with this kind of categorization is that the ads within any of these groupings can still exhibit very different advertising strategies and therefore be expected to have different effects on different people at different times. Neither the Miller Lite ad of figure 23 nor the Heineken-Amstel ad of figure 24 portrays any people. In fact, they both show bottle tops and water spills. But the strategy behind these two ads is quite different. The Miller Lite ad is designed to remind us of good times with our "social circle." The color is warm and inviting. The copy contains three slogans that appeared in former advertising: "The great beer that's less filling," "It's everything you want a beer to be," and "It's it and that's that." Repeating these slogans is done to remind consumers of all the beer ads they have seen in which males were shown socializing with one another. The Heineken-Amstel ad is blue and gray and is much more subdued, colder, and more sophisticated than the Miller Lite ad. The copy focuses on the intrinsic attributes of the beers, and lectures the consumer. The headline is a pun—a linguistic form intended only for the more sophisticated consumer. Thus the strategy and targeting behind these ads is very different. Furthermore, the Miller Lite ad was in *Philip Morris Magazine* (predominantly lower-income, blue-collar readers). The Heineken-Amstel ad was in *Sports Illustrated*, which has a more educated, upscale audience. Thus, while these two ads would be categorized as identical in virtually all the content analyses cited above, the advertising strategist would expect them to talk to very different audiences and make very different promises. A 15-year-old might respond to the Miller Lite ad but would be much less likely to respond to the Heineken-Amstel ad. When content analysis categories fail to capture these kinds of differences, their utility for gaining understanding of the impact of the ads is low or nil.

Given this reasoning, it can be seen that content analyses of the type that have been typically carried out do not provide the proper categorizations to aid understanding of the sophisticated variations in ads that are guided by strategic planning. In addition, the content analyses that have been done do not examine the cultural meanings of alcohol ads. It will be suggested here that these meanings may provide the best possibility for understanding both the intended and unintended effects of alcohol advertising.

What are cultural meanings of messages? Although definitions vary within the cultural literature itself (e.g., Barthes

1972; Fiske 1987; Williamson 1978), the approach basically looks at messages in terms of the cultural themes and images that they evoke in viewers and readers. These themes and images (often called "myths") are usually not denoted, but are rather connoted. Often they are generally assumed truths and unconscious assumptions. In the United States, for example, the Western cowboy image has a set of meanings for people: The cowboy is masculine, tough, good, individualistic, and brave. He fights nature and usually masters it.

Images and themes are expressed via many types of messages in societies. The cowboy image is expressed in books and films, in games (like cowboys and Indians), in newspapers, and of course, in commercials. Many beer campaigns, for example, have associated beer with the cowboy myth. Other myths commonly seen in alcohol advertising include (1) the mystery of the "exotic" (note the mask in the Kamora ad [figure 26] and the Jamaican fruit seller in the Tia Maria ad [figure 5]); (2) Norse warriors (oddly translated to a female representing a German liquor [figure 9]); and (3) the purity of nature (note the figure of the reindeer and fisherman on the lake [figure 25]).

Cultural theorists suggest that associating alcohol with powerful mythic images gets at the heart of the impact of the advertising (Strate 1991). For example, when alcoholic products like beer are for many years associated with the cowboy myth, then drinking becomes a symbolic reenactment of the strength and courage that we attribute to the cowboy's taming of nature. Given how extensively beer has been associated with the cowboy myth, sports myths such as the underdog coming from behind to win the big game, the blue-collar myth, and many back-to-nature myths (e.g., "from the land of sky blue waters"), it would not be surprising to find that to males of many ages and demographic groups, beer drinking means mastery of challenge, tough masculinity, bravery, competitive edge, and having power over females (Postman et al. 1987). Beer drinking is also likely seen as an initiation rite into adulthood (Strate 1991).

Most of what the cultural researchers present is, of course, hypothetical. They claim that mythic meanings are derived from media messages such as advertising, but they do not test for the presence of these meanings in human thought or experience. Nevertheless, if such meanings are being derived from alcohol advertising, they are important to study. As noted above, the content analyses carried out so far on American alcohol advertising have largely ignored these kinds of meanings. Certainly the experiments examining alcohol ad impact (see the review by Atkin, in press) have not asked for cognitive and affective responses that could indicate whether these kinds of meanings for alcohol are being developed in the belief systems of people. Analyzing alcohol advertising from a cultural perspective and then testing for the presence and impact of those meanings would seem an excellent field for future study by alcohol advertising researchers.

SUMMARY AND CONCLUSIONS

It has been argued here that in order to better understand the impact of alcohol advertising on people, there should be considerable attention paid to two important aspects of advertising research that have proved helpful for our general understanding of how advertising works, but are missing in the experimental and survey literature on alcohol advertising effects. First, perhaps both advertising effects research in general and alcohol advertising effects research specifically can be accused of paying too little attention to the various strategic positionings of ads and commercials. Just as even the most inexperienced ad practitioner would not fail to ensure that the promises and supports in an ad will appeal to a particular target audience, ad researchers must look for ad effects where they are likely to occur—with the right message for the right person at the right aperture. The failure to do so may well explain the puzzlingly small effects found in experimental studies of alcohol ad effects.

Finally, although cultural researchers have begun to turn some attention to the meanings in alcohol advertising, much is left to be done. It seems likely that experimental (or survey) research could help to verify the existence of alcohol myths of various types and explore their impact on purchase and consumption.

REFERENCES

Atkin, C. Media effects on alcohol consumption. In: Comstock, G., ed. *Public Communication and Behavior, Vol. 3.* New York: Academic Press, in press.

Atkin, C.; Hocking, J.; and Block, M. Teenage drinking: Does advertising make a difference? *J Commun* 34:157–167, 1984.

Barthes, R. *Mythologies.* Translated by J. Cape Ltd. New York: Hill and Wang, 1972.

Breed, W., and DeFoe, J. Themes in magazine alcohol advertisements: A critique. *J Drug Issues* 9:511–522, 1979.

Brown, R.A. Educating young people about alcohol use in New Zealand: Whose side are we on? *Br J Alcohol Alcohol* 13:199–204, 1978.

DeFoe, J., and Breed, W. The problem of alcohol advertisements in college newspapers. *J Am Coll Newspaper Assoc* 21:195–199, 1979.

Finn, T.A., and Strickland, D.E. A content analysis of beverage alcohol advertising. *J Stud Alcohol* 43:964–989, 1982.

Finn, T.A., and Strickland, D.E. The advertising and alcohol abuse issue: A cross media comparison of alcohol beverage advertising content. In: Burgoon, M., ed. *Communication Yearbook 6.* Beverly Hills: Sage Press, 1983. pp. 850–872.

Fiske, J. *Television Culture.* London: Rutledge, 1987.

Kohn, P.M., and Smart, R.G. The impact of television advertising on alcohol consumption: An experiment. *J Stud Alcohol* 45:295–301, 1984.

Kohn, P.M.; Smart, R.G.; and Ogborne, A.C. Effects of two kinds of alcohol advertising on subsequent consumption. *J Advert* 13:34–41, 1984.

McCarty, D., and Ewing, J.A. Alcohol consumption while viewing alcoholic beverage advertising. *Int J Addict* 18:1011, 1018, 1983.

Pollay, R.W. The distorted mirror: Reflections on the unintended consequences of advertising. *J Market* 51(2):18–36, 1986.

Postman, N.; Nystrom, C.; Strate, L.; and Weingartner, C. *Myths, Men & Beer: An Analysis of Beer Commercials on Broadcast Television.* Washington, DC: AAA Foundation for Traffic Safety, 1987.

Strate, L. The cultural meaning of beer commercials. In: Holman, R.H., and Solomon, M.R., eds. *Advances in Consumer Research Vol. 18.* Provo, UT: Association for Consumer Research, 1991. pp. 115–119.

Wells, W.D. *Planning for R.O.I.: Effective Advertising Strategy.* Englewood Cliffs, NJ: Prentice-Hall, Inc., 1989.

Williamson, J. *Decoding Advertisements: Ideology and Meaning in Advertising.* London: Marion Boyars, 1978.

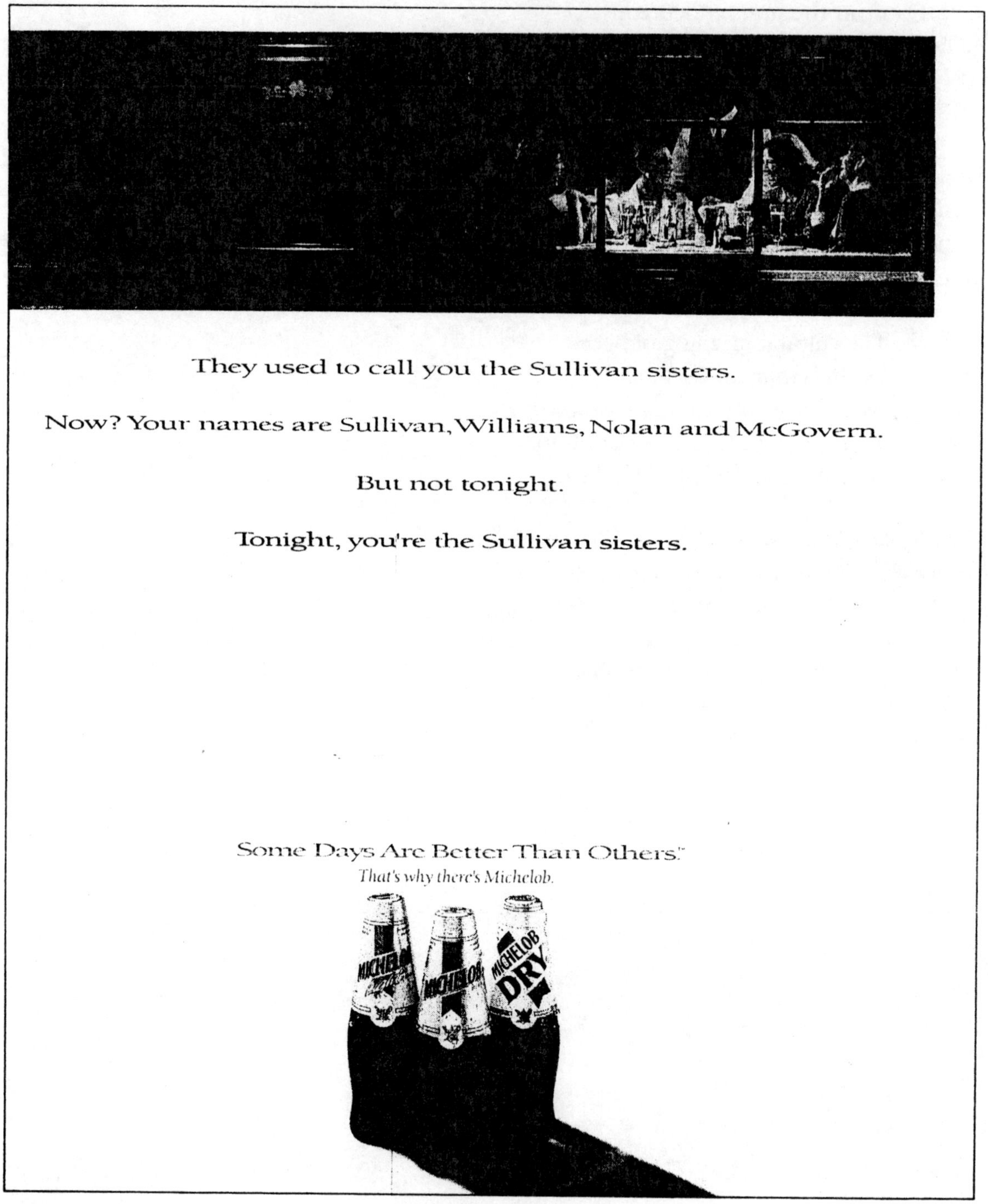
They used to call you the Sullivan sisters.
Now? Your names are Sullivan, Williams, Nolan and McGovern.
But not tonight.
Tonight, you're the Sullivan sisters.
Some Days Are Better Than Others.™
That's why there's Michelob.
MICHELOB DRY

Figure 1

PLAY THAT FUNKY MUSIC
SPUDS BOY.
Party Right with Bud Light!
SPUDS MACKENZIE. THE ORIGINAL PARTY ANIMAL.
©1987 Anheuser-Busch, Inc.
For a copy of this ad in poster form, send $2.50 to: Funky Music Poster Offer, Box 93292, Atlanta, GA 30377-0292. Allow 4-6 weeks for delivery.

Figure 2

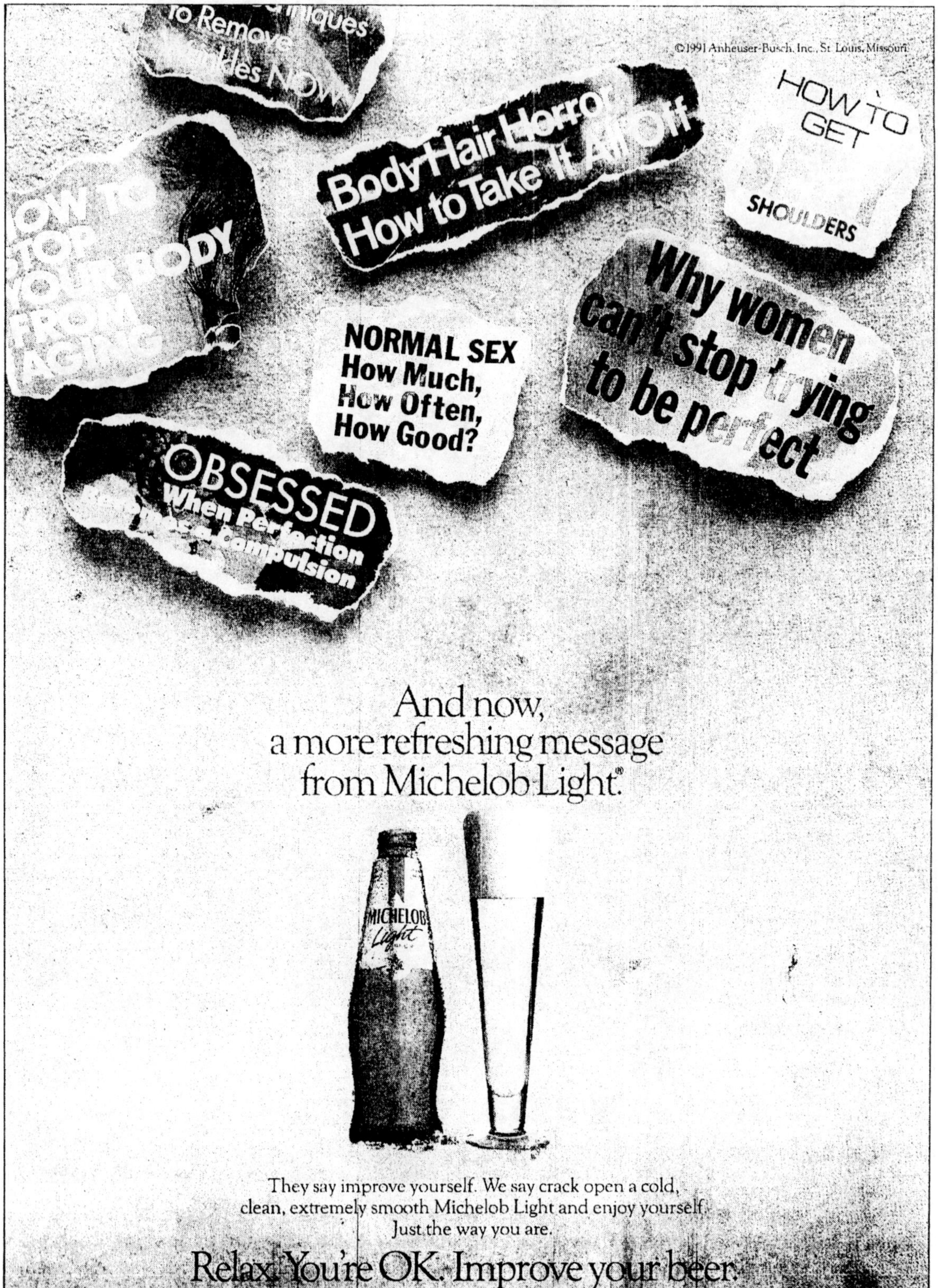

to Remove
©1991 Anheuser-Busch, Inc., St. Louis, Missouri
Body Hair Horror
How to Take It All Off
HOW TO GET
SHOULDERS
YOUR BODY
FROM
AGING
NORMAL SEX
How Much,
How Often,
How Good?
Why women can't stop trying to be perfect
OBSESSED
When Perfection
And now,
a more refreshing message
from Michelob Light.
MICHELOB
Light
They say improve yourself. We say crack open a cold,
clean, extremely smooth Michelob Light and enjoy yourself.
Just the way you are.
Relax. You're OK. Improve your beer.

Figure 3

©1991 Anheuser-Busch, Inc., St. Louis, Missouri
Does He Bore You? How to Stay Interested
BLAST JIGGLY HIPS & THIGHS
5 Great Exercises That Get Results—FAST!
PERFECT SKIN FIXING EVERY FLAW
And now, a more refreshing message from Michelob Light.
They say improve yourself. We say crack open a cold, clean, extremely smooth Michelob Light and enjoy yourself. Just the way you are.
Relax. You're OK. Improve your beer.

Figure 4

July 16, 1954
Tia Maria
The recent discovery of a lost journal sheds new light on the 300-year-old legend of Tia Maria liqueur. It reveals how, in the early 1950s, an adventurous young American named Cynthia Andrews went on a journey in search of the legend of Tia Maria she'd heard her grandfather describe. We share excerpts of her journal and letters with you here and invite you to taste the legendary Tia Maria. Smooth. Delicate. Flavorful. Straight or over ice. To learn more about Cynthia Andrews and the Tia Maria legend, write to: Tia Maria, 501 Brickell Key Dr., Miami, FL 33131.
Tia Maria

Figure 5

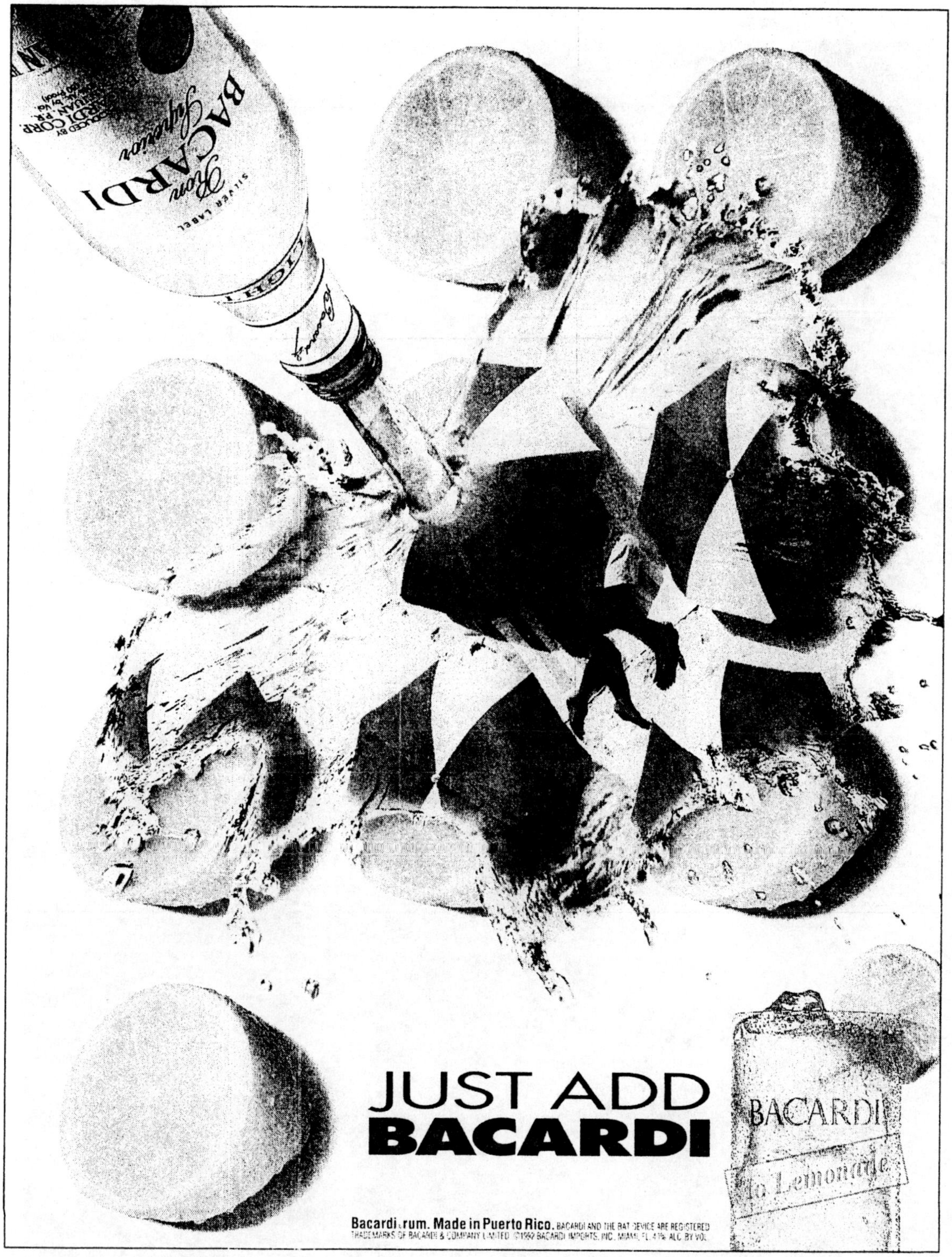
JUST ADD
BACARDI
BACARDI
to Lemonade
Bacardi rum. Made in Puerto Rico. BACARDI AND THE BAT DEVICE ARE REGISTERED TRADEMARKS OF BACARDI & COMPANY LIMITED ©1992 BACARDI IMPORTS, INC. MIAMI, FL 41% ALC BY VOL

Figure 6

If
YOU'VE
EVER
BEEN
KISSED
you
ALREADY
KNOW
THE
FEELING
of
COGNAC
HENNESSY
ESTD 1765
COGNAC
Hennessy

Figure 7

LIGHT
RIGHT BEER NOW!
Choosing the right
color was hard—
the beer was easy.
Coors Light—because
for friends like mine
only the best will do.

Figure 8

Rumple Minze.
Primal Peppermint Schnapps.
Rumple Minze
PRODUCT OF GERMANY
IMPORTED
100 proof
Rumple Minze
ORIGINAL-REZEPT
PEPPERMINT SCHNAPPS
LIQUEUR
50% alc. by vol.
(100 proof)
BY SCHARLACHBERG DISTILLERY ESTB.1898
CORPORATION. FORT LEE; N.J.
Imported by The Paddington Corporation, Fort Lee, NJ © 1990
AUTHENTIC. GERMAN.
RUMPLE MINZE. 50% ALCOHOL BY VOLUME PEPPERMINT FROM GERMANY.
FOR AN 18"X22" POSTER OF THIS AD, PLEASE SEND $4 TO RUMPLE MINZE.

Figure 9

DeKuyper
Original
BUTTERSHOTS
Buttershots Butterscotch Schnapps. And a herd of over 40 other flavors.
CACTUS JUICE KEY LARGO BUTTERSHOTS RAZZMATAZZ HOT DAMN!
DEKUYPER

Figure 10

Guess Who's Holland's #1 Premium Beer?
Non-Pasteurized
Triple Cold Filtered
All Natural Ingredients
Four Centuries of Family Brewing Heritage
Grolsch
PREMIUM LAGER
Excellence in Brewing Since 1615
Grolsch Importers, Inc., Atlanta, GA 30339

Figure 11

Figure 12

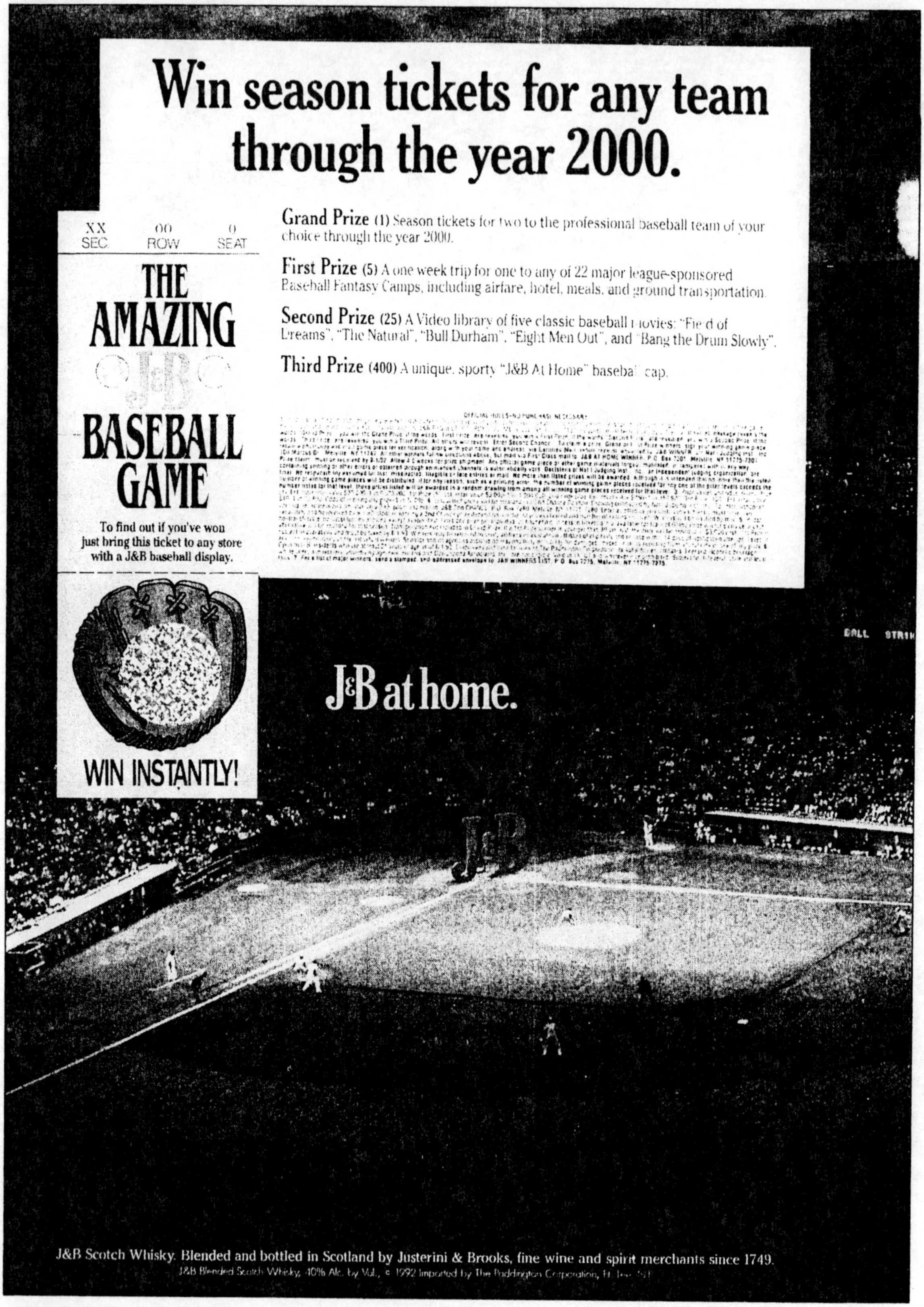
Win season tickets for any team through the year 2000.
Grand Prize (1) Season tickets for two to the professional baseball team of your choice through the year 2000.
First Prize (5) A one week trip for one to any of 22 major league-sponsored Baseball Fantasy Camps, including airfare, hotel, meals, and ground transportation.
Second Prize (25) A Video library of five classic baseball movies: "Field of Dreams", "The Natural", "Bull Durham", "Eight Men Out", and "Bang the Drum Slowly".
Third Prize (400) A unique, sporty "J&B At Home" baseball cap.
XX SEC
00 ROW
0 SEAT
THE AMAZING J&B BASEBALL GAME
To find out if you've won just bring this ticket to any store with a J&B baseball display.
WIN INSTANTLY!
J&B at home.
J&B Scotch Whisky. Blended and bottled in Scotland by Justerini & Brooks, fine wine and spirit merchants since 1749.

Figure 13

IMPORTED BY VAN MUNCHING & CO., INC., NEW YORK, NY
SECRET BREWING PROCESS
Sudz
Nope.
Nobody's ever proven that a catchy jingle makes a beer taste better. Or scenes of beautiful people playing volleyball. Or endorsements by retired third basemen.
We believe people choose a beer because of what's in the bottle rather than what's in the ad. Which just might explain why Heineken is the number one imported beer in America.
Heineken. Just being the best is enough.
Heineken

Figure 14

This is a glass of Cutty Sark.
If you need to see a picture of a guy in
an Armani suit sitting between two fashion models
drinking it before you know it's right for you,
it probably isn't.
CUTTY SARK
SCOTS WHISKY
UNCOMMONLY SMOOTH

Figure 15

Drinking Cutty Sark
won't make you seem more attracti
Or help you get a date.
But if you really want to score points at a
there are other ways.
CUTTY SARK
SCOTS WHISKY
UNCOMMONLY SMOOTH

Figure 16

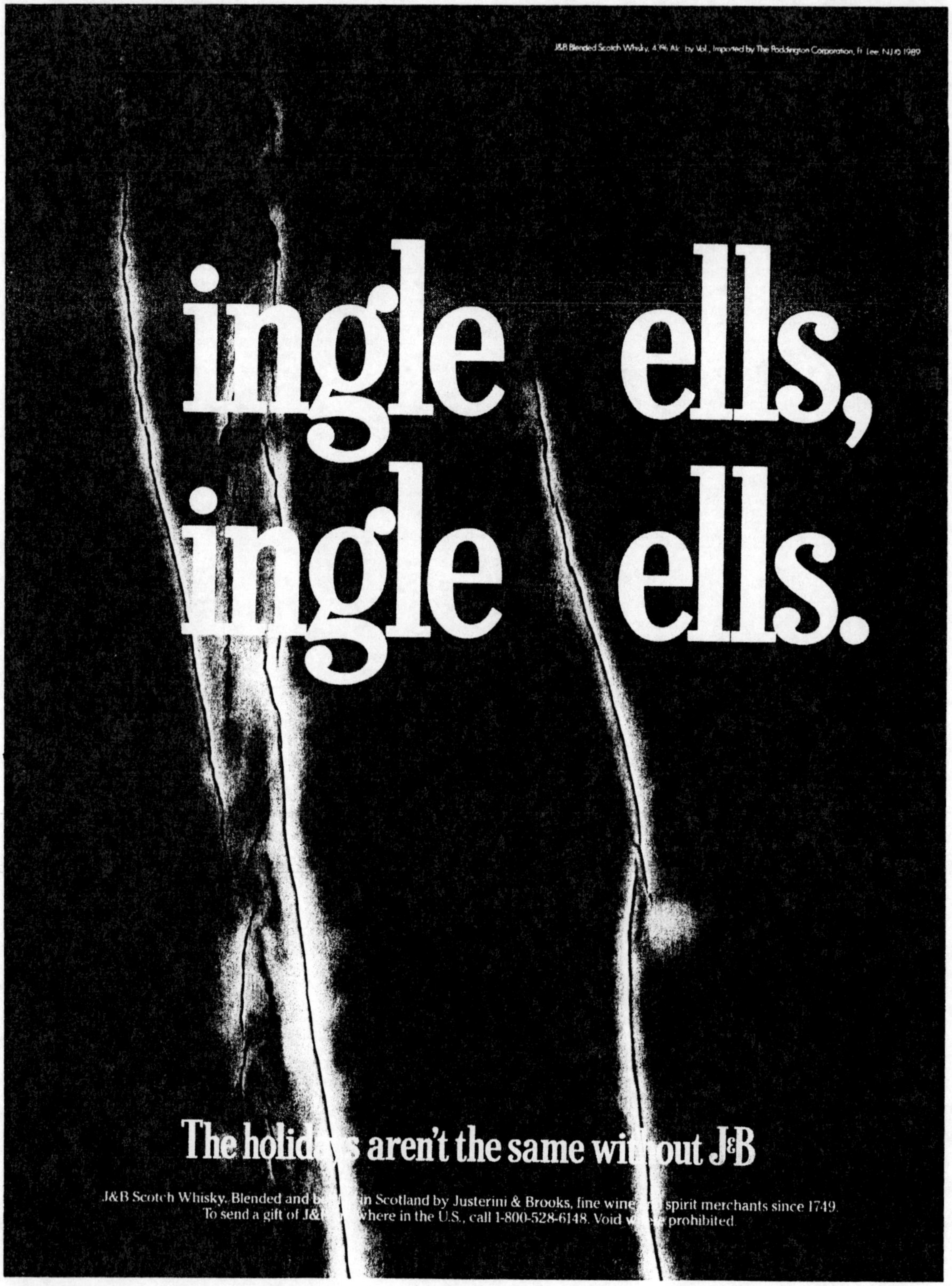
J&B Blended Scotch Whisky, 43% Alc. by Vol., Imported by The Paddington Corporation, Ft. Lee, NJ © 1989
ingle ells,
ingle ells.
aren't the same
J&B Scotch Whisky. Blended and
in Scotland by Justerini & Brooks, fine
spirit merchants since 1749.
To send a gift of
in the U.S., call 1-800-528-6148. Void
prohibited.

Figure 17

Figure 18

SUMMER IS THAT
TIME OF YEAR
WHEN YOU LOOK
FORWARD TO
GOING BAREFOOT
AND HOLDING
SOMETHING OTHER
THAN MEETINGS.
THE SUMMER GIN
BEEFEATER
DRY GIN
BEEFEATER
SUMMER GIN

Figure 19

PEOPLE SWEAR THAT ON
SOME WARM SUMMER NIGHTS
THE DISTANCES BETWEEN THEM MELT.
BACARDI BLACK
THE TASTE OF THE NIGHT
ENJOY OUR GOOD TASTE WITH YOUR GOOD JUDGMENT. BACARDI® RUM, MADE IN PUERTO RICO.
BACARDI AND THE BAT DEVICE ARE REGISTERED TRADEMARKS OF BACARDI + COMPANY LIMITED. ©1991 BACARDI IMPORTS, INC. MIAMI, FL. RUM 40% ALC. BY VOL.

Figure 20

Doing the town is more delicious with a touch of Comfort.
Distinctive and delicious. The special taste of Southern Comfort makes any night on the town a night to remember.
SOUTHERN COMFORT
Comfort
Dry Manhattan

Figure 21

Figure 22

Social Circle.
MILLER BREWING COMPANY REMINDS YOU TO PLEASE:
THINK WHEN YOU DRINK
The great beer that's less filling.
It's everything you want a beer to be.
Miller Lite. It's it and that's that.
© 1992 Miller Brewing Co., Milwaukee, WI

Figure 23

QUALITY PRODUCT
AMSTEL
light
BREWERY
Heineken®
Beer
THE TOPS.
Heineken is America's number one selling imported beer.
Amstel Light is America's number one selling imported light beer.
For one simple reason: taste.
Imported by Van Munching & Co., Inc., New York, NY

Figure 24

There are three indispensable items for every Finnish fishing excursion: a fishing pole, a fishing buddy, and, of course, Finlandia. (As you might guess, one of these items may be a little more essential than the other two.)
FINLANDIA
VODKA OF FINLAND
Finlandia. Vodka From The Top Of The World.

Figure 25

How will your guests feel if you don't serve Kamora?
KAMORA
The hidden treasure of Mexico.
KAMORA
IMPORTED COFFEE LIQUEUR
MAKE RESPONSIBILITY PART OF YOUR ENJOYMENT. Kamora® Coffee Liqueur, 20% and 26.5% Alc./Vol. Imported & Bottled by Beam Import Co., a division of Jim Beam Brands Co. Deerfield, IL © 1992

Figure 26

Chapter 12

Advertising Principles, Practices, and Outcomes: Applicability to Alcohol Marketing

Jerome D. Williams[1]

Thorson's chapter provides an excellent integration of the reasons why the alcohol advertising research literature fails to find many effects, while conversely the broader advertising research literature[2] tends to find many significant effects. Her chapter develops four points for future research directions. She suggests that researchers should (1) use different theories to more fully understand alcohol advertising effects, (2) put more emphasis on the intervening variables between exposure and consumption, (3) emphasize a strategic focus, and (4) pay greater attention to the importance of cultural meanings.

The perspective presented in this chapter is shaped by my background in marketing. Marketing has borrowed many theories from other disciplines, and researchers should be skeptical about borrowing and applying these theories indiscriminately because they often do not work the same way in marketing as they do in other disciplines, like psychology. Therefore, researchers should broaden their thinking and be more open to alternative approaches to analyzing advertising.

THE NEED FOR SKEPTICISM

This section provides information based on my personal background and empirical studies that may help the reader to appreciate the need for skepticism about traditional theories and approaches to explaining advertising effects. The inner city Philadelphia neighborhood where I grew up had about 60 to 80 percent of the billboards with advertising for alcohol or tobacco products—as is true of many inner

[1]Department of Marketing, 707C Business Administration Building, Penn State University, University Park, PA 16802

[2]In this chapter, "alcohol advertising research literature" refers to research on the many issues related to alcohol, one of which happens to be the effects of advertising, while "advertising research literature" refers to research on the many issues related to advertising products, one of which happens to be alcohol.

city neighborhoods today (McMahon and Taylor 1990; Scenic America 1989; *National Medical Association News* 1991; Schooler and Basil 1989). Also this was a time when many youth "smoked" candy cigarettes in imitation of adults. Yet today very few of those youth who grew up in that same environment with me smoke or drink alcohol. This personal experience of growing up under these conditions raises questions about how effective these influences actually were on me and my contemporaries—and more specifically today, how effective alcohol product target marketing strategies are in influencing minorities, especially minority adolescents.

Some statistics suggest a cause for skepticism concerning the effectiveness of these promotional efforts. The National High School Senior Surveys (NHSSS) from 1985 to 1989, conducted by the University of Michigan's Institute for Social Research, asked, "Have you consumed alcohol during the past month?" Based on combined data for the 5-year period, 72.3 percent of white male seniors but only 49.2 percent of black male seniors responded yes; similarly, 66.6 percent of white female seniors and 32.8 percent of black female seniors answered in the affirmative (table 3 in Bachman et al. 1991, p. 374).

Data also indicate that among underage drinkers, whites consume in heavier quantities than blacks (U.S. Department of Health and Human Services 1993). Based on the University of Michigan's Monitoring the Future Project, approximately 32 percent of white high school seniors are heavy drinkers, compared with 11 percent of black seniors (Reynolds 1994). These responses seem to argue against the notion that black youth are more likely to consume alcohol than youth of other races or are heavier users of alcohol. They certainly raise additional research questions regarding the impact of concentrated billboard advertising for alcohol products in inner city ethnic minority areas and of target marketing of malt liquors to minority consumers; the effects of these promotional strategies on minority adolescents might not be as significant as generally thought.

Some have suggested that the lower consumption rate of alcohol among black adolescents is due to lower household income in minority families compared with the general population or, alternatively, that studies of high school seniors might not be tapping into the most significant segment for alcohol consumption, namely, those youth who have dropped out of school. However, another study, referred to by then-U.S. Secretary of Health and Human Services Dr. Louis W. Sullivan (1992), which looked at junior high students and controlled for income asked, "Have you had a beer?" Among whites the proportion answering yes was 35.1 percent and among blacks it was 30.6 percent.

The pattern for drug use is also significantly lower among black youth compared with whites. For example, data from the Parents Resource Institute on Drug Education (PRIDE) of Atlanta show that 5.4 percent of white male junior high school students had used marijuana compared with 3.4 percent of black male students (Sullivan 1992). NHSSS and PRIDE surveys also show lower alcohol and drug use by black females than white females, although in all cases the proportion of females using alcohol or other drugs was less than that of males. Similarly, data indicate lower rates of smoking among black youths compared with whites (U.S. Department of Health and Human Services 1993).

These data on lower consumption among black adolescents should not be construed to mean that alcohol promotion does not have any adverse effects. One counter-argument to these survey results that needs to be considered is that studies based on broad random samples of the population do not take into account the effects of targeted promotion on those segments that are at greater risk. For example, while it is generally accepted that among blacks of all ages and both sexes the likelihood of consuming alcohol is lower than among whites (U.S. Department of Health and Human Services 1992), problem drinking is more prevalent among blacks in specific market segment categories (Hacker et al. 1989). Therefore, the adverse effects of target marketing on specific segments of the black community might be somewhat disguised by survey results reporting general consumption patterns.

Furthermore, these general survey results do not explain the "crossover effect" in the adult population. Although blacks show lower alcohol and drug use rates than whites in adolescence, the differences get smaller in early adulthood; and by middle adulthood, the abuse rates are generally higher among blacks (Bachman et al. 1991). We do not understand when, how, or why this occurs or what effect alcohol advertising plays in the process. One hypothesis is that the "crossover effect" is the result of sustained promotion targeted toward younger blacks (Scott et al. 1992) and that sustained exposure to this heavy promotion effort eventually results in greater alcohol misuse/abuse problems among blacks compared with whites as they get older. Alternatively, the effect might be due to unhealthy coping habits that some blacks might develop in order to deal with difficult life circumstances, including the effects of racism, discrimination, and prejudice (Odom 1994).

CONTRASTING ALCOHOL ADVERTISING RESEARCH AND ADVERTISING RESEARCH

To address and expand on some of Thorson's specific points, there appear to be differences in the results found in the alcohol advertising research literature and the advertising research literature, because there is a basic difference in the starting point of researchers in these two groups. In initiating a project, a researcher must ask, "What is the objective of my research?" and the two groups of researchers generally set out with different objectives. Researchers in advertising are particularly brand oriented. They focus on the attributes of a brand and the process that leads to a positive evaluation of those attributes by prospective purchasers of the brand. Individuals involved in alcohol research, on the other hand, usually come from a public policy perspective and tend to be more concerned with health effects and other social concerns.

This translates into greater concern about aggregate consumption and the relationship of product promotion to public policy issues on the part of alcohol advertising researchers, while commercial advertising researchers are more concerned about brand consumption and the factors that lead to brand consumption.

In marketing, this is called the difference between primary demand and selective demand. Primary demand is related to the effects of alcohol promotion in general. Selective demand is related to the effects of promoting a specific brand to a specific target audience. This is directly related to Thorson's discussion of aperture as part of strategic planning and execution.

In examining the connection between media advertising exposure and consumption, alcohol and public health researchers and advertising researchers are looking at different types of consumption. The former focus on aggregate consumption; the latter are more concerned about advertising for specific brands, brand promotion strategies, and brand attributes. For this reason, advertising researchers tend to use many of the types of models Thorson identified (e.g., multi-attribute, expectancy-value, and attitude-toward-the-ad models). They assume that if the viewer has a positive attitude toward the ad, there will be a spillover effect toward the brand, and that is what is going to lead to consumption. The point is that it is important to recognize that in measuring alcohol advertising effects, there are different research objectives, and these lead to examining different types of dependent measures. This probably accounts for many of the conflicting results reported by alcohol-oriented researchers and advertising researchers.

Most researchers involved in alcohol advertising studies from a public policy perspective do not believe that exposure to alcohol messages in the media alone is responsible for all the negative social effects associated with alcohol misuse and abuse. However, many researchers are quick to accept the simplistic assumption that advertising exposure leads directly to misuse, abuse, and negative health effects. This might be due to their concern about the role of the media and advertising in contributing to consumption and abuse, as well as their desire to identify causes and rectify problems.

THE INTERVENING VARIABLES ISSUE

As Thorson's chapter suggests, there are a host of intervening variables between advertising and consumption that need to be examined, particularly in the context of hierarchy-of-effects models, which focus on stages such as attention, awareness, and preference and other variables, all of which precede consumption. It is important for researchers to put more emphasis on understanding *how* these intervening variables relate to consumption, rather than focusing primarily on the exposure–consumption link. Research suggests that most of the direct effects of advertising on alcohol consumption are fairly weak until one examines the effect of a message specifically targeted to a particular segment.

Examples from smoking research might help to illustrate how researchers sometimes jump from exposure to consumption, bypassing the intervening variables. A number of recent studies have examined the effects of tobacco promotion—specifically Camel's "Old Joe" cigarette cartoon character campaign—on underage smokers. Implicit in most of these studies is the assumption that if children are exposed to tobacco promotion, this will lead to smoking behavior as they grow older. However, researchers need to exercise more caution in making causal assertions when conducting studies that merely measure exposure to advertising and its correlation with smoking behavior. Although such research designs and conclusions may be laudable in their objectives (i.e., to identify the adverse effects of tobacco advertising), these studies have been criticized as biased and conceptually and methodologically flawed.

For example, Mizerski et al. (1993) criticized several tobacco advertising studies that appeared in the *Journal of the American Medical Association*. In the study of DiFranza et al. (1991), for example, one of the objectives was to determine if children see, remember, and are influenced by cigarette advertising. The outcome measures were recognition of Camel's Old Joe cartoon character, product and brand name recall, brand preference, and appeal of advertising themes. Brand preferences prior to the Old Joe campaign, which was initiated in 1988, were obtained from seven adolescent surveys collected between 1976 and 1988 in three States. Following the campaign introduction, brand preference and intent-to-smoke measures were taken from students in grades 9 through 12 after they were exposed to six Camel ads in succession and quizzed about them; similar data were collected from a sample of adults age 21 and older. Youth were more likely than adults to report prior exposure to the Old Joe cartoon character, to be able to identify the type and brand of product being advertised, and to find the Camel cigarette advertisements appealing. Camel was given as the preferred brand of 33 percent of smokers under 21 but only 8 percent of smokers 21 years of age and over. Based on these findings, DiFranza et al. (1991) concluded that "tobacco advertising promotes and maintains nicotine addiction among children and adolescents" (p. 3152).

In their review of the study, Mizerski et al. (1993) criticize DiFranza et al.'s conclusion, noting that their method "reeks of cues promoting subject expectations of what is appropriate to say to the interviewer" (p. 10).

In a second study, Pierce et al. (1991) sought to evaluate whether tobacco advertising encourages teenagers younger than 18 years of age to start smoking. Using survey data from a national probability sample in 1986 and from a similar survey sample of California residents in 1990, they tested three hypotheses: (1) youth are more likely to notice the most heavily advertised brands than are persons over 21, (2) the pattern of market share in minors reflects the pattern of their perceived advertising, and (3) "the market share of a cigarette brand that only recently has targeted young people [Camel] has increased disproportionately in the young" (Pierce et al. 1991, p. 3152).

The study found that the perception that Camel was the most advertised brand was highest among 12- and 13-year-olds (34 percent), declining as the age of respondents increased. In addition, the pattern of cigarette brand purchases by California smokers paralleled the reported perception of the most advertised brands. Further, the study found that the market share increase between 1986 and 1990 among Camel smokers was greatest among the age group 12 to 17 years. On the bases of these findings, the investigators conclude that "our results suggest that tobacco advertising is *causally* related to young people becoming addicted to cigarettes" (Pierce et al. 1991, p. 3158) [emphasis added].

However, as Mizerski et al.'s (1993) critique of Pierce et al.'s conclusion points out, the link between recognition/awareness and the causation of usage behavior for any product is tenuous at best, and the study did not rule out an equally plausible alternative explanation, namely that "smoking behavior may be 'causing' the respondent to state that Camel was the brand that advertised the most" (Mizerski et al. 1993, p. 14).

Some studies are more cautious about making causal links between advertisement exposure and consumption. For example, in the tobacco area, Fischer et al. (1991) sought to measure 3- to 6-year-old children's ability to match brand logos and trade characters to pictures of products. They used 22 logos including those representing children's products, adult products, and two popular cigarette brands. Recognition rates increased with age, were highest for children's brands, but were higher for cigarette brands than adult brands. To the researchers' credit, they identify several limitations of their study and acknowledge that "it is obviously impossible to predict how the exposure of children to environmental tobacco advertising might influence their later smoking behavior" before concluding that cigarette advertising "may be an important health risk for children" (Fischer et al. 1991, p. 3148).

Similarly, some recent studies in the area of alcohol seem to be addressing these types of criticisms by focusing more clearly on the intervening steps rather than forcing the link between exposure and consumption. For example, Grube and Wallack (1994) studied the impact of awareness of beer advertising on children's beliefs, knowledge, and intentions. They found that those most familiar with the advertisements are more likely to express positive beliefs about alcohol and an intention to drink more heavily as adults, hence suggesting that alcohol advertising may "predispose" young people to drinking. Just as important as focusing on the intervening steps of beliefs, knowledge, and intentions, the authors also investigated the alternative explanation (i.e., the possibility that those predisposed to drink seek out information about alcohol and thus are more attentive to relevant advertising). Such an approach will be much more useful in gaining a greater understanding of the effects of alcohol advertising.

ALTERNATIVE THEORIES

As Thorson suggests, perhaps researchers should start looking at a broader array of theories to explain the effects of alcohol advertising. Without necessarily discarding the old theories, researchers might have to adapt them for specific situations such as alcohol advertising. As Thorson noted, the theory of cognitive dissonance is not widely regarded as relevant for advertising research; however, it actually could be very relevant for understanding alcohol advertising research. According to a cognitive dissonance approach, consumption behavior occurs first, and then consumers justify their behavior by seeking out and paying greater attention to the advertising supporting that behavior. For example, in the consumer-behavior literature, studies have shown that people pay more attention to advertising after they buy a car than before they buy it. This is because after they have already made the purchase, they must justify it in order to reduce dissonance (i.e., the dissonance between their cognitive state of knowledge and attitude about the car and their actual behavior of having already purchased the car). Therefore, they will seek out and pay attention to commercial messages that reinforce a positive cognitive state about the car in order to justify their purchase behavior rather than change the behavior (i.e., return the car). The advertising acts to bring the cognitive state in line with the behavior, hence reducing any cognitive dissonance.

Perhaps this same theoretical model might be appropriate in explaining certain effects of alcohol promotion. For example, if adolescents are at a party and begin drinking because of peer pressure, cognitive dissonance theory would suggest that after they have already engaged in alcohol consumption behavior, they would seek to justify this behavior, perhaps by paying more attention to alcohol advertising.

This theory merits consideration as an alternative explanation, particularly in studies that first examine the correlation between alcohol advertising exposure, awareness, or recognition and consumption, and then draw conclusions regarding the causal effect of alcohol advertising on consumption. Because correlation does not equal causation, it is possible, reversing the causal relationship, that the alcohol consumption behavior came first and caused the individual to pay more attention to the advertising. This alternative explanation certainly needs to be investigated more frequently in alcohol advertising studies, as was done by Grube and Wallack (1994).

Researchers typically assume that "pro-social" messages delivered through public education campaigns (e.g., "Don't drink and drive" or "Just say no to drugs") have the intended effect on recipients. Although this may be true in many cases, researchers must be cautious about making assumptions regarding the effectiveness of these messages. In some instances they may have the opposite effect, particularly with alcohol products and adolescents.

Commodity theory (Brock 1968), for example, offers an alternative explanation of advertising effects that has been largely ignored. This theory suggests that the scarcer the commodity, the more the demand. In marketing this sometimes is referred to as the "marketing mystique." It is illustrated by the higher demand for Coors beer when it was not available in certain regions of the country than when it became available. This theory suggests that placing more restrictions on alcohol advertising has the potential to have the opposite of the intended effect; if people are told they cannot have something, often they want it even more.

Consider the case of the Hornell Brewing Company, which introduced Crazy Horse malt liquor in March 1992. Although the product proved to be highly successful in the marketplace, it also received a great deal of negative publicity when then Surgeon General Antonia Novello denounced the brand's "insensitive and malicious" marketing strategy. Critics also pointed to the new malt liquor's name, which could be interpreted to appeal to drinkers who want to "go crazy." In addition, because Crazy Horse was a noted Native American Chief and problems associated with alcohol abuse have afflicted the Native American community, many viewed this marketing strategy as exploitative.

However, an editorial in the *Wall Street Journal* (Bovard 1992) alluded to the fact that all of the negative publicity about Crazy Horse beer may have actually increased demand for it. For example, in

South Dakota, where Crazy Horse is not licensed to be sold, people were paying as much as $14.00—more than five times the retail price elsewhere—just for the empty bottle. While this particular instance of the "marketing mystique" phenomenon reflects a greater demand for the bottle as a collector's item as opposed to the beer in the bottle, other instances indicate that demand for the actual product has increased when scarcity occurs, as in the case of Coors noted above.

Another example of commodity theory at work is the significant increase in sales of Camel cigarettes despite vitriolic attacks on the use of "Joe Camel" as a target marketing strategy designed to appeal to young consumers. Several articles have noted that antismoking groups are accomplishing the exact opposite of their mission and are glorifying "Old Joe" in the eyes of rebellious preteens and teenagers by publicly campaigning against him (Lipman 1992). Similarly, it has been observed that restricting alcohol advertising and consumption has made it more desirable among the underage population, transforming alcohol into a "forbidden fruit" and drinking into a rite of passage (Rockoff 1991).

This "forbidden fruit" syndrome calls to mind a newspaper cartoon in which a teacher comes into the teachers' lounge and proclaims, "It worked. I told them that the multiplication table was none of their business and they learned it in a week." Similarly, if you put a warning label on a record because of its explicit lyrics, or you tell adolescents that certain books are banned from the school library, it is more likely that they are going to try to get them.

This is not to suggest that we tell young people to go out and consume alcohol and assume they will do the opposite, but merely to suggest that our standard theories and media and message approaches to control/reduce alcohol use and abuse may not be as applicable as we have assumed. There are a number of alternative theories, such as commodity theory and cognitive dissonance theory, that might offer alternative explanations for how alcohol commercial messages and public service communications actually work in certain situations and among certain market segments.

TARGET MARKETING

Thorson's comments about targeting and target marketing were especially valid. There are a number of ways to target a product depending on (1) the medium selected (e.g., ethnic newspapers, magazines, or radio stations); (2) the neighborhoods in which the advertising occurs (e.g., malt liquor billboards in urban inner city areas); (3) the people selected to be put in the ads (e.g., using a black celebrity such as Billy Dee Williams for Colt 45 malt liquor); and (4) the appeal used (e.g., rap music to reach urban youth).

The effect of each tactical decision may vary depending on aperture, a critical area for additional research on the effects of alcohol promotion. For example, there is a dilemma in choosing the right sample to measure effects. Showing a *random* sample of the general population ads for alcohol products neglects the strategic focus that was employed in designing the ads for *specific* target groups. Thus it will be difficult to tease out hypothesized effects. For example, what would one learn from an experiment where subjects were drawn from the general population and viewed the ad for Colt 45 malt liquor that features Billy Dee Williams? That ad was strategically designed to target a specific segment, namely black consumers who have a very high consumption rate of malt liquor.

One way to circumvent this sample problem is to choose a random sample of subjects only from among the targeted segment (e.g., measure the effect of the Billy Dee Williams ad only on black consumers). Alternatively, generic ads might be used to appeal across market segments. However, such ads might be so bland that they fail to produce any measurable effects.

MEDIA INFLUENCES BEYOND ADVERTISEMENTS

Researchers at Penn State University have been conducting a content analysis of movies, assessing what has been labelled "advertainment" (i.e., the placement of products in entertainment media to achieve the effect of advertising) (Williams et al., unpublished observations). This content analysis of the top 100 movies in 1991 found a surprising number of product placements of alcoholic beverages in these films. In many cases these placements were paid for by the company that produces the product; in others, alcoholic beverages were put there by writers, producers, and directors to add realism. Although these placements might not appear very prominent when viewers watch the movie for entertainment, on a video clip where all of these placements had been aggregated on one tape, the effect was quite powerful.

This study examines what impact these placements have in fostering an attitude of social acceptability of alcohol consumption in our society among all ages of consumers. The findings also suggest that even if alcohol advertising were totally eliminated in the commercial media, consumers would still be exposed to an overwhelming and ubiquitous promotion of alcohol through exposure in the entertainment media.

THE LIMITATIONS OF ALCOHOL ADVERTISING RESEARCH

This chapter concludes with an assessment of four major limitations of alcohol advertising research, extending Thorson's comments (Williams 1993). First, researchers pay too little attention to the interaction of advertising with many other variables that intervene between it and consumption, and to measuring these variables (e.g., the various stages in hierarchy-of-effects models). Researchers also need to recognize that to a certain extent they may be "swatting at gnats while being swallowed by a tiger" by spending so much time focusing on advertising while ignoring factors such as family and peer pressure, which account for the greatest impact on consumption, particularly among adolescents.

Second, researchers have relied too much on "one shot" studies that bring people into a room, expose them to ads, and then measure the immediate effect. That is not what happens in the real world; the effect of advertising is actually cumulative. Therefore, there is a need to develop more longitudinal studies that examine what happens over a period of time.

Third, context is important. If a certain ad is targeted toward a group of people who may be watching a sports game in a bar, there is a certain context involved there. Researchers need to look more at those kinds of situations in which people are actually exposed to the advertising.

Finally, researchers need to be a little more iconoclastic and not necessarily accept the traditional theories, most of which were borrowed from other disciplines and in some cases may not apply to marketing without major adaptation. Even theories that do apply in a general sense may not be applicable for alcohol promotion, or for alcohol promotion in specific strategic situations and to specific target segments. Therefore, alternative explanations such as cognitive dissonance theory and commodity theory deserve greater consideration. By recognizing the limitations of their research and taking steps to overcome them, researchers will emerge with a richer understanding of the effects of alcohol promotion on both consumption and the intervening stages leading up to consumption.

REFERENCES

Bachman, J.G.; Wallace, J.M.; O'Malley, P.M.; Johnston, L.D.; Kurth, C.L.; and Neighbors, H.W. Racial/ethnic differences in smoking, drinking, and illicit drug use among American high school seniors, 1976–89. *Am J Pub Health* 81:372–377, 1991.

Bovard, J. The Second Murder of Crazy Horse. *Wall Street Journal.* Sept. 15, 1992. p. A15.

Brock, T.C. Implications of commodity theory for value change. In: Greenwald, A.G.; Brock, T.C.; and Ostrom, T.M., eds. *Psychological Foundations of Attitudes.* New York: Academic Press, 1968. pp. 243–275.

DiFranza, J.R.; Richards, J.W.; Paulman, P.M.; Wolf-Gillespie, N.; Fletcher, C.; Jaffe, R.D.; and Murray, D. RJR Nabisco's cartoon camel promotes Camel cigarettes to children. *JAMA* 266(22):3149–3152, 1991.

Fischer, P.M.; Schwartz, M.P.; Richards, J.W.; and Goldstein, A.O. Brand logo recognition by children aged 3 to 6 years. *JAMA* 266(22):3145–3148, 1991.

Grube, J.W., and Wallack, L. Television beer advertising and drinking knowledge, beliefs, and intentions among school children. *Am J Pub Health* 84:254–259, 1994.

Hacker, G.A.; Collins, R.; and Jacobson, M. *Marketing Booze to Blacks.* Washington, DC: Center for Science in the Public Interest, 1989.

Lipman, J. Joe Camel's Bad Press Could Be Boosting Brand. *Wall Street Journal.* May 14, 1992. pp. B1, B5.

McMahon, E.T., and Taylor, P.A. *Citizens' Action Handbook on Alcohol and Tobacco Billboard Advertising.* Washington, DC: Center for Science in the Public Interest, 1990.

Mizerski, R.; Sonner, B.S.; and Straughn, K. "A Re-evaluation of the Reported Influence of the Joe Camel Trade Character on Cigarette Trial and Use by Minors." Paper presented at the 1993 American Academy of Advertising Annual Conference, Montreal, Canada, Apr. 16–19, 1993.

National Medical Association News. Outdoor Cigarette and Alcohol Advertising Is Targeted Toward the Minority Populations. May/Jun., 1991. pp. 1–2.

Odom, M. Change of Habits, Diet Helps Black Americans. *Centre Daily Times*. Mar. 7, 1994. p. 6B.

Pierce, J.P.; Gilpin, E.; Burns, D.M.; Whalen, E.; Rosbrook, B.; Shopland, D.; and Johnson, M. Does tobacco advertising target young people to start smoking? *JAMA* 266(22):3154–3159, 1991.

Reynolds, B. Black Teens Are Leaders in Saying No to Drugs, Cigarettes. *USA Today*. Mar. 14, 1994. p. 9A.

Rockoff, J.D. Raising Legal Age Does Little To Cut Drinking at Colleges, Studies Show. *The Philadelphia Inquirer*. Jan. 1, 1991. pp. 1A, 6A.

Scenic America. *Billboards in Baltimore: A Blight on Beauty and a Scourge on Health in Our City*. Report to the Abell Foundation, Washington, DC, 1989.

Schooler, C., and Basil, M.D. "Alcohol and Cigarette Advertising on Billboards: Targeting with Social Cues." Paper pre sented at the International Communication Association Conference, Dublin, Ireland, 1989.

Scott, B.; Denniston, R.W.; and Magruder, K.M. Alcohol advertising in the African-American community. *J Drug Issues* 22(2):455–469, 1992.

Sullivan, L.W. Don't Believe the Hype About Black Youths. *The Philadelphia Tribune*. Jul. 3, 1992. p. 7A.

U.S. Department of Health and Human Services. *National Household Survey of Drug Abuse: Highlights 1991*. DHHS Pub. No. (SMA)93-1979. Rockville, MD: Substance Abuse and Mental Health Services Administration, 1993.

U.S. Department of Health and Human Services. *National Household Survey of Drug Abuse: Population Estimates 1991*. Revised Nov. 20, 1992. DHHS Pub. No. (ADM)92-1887. Rockville, MD: National Institute on Drug Abuse, 1992.

Williams, J.D. Minority adolescents, alcohol consumption, and media effects: A review of issues and research. In: Lerner, R., ed. *Early Adolescence: Perspectives on Research, Policy, and Intervention*. Hillsdale, NJ: Lawrence Erlbaum Associates, 1993. pp. 431–446.

Chapter 13

Nontraditional Media and Promotions in the Marketing of Alcoholic Beverages

David W. Stewart[1] and Ronald Rice[2]

There have been profound changes in the marketing of goods and services during the past decade. The ratio of expenditures on advertising versus promotions has been reversed (Naber 1986). Whereas traditional media advertising expenditures exceeded promotional expenditures by two to one only a few short years ago, promotional expenditures now dominate advertising by an even greater ratio. According to the *Fourteenth Annual Survey of Promotional Practices* (Donnelley Marketing 1992), manufacturers of consumer products spent half of their marketing dollars on trade promotions, 25 percent on consumer promotions, and 25 percent on media advertising. During the 5-year period between 1987 and 1991, trade promotions showed consistent gains at the expense of media advertising (Miller 1992).

The nature of expenditures on advertising has also changed. Mass print and broadcast media have experienced declines in usage associated with the rise of new media and the proliferation of options within the print and broadcast arena. There has also been rapid growth in the use of so-called "unmeasured media" such as direct response marketing, event sponsorships, catalogs, place-based media, and product placements in videos, television programs, films, and cultural and sporting events. Traditional mass media advertising, such as ads in network television, magazines, newspapers, and radio, now accounts for less than half of all advertising expenditures, with the remainder of expenditures allocated to unmeasured media (Endicott and Brown 1990; Burgi 1991).

The traditional distinction between advertising and promotions has also blurred (Stewart 1992). As a result of this blurring, some scholars have suggested that it may no longer be appropriate to

[1]Department of Marketing, College of Business Administration, University of Southern California, Los Angeles, CA 90089-1421

[2]Now affiliated with the United Parcel Service (UPS).

examine advertising effects in isolation from other types of marketing tools. There have been calls for placing all of marketing communications and promotions under a general umbrella that is known as integrated marketing (Schultz 1991). Many marketing vehicles have characteristics of both promotions and advertising.

These changes also indicate that the conceptualization of advertising and promotions as communication through "mass media" may be obsolete. Many communications vehicles, from cable television to catalogs, can be customized at the level of the individual household, and customization of advertising messages and promotions for specific and well-defined audiences has become commonplace. Furthermore, unlike traditional advertising, some of the newer marketing vehicles consist of little more than the placement of a product, brand name, or brand logo in particular situations or locations. There is no explicit product message. Thus, there exists a very diverse array of advertising and promotions vehicles that do not meet the traditional characterization of advertising. These vehicles are finding increasing use by marketers of consumer products.

Widespread use of these nontraditional marketing communications and promotional vehicles is of relatively recent origin. As a result, there has been less systematic research on the effects of such vehicles than on the effects of more traditional vehicles. Nevertheless, some business organizations have used such marketing tools for many years. Use of nontraditional marketing communications tools was pioneered by firms that found the use of more traditional approaches inefficient or restricted by regulation or law. Among the firms with long histories of using nontraditional communications tools are producers and distributors of alcoholic beverages, who face significant restrictions on their use of more traditional media such as radio and television (but not print media). Use of nontraditional media by marketers of alcoholic beverages has been the object of growing criticism by individuals and organizations who believe that such marketing techniques contribute to the use and abuse of alcohol (Atkin 1989). Regardless of one's attitude toward advertising in general or the advertising of specific products, the use of nontraditional advertising and promotion raises important questions about the use and regulation of marketing communications in general and for specific types of products.

The purpose of this chapter is to review the changing character of advertising and promotions, with special emphasis on nontraditional advertising and promotions, and to place current practices in the alcoholic beverage industry within the broader context of general marketing practices. The chapter begins with a review of the changes in audience composition and in technology that have radically altered the media environment. It will then briefly review what is known about the effects of nontraditional media and their use as vehicles for advertising and promotion. Nontraditional advertising and promotion will also be compared to more traditional forms of advertising and promotion. The chapter concludes with a discussion of the implications and potential effects of the use of nontraditional media on the consumption of alcoholic beverages. The latter discussion will address consumption in the general population and within specific segments of consumers.

ADVERTISING EFFECTS IN A FRAGMENTED MEDIA ENVIRONMENT

Any discussion of the effects of nontraditional advertising and promotions, in general or for a specific product such as alcoholic beverages, must start by placing such advertising in its larger context. Even a cursory reading of the popular and trade press suggests that advertising is in a state of transition. Advertisers have become increasingly skeptical of the efficacy of traditional advertising as a marketing tool. For example, a story about one particular advertising study reported in the *Wall Street Journal* in February 1989 concluded that "TV exposure has very minimal effect . . . difficult to find at all . . . . The most important factors affecting consumers' choices . . . were in-store displays and coupons . . . . TV advertising wasn't even effective over the long run" (Lipman 1989, p. B6). Recent articles in *The Economist* (1990) and in the *Journal of Advertising Research* (Clancy 1990) have suggested that the role of advertising within the marketing mix, and perhaps even the definition of advertising, must change. *Advertising Age*, the respected weekly trade publication for the advertising industry, ran a front-page headline on February 27, 1989, that read, "The Party's Over."

While there have been doubts about the efficacy of advertising since its inception, these doubts have increased in the past 5 years. Nevertheless, there is considerable evidence that advertising can have an effect in the marketplace. A rather large literature created by both academic and industry sources has documented these effects for more traditional forms of advertising (see Stewart and Ward 1994; Lodish 1991; Abraham and Lodish 1989; Stewart et al. 1990; Lambin 1976; Ehrenberg 1974), and an array of techniques and measures have been used to assess these effects (for a review, see Stewart et al. 1985; Stewart 1989). This literature suggests several conclusions: (1) advertising may induce trial of products by making people aware of them, by suggesting new uses, and by creating interest; (2) for mature products, the primary, and perhaps only, effect of advertising is on choice of brand or product form; (3) people tend to pay attention to advertising that is personally relevant, which means they are most likely to attend to advertising for products and brands they already use or for which they are seeking information; and (4) people tend to ignore much of the advertising to which they are exposed and discount that to which they do attend.

These conclusions reflect a movement away from earlier notions of advertising as a powerful persuasive force and toward a more realistic view of advertising as a source of information that is acted upon by recipients. This does not mean that advertising cannot contribute to other effects, particularly if it is used in association with other marketing techniques. For example, advertising may help stimulate demand by making consumers aware of price reductions or product extensions. Nevertheless, the weight of the evidence suggests that advertising is not a particularly powerful tool for persuasion. This is particularly true for the creation of primary demand (Lambin 1976; see also the discussion later in this chapter), but doubts have also arisen concerning the ability of advertising to alter brand choice (Raj 1982; Tellis 1988). The latter doubts are in part responsible for the changes in marketing expenditures discussed at the beginning of this chapter.

Among the reasons for recent doubts about the efficacy of advertising are changes in the media environment that make it increasingly difficult to get the attention of consumers. Even if advertising has an effect, the effect will not occur if consumers are not exposed to the advertising. Furthermore, the likelihood of paying attention to advertising is reduced when consumers rather than advertisers have control over exposure. Today's media environment has become highly fragmented. Statistics tell a part of this story. Twenty years ago, 90 percent of all households watched prime-time television on any given night; today only 68 percent do so (Russell 1989). Similarly, 78 percent of all households regularly read the daily newspaper 20 years ago; today that figure is only 64 percent (Russell 1989). And it appears that only the leading edge of this fragmentation is currently visible.

Cable television has vastly expanded the number of channels from which a household can select. Low-power television stations, which will have a broadcast radius of 15 miles or less, are already on the horizon. Television broadcasting has become a fragmented medium with increasingly specialized programming for smaller and more selective audiences. The fragmentation of such traditional media as television, radio, magazines, and newspapers has resulted in the coining of the term "narrowcasting" to refer to editorial content, broadcast programming, and marketing communications that are designed for highly specialized and selective audiences. Examples of such narrowcasting include Black Entertainment TV, MTV, and the Health and Weather channels. Yet these events in the traditional media are only a portion of more profound changes. Whole new media have arisen in recent years, and more are on the way.

New technologies and formats of media are rapidly coming into being. These technologies and formats—actually new media—include such things as 1-900 telephone services, interactive television, computer bulletin boards, online information services, and place-based media like SRTV and Channel M. Each of these new technologies and formats serves to reduce exposure to more traditional broadcast and print media. For example, a television screen featuring SRTV in a doctor's waiting room competes with the traditional magazines that have long been a fixture in waiting rooms. On the other hand, each of these new technologies and formats offers new opportunities for the placement of advertising and the promotion of products.

While these new media are increasingly being employed for marketing communications—and in some cases exist solely for the purpose of promoting products and services—very little is known about their effectiveness as channels of communication. One thing is clear: these new media—and to a growing extent the more traditional media—are increasingly under the control of consumers. Consumers not only have more choices among media, but they also have greater control over their own responses to those media and when they will use them. An important implication of this control by consumers is that marketers can no longer expect consumers to regularly have opportunities for exposure to product messages in a relatively few media. Marketers have responded to this problem by employing a variety of nontraditional media and approaches to advertising and promotion within the more traditional media, such as the use of more channels of communication and different types of media and messages to reach consumers. This response is particularly well illustrated by the advent of what has come to be called event marketing.

THE RISE OF EVENT MARKETING

At the same time that new media technologies and formats have arisen, other existing forms of media have been adopted as advertising vehicles. Sponsorships and product placements at cultural and sporting events have become common. These events represent opportunities to attract the attention of a particular group of consumers in an environment that is relatively uncluttered by other commercial messages. Events may be exclusively sponsored by a single firm and can be matched with a particularly appropriate product, for example, a running shoe as sponsor of a 10-K race or a building materials manufacturer as sponsor of a home show.[3]

These events provide a means for reaching consumers with very specific interests and characteristics. Although such events offer only limited opportunities for communicating specific product messages, they do provide a means for increasing the visibility of product names and for building and reinforcing consumer goodwill through association with the event. They may also provide a means for associating the product with the event and thus potentially transferring part of the image of the event to the product.

Events may be created and sponsored by one or more organizations. They may differ in the degree to which sponsors are identified and in the amount and number of overt product messages. They may be one-time or ongoing affairs. Events need not be constructed, however; there are numerous events in the lives of consumers that can provide opportunities for product associations. Thus, Lexus automobiles were placed in the lobbies of theaters featuring operas, ballet, and similar events because the type of customer likely to purchase them tends to frequent such events. Automobile and boat races tend to attract a disproportionate number of frequent consumers of beer, so sponsorship of such races or of participants in these races represents a viable means for reaching these consumers.

The decision to sponsor an event or to place a product is often based on a careful evaluation of the relationship between attendance at specific types of events and consumption of particular products. Events differ with respect to the types and sizes of the audiences they attract. Thus, different types of events are not interchangeable as promotional tools. Events frequently have multiple audiences. There may be active participants and local spectators. When the event is broadcast, there is also a media audience, which may be very large or rather small. Abratt et al. (1987) note that some events have the potential for attracting worldwide audiences. For example, it is estimated that the 1994 World Cup soccer competition will attract

[3]Not all event sponsorships represent a good match between product and event. This is probably due to the complexity of the sponsorship decision, as well as the current lack of understanding about the full impact of such events.

a cumulative audience of more than 20 billion people. This audience may be exposed to traditional product advertising through live television or reruns and may also be exposed to advertising and product or brand name placements associated with sponsorship of the event. At the same time, certain events attract very selective audiences that can be targeted with efficiency and a minimum of leakage into audiences of little interest to the marketer. It is likely that these two types of audiences are influenced differently, although there is little empirical evidence on this. In one case history, however, Hastings (1984) found that a racing event had more impact on participants and local spectators than on a larger media audience.

Although event marketing has a long history, its frequency of use and sophistication have increased dramatically during the past 10 years. This has been attributed to the 1984 Olympics, which demonstrated the potential of sponsorship for both event managers and event sponsors (Wilber 1988). Evidence of this potential for the sponsoring organization is found in a 1987 SRI Research Center poll, which revealed that 51 percent of one thousand surveyed adults recalled advertising that mentioned a company's status as an Olympic sponsor or supplier, and 46 percent said a company's Olympic sponsorship raises their opinion of the company. Thirty-seven percent said they would be more inclined to buy a product because its manufacturer is an Olympic sponsor (Swenson and Seagren 1988). During the 1980s there was also a growth in paid product placement in motion pictures, which was precipitated in part by the success of "Reese's Pieces" after its appearance in the movie *ET*.

There has been a tendency to treat event marketing as a form of advertising. It is useful to note, however, that very little research has examined the efficacy of these various forms of communications. Hastings (1984) has urged caution in concluding that event sponsorship, in particular, is an effective mode of communication. He notes that awareness of an event is not necessarily the same as awareness of a brand that is associated with the event. Furthermore, whereas in more traditional advertising the advertiser can directly influence the product message received by the consumer, in event marketing the message is not under the direct control of the marketer unless the marketer also uses some form of more traditional advertising. Otherwise, to the extent that a message is communicated at all, it usually must be by association.

It may be the case that event sponsorship or association increases awareness of a sponsor and its products and creates positive associations with the product. It is also possible in some circumstances that the "event" may serve to disarm the consumer and reduce counterarguing, because the event distracts the consumer from the task of evaluation of information. On the other hand, such distraction would occur only when there was information to process. Many sponsored events involve little more than the presence of a brand name, logo, or product to remind participants of the sponsor. Presentation of additional information frequently takes a form that resembles more traditional advertising or personal selling. Whether such communication is attended to is as much under the control of the spectator as a television commercial, which can be readily switched off. Indeed, the event itself may distract the consumer from the advertiser's intended message. Furthermore, any message that is offered in the form of a more traditional advertisement will carry cues that suggest that it is, indeed, an advertisement. Thus, it is not at all clear that most events provide a particularly powerful forum for communications about products and services.

Events also carry a significant risk associated with the lack of control over the message. The marketer is vulnerable to negative publicity. For example, if a firm were identified with an event that excluded certain minority groups, as has happened in a number of circumstances, it might well find its image damaged.

Although the efficacy of event sponsorship remains an empirical question, there is no doubt that there is value in such sponsorships for viewers and event managers. Steve Ryan, president of National Hockey League Services, has noted that the "influx of sponsor dollars helps keep prices down for consumers" (Wilber 1988, p. 9). Neither is there any question about the desire of companies to sponsor events of various types. Wilber (1988) notes that over 3,500 companies are involved in sports marketing programs in the United States alone. *Special Events Report*, a Chicago-based newsletter that monitors the industry, indicates that these companies spent $1.75 billion on sports marketing in 1988, a 30-percent increase over 1987 and more than five times the amount spent in 1983 (Wilber 1988).

The rise of event marketing makes it clear that almost anything is a potential medium. Any event is a potential opportunity for advertising and promotion. The presence of a product in the home, in the office, in a movie, or in the context of a television program or live theater has the potential to create product awareness and product associations. The power of any given medium to create awareness or associations with a product varies considerably, however. A sign in a stadium is likely to have less influence than a well-crafted 30-second television commercial, since it often provides little or no product information beyond a brand name. On the other hand, the use of a given product by a well-known and respected celebrity, whether real or fictional, may be a particularly strong endorsement.

TOWARD UNDERSTANDING MEDIA EFFECTS ON MARKETING COMMUNICATIONS

When individuals in an audience can be highly selective within a medium (or even select a vehicle within a medium), as is increasingly the case, the already tenuous link between media exposure and advertising exposure is further weakened. Opportunities for exposure to product messages are not the same as actual exposure. It is the nature of the consumer's interaction with media that increasingly determines its efficiency and effectiveness as a communications tool. While such interaction must be considered in all forms of advertising and promotion, it may be more important in the case of nontraditional media, where there can be far greater variability.

There are currently few systematic measures of the use of most media. This is most clearly the case for newer media and for events, but surprisingly little is known even about more traditional media.[4] Such tools are clearly needed and necessary. Several conferences and surveys of the advertising community have suggested the need for such measures as a means for making decisions among different media (Advertising Research Foundation 1961, 1983; Schultz 1979; Schmalensee 1983). More than a decade ago, Raymond (1976) noted that "While acceptable methods exist for measuring target audience *exposure* to the vehicle, few equally acceptable measures permit valid *comparisons* of exposures in *different* media, and no acceptable measures of *response to advertising* exist for comparing vehicles in different media" (p. 53–54). Raymond was referring only to traditional advertising media, but his comment is even more valid when newer media forms are considered.

This would be a significant problem for researchers even if there were only a few simple dimensions along which media differed. Media differ on many dimensions, however, and the number of these dimensions is growing with the number of media. Furthermore, the form that a medium takes is increasingly under the control of the individual audience member. This would not be a problem if the influence of differences in media could be modeled with the judgment of experienced media professionals, but research indicates that decisions by media professionals about qualitative differences in media are not particularly reliable (Haley 1985).

THE MEDIATING ROLE OF SELF-SELECTION

More than 20 years ago, Marshall McLuhan (McLuhan and Fiore 1967) suggested that the medium is the message. Even if the medium is not the message, it is certain that the medium influences the way the message is perceived, processed, and stored. Empirical studies consistently reveal that more involving media are better vehicles for delivering product messages (Lloyd and Clancy 1989; Audits and Surveys 1986). This is the case regardless of whether the measure of performance is recall, persuasion, or message credibility. Numerous studies have shown that the medium in which a message is embedded can serve to prime responses to marketing communications (Higgins and King 1981; Wyer and Srull 1981; Herr 1989; Yi 1990*a,b*). Still other media effects have been identified by researchers (see, for example, Kennedy 1971; Soldow and Principe 1981; Krugman 1983; Chook 1985; Singh and Churchill 1987). It is not at all clear that these effects are directly attributable to the characteristics of the media or a particular medium. It is more likely that they are attributable to the way in which people interact with the media. The appropriate question is no longer What does media do to people? but rather, What do people do with media? (See Zillman and Bryant [1985] for a discussion of some of the implications of this change in perspective.) This perspective is well illustrated in research on advertising, persuasive communication, and decision-making that has emphasized the role of message recipients as active processors of information who elaborate, modify, and edit information (Payne and Bettman 1992; Petty et al. 1983). Consumers do

[1]Until very recently, much of the research on advertising effects at the level of the individual consumer was carried out in carefully controlled settings where the effects of media were held constant. This was true of both industry and academic research.

not respond passively to information in advertising; rather, they act on it based on their beliefs, needs, and personalities.

There is growing evidence of differential loyalty to media types among consumers. In addition, there are selective patterns of exposure and preferential attitudinal dispositions toward certain kinds of media and vehicles within media that are not constant across all viewers (Gunter 1985). There is also strong evidence that people selectively attend to information based on its relevance to them at a given point in time (Broadbent 1977; Greenwald and Leavitt 1984; Krugman 1988; Pechmann and Stewart 1990; Tolley 1993). Thus, consumers not only have characteristic patterns of interaction with and preferences for media in general, but they also have characteristic patterns of information search and preferred modes for obtaining information about products. These characteristics and preferences influence whether consumers attend to advertising and how they process it. Thus, the influence of advertising on a given consumer cannot be understood apart from an understanding of that consumer's characteristics and preferences. There is a need to better understand why individual consumers and aggregate audiences behave as they do toward specific types of messages and the media used to deliver these messages (Stewart 1992).

Individuals with a need for information watch more information programs. Those with social and personal identity needs watch more programs such as popular dramas and movies, which can be seen to serve needs related to vicarious social contact. There are no specific programs that particularly serve individuals with escapist needs; for such persons, there are a number of program options (Murray 1980). The effect of commercial messages will differ substantially depending on the use a particular consumer is making of a given medium. Some commercial messages will not even register since they may be inconsistent with the consumer's purpose; they may spoil the mood, distract from the flow of thought, etc. Thus, in the future it will be important to identify those media, and the purposes for using them, that are consistent with and supportive of the commercial message.

Greater selectivity exercised by consumers means, on the one hand, that consumers are more difficult to reach through traditional mass media. On the other hand, the increase in the number of media vehicles available to consumers and consumers' selectivity in using these vehicles may also provide more opportunities for the marketer to reach consumers with the optimal message for the medium and medium-use occasion. Note that what is needed is not a better understanding of *media*, but a better understanding of how people interact with media and embedded commercial messages.

MEDIA AND MARKET SEGMENTS

Marketing communications channels will have different roles depending on who the consumer is, and the consumer's relationship to the product. Obviously, these roles will vary considerably with the specific product, but it is possible to identify some very general hypotheses about the effects of marketing communications on particular sets of customers. There are four distinct groups of consumers that may be identified: (1) nonusers of the product category, (2) brand-loyal users, (3) brand switchers, and (4) emergent users. Each of these will be discussed below.

Nonusers

Nonusers of a product category have either rejected the need for the product and the benefit(s) it provides, perhaps because they use an alternative type of product, or have decided that they have no need for the product. Marketing communications will not change this circumstance. Aside from the identification of new uses for or benefits of the product, communications directed at this group are a waste of money. These individuals may be aware of advertising for the product, but awareness is insufficient to induce product use among these individuals. These individuals may even enjoy the advertising for the product, but this enjoyment does not induce product use. On the other hand, these individuals may find marketing communications for such unwanted products highly irritating. Greater numbers of options for communications and consumer self-selection should enable marketing organizations to reduce the frequency with which unwanted and intrusive product information reaches these consumers. One reason for the increasing use of alternative forms of media and promotion is to avoid both the cost and the consumer irritation associated with advertising to nonusers.

Loyal Users

Within any given product category, there are individual users of the product who are highly loyal to a particular brand or set of brands. The proportion of these individuals appears to vary from product category to product category (Ehrenberg 1972); there are many loyal consumers in categories such as bleach and cigarettes and relatively few in categories like paper towels. These individuals are already persuaded that a given brand is best (or at least no worse than others), and they have high levels of brand awareness and relatively positive brand attitudes. Marketing communications directed at these individuals are unlikely to raise awareness very much, particularly for well-known, frequently purchased brands. Neither are marketing communications likely to change attitude or the propensity to purchase.

Loyal consumers may need to be reminded that they have made a good choice and that they should remember to purchase their regular brand. A substantial body of research suggests that consumers are most likely to attend to information about their preferred brands and to ignore information about other products. (See Stewart et al. [1990] for a review of this literature. See also Zillman and Bryant 1985; Pechmann and Stewart 1990; Tolley 1993.) Indeed, research by Raj (1982) and by Tellis (1988) suggests that advertising, at least for mature brands, may be more likely to maintain consumers' loyalty to a brand than to cause consumers to switch from one brand to another. This makes marketing communications to these consumers a rather easy task since the audience is attentive, and a simple reminder, perhaps just the name, may be sufficient as a reinforcer.

Nontraditional media, particularly those that are routinely used by the consumer, may be particularly effective and efficient for reinforcing loyalty to a given brand of product. There is little need to communicate a detailed product message. Maintaining top-of-mind awareness[5] of the brand may be sufficient for reinforcing use. Event marketing, product placements, outdoor advertising, and other forms of marketing communications and promotions that provide an opportunity to identify the preferred brand by name or by some other well-known feature may be particularly well suited for advertising to loyals.

Research is quite clear that advertising has little or no effect on the *creation* of product demand, except insofar as it may create awareness or generate trial of a product with which the consumer is otherwise unfamiliar (Fisher 1993; Lambin 1976; Ehrenberg 1972, 1974). In one of the most comprehensive studies of this issue, Lambin (1976) examined the effects of advertising for 16 different product categories in as many as 9 different countries over a 10-year period. Regarding the question of advertising's effects on aggregate category demand, Lambin concluded that "Limited empirical support is given to the view that advertising increases primary demand" (p. 136). In the four product categories in which advertising did have a significant effect on primary demand, the effect occurred early in the product life, when creation of awareness and trial are important determinants of demand.

It is useful to note that some advertising campaigns that appear directed at increasing sales for a product category as a whole are, in fact, competitive advertisements within a broader context of competition among seemingly dissimilar products. Examples of such campaigns include the California Raisins campaign (the dancing raisins) and the V-8 vegetable juice campaign ("Wow! I could have had a V-8.") Similarly, Fisher (1993) summarizes data on the advertising of alcoholic beverages and concludes that much of the apparent (small) effect of advertising on aggregate consumption is accounted for by consumers switching from one type of alcoholic beverage to another. Thus, an increase in beer advertising may produce a modest increase in beer consumption, but it also appears to decrease consumption of wine and spirits. Two other instances in which advertising may stimulate product demand are when advertising suggests new uses for an established product (the well-known Arm and Hammer baking soda campaign is an example) and when a product with a low level of top-of-mind awareness is made more salient to consumers by means of advertising (again, the California Raisins campaign is an example). In all of these instances, the advertised product is more like a new product than an established product. The suggestion of new uses for a product is essentially the same as developing a new market. In the case of a product or brand with low awareness and usage, the influence of advertising is also more closely akin to the development of a new market.

Several of the empirical studies that suggest that advertising has an effect on primary demand have, in fact, been carried out in markets for various agricultural products, where low levels of awareness or indirect substitutes exist (Hoofnagle 1963; Henderson and Brown 1961; Henderson et al. 1961). Thus, these studies are consistent with the proposition that advertis-

[5]Top-of-mind awareness refers to a measure of the frequency with which a group of consumers mention a given product when asked to identify products in a given category.

ing has an effect on aggregate demand only under a narrow set of circumstances.

It is less clear whether advertising and promotions serve to reinforce the use of a product category per se, as opposed to reinforcing the choice of a particular brand. There has been little research that has directly addressed this issue. Empirical research that demonstrates an association between attention to and memory for advertising for a product and product use merely confirms the well-known phenomenon of selective exposure discussed above, although such findings have occasionally been interpreted to mean that advertising is the causal agent (see, for example, Aitken et al. 1986). On the other hand, to the extent that advertising reflects cultural acceptance of a product, there is reason to believe that advertising will have some reinforcing effect on consumption, just as the observation of important others engaged in a practice or using a product may serve as a reinforcer. Fisher (1993) has reviewed research on the reinforcing effects of advertising for alcoholic beverages and concludes that such reinforcing effects account for 1 to 3 percent of the variability in drinking and that these effects are confined to a small number of individuals who seek out media with unusually high levels of advertising for alcoholic beverages.

There is no reason to believe that advertising embedded within new media, such as product placement in movies or event sponsorship, is any more effective than advertising in more traditional media except insofar as the audience may better match the characteristics of the advertiser's target audience. Indeed, to the extent that product messages are incidental to exposure to a medium or event, it is unlikely that such messages will attract much attention, and thus they will generally have less impact. The reinforcing effects of such exposure will almost certainly be weaker than more salient cultural influences such as family and friends.

Brand Switchers

Much of the research on marketing communications that has been carried out in both industry and academe has focused on this group of consumers. Switchers have little or no brand loyalty. They most certainly make purchase decisions on the basis of something other than brand. Switching may be associated with price, availability, top-of-mind awareness, or any number of other factors. In cases where price is the determinant characteristic, price promotions are likely to be the most effective vehicle for inducing switching. Where the determinant factor is familiarity, top-of-mind awareness, image, or other communications-driven element, advertising may play an important role. When familiarity or top-of-mind awareness is an important determinant of brand choice, nontraditional advertising may be an effective mode of communication. Consumers often use familiarity as a heuristic when making choices among brands; thus, the product that most readily comes to mind is often the one selected by a consumer. Indeed, empirical evidence suggests that the brand that enjoys the highest level of top-of-mind awareness is likely to enjoy the largest market share (Holman and Hecker 1983).

It is useful to note, however, that the effect of advertising on switchers is likely to be short-lived and readily influenced by the actions of competitors. Switchers are the most expensive group of consumers to attract, and they are virtually impossible to hold. Unfortunately for marketers, this group cannot be ignored since doing so leaves competitors with an unobstructed opportunity to reinforce decisions favorable to their product. As in the case of loyals, research on the extent to which advertising reinforces consumption of a product category is quite limited.

Emergent Users

The fourth group of consumers consists of members of the emergent market. Even in a mature market, there are new consumers entering the market as others leave. The characteristics and composition of an emergent market will vary by product class, but there are two groups that are particularly important for a wide range of consumer markets, at least in the United States. These two groups are young people (teens and young adults) and immigrants. Both groups are in the process of forming preferences for numerous products, and both represent a market for products over a long time horizon.

Marketing communications targeted at an emergent market are closely akin to advertising for a new product. There is a need to create awareness, build brand image, and induce trial. There is a need to create in the consumer a sense of identity with the product and to reinforce trial. The emergent market is very vulnerable to competitive activity and, at the same time, very important for the long-term viability of a firm. Marketing communications that specifically serve this market are particularly important to a firm, as they represent tools for building a brand franchise for the long term.

Nontraditional media, including events, may help build brand awareness and image or induce trial of a given brand. The extent to which advertising (or media in general) influences the trial of a product category is less clear. Such influence probably varies by product category, but insofar as product use is encouraged or made appealing by advertising or by use in the media, there is likely to be some effect in some categories, although virtually all published research reveals that word-of-mouth communications, the example of parents, and peer influence exert far more influence on product use (and brand choice) than advertising (Ward et al. 1977). Nevertheless, to the extent that advertising contributes to awareness of a product, it has some effect on product trial and long-term consumption.

EFFECTS OF PROMOTIONS AND NONTRADITIONAL ADVERTISING ON THE CONSUMPTION OF ALCOHOLIC BEVERAGES

Although the use of new media, promotions, event marketing, and other forms of nontraditional advertising is widespread, the use of these tools by marketers of certain types of products has created controversy and criticism. Manufacturers of tobacco products and alcoholic beverages have been among the most frequent objects of such criticism. The remainder of this chapter will consider the use of nontraditional marketing tools by the alcoholic beverage industry. Before turning to more specific issues, however, it is useful to place that industry's use of nontraditional marketing tools within the larger context of the changing marketing practices discussed earlier.

It is certainly the case that marketing of alcoholic beverages involves a wide array of newer media, promotions, and event sponsorships. Expenditures on traditional media advertising for alcoholic beverages have declined in recent years, although there is some evidence that total expenditures for these products has not decreased by the same percentage and in some cases has not declined at all (M. Shanken Communications 1990, 1991). This suggests that marketers of alcoholic beverages have been shifting from traditional media to less traditional media and promotions.

The use of nontraditional marketing programs does not appear to work any differently for alcoholic beverages than for other products. The shift in media usage among marketers of alcoholic beverages is being driven in part by the same factors that have caused the shift among other marketers: the rising costs of traditional media, declines in consumer usage of more traditional media, and the desire for more selective and targeted communications. At the same time, there is no doubt that marketers of alcoholic beverages use nontraditional media and advertising partly as a result of the greater restrictions on their use of traditional media such as radio and television. As the earlier sections of this chapter make clear, little is known about the effects of these new media, and their effectiveness as communications vehicles is a very complex issue. Thus, in the absence of direct empirical research, it is useful to consider the probable effects of nontraditional media within the context of what is known about the effects of traditional advertising for alcohol, and then consider the factors unique to nontraditional media that might increase or reduce effectiveness relative to more traditional media.

Effects of Advertising for Alcoholic Beverages

Extant empirical research is quite clear about the conclusion that advertising has little influence on the total consumption of alcoholic beverages (Fisher 1993). Nonprice advertising has been shown to have little or no effect on a consumer's decision to consume alcoholic beverages (Ornstein and Hanssens 1985). For example, Warburton (1932) found little evidence that the absence of advertising during Prohibition lowered consumption, although reduced availability and the illegality of consumption did decrease total consumption. In a review of econometric studies of the relationship between advertising and consumption of alcoholic beverages, and in their own study using State-level historical data, Ornstein and Hanssens (1985) found no evidence of a positive relationship between nonprice advertising and consumption. Rather, such studies consistently find that the effects of advertising are limited to intraindustry sales, that is, shifts in sales across brands (Duffy 1982; Grabowski 1976; McGuinness 1980).

As noted above, even those studies that find a relationship between advertising expenditures and consumption report very small relationships. Such relationships may be attributable, at least in part, to product switching within the more general alcoholic beverage category. Selvanathan (1989), Clements and Selvanathan (1987), Johnson (1985), and Duffy (1987) all report evidence that increases in consumption of one type of alcoholic beverage product (beer, wine, or spirits) that were associated with increased advertising expenditures were accompanied by decreases in consumption of other categories of alcoholic beverages. This finding suggests that alcoholic beverage products are generic substitutes and that advertising for these products appears to create a very modest shift in demand from one product type to another. The very small variance associated with such effects makes it impossible to determine whether any increase occurs in absolute demand for all alcoholic beverages, but it does appear safe to conclude that such effects are minuscule if they exist at all.

While most econometric studies have examined aggregate advertising expenditures or expenditures on print and broadcast advertising, Ornstein and Hanssens (1985) also examined the effect of billboard advertising on consumption. They found no increase in consumption associated with billboards that did not contain price information. Such findings do not necessarily imply that billboards do not reinforce consumption among current users or influence brand choice, but they are consistent with the view that nonprice advertising does not increase consumption.

Evidence is also fairly consistent regarding the determinants of alcohol consumption. Economic and sociodemographic variables, along with price, account for most of the variance in consumption. In one of the more comprehensive studies of the issue, Ornstein and Hanssens (1985) demonstrated the importance of economic and socioeconomic factors and price, but also found factors associated with demand that differ according to product type. For example, they found that aggregate consumption of beer was strongly related to the number of younger consumers in the market but that consumption of distilled spirits was unrelated to youth. Price and income were far more inelastic for beer consumption than for consumption of distilled spirits. Income was unrelated to beer consumption. Availability on Sundays was an important determinant of the consumption of beer but not of distilled spirits. This suggests that beer may be more of an impulse purchase. Tourism was also highly related to consumption of beer, but not other types of alcoholic beverages. A lower legal drinking age was associated with greater consumption of beer but not other types of alcoholic beverages. Finally, directly relevant to the question of the efficacy of nontraditional media and promotions, Ornstein and Hanssens (1985) found that novelty give-aways appeared to affect consumption of distilled spirits but not other types of alcoholic beverages. The mechanism by which such novelties had their effect was not identified.

The weight of the evidence suggests that advertising has its primary effect on brand and product form preference rather than consumption. Such evidence appears contrary to research that has reported reductions in alcohol consumption associated with bans on the advertising of alcoholic beverages (Saffer 1991). Findings of lower consumption following advertising bans are the exception, however (see Fisher 1993 for a review). Indeed, where advertising bans have been associated with decreases in consumption, other factors have been confounded with the ban. Such confounding led the author of one of the more comprehensive studies to conclude that "These models cannot explicitly distinguish between the effects of alcohol advertising bans, other alcohol policies, and alcohol sentiment" (Saffer 1991, p. 73). Thus, there appears to be little evidence that advertising bans alone influence consumption of alcoholic beverages. Similar findings have been reported with respect to bans on tobacco advertising (Smith 1990; Boodewyn 1986, 1987).

It is reasonable to suppose that promotions and nontraditional advertising would have effects similar to those identified for more traditional forms of advertising. The question then arises as to whether promotions, sponsored events, or nontraditional media might have effects beyond those obtained with more traditional advertising. While the evidence is limited, it would appear that promotions that include a lowering of price, and particularly those that explicitly communicate the lowering of price to consumers, are more likely than traditional advertising to produce an increase in consumption. Promotions that increase the availability or accessibility of alcoholic beverages are also likely to increase consumption. This latter effect is likely to be more strongly associated with beer and wine than distilled spirits. The effect of increased accessibility may also be potentiated by lower prices. Finally, promotions or merchandising programs that add value for the consumer, such as when novelty items are included in the purchase price of the beverage, may increase consumption, at least in the case of distilled spirits.

Thus, price reductions and increased availability are two dimensions that may differentiate nontraditional media and promotions from traditional advertising. Even when promotions lower price or increase accessibility, it not clear whether the effects are restricted to current users of the product or carry over to nonusers who might be encouraged to try a product they have not previously used. The latter issue requires empirical study. Neither is there direct evidence on the question of whether certain types of promotional activities, particularly those associated with various "events," may facilitate consumption. It would seem reasonable considering the available evidence that event-related marketing activities that offer lower prices or facilitate purchase of a product may increase consumption. For example, vendors at a sports event may bring alcoholic beverages directly to consumers, although increasingly there are restrictions on how much can be purchased and on availability during the latter portions of an event.

Some nontraditional advertising or promotions may facilitate consumption of alcoholic beverages through less direct means than price reduction or accessibility, although little research has focused on these indirect effects. Such facilitation effects may occur when there is a cultural (or subcultural) association between a given event and the consumption of alcoholic beverages, when consumption of alcoholic beverages is perceived to be a part of the event experience or to add enjoyment to the experience, or when the event involves a social setting conducive to the development of group pressure to consume alcoholic beverages. Such events are generally not commercially sponsored, although promotions and marketing communications may be associated with these events. Whether such associations increase consumption of alcoholic beverages is an empirical question.

It is important to note that nontraditional advertising, events, and promotions may take many forms, such as graduation parties and the week-long spring break holiday enjoyed by some college students. Promotions by marketers of alcoholic beverages that have been associated with such events have been widely criticized. On the other hand, there are events that are frequently associated with the consumption of alcoholic beverages that are seldom involved in commercial promotions but may be powerful factors in the initial decision to consume alcoholic beverages. Many adolescents have their first experience with alcohol with the family during special occasions (weddings, birthdays, etc.) or with peers during or following events that do not promote consumption of alcoholic beverages (high school football games, class trips, etc.).

Although nontraditional communications and promotions may differ in many ways from traditional advertising, two dimensions appear particularly relevant considering the empirical evidence that is available. One dimension is related to the extent to which a product association or message is incidental to an event that is central to the consumer's interests and agenda. For example, the placement of a sign for a particular brand of product on the scoreboard of a football stadium is largely incidental to a fan's interest in the game. Such incidental messages have the advantage of eliminating consumer control over exposure to a message, given the consumer's choice to attend a given event. On the other hand, the more incidental the message, the less likely it will be attended to or processed by the consumer. The more incidental the association, the less effective the medium of message delivery will be relative to more traditional advertising. It would seem that incidental communications are very weak communication vehicles indeed. Any effects that do exist are likely to be related to reinforcing brand awareness and preference among current users.

A second dimension of nontraditional marketing communications is the selectivity of the communications vehicle (Haley 1985). Media vehicles vary considerably in their ability to reach targeted audiences. The more targeted the vehicle, the more involving and relevant the product message can become. Consumers are more likely to attend to and process such messages. On the other hand, the more targeted the medium, the more exposure to the medium is under the control of the consumer because the consumer chooses to place himself or herself in a situation where the advertising message may appear. Thus, nontraditional media may be able to deliver more relevant messages to consumers than traditional advertising media, but the consumers who receive them are likely to be a narrow group who are already interested in the messages.

It would appear that nontraditional media are less likely to influence consumption of alcoholic beverages than more traditional media. It is almost a certainty that nontraditional media communications have at best a very modest direct influence on the initial decision to consume alcoholic beverages, given the limitations of such media and the empirical evidence on the efficacy of more traditional media. Such media may influence brand choice and the circumstances under which products are consumed, however.

There are those who would argue that certain groups of consumers are particularly vulnerable to marketing communications and that nontraditional advertising may powerfully affect them because it can carefully target these vulnerable groups with subtle, but persuasive, communications. Two groups of consumers have been the principal sources of concern: minorities and youth.

Advertising, Marketing Communications, and Minorities and Youth

The arrival of new media, event marketing, and other forms of nontraditional advertising and promotions has certainly increased the ability of marketers to more selectively target their communications. The fact that marketers, including the makers and distributors of alcoholic beverages, have targeted marketing campaigns at minorities is well documented. Since the media-consuming habits and lifestyles of 17-year-olds and 22-year-olds are similar, it is almost certain that messages targeted at consumers of legal drinking age also reach youth below the minimum drinking age. Nonetheless, these facts must be placed in proper perspective.

Target marketing is a common marketing technique, and its use by marketers of alcoholic beverages is not surprising. The important issue in the case of minorities is not what type of advertising or promotions are used, but whether minorities are inherently more vulnerable to marketing communications. It may be the case that certain individuals are more or less vulnerable to marketing communications or other persuasive communications, but there is no evidence to suggest that such vulnerability is associated with race, ethnicity, or gender. Thus, issues related to target marketing and the use of highly selective media and promotions merely add unnecessary complexity to the question of media effects. While it is likely that product messages that are more relevant to the consumer are more effective, this is not an issue of minority vulnerability. Rather, it is a question of whether target marketing, with its emphasis on creating products and product messages that more closely match consumers' desires, is appropriate. This is a question well beyond the scope of this chapter.

While the issue of targeting members of minority populations is difficult to address, and may be regarded as insulting to members of minority populations, the question of whether youth might be more vulnerable to advertising and promotions than adults is an important question, particularly in the context of marketing alcoholic beverages. There is evidence that young adults are among the more frequent users and abusers of alcoholic beverages, especially beer (Lastovicka et al. 1987), even though it is illegal for persons under 21 to drink or purchase alcohol. The more specific question of import is whether advertising and promotions, by whatever means, increase the likelihood that underage youth will initiate drinking or increase their consumption of alcoholic beverages. In order to address this question, it is necessary to examine the literature on advertising effects on children and adolescents.

Research over the past 20 years on children and advertising has examined the variables of attention, recall and recognition, and product preferences. The groups that have received the most attention have been children between the ages of 6 and 10 years old and those between the ages of 10 and 12 years old. The major medium investigated has been television. The general findings for children below the age of 10 suggest that these children have difficulty distinguishing commercials from programs (Ward 1972; Ward et al. 1972*b*; Robertson and Rossiter 1974; Adler 1978). They are also unaware of the purpose of advertising, i.e., the selling aspect (Ward et al. 1972*b*; Ward et al. 1977;

Adler 1978), and tend to pay more attention to commercials than adults (Ward 1972; Ward et al. 1972*a*; Ward et al. 1977). In addition, young children fail to remember much product-related information from commercials (Blatt et al. 1972; Ward 1972, 1974; Ward et al. 1972*b*; Ward et al. 1977; Ratner 1978; Wartella 1980; Stoneman and Brody 1983), and they desire and request more advertised products (Frideres 1973; Goldberg and Gorn 1974; Robertson and Rossiter 1976, 1977; Barry 1977; Gorn and Goldberg 1980, 1982; Goldberg et al. 1978; Ratner 1978; Rossiter 1979; Atkin 1980).

A very different picture emerges for children above the age of 10. These children can distinguish between commercials and programming and know the purpose of advertising. Research has also shown that these older children are less trusting of commercials and feel that commercials do not indicate much about the product or its quality (Ward et al. 1977). In addition, these children pay less attention to commercials (Ward 1972; Ward et al. 1972*a*; Ward et al. 1977). Older children's attention patterns appear to be comprehension-guided. That is, they only pay attention to commercials that they understand and that they can relate to, either through the content of the advertisement or the product being advertised (Anderson and Lorch 1983). Thus, selective exposure appears to be operating in these instances. In addition, communication with peers seems to condition adolescents' perception of and interests in products.

Memory for advertisements also increases as a function of age. This is true for both recall and recognition measures of memory (Blatt et al. 1972; Ward et al. 1972*b*; Ward 1972, 1974; Ward et al. 1977; Ratner 1978; Wartella 1980; Stoneman and Brody 1983). However, no correlation between memory and product preference has been found.

The effect of advertising on adolescents' brand preferences is less clear. In most empirical studies, product preference has been defined as the desire for and request for an advertised product. Several studies have reported finding that exposure to advertising increases desire for, requests for, and consumption of advertised products (Barry 1977; Atkin 1980). However, all of these studies examined children's products advertised to children on children's television shows. There is little research that has directly examined the effect of advertising on adolescents' product preferences and virtually no evidence on the causal linkage between exposure to advertising and the initiation of product consumption. There is literature, however, that suggests that adolescents may find advertising unconvincing.

Moore and Moschis (1978) studied adolescents' reactions to advertising by examining both general attitudes toward advertising and perceived credibility of advertising. Attitudes toward advertising were based upon adolescents' liking or disliking of advertising. Perceived credibility of advertising was based on adolescents' perception of the honesty of television, newspaper, radio, and magazine ads. They reported that adolescents have negative attitudes toward advertising and that advertising has low perceived credibility. In addition, these results were not related to amount of television viewing or communications with family and peers. Thus, it appears that a negative attitude toward advertising is already developed by adolescence.

Similar results were found in another study investigating adolescents' attitudes toward advertising that focused on adolescent skepticism of advertising and their responses to ads reporting product tests (Linn et al. 1982). This study found that adolescents display substantial skepticism of advertisers and tests conducted by advertisers. Almost two-thirds of the adolescents studied believed that advertisers often or always lie or cheat. They based this view primarily on personal experience. In addition, more than three-quarters of the adolescents studied generally believe that tests reported by advertisers are unfair and untrue. Such findings do not mean that adolescents are unaffected by advertising, however. Adolescents may still accept the claims made in an advertisement even while expressing skepticism (Linn et al. 1982).

On the other hand, the general dislike and skepticism of advertising may result in adolescents tuning out most advertising they are exposed to, and may result in increased vigilance regarding advertising claims. This could result in adolescents being less influenced by advertising than adults. This is an empirical question that has not been answered to date. However, adolescents' distrust and disbelief of advertising should result in weaker product preferences after exposure to advertising. Perhaps this distrust is why adolescents rely on advertising less than on other sources of information.

Several studies (Jessor and Jessor 1977; MEE Productions 1992) suggest that most studies of adolescent response to advertising may understate adolescent cynicism among inner-city youth. A recent study sponsored by the Robert Wood Johnson Foundation (MEE Productions 1992) concludes:

> The African-American urban teenager may well be the most difficult audience to reach. . . . Mainstream society has virtually no credibility with these young people; they are alienated from their own heritage . . . . The most popular media—movies and rap music/videos—are not well suited for conventional . . . campaigns. Broadcast television is perceived as a mainstream medium, and behavioral messages it promotes are suspect (p. xii).

This same report suggests that the use of sports figures and other celebrity spokespersons are ineffective unless the spokesperson has a reputation within the street culture. Thus, Magic Johnson is not a credible spokesperson, but members of the rap group Public Enemy may be persuasive. In addition, these youths find attempts to co-opt counter-culture figures highly offensive.

The latter finding suggests that sponsored events and sports marketing programs may have little influence on inner-city youth unless there is a strong identification with the event. Such events do exist, however. They include rap concerts, movies such as *Boyz in the Hood* and *Malcolm X*, step shows, Kwanzaa celebrations, and other manifestations of urban street culture. It is unclear how the involvement of alcoholic beverage marketers in activities that are more mainstream, such as Anheuser-Busch's sponsorship of Black History Month events, influences minority youth.

It is certainly the case that marketers of alcoholic beverages offer products and advertising for black consumers. Such consumers have distinctive product preferences and are especially heavy consumers of malt beverages. Less clear is the direction of causality. Advertisers frequently advertise products to those consumers who have already demonstrated an interest in them. Such advertising no doubt contributes to inner-city youths' awareness and image of these products. It is less clear whether advertising of either the traditional or nontraditional variety has other effects. It is unlikely, however, that advertising for alcoholic beverage products that do not already enjoy some acceptance within the urban culture will be perceived as relevant to such youths.

Thus, a case can be made that rather than being among the most vulnerable targets for advertising and promotions, inner-city youths may be among the most resistant. It should be noted that such resistance applies to both product messages and public service messages designed to foster more responsible and healthy behavior. No research has addressed this issue in the specific context of alcoholic beverages, and the issue is an especially deserving topic for future research.

SUMMARY AND CONCLUSIONS

There is no doubt that marketers of alcoholic beverages are making greater use of new media, nontraditional advertising vehicles, and promotions to sell their products. The movement away from traditional media toward innovative forms of marketing is not unique to the alcoholic beverage industry. Rather, this trend is a general phenomenon occurring within the entire consumer products industry. Shifts in communication and promotion strategies are related to the increasing fragmentation of media, to the increasing control consumers are able to exercise over exposure to media and advertising, and to the desire of marketers to find less costly alternatives to traditional media. Marketers of alcoholic beverages have been subject to these same trends, and they have also had fewer options available to them in more traditional media as a result of restrictions on their use of television and radio.

While it is clear that marketing organizations are moving expenditures to nontraditional forms of communications, it is unclear whether these forms of communication and promotion are more effective than those appearing in more traditional media. Indeed, the influence of media on advertising effects is not well understood, nor has it been well researched. What is well understood is that advertising is not a particularly strong force, regardless of the medium in which it appears. The limited data that do exist suggest that nontraditional marketing communications may be less effective than traditional advertising media when the objective of the communication is to persuade a nonuser to try a product or brand. Nontraditional advertising is a more cost-effective means of reinforcing brand loyalty among users and may be more carefully targeted at selected groups of consumers than traditional advertising. Marketing communications in nontraditional advertising would appear to have a direct effect on product consumption only when they involve price reductions or when they occur in a setting that facilitates and encourages consumption. The latter types of events are not restricted to commercially sponsored activities, however.

There is little empirical evidence that nontraditional advertising directed at minorities or youth is more effective than other forms of advertising. There is considerable evidence that advertising of all types is less credible among adolescent consumers. There is no reason to believe that advertising in nontraditional media—whether specific event sponsorships, product placements, or other vehicles—will be any more effective with this group than advertising in traditional forms of media. Some advertising in nontraditional media will no doubt be particularly well suited for reaching adolescent consumers, but traditional media also have vehicles that have special appeal for adolescent consumers. Thus, the issue is not whether advertising in nontraditional media is more effective than advertising in traditional media. The question is the following: Which media are most effective for communicating with a given audience?

Two questions remain unanswered by the current review. First, extant empirical evidence does not indicate the extent to which advertising and promotions of any type reinforce continued use of a product by current users or increase consumption. It is known that advertising and promotions can reinforce brand loyalty. It is not unreasonable to assume that advertising and promotions might, under certain circumstances, also reinforce the continued use of the product class, although the magnitude of this effect is unknown. The particular circumstances under which advertising and promotions might maintain product use remain to be determined, if indeed they exist. Alcoholic beverages, like soft drinks and snack foods, are products for which availability tends to increase consumption. Thus, promotions that encourage stocking behavior or ready accessibility may increase the aggregate consumption of alcoholic beverages. This conclusion is consistent with empirical research that price promotions and increased product availability are associated with higher consumption. On the other hand, there is little evidence that advertising and promotions that do not increase availability or include pricing information can influence consumption of alcoholic beverages as a product class, although they may influence switching from one product form to another (e.g., from beer to wine). This is an area of research that has received very little attention and could benefit from further research.

A second question revolves around the use of nontraditional media for delivering messages designed to reduce product consumption or encourage more responsible use of alcoholic beverages. The same problems that confront the marketing organizations within the alcoholic beverage industry also confront health administrators, educators, and others concerned with persuading consumers to modify their behavior. Media fragmentation, consumer selectivity, and a lack of credibility among certain groups of consumers make the task of these agents more difficult than ever. There is a role for nontraditional media in these activities, but that role is not easy to identify given the current lack of knowledge about these media.

Answers to these questions await additional research on the use of new media and nontraditional advertising and promotion practices. The present review has identified a number of research issues that deserve attention and for which little empirical data exist. The most fundamental issue is the need for a better understanding of how audiences interact with various media and the messages that are embedded within these media. The development of such an understanding requires a recognition of the message recipient as an active seeker and processor of information rather than a passive receiver. Research that examines message content alone is insufficient for identifying how consumers influence and are influenced by advertising messages. Since advertising and promotions that appear in nontraditional media differ from advertising and promotions in more traditional advertising, there is a need for research that specifically focuses on the effects of nontraditional media to determine whether and for what purposes such media might be effective. To date, very little empirical research has focused on the use of such media in a marketing context.

Historically, advertising has been viewed as a means for creating demand for products and brands. In growing markets, where the creation of awareness and product trial is strongly linked to product demand, this view may be appropriate. In mature markets, where product and brand awareness are well established, the role of advertising must be rather different. In such markets advertising may serve to reinforce brand loyalty or encourage switching from one brand to another or from one product form to another. It may also serve to reinforce consumption of the product category. Few studies have focused on the role of advertising as a reinforcer of brand loyalty or product consumption, and this issue could benefit from additional research. Such research would be particularly germane for understanding the effects of nontraditional advertising, which often includes little more than a brand-name identifier. Whether and how such identifiers reinforce brand and product loyalty and whether such identifiers influence brand switching are issues that have not been addressed in the published literature on advertising effects.

Finally, research that examines the effects of promotions and increased availability on current users and nonusers of products would be particularly useful. While it is certain that price promotions and increased availability play a role in increased consumption, the nature of that role is not well defined by empirical research. Furthermore, the role of promotions and product availability in the decision to begin the use of a product and in reinforcing the use of a product has not been well examined.

All of the research issues and questions identified in this chapter represent opportunities for expanding the general understanding of how advertising and promotions work. Examination of these issues will also be useful for informing the management and regulation of marketing activities for specific products, including alcoholic beverages. Although there remain numerous questions for future research, it is useful to conclude by noting that advertising is a relatively weak force in shaping consumption patterns. Factors such as family and friends are far more important determinants of consumption, and price and availability are far stronger marketing tools for influencing consumption. Thus, these factors and tools represent far stronger levers for influencing the consumption of alcoholic products.

REFERENCES

Abraham, M., and Lodish, L. *Advertising Works!* Chicago: Information Resources, 1989.

Abratt, R.; Clayton, B.C.; and Pitt, L.F. Corporate objectives in sports sponsorship. *Int J Advert* 6:299–311, 1987.

Adler, R.P. *Research on the Effects of Television Advertising on Children: A Review of the Literature and Recommendations for Future Research.* Washington, DC: National Science Foundation, 1978.

Advertising Research Foundation, Audience Concepts Committee. *Toward Better Media Comparisons.* New York: The Foundation, 1961.

Advertising Research Foundation. "1983 Member Representative Questionnaire." Report 1R, Apr. 1983.

Aitken, P.P.; Leathar, D.S.; O'Hagan, F.J.; and Squair, S.I. Children's awareness of cigarette advertisements and brand imagery. *Br J Addict* 82:615–622, 1986.

Anderson, D.S., and Lorch, E.P. Looking at television: Action or reaction? In: Bryant, J., and Anderson, D.R., eds. *Children's Understanding of Television: Research on Attention and Comprehension.* New York: Academic Press, 1983.

Atkin, C.K. Effects of television advertising on children. In: Palmer, E.L., and Dorr, A., eds. *Children and the Faces of Television: Teaching, Violence, Selling.* New York: Academic Press, 1980.

Atkin, C.K. Mass communication effects on alcohol consumption. In: *Surgeon General's Workshop on Drunk Driving.* Washington, DC: U.S. Department of Health and Human Services, 1989. pp. 15–34.

Audits and Surveys, Inc. *A Study of Media Involvement.* New York: Audits and Surveys, 1986.

Barry, T.E. *Children's Television Advertising.* Monograph Series #8. Chicago: American Marketing Association, 1977.

Blatt, J.; Spencer, L.; and Ward, S. A cognitive developmental study of children's reactions to television advertising. In: Rubinstein, E.A.; Comstock, G.A.; and Murray, J.P., eds. *Television and Social Behavior, Volume 4, Television in Day-to-Day Life.* Washington, DC: U.S. Department of Health, Education, and Welfare, 1972. pp. 452–467.

Boodewyn, J.J. *Why Do Juveniles Smoke?* New York: International Advertising Association, 1986.

Boodewyn, J.J. *Why Do Juveniles Start Smoking? An International Study of the Role of Advertising and Other Contributory Factors in Argentina, Australia, Canada, Hong Kong, Norway, Spain, Sweden, Switzerland, Turkey, and the United Kingdom.* New York: International Advertising Association, 1987.

Broadbent, D. The hidden pre-attentive processes. *Am Psychol* 32(2):109–118, 1977.

Burgi, M. Cable's Double Digit Dollars Offset Ad Slide. *Multichannel News,* Issue 12, Dec. 16, 1991. p. 50.

Chook, P.H. A continuing study of magazine environment, frequency, and advertising performance. *J Advert Res* 25(4):23–33, 1985.

Clancy, K.J. The coming revolution in advertising: Ten developments which will separate winners from losers. *J Advert Res* 30(Mar./Apr.):47–52, 1990.

Clements, L., and Selvanathan, E. Chapter 5. In: Theil, H., and Clements, K., eds. *Applied Demand Analysis: Results from System-Wide Approaches.* Cambridge, MA: Ballinger Publishing, 1987. pp. 185–264.

Donnelley Marketing. *Fourteenth Annual Survey of Promotional Practices.* Stamford, CT: Donnelley Marketing, 1992.

Duffy, M. The effect of advertising on the total consumption of alcoholic drinks in the United Kingdom: Some econometric estimates. *J Advert* 1(Apr.–Jun.):105–117, 1982.

Duffy, M. Advertising and the inter-product distribution of demand: A Rotterdam model approach. *Eur Econ Rev* 31:1051–1070, 1987.

The Economist. A Survey of the Advertising Industry. Jun. 9, 1990. pp. 3–18.

Ehrenberg, A.S.C. *Repeat-Buying: Theory and Applications.* New York: American Elsevier, 1972.

Ehrenberg, A.S.C. Repetitive advertising and the consumer. *J Advert Res* 23(Sept.):25–34, 1974.

Endicott, R.C., and Brown, K. Top 100 Boosts Ad Spending 6.4% to Almost $34 Billion. *Advertising Age.* Sept. 26, 1990. pp. 1–2.

Fisher, J. *Advertising, Alcohol Consumption, and Abuse. A Worldwide Survey.* Westport, CT: Greenwood Press, 1993.

Frideres, J.S. Advertising, buying patterns and children. *J Advert Res* 13(1):34–36, 1973.

Goldberg, M.E., and Gorn, G.J. Children's reaction to television advertising: An experimental approach. *J Consum Res* 1(Sept.):69–75, 1974.

Goldberg, M.E.; Gorn, G.J.; and Gibson, W. TV messages for snack and breakfast foods: Do they influence children's preferences? *J Consum Res* 5(Sept.):73–81, 1978.

Gorn, G.J., and Goldberg, M.E. Children's responses to repetitive television commercials. *J Consum Res* 6(Mar.):421–424, 1980.

Gorn, G.J., and Goldberg, M.E. Behavioral evidence of the effects of televised food messages on children. *J Consum Res* 9(Sept.):200–205, 1982.

Grabowski, H.G. The effects of advertising on the interindustry distribution of demand. *Explor Econ Res* 3(Winter):21–75, 1976.

Greenwald, A.C., and Leavitt, C. Audience involvement in advertising: Four levels. *J Consum Res* 11(Jun.):581–592, 1984.

Gunter, B. Determinants of television viewing preferences. In: Zillmann, D., and Bryant, J., eds. *Selective Exposure to Communication.* Hillsdale, NJ: Lawrence Erlbaum Associates, 1985. pp. 93–112.

Haley, R.I. *Developing Effective Communications Strategy.* New York: John Wiley, 1985.

Hastings, G.B. Sponsorship works differently from advertising. *Int J Advert* 3(2):171–176, 1984.

Henderson, P.L., and Brown, S.E. Effectiveness of a Special Promotional Campaign for Frozen Concentrated Orange Juice. Report No. 356. Washington, DC: U.S. Department of Agriculture Economic Research Service, 1961.

Henderson, P.L.; Hind, J.F.; and Brown, S.E. Sales effects of two campaign themes. *J Advert Res* 6(Dec.):2–11, 1961.

Herr, P.M. Priming price: Prior knowledge and context effects. *J Consum Res* 16(Jun.):67–75, 1989.

Higgins, E.T., and King, G. Accessibility of social constructs: Information processing consequences of individual and contextual variability. In: Cantor, N., and Kihlstrom, J., eds. *Personality, Cognition, and Social Interaction.* Hillsdale, NJ: Lawrence Erlbaum Associates, 1981. pp. 69–122.

Holman, R.H., and Hecker, S. Advertising impact: Creative elements affecting brand saliency. In: *Current Issues and Research in Advertising.* Ann Arbor, MI: University of Michigan School of Business, 1983.

Hoofnagle, W.S. The effectiveness of advertising for farm products. *J Advert Res* 3(4):2–6, 1963.

Jessor, R., and Jessor, S.L. *Problem Behavior and Psychosocial Development: A Longitudinal Study of Youth.* New York: Academic Press, 1977.

Johnson, L. Alternative economic estimates of the effect of advertising on the demand for alcoholic beverages in the United Kingdom. *Int J Advert* 4(1):19–25, 1985.

Kennedy, J.R. How program environment affects TV commercials. *J Advert Res* 11:33–38, 1971.

Krugman, H.E. Television program interest and commercial interruption: Are commercials on interesting programs less effective? *J Advert Res* 23(1):21–23, 1983.

Krugman, H.E. Point of view: Limits of attention to advertising. *J Advert Res* 28(Oct./Nov.):47–50, 1988.

Lambin, J. *Advertising, Competition and Market Conduct in Oligopoly Over Time: An Econometric Investigation in Western Countries.* Amsterdam: North-Holland, 1976.

Lastovicka, J.L.; Murry, J.P., Jr.; Joachimsthaler, E.A.; Bhalla, G.; and Scheurich, J. A lifestyle typology to model young male drinking and driving. *J Consum Res* 14(Sept.):257–263, 1987.

Linn, M.C.; de Benedictis, T.; and Delucchi, K. Adolescent reasoning about advertisements: Preliminary investigations. *Child Devel* 53:1599–1613, 1982.

Lipman, J. Television ads ring up no sale in complex study of consumers. *Wall Street Journal.* Feb. 15, 1989, p. B6.

Lloyd, D.W., and Clancy, K.J. The effects of television program involvement on advertising response: Implications for media planning. In: *Transcript Proceedings of the First Annual Advertising Research Foundation Media Research Workshop.* New York: Advertising Research Foundation, 1989. pp. 177–192.

Lodish, L. *How Advertising Works.* Chicago: Information Resources, 1991.

M. Shanken Communications. U.S. Drinks Marketers Cut Ad Spending 9% in 1989. *Impact.* Oct. 1, 1990. p. 1.

M. Shanken Communications. Ad Spending Shrinks 11.5% in 1990 as Drinks Marketers Pull in the Reigns. *Impact.* Oct. 15, 1991. p. 1.

McGuinness, T. An econometric analysis of total demand for alcoholic beverages in the U.K., 1956-75. *J Ind Econ* 29(Sept.):85–108, 1980.

McLuhan, M., and Fiore, Q. *The Medium Is the Message.* New York: Bantam Books, 1967.

MEE Productions. *The MEE Report: Reaching the Hip-Hop Generation.* Philadelphia: MEE Productions, 1992.

Miller, C. Moves by P&G, Heinz Rekindle Fears That Brands Are In Danger. *Marketing News* 26(12):1–15, 1992.

Moore, R.L., and Moschis, G.P. Teenagers' reactions to advertising. *J Advert* 7(4):24–30, 1978.

Murray, J.P. *Television and Youth: 25 Years of Research and Controversy.* Boys Town, NE: Boys Town Center for the Study of Youth Development, 1980.

Naber, J. "The Sales Promotion Explosion." The James Webb Young Fund Address, Department of Advertising, University of Illinois, Urbana, IL, 1986.

Ornstein, S.I., and Hanssens, D.M. Alcohol control laws and the consumption of distilled spirits and beer. *J Consum Res* 12(2):200–213, 1985.

Payne, J.W., and Bettman, J.R. Behavioral decision research: A constructive processing perspective. *Ann Rev Psychol* 43:87–131, 1992.

Pechmann, C., and Stewart, D.W. The role of comparative advertising: Documenting its effects on attention, recall, and purchase intentions. *J Consum Res* 17(Sept.):180–191, 1990.

Petty, R.; Cacioppo, J.; and Schumann, D. Central and peripheral routes to advertising effectiveness: The moderating role of involvement. *J Consum Res* 10(Sept.):135–146, 1983.

Raj, S.P. The effects of advertising on high and low loyalty segments. *J Consum Res* 9(Jun.):77–89, 1982.

Ratner, E. *FTC Staff Report on Television Advertising to Children.* Washington, DC: Federal Trade Commission, 1978.

Raymond, C. *Advertising Research: The State of the Art.* New York: Association of National Advertisers, 1976. pp. 57–58.

Robertson, T.S., and Rossiter, J.R. Children and commercial persuasion: An attribution theory analysis. *J Consum Res* 1(1):13–20, 1974.

Robertson, T.S., and Rossiter, J.R. Short-run advertising effects on children: A field study. *J Market Res* 13:68–70, 1976.

Robertson, T.S., and Rossiter, J.R. Children's responsiveness to commercials. *J Commun* 27:101–106, 1977.

Rossiter, J.R. Does TV advertising affect children? *J Advert Res* 19(1):49–53, 1979.

Russell, C. People Who Lust After Big Numbers. *American Demographics* 11(May):2, 1989.

Saffer, H. Alcohol advertising bans and alcohol abuse: An international perspective. *J Health Econ* 10:65–79, 1991.

Schmalensee, D.H. Today's top priority advertising questions. *J Advert Res* (Apr./May):49–60, 1983.

Schultz, D.E. Media research users want. *J Advert Res* (Dec.):13–17, 1979.

Schultz, D.E. Integrated marketing communications. *J Promotion Manage* 1(1):99–104, 1991.

Selvanathan, E. Advertising and alcohol demand in the UK: Further results. *Int J Advert* 8(2):181–188, 1989.

Singh, S.N., and Churchill, G.A. Arousal and advertising effectiveness. *J Advert* 16(1):4–10, 1987.

Smith, G. The effect of advertising on juvenile smoking behavior. *Int J Advert* 9(1):57–79, 1990.

Soldow, G.F., and Principe, V. Response to commercials as a function of program context *J Advert Res* 21(2):59–65, 1981.

Stewart, D.W. Measures, methods, and models of advertising response. *J Advert Res* 29(Jun./Jul.):54–60, 1989.

Stewart, D.W. Speculations on the future of advertising research. *J Advert* 21(Sept.):1–18, 1992.

Stewart, D.W.; Pechmann, C.; Ratneshwar, S.; Stroud, J.; and Bryant, B. Methodological and theoretical foundations of advertising copy testing: A review. In: *Current Issues and Research in Advertising.* Ann Arbor, MI: University of Michigan School of Business, 1985. pp. 1–74.

Stewart, D.W.; Tellis, G.; and Sanft, H. "Advertising Effects in the Market Place: What We Know About How Advertising Does (and Does Not) Work." Working Paper, Department of Marketing, University of Southern California, 1990.

Stewart, D.W., and Ward, S. Media effects on advertising. In: Bryant, J., and Zillman, D., eds. *Media Effects: Advances in Theory and Research.* Hillsdale, NJ: Lawrence Erlbaum Associates, 1994. pp. 315–363.

Stoneman, Z., and Brody, G.H. Immediate and long-term recognition and generalization of advertised products as a function of age and presentation mode. *Develop Psychol* 19(1):56–61, 1983.

Swenson, C.A., and Seagren, B. Marketing Issues of Sports Tie-ins. *Bank Marketing*. Dec. 1988. pp. 34–36.

Tellis, G.J. Advertising exposure, loyalty, and brand purchase: A two stage model of choice. *J Market Res* 25(May):134–144, 1988.

Tolley, B.S. The search. In: Clark, E.; Brock, T.; and Stewart, D.W., eds. *Attention, Attitude, and Affect in Response to Advertising*. Hillsdale, NJ: Lawrence Erlbaum Associates, 1993.

Warburton, C. *The Economic Results of Prohibition*. New York: Columbia University Press, 1932.

Ward, S. Effects of television advertising on children and adolescents. In: Rubinstein, E.A.; Comstock, G.A.; and Murray, J.P., eds. *Television and Social Behavior, Volume 4, Television in Day-to-Day Life*. Washington, DC: U.S. Department of Health, Education, and Welfare, 1972. pp. 432–451.

Ward, S. Consumer socialization. *J Consum Res* 1(1):1–14, 1974.

Ward, S.; Levinson, D.; and Wackman, D. Children's attention to television advertising. In: Rubinstein, E.A.; Comstock, G.A.; and Murray, J.P., eds. *Television and Social Behavior, Volume 4, Television in Day-to-Day Life*. Washington, DC: U.S. Department of Health, Education, and Welfare, 1972*a*. pp. 491–515.

Ward, S.; Reale, G.; and Levinson, D. Children's perceptions, explanations and judgments of television advertising: A further exploration, attention to television advertising. In: Rubinstein, E.A.; Comstock, G.A.; and Murray, J.P., eds. *Television and Social Behavior, Volume 4, Television in Day-to-Day Life*. Washington, DC: U.S. Department of Health, Education, and Welfare, 1972*b*. pp. 468–490.

Ward, S.; Wackman, D.B.; and Wartella, E. *How Children Learn to Buy: The Development of Consumer Information Processing Skills*. Beverly Hills: Sage, 1977. pp. 307–322.

Wartella, E. Individual differences in children's responses to television advertising. In: Palmer, E.L., and Dorr, A., eds. *Children and the Faces of Television: Teaching, Violence, Selling*. New York: Academic Press, 1980. pp. 307–322.

Wilber, D. Linking sports and sponsors. *J Bus Strategy* (Jul./Aug.), 1988. pp. 8–10.

Wyer, R.S., and Srull, T.K. Category accessibility: Some theoretical and empirical issues concerning the processing of social stimulus information. In: Higgins, E.T.; Herman, C.P.; and Zanna, M.P., eds. *Social Cognition: The Ontario Symposium*. Hillsdale, NJ: Lawrence Erlbaum Associates, 1981. pp. 161–197.

Yi, Y. Cognitive and affective priming effects of the context for print advertisements. *J Advert* 19(2):40–48, 1990*a*.

Yi, Y. The effects of contextual priming in print advertisements. *J Consum Res* 17(Sept.):215–222, 1990*b*.

Zillmann, D., and Bryant, J. *Selective Exposure to Communication*. Hillsdale, NJ: Lawrence Erlbaum Associates, 1985.

Chapter 14

Conducting Research on Nontraditional Media in the Marketing of Alcoholic Beverages

Michael B. Mazis[1]

The use of nontraditional media to promote alcoholic beverages is an emerging public policy topic of great interest to consumer groups and government agencies. On September 3, 1992, the Center for Science in the Public Interest and nearly two dozen consumer groups asked the Federal Trade Commission to stop a number of nontraditional promotional practices. Among those cited was product placement of alcoholic beverages in movies, television programs, and music videos, noting that "it is illegal for many viewers to even purchase some of these products that are being subliminally marketed to them" (Center for Science and the Public Interest, p. ii). Also mentioned was the use of alcoholic beverage advertising on billboards and scoreboards at high school and college sporting events.

My comments about nontraditional media address four issues. First, I will comment on four myths about the effects of advertising and nontraditional media. Second, I will discuss what the research shows about the effects of alcohol advertising. Third, I will examine the difficulties of conducting research on nontraditional media effects. And, fourth, I will indicate how such research might be conducted.

MYTHS ABOUT THE EFFECTS OF NONTRADITIONAL MEDIA

There are several myths about the effects of advertising and nontraditional media. The first myth is about the advertising–sales relationship. The myth is that for mature products, such as alcohol or cigarettes, that advertising affects brand choice but does not affect overall category demand. Mature products have slower growth than new products, and advertisers often focus on shifting demand from one established brand to other brands on the market. This is a well-established marketing principle.

[1]Department of Marketing, College of Business, American University, Washington, DC 20016-8044

However, new alcohol and cigarette users tend to be young, and older users literally die off, stop their use, and reduce product use as they age. Thus, heavy consumption of beer occurs primarily among people under 30 years of age. Therefore, to maintain demand for a mature product, an alcoholic beverage company that sells beer must cultivate many new users, or sales will decline substantially. As a result, an alcoholic beverage company or a cigarette firm must be concerned with attracting new, young users, and it must focus on maintaining primary demand as well as on cultivating demand for specific brands. In oligopolistic industries, the larger companies must take the lead in assuring their stockholders that product category demand will be maintained.

A second myth is that advertisers are able to target their efforts to legal-age drinkers. Beer consumers, in particular, tend to be young. When advertisers direct their appeals to young adults 21 to 30 years of age, there is a natural "spillover" effect. That is, by targeting 21- or 23-year-olds, the advertising campaign is likely to have an effect on underage viewers as well. There has been much criticism of Budweiser's Spuds McKenzie and some of the recent cartoon-type characters, such as Bud Man and Miller's extraterrestrials. Considerable caution is needed with this type of advertising because of the possible spillover effect to young viewers. Even though ads may be targeted to legal-age drinkers, the spillover to youth must be carefully monitored.

A third myth is that new technologies and nonmedia promotion for alcoholic beverage products are unlikely to have an effect on demand stimulation. Stewart and Rice (chapter 13, this volume) claim that these nontraditional media are likely to have much less effect than traditional advertising on total alcoholic beverage demand.

There are two issues to consider. There are many types of nontraditional media. Some forms of these media would be unlikely to affect demand, while other types might stimulate demand. For example, strategies like including a beer company's name on tee-shirts and sponsoring auto racing and cultural festivals are likely to promote high audience involvement with the brand and the product category. These strategies may influence underlying demand because audiences are closely associated with the product. On the other hand, approaches such as product placement in movies are less likely to increase long-term sales because they do not promote high audience involvement.

In addition, we must consider whether demand stimulation is the right dependent variable. Sales or product demand is not the focus of commercial advertising research. Advertising research typically examines other dependent measures, such as recall, recognition, brand image, and brand attribute associations. Stewart and Rice's assertion that nontraditional media are unlikely to have an effect on demand stimulation is difficult to disprove, because definitive evidence is difficult to collect and carefully controlled research is difficult to conduct.

The fourth myth is that adolescents are skeptical of advertising, and therefore they are unlikely to be affected by advertising and by nontraditional media. When questioned in surveys, most people claim that they are skeptical of ads. However, even if consumers have learned to be skeptical of advertising, it may still ultimately influence their behavior. In some cases, nontraditional media may have a greater impact on behavior than traditional advertising because consumers' usual defenses against advertising may not be raised against nontraditional forms of promotion.

RESEARCH ON THE EFFECTS OF ALCOHOL ADVERTISING

Advertising research has shown that low-involvement learning from repetitive advertising exposures tends to take place over time. That is, adolescents and adults form associations between alcohol use and important values, goals, and lifestyles, even though they may not agree with the ads, may not like them, or may be skeptical of them. Through repeated exposure to advertising images they may still learn to make important associations.

Low-involvement learning may be even more extensive from exposure to nontraditional media than from exposure to advertising. Promotion of alcoholic beverages through nontraditional media may not be viewed by consumers as advertising. Inherent skepticism toward advertising may result in counterarguing, thereby reducing an ad's impact. Whereas consumers might argue mentally against assertions made in advertising, they might not engage in such a process when exposed to nontraditional media because promotions such as event sponsorships might not be viewed as persuasive communications.

At present, there is no comparative evidence about the amount of counterarguing that takes place when consumers are exposed to advertising and to nontraditional media. This is a fruitful area for research. When consumers are confronted with various media forms, what mental processes take place?

PROBLEMS WITH CONDUCTING RESEARCH ON THE EFFECTS OF NONTRADITIONAL MEDIA

Researchers have not had great success in studying the effects of traditional media. Studies of nontraditional media effects are likely to be even more challenging. There are several issues to consider when designing studies on the impact of nontraditional media.

First, alcohol advertising research must be contrasted with nontraditional media studies. The typical experimental research study uses advertising as an independent variable and alcohol consumption or abuse as a dependent variable. These experimental studies generally find that alcohol ads do not affect consumption or abuse. There are a number of reasons for the failure to find a consistent relationship between alcohol advertising and alcohol consumption or abuse. It is difficult to uncover an effect in a laboratory experiment in which subjects are given a few exposures to advertising. They have had thousands of exposures previously, and researchers are likely to find that a small number of additional exposures to alcohol advertising has little impact on alcohol-related consumer behavior. In addition, the dependent variable, consumption, that is used in many of these studies is difficult to influence in a laboratory setting. As a result, researchers have developed contrived situations to simulate "normal" consumption behavior.

What is the potential application of traditional laboratory research methods to studying the effects of nontraditional media? Laboratory studies for nontraditional media are even more difficult to develop than laboratory studies on advertising effects. How does a researcher expose subjects to tee-shirts? How can research simulate an "event" in a laboratory? It is, therefore, difficult or impossible to conduct meaningful laboratory experiments on the effects of nontraditional media.

Field experiments on advertising effects are also very difficult to conduct. How would a researcher conduct such research without the cooperation of leading alcoholic beverage manufacturers? Similar problems are also evident for field experiments involving nontraditional media.

Cross-sectional surveys may also be ineffective as a method of studying advertising effects. Researchers typically survey several hundred people, classify consumers as heavy, light, or nondrinkers, and then examine the correlation between advertising exposure and alcohol consumption levels.

Not surprisingly, some studies have reported greater advertising exposure for heavy drinkers than for light drinkers. As a result, some researchers have assumed that this finding "proves" that advertising causes people to drink alcoholic beverages. No matter how many covariates are used in the analysis of these data, it is difficult or impossible to eliminate the possibility of reverse causation; drinkers of alcoholic beverages are likely to expose themselves to more alcoholic beverage advertising.

For example, adolescents who are less likely to watch television and more likely to read books are probably also less likely to drink alcoholic beverages. As a result, survey research that has been conducted using survey methods has not been useful in assessing advertising–demand effects, and such research may be misleading. Investigators often report "causal" relationships, but in fact, such studies are attacked by critics for their methodological flaws.

What about the prospects of conducting survey research on the effects of nontraditional media? The same problems are likely to occur. Studies that investigate adolescents wearing tee-shirts with alcoholic beverage insignia or attending motorcycle races sponsored by alcoholic beverage manufacturers are likely to find that many of these adolescents drink alcoholic beverages. However, the causal link between exposure to these forms of nontraditional advertising and consumption of alcoholic beverages cannot be proven. Therefore, such cross-sectional studies will not advance knowledge about the impact of nontraditional media.

What are the prospects of conducting econometric research on the effects of advertising or nontraditional media? Most econometric research studies conclude that alcohol advertising expenditures are not correlated with demand for alcohol. One of the reasons for these findings is that in any given period, ad expenditures and demand do not show much variation, thereby making it difficult to detect any relationship between changes in advertising spending and changes in alcoholic beverage consumption. In addition, a substantial portion of users are habituated, and any change that might result from advertising is likely to occur to a small segment of people. These econometric studies are not sufficiently sensitive to detect effects for a narrow market segment.

Cross-sectional studies comparing alcohol abuse in countries with alcoholic beverage ad bans and countries without ad bans have also been criticized. Public attitudes toward alcohol use and abuse may differ in countries with and without ad bans. Such attitudinal differences and usage patterns may affect alcohol abuse more strongly than any advertising prohibitions. As might be expected, econometric studies on nontraditional media effects are even more difficult to conduct because expenditures on these forms of media are not reported.

CONDUCTING RESEARCH ON NONTRADITIONAL MEDIA EFFECTS

What types of research should be conducted on the effects of nontraditional media? First, the major focus should be on areas such as event marketing, where there is high audience involvement and where there are associations between the brand, the product category, and the event. Also, the effects of these practices on vulnerable groups, such as children and adolescents, should be explored.

Second, in conducting research on nontraditional media, attention should be devoted to exploring theories about how a particular nontraditional medium is likely to work. That is, a hypothesized mechanism should be posited, such as a hierarchy-of-effects model, a cognitive-response model, or an attitude-toward-the-ad model, and effects should be measured across different levels of that model.

Third, attention needs to be devoted to selecting the appropriate dependent variable. Alcohol consumption and alcohol abuse are not useful criterion variables because they are not sufficiently sensitive to variations in advertising or promotion, especially in laboratory experiments. Increased attention should be devoted to the selection of "intermediate" variables, such as perceptions, attitudes, cognitive responses, and emotional responses. The key focus should be on the development of associations between alcohol and a particular lifestyle, a particular emotion, or a particular value that is emphasized in advertising or promotions. Academic researchers need to employ the same variables that advertisers consider in message creation and evaluation. Laboratory experiments can employ these "intermediate" dependent variables much more effectively than they can employ alcoholic beverage consumption behavior as a criterion measure.

Fourth, studies should focus on how children and adolescents learn about alcohol use, and the role that advertising plays in this learning process. This developmental perspective has been useful in other areas, such as understanding children's viewing of advertising on television. Both laboratory studies and ethnographic methods would be effective for investigating these issues. Cross-sectional surveys also may be developed to question different age groups about their exposure to advertising and promotion and about the impact of marketing techniques on their perceptions of alcoholic beverage products.

Research on how children and adolescents learn about alcohol and how to use it should focus attention on understanding the impact of advertising and promotions on African Americans, Hispanics, and Native Americans. These groups have been the frequent targets of alcoholic beverage promotions. A recent *Washington Post* article (Halken 1992) points out efforts to target Native Americans at a 1990 Labor Day Weekend celebration. A local beer distributor hired two men dressed as the Budweiser mascots Spuds McKenzie and Bud Man, who tossed to children miniature rolls of candy packaged to look like tiny beer cans.

The article goes on to discuss the role of advertising and promotion in initiating drinking among Native-American youth. One 13-year-old Native-American girl described how alcohol and alcohol advertising were a way of life from early childhood. She noted that beer bumper stickers were pasted on school binders and rodeo prize jackets were decorated with beer logos. "Now beer ads are a temptation," she said, "because they are everywhere, and they make me think about how good I felt when I was getting drunk and forgetting everything" (p. 11). These comments point to the need for research on the role that advertisements and promotions play in adolescent drinking initiation.

In conclusion, effective research on the impact of traditional advertising and nontraditional media is needed. However, research that focuses on establishing a direct link between advertising or nontraditional media and alcoholic beverage sales or consumption will continue to be unsuccessful. Successful research will emphasize the processes used by adolescents and children in learning about alcoholic beverages. Such research will be based on theories about how a particular medium is likely to work. Although research on the effects of nontraditional media is difficult to carry out, it can lead to more effective alcohol prevention strategies if it is carefully conducted.

REFERENCES

Center for Science and the Public Interest. Petition to the Federal Trade Commission, September 3, 1992. p. ii.

Halken, M. Liquor Ads Targeted at Indians Dismay Some Tribal Leaders. *Washington Post.* Sept. 22, 1992, Health Section. p. 11.

Chapter 15

Reconceptualizing Alcohol Advertising Effects: A Consumer Psychology Perspective

Joel B. Cohen[1]

My approach to alcohol advertising comes from a background in consumer behavior research and from the perspective of about 12 years of involvement in the relationship between cigarette marketing and advertising (and their proposed regulation) and smoking behavior.

It is important, at the outset, to call attention to some important differences—as well as some similarities—between tobacco and alcohol advertising issues. In terms of public policy interest, there is a stated commitment to the goal of a smoke-free society. (By many estimates, about one out of four regular smokers die from tobacco use.) Moreover, there is a firm commitment to shield nonsmokers from the deleterious effects of cigarette smoke. Hence, existing public policy seeks to confine use of the product to existing users who do not or cannot quit, and to reduce risks among nonsmokers.

With respect to alcohol, public policy appears to have a more limited agenda. The behavioral outcomes that are apparently of greatest interest to the National Institute on Alcohol Abuse and Alcoholism are such things as deaths from highway accidents, domestic violence, and health problems such as cirrhosis of the liver and fetal alcohol syndrome. Hence, the current public policy concern appears to be over such issues as curbing irresponsible use and underage use.

Accordingly, the areas of interest in advertising content should also be somewhat different. With cigarettes, advertising that increases the attractiveness of smoking or its social acceptability may be counter to the public interest because of the potential effect of these ads on new smokers. There is also a legitimate concern about ads that imply health reassurance, since people might then continue to smoke instead of quitting.

[1]Center for Consumer Research, College of Business Administration, Bryan Hall, University of Florida, Gainesville, FL 32611

The substantive interest in advertising content for alcohol, on the other hand, may well be limited to advertising that enhances the likelihood of underage drinking or that leads to irresponsible or excessive use of alcohol. Other than concerns of this type, there may be little justification or public support for efforts to restrict alcohol advertising.

A perplexing issue concerning both products is the difficulty of isolating new smokers or underage drinkers from advertising that society is prepared to accept or tolerate for other consumers (e.g., existing smokers, people legally entitled to use alcohol). It is exceedingly difficult to draw a magic curtain separating these groups. However, because of the risks inherent in even moderate use of cigarettes, society may be willing to accept broader restrictions on cigarette advertising content, as well as on medium, time, or location.

For alcohol, society seems willing to accept advertising restrictions for some types of products (e.g., hard liquor) in media or locations likely to attract a high proportion of underage people. However, unless the advertising content is aimed specifically at a disapproved audience (as judged by either placement or executional tactics) or at an unacceptable outcome (e.g., drinking to get drunk), there may be little widespread support for restrictions on an advertiser's perceived right to present the product so as to heighten its appeal. It is beyond the scope of this chapter to discuss the regulatory domain of unfair and/or deceptive practices, although the omission from advertising of information clearly relevant to one's decision to use alcohol (and in particular amounts and under particular conditions) may convey an inaccurate and potentially misleading impression of the product and its risks.

Most current conceptualizations of advertising effects are predicated on models that link advertising directly to certain communications objectives (e.g., increasing product awareness/accessibility, informing potential customers of particular offerings, establishing associations between products and attributes/benefits, developing favorable attitudes and interest in using the product). These are generally referred to as hierarchical models of advertising effects—as also discussed by Thorson (chapter 11, this volume). These models implicitly recognize that effective advertising serves to increase the likelihood of purchase by creating a state of readiness to respond favorably to the product itself or to environmental cues relevant to product purchase or use. Such a favorable readiness to respond is often undermined by a variety of factors including a lack of opportunity or ability to take the necessary steps (e.g., due to product unavailability or inadequate funds or time), unforseen or changed circumstances (e.g., exposure to new information or social pressure, changes in goals), and the availability of alternative actions (e.g., competing or substitute products).

If the advertising has targeted appropriate communications objectives (i.e., those most likely to increase the likelihood of purchase, such as developing a favorable attitude toward visiting a car dealer's showroom or creating "top of mind" brand awareness for a frequently purchased supermarket item) and succeeds in accomplishing its objectives, marketers know to look elsewhere for the problem if sales are disappointing (e.g., at product weaknesses or pricing).

It is important to begin with a similarly meaningful conceptualization of alcohol advertising effects at the individual level. There is no reason to expect a strong relationship between marginal changes in yearly advertising expenditures (as a proxy for advertising exposure) and the amount of alcohol consumed. People probably do not drink proportionately more beer, liquor, or wine as a result of small departures from a rationally determined baseline amount of advertising. Such proportional effects as could be observed statistically would hinge on converting nonusers to users as a result of incremental changes in advertising expenditures. Even ignoring the fact that new users' consumption would be such a small proportion of the total that the effect would be hard to detect, such marginal analyses simply do not fit into a good working model of advertising effects.

To look beyond alcohol consumption as a dependent variable and expect to find any sort of year-to-year relationship between changes in advertising expenditures and alcohol-related health problems or fatalities is a near impossibility. The kind of long-term controlled experiment necessary to estimate the effects of exposure to advertising on such dependent variables (i.e., to isolate advertising effects apart from broad social trends, background factors, and so on) simply cannot be run.

Researchers are faced with a choice. The first option is to sift through extremely "noisy" behavioral data trying to detect signs of an "input–output" relationship. The difficulty of this task insures that the best one can hope for is evidence of a weak relationship. This type of evidence is generally translated into a conclusion that advertising plays only a weak role in the use and abuse of alcohol. The irony is that advertising effects on attitudinal variables may in fact be quite strong and therefore instrumental in *contributing* to product use.

The second option for researchers is to actually study what alcohol advertising does. A simplified model might imagine that advertising first produces a set of communications effects, which can be loosely described as object–concept associations, and that these in turn produce a set of behaviors toward alcohol as an "object." These object–concept associations can be grouped into six general categories. One category would be product–performance associations, such as the belief that a product does something and/or provides a certain benefit.

A related category comprises product attribute or component associations, the belief that a product contains or has certain features or ingredients. These associations are sometimes considered to be subservient to product performance associations in that attributes are often valued largely as a means to a desired end.

A third type of association is product–product associations; for example, the belief that brand X is similar to brand Z. A new entrant into the marketplace, for example, may have the advertising objective of trying to have its brand perceived as similar to another well-established product or brand. A related type of product–product association would be brand superiority claims.

The fourth category is product–social identity associations. The intent is to link the shared meaning of a product symbol with one's personal identity; for example, this product is for "macho men."

A fifth category is product–emotionality associations; for example, the affective tone of an ad may be designed to associate a product with feelings of pride, love, or some other important emotion. The last category is product–personal history associations. The old Campbell soup ads were an excellent example; they were marvelous at bringing to mind childhood memories of mother, winter, and warmth.

All advertising is designed to create specific object–concept associations, and a considerable amount of research is often done to decide which associations are most appropriate. In carrying out this type of analysis, the advertiser will typically work backward from the behavior of interest and consider which associations, if learned (and in *some* cases if believed), will support the behavior that the advertiser wants. The belief in or acceptance of an object–concept association is not essential for every category of object–concept associations. If an advertiser is making a product performance claim, it is very important that it be accepted and believed, as people may well discount such claims in the absence of supporting evidence or a credible communicator. But associations to social identity or emotionality are often delivered indirectly (e.g., by showing certain kinds of people or settings in ads) rather than presented as factual claims. People do not generally analyze or question their own decoding of sensory input. The conceptual models that apply to traditional forms of persuasion, such as rhetoric or political speeches, do not apply very well to forms of modern advertising that rely on low involvement formation of associations.

In terms of research on advertising and the use of alcohol, it is useful to ask, "What evidence is needed that we do not have?" and "Where do we go from here?" As already indicated, looking for evidence that directly links advertising to product consumption and resulting behavioral outcomes is not likely to be productive. But if we break this larger issue down, there is a great deal of meaningful research that can be and is being done.

As has been discussed, advertising professionals understand that even good ads often cannot be expected to generate behavior (ads announcing special sales would be an exception). Advertisers are willing to rely on a theory that presumes that there is a probabilistic relationship between intermediate communications effects and behavior. Advertising practitioners, in essence, focus their attention on developing advertising that increases the likelihood of the behavior, and their ads do this either by generating necessary object–concept associations or by strengthening already existing associations.

With this in mind let's return to what it is that alcohol researchers know and don't know about the initial link between alcohol advertising and relevant object–concept associations and the second link between these object–concept associations and alcohol-related behavior. There is simply no reason *not* to proceed on the same premise that advertising researchers have followed for years: that the link between object–concept associations and behavior toward the object is well established. Policymakers should simply face the fact that this relationship is probabilistic. People in business understand that by spending advertising dollars they can change the odds: creating desired associations for a large group of people (other things staying pretty much the same) leads to an increase in sales.

So if we accept this basic premise, what kind of research *is* needed? Useful content analysis work has already been carried out in this area, and this is a good way to examine the types of associations appearing in alcohol advertising over time, as well as for specific products and specifically targeted audiences. The parallel—on the consumer side—would be to examine what was actually conveyed. There are many ways of looking at the latter issue, including qualitative investigations, multidimensional scaling and other meaning-based measurements, and even reaction-time measures of the strength of object–concept associations. A further step would be to examine any link between these conveyed associations and product-use beliefs, especially those beliefs that may lead to risky behavior (e.g., "demonstrating you can hold your liquor is a sign of strength").

A key difference between standard advertising research studies and the issues addressed in many of the chapters in this monograph is that the latter appropriately focus on the cumulative impact of years of exposure to alcohol "messages." Clearly, studies that examine the effects of individual ads have a much more limited objective. However, the same general approach (i.e., categorizing ad content and investigating whether it has been translated into similar product associations and correlated product beliefs) can be employed in larger scale investigations. Consistent evidence of successful communication of object–concept associations carries the strong presumption that alcohol advertising is achieving its desired communications objectives. The research goal would be to focus explicitly on what has been conveyed and the effect on related beliefs and attitudes (assuming the subsequent probabilistic link to behavior). Furthermore, since the public policy interest is most strongly concerned with advertising targeted to vulnerable audiences and that encourages irresponsible use, this approach should be helpful in identifying the most problematic types of portrayals of alcohol.

The final point discussed here relates to the frequently heard comment that both cigarette and alcohol advertising function primarily to foster brand switching. Those who take this position support it by relying on the unavoidably weak evidence linking overall advertising expenditures to increases in consumption (an ironic outcome of "buying into" an inappropriate conceptual model). Whenever advertising is effective in positioning individual brands as having more or less optimal collections of features, benefits, or associations for each clustering of consumers (i.e., reducing the psychological distance between what a product has to offer and what specific people most want a product to do, be, or convey), each consumer's likelihood of using the product (through one of many brands) is optimized. Therefore, strengthening each brand's appeal does far more than give it an advantage for the competitive battle; summed over all brands, the likelihood of *product use* increases as well.

Health Promotion: Public Service Announcements, Media Campaigns, and Media Advocacy

Chapter 16

Mass Media and Public Health: Moving the Focus From the Individual To thc Environment

Lawrence Wallack[1] and William DeJong[2]

While a woman sings, accompanied by soft acoustic music, the camera pans a horribly polluted river. A male announcer intones, "Thirty years ago children played on its bank. Striped bass, salmon, and more than 30 species of fish streaked through its crystal waters." The announcer goes on to say that the corporation whose factory is located on the banks of this once-great river "understands its responsibility" and is doing something about the problem. Several years ago, he explains, the corporation "hired thirty men, highly respected in their fields, and one million dollars later they came up with this new advertising campaign."

This satirical public service announcement (PSA) was never seen on television, but it cuts to the heart of public service advertising, the real function of which may have little to do with meaningfully addressing important problems, but a lot to do with image promotion and shifting blame. Using public service advertising as a public relations tool, entities such as the tobacco industry, the alcohol industry, and other manufacturing companies position themselves as not only part of the solution to the problem, but as the very ones to *define* what the solution should be. Often these types of campaigns are done in conjunction with or with the tacit approval of public health professionals.

Virtually all would agree that the mass media can play a significant role in promoting health in our society. Public service advertising campaigns are a legitimate part of that role, but it is questionable whether such campaigns should be the primary means of media involvement.

This chapter will describe three general approaches to using the media in the prevention of alcohol problems. The first is the public service advertising campaign,

[1]School of Public Health, University of California at Berkeley, 516 Warren Hall, Berkeley, CA 94720

[2]School of Public Health, Harvard University, Boston, MA 02115

the most widely used and least effective approach. The second is the comprehensive health communication campaign, a less frequently used approach that has produced positive results in some cases. The third approach, media advocacy, addresses public health problems as collective phenomena and uses the tools of political activism. This approach is new to the health field, and examples of it are just beginning to be documented (Wallack et al. 1993). In reviewing these strategies, this chapter focuses on the basic but often unstated assumptions that underlie each approach and raises both conceptual and practical issues about their use.

CHANGES IN THE PUBLIC HEALTH PERSPECTIVE

To establish a context for this review, we first must consider the evolution of a new environmental perspective in understanding the nature of public health problems. Originally, the field of public health focused largely on broad social and environmental factors as causes of disease. Then, beginning in the latter part of the 18th century with the advent of a germ theory of disease, attention shifted to individual-level explanations for disease causation. In the 20th century, as infectious diseases receded and chronic diseases emerged as the primary health problem, a focus on lifestyle and behavioral factors became more pronounced, a shift that resulted in an even stronger focus on individual responsibility for disease. In recent years, however, a new environmental perspective has emerged that has redirected attention to the role of policy- and community-level factors in health promotion (Dubos 1959; Tesh 1988).

This new environmental perspective includes both a physical and a social element. For example, policies and practices that support product availability and marketing of tobacco also help cultivate positive social perceptions about this product. As a result, key objectives of the tobacco control movement include limiting billboard advertising, sponsorship of community activities, and cigarette vending machines, while also promoting clean indoor air legislation. In essence, tobacco control advocates have sought to shift the focus from the behavior of the smoker to the behavior of the tobacco industry and to the policies that support its marketing activities.

This shift to an environmental perspective is also being seen increasingly in the alcohol field, particularly among minority communities. Advocacy and political action are emerging as fundamental weapons for health promotion, while individual health behavior change remains an important, but secondary, focus. It has come to be understood that prevention and health promotion is a process of changing political behavior in order to make personal behavior change more feasible. The likelihood of accomplishing personal behavior change is now being linked to the overall quality of the social and physical environment.

A focus on the immediate marketing and community-level environment is important but still fails to address the most significant variable regarding health status. An extensive body of literature clearly indicates that social class is the single most important determinant of health, with virtually every disease showing an association with measures of economic standing. This is not a simple rich–poor dichotomy, but a *graded* response that can be seen even within the upper quadrant of society (e.g.,

Haan et al. 1987; Smith and Egger 1992; Kitagawa and Hauser 1973). Recent work suggests that the most important factor within the social class construction may be level of education (Winkleby et al. 1992).

In cross-cultural comparisons, it appears that a society's health status is not linked solely to per capita income but also to its variability and therefore to the extent of deprivation within a society (Wilkinson 1992). The United States, for example, fares poorly on a number of key health indicators when compared to several countries that are less affluent but also show less variability in income.

The key point is that our ability to promote health is not linked so much to our capacity to disseminate information as to our ability to establish a more just and equitable society. The public health profession has always had a strong focus on stimulating social change. Indeed, the recent Institute of Medicine report on the future of public health defined the mission of public health as "the fulfillment of society's interest in assuring the conditions in which people can be healthy" (Institute of Medicine 1988, p. 40). Certainly, accurate health information helps foster these conditions, but it does little to address poverty, unemployment, or inadequate housing, which are the most important risk factors for disease. Promoting exercise and diet will do little good when people are poor, unemployed, or without shelter. The best, most expensive medical care in the world, as we have found out, cannot compensate for the adverse effects of poor living and working conditions.

PUBLIC SERVICE CAMPAIGNS

Most public service advertising represents the perspective of those who see individual choice as the crux of public health problems. And because choice is thought to result from a rational consideration of self-interest, problems of drinking and driving, tobacco use, drug use, poor diet, or lack of exercise are seen to be the result of failing to get the right information presented in the right way to the right people. The underlying theory appears to be that if people just knew better, they would not use drugs, drink to excess, smoke, and so forth. In a very specific way, these campaigns represent propaganda for the status quo in the sense that they exonerate the political-economic system from significant responsibility for addressing the problem (Wallack 1990*a*).

For example, in a recent review of PSA campaigns for reducing alcohol-impaired driving, DeJong and Atkin (1992) assessed 137 PSAs that were produced between 1987 and 1992 for national distribution. They found that these spots were targeted to a general audience and not necessarily to those at greatest risk; focused on increasing awareness or motivating personal behavior change; and ignored the social, legal, and economic environment that shapes individual behavior. Despite research data supporting the role of excise taxes in reducing alcohol-related traffic crashes, and despite the concern of the past two Surgeons General about the potential role of alcoholic beverage advertising, one is unlikely to see a media campaign that focuses on those environmental factors.

Campaigns that focus on individual choice give the appearance of being apolitical but are in fact providing a potent political message. One of the most frequently aired public service messages in the United States is produced by the privately funded

Partnership for a Drug-Free America (Buchanan and Wallack 1994). Far from taking a public health approach that focuses attention on environmental factors, this campaign instead reinforces the view that alcohol and other drug use is a problem that can best be solved through personal rather than social or political action. The Partnership's well-known "frying egg" spot ("This is your brain. This is drugs. This is your brain on drugs. Any questions?") promotes the idea that a complex social problem can be reduced to individual behavior deficits: If people just knew how bad drugs are, and if they had the proper self-discipline, they would not use them. A message like this, or one that tells us that designating a driver is the best solution to alcohol-impaired driving (DeJong and Wallack 1992), is really a commercial for the status quo. In essence, such messages suggest that the social system is working and that the fault for these problems resides solely with the persons themselves.

Public service campaigns of this type can serve the interests of those who seek to distance themselves from a problem or to discharge easily their responsibility to do something about it. For example, the Partnership, partially funded by alcohol and tobacco producers (Cotts 1992), focuses on marijuana and cocaine while ignoring alcohol and tobacco—drugs that kill far more people every year. Unfortunately, these two major killers have received relatively little attention in public service advertising.

When sponsored by private industry, public service campaigns can easily be confused with public relations efforts, where looking good rather than doing good is a key outcome. A recent analysis of beer industry-sponsored "moderation" campaigns concluded that such ads might be counterproductive, in that they improve public perception of the industry's image, while at the same time glamorizing beer consumption and increasing brand recognition (DeJong et al. 1992). A study of audience reactions to these ads showed that many college and high school students perceived them as sales-oriented messages, but still saw the brewers as more "responsible" and "respectable" for having produced them (Atkin et al. 1992).

The lack of critical attention to the social, legal, or economic environment that drives public health problems also serves the interest of media outlets that support public service campaigns. Because the public service function is seen as a way to enhance a station's image (Bollier 1989), local media outlets are pleased to participate in developing and airing a PSA campaign that is nonthreatening to their advertisers yet positions them as good community citizens.

Addressing public health issues is inherently political and controversial, yet public service campaigns are purposely noncontroversial. Indeed, in a survey of media gatekeepers, Freimuth (1985) found that "too controversial" was one of the factors that defined a poor PSA. Controversy can lead to audience loss, which can lead to advertiser flight, which can lead to reduced revenue for the media outlet. Whether a PSA will alienate viewers or sponsors is clearly a matter of importance.

Consider the role of public service advertising in the HIV/AIDS epidemic. The Centers for Disease Control and Prevention (CDC), stressing the need for prevention, has pronounced that condom use can significantly reduce the risk of infection and death. Research indicates a public uneasiness about condom use, a widespread lack of knowledge about proper use, and a lack of social support for use among some populations. Thus, although most prevention specialists would argue that clear communication about condom use must be the cornerstone of any comprehensive approach to HIV/AIDS, few PSAs mention condom use (DeJong and Winsten 1992). In a CDC-sponsored PSA that appears symbolic of government and media policy on this significant public health issue, condom use was alluded to through the metaphor of putting on a sock: "What if something as simple as putting on a sock could save your life?" Similarly, the most recent U.S. Department of Health and Human Services campaign, developed by the Advertising Council, "Get High, Get Stupid, Get AIDS," does little to address the key prevention issues identified by AIDS specialists.

Even though most broadcasters are reluctant to air PSAs that are controversial or argue for specific changes in public policy, there still may be a role for public education campaigns in helping achieve policy change. First, PSAs can help increase public recognition of a problem and establish it as a primary concern. For example, when confronted by the AIDS epidemic, U.S. public health officials turned to the mass media as a means of quickly educating the American general public about the disease. While PSAs from the "America Responds to AIDS" campaign have not explored public policy options, they have helped to keep AIDS in the forefront of public attention (DeJong and Winsten 1992).

Second, PSAs can position a sponsoring organization as an agent of change (Skirrow 1987). Then, through a telephone hotline number that the organization publicizes, callers can get further information about a health problem, various policy proposals for addressing it, and how to get more involved in fighting for policy change (DeJong 1991). As one example, a public education campaign could be devised to promote parents' groups that would work to change local school policies regarding substance use, tighten up local enforcement of alcohol control laws, and push for new laws to eliminate cigarette vending machines.

Third, PSAs can be expressly designed to provide factual information that will bolster public receptivity to proposals announced through press conferences and other means. For example, the need for a lower per se limit on driver blood alcohol levels could be substantiated by a PSA that shows how driving is severely impaired at blood alcohol levels far lower than the standard U.S. limit of .10 percent (DeJong and Atkin, 1992). Similarly, regulatory proposals for reducing the availability of alcohol to youth, such as keg identification tags, could be bolstered by a public education campaign that highlights the role of adults in providing alcohol to underage drinkers.

In sum, typical public service campaigns can raise awareness about public health problems and contribute to attitude change, but generally do little to affect behavior. Indeed, these campaigns may serve the political status quo by maintaining a narrow definition of the problem and deflecting concerns about the environmental factors that contribute to it, including production and marketing practices. Finally, these campaigns may also serve to minimize government responsibility for addressing the broader social and economic conditions that contribute to public health problems.

COMPREHENSIVE HEALTH COMMUNICATION CAMPAIGNS

Several community-based campaigns have produced promising results in the prevention of heart disease, smoking, and alcohol problems. The mass media play an important role in these campaigns, but within a framework of community-level involvement and support. The prototype for the comprehensive community approach to health promotion is the Stanford Three Community Study, which tested the impact of a mass media campaign to reduce cardiovascular disease among adults living in a small California city (Farquhar 1984; Farquhar et al. 1977; Maccoby et al. 1977; Stern et al. 1976).

In the "treatment community," the researchers used a variety of mass media strategies for 2 years to create problem awareness, to market the project's key messages, and to teach cardiovascular risk reduction skills. Specific target behaviors included reduced dietary fat consumption, smoking cessation, and increased physical activity. The campaign's armamentarium included 50 television spots, over 100 radio spots, several hours of television and radio programming, weekly newspaper columns, newspaper advertisements and stories, billboards, bus posters, and mailed print materials. The researchers used the broadcast media and billboards to alert the public to the campaign, while relying on print media to provide indepth health information.

In a second, highly similar community, the media campaign was combined with face-to-face instruction provided to a small subset of high-risk individuals identified through a baseline survey. Methods used included standard techniques of behavior modification and self-control management: personal analysis of existing behavior, modeling of skills, guided practice, and gradual withdrawal of instructor participation to ensure self-maintenance. A third community, where no intervention was introduced, served as a control site.

People from each of the three communities were interviewed and examined by appointment at special survey centers before the campaign began and 1 and 2 years afterward to assess knowledge and behavior and to measure physiological indicators of cardiovascular risk. In the control community, the risk of cardiovascular disease for the general adult population increased during the 2-year study. In the treatment community exposed to the mass media alone, there was a substantial decrease in risk, between 15 and 20 percent across different subgroups (Farquhar et al. 1977).

Substantial improvement in behavior was documented for daily saturated fat intake, which was estimated from subjects' dietary reports (Farquhar et al. 1977; Maccoby et al. 1977). The mass media campaign alone increased smoking cessation somewhat during its first year, but the effect was not long-lasting (Farquhar 1984). Reductions in the number of cigarettes smoked were smaller than expected across both years of the campaign (Maccoby et al. 1977). The expected changes in reported leisure time physical activity also failed to occur (Farquhar et al. 1977).

The Stanford study demonstrates that a public education campaign can be used to influence health-related behaviors that depend on the acquisition of new knowledge, such as better eating habits (Flora et al. 1989*a*). On the other hand, altering more ingrained or complex behaviors (e.g., smoking, sedentary lifestyle) seems to require more intensive instruction that encourages the learner's active participation and provides corrective feedback (Alcalay 1983). In these cases, a public education campaign can be used to stimulate the development and coordination of community-based programs and to provide specialized instruction through news stories or documentaries (Maccoby and Solomon 1981; Flay 1987).

Subsequent community-based campaigns have tried to build on the Stanford approach with varying degrees of success. The Stanford group itself went on to implement a five-city study, which was recently completed. The Stanford Five City Project (FCP) has reported some success in reducing community-wide levels of plasma cholesterol, blood pressure, resting pulse rate, and smoking. Total mortality risk declined 15 percent, while coronary heart disease risk declined 16 percent (Farquhar et al. 1990; Fortmann et al. 1990). The FCP combined media with a wide range of community activities and planned changes in the community environment. Over a 5-year period, the average adult was exposed to approximately 26 hours of education coming from television, radio, newspapers, community classes, training, and kits and booklets.

The "Winners Quit When They're Ahead" campaign implemented in California in the late 1970's focused on the prevention of alcohol-related problems. Funded by the State of California, this 3-year program used paid media in conjunction with school programs and community organization in an effort to reduce drinking to intoxication among both youth and adults. An extensive evaluation indicated a high level of campaign awareness and some gain in public knowledge, but no attitudinal or behavioral change. An interesting aspect of the campaign was the controversy generated when the Governor intervened to stop the airing of two of the paid advertisements after they were being previewed by the Wine Institute. The launch of the campaign was delayed, and substitute advertisements were hastily developed (Wallack and Barrows 1982–83).

The Community Action Project (CAP) in New Zealand (Casswell and Stewart 1989) also focused on the prevention of alcohol-related problems. What was new about the CAP was its explicit focus on alcohol policy and political action as well as on individual behavior. For example, the campaign used full-page newspaper advertisements to raise the issue of alcohol availability in supermarkets and the need for limits on alcohol advertising. Evaluation evidence suggested that the project was effective in getting policy issues on the public agenda. One interesting sidelight was that by the end of the project, journalists were routinely seeking out the community organizers for comments on breaking health-related news stories.

Media interventions appear to show the most promise for creating behavior change in the area of smoking cessation. Flay's (1987) review of 56 mass media programs to reduce cigarette smoking among adults showed that such programs can cause widespread changes in knowledge and attitudes, and small but meaningful changes in smoking behavior. The results from televised smoking cessation clinics are very encouraging, especially when such programs are enhanced by supplementary written materials and strong social support. Although the quit rates for these programs may be somewhat lower than for walk-in clinics, the rates are substantially higher than would normally occur with no intervention. Hence, the ability to reach much larger numbers of people (at a lower cost per quitter) makes the televised clinic a very attractive part of smoking control efforts. Recent evidence from Australia (Pierce et al. 1990) suggests that paid media placements, coordinated with school- and community-based activities, can lower smoking prevalence in both the short- and long-term.

Recently, an extensive tobacco education program was funded in California with revenue from an increased excise tax on tobacco. The program included a large-scale paid media campaign, public service advertising, and extensive resource development at the community level for both cessation and advocacy activities (Bal et al. 1990). A $28.6 million media campaign was launched in April 1990 and played over an 18-month period. Various target groups defined by age, gender, and racial/ethnic variables were addressed through a wide range of communication strategies. Despite the high level of media activity, these efforts were roughly equivalent to only 6 weeks of tobacco industry advertising in California (Bal et al. 1990).

The California campaign continues to break new ground by combining policy and individual behavior messages in a dramatic way. Particularly noteworthy were hard-hitting television, radio, and newspaper ads and billboards that used shaming and ridiculing to attack the legitimacy of the tobacco industry. For example, several messages questioned the ethics of tobacco industry executives with themes such as "Warning: Some People Will Say Anything To Sell Cigarettes," and "Warning: The Tobacco Industry Is Not Your Friend."

Preliminary evaluation results are inconclusive. The media campaign was widely recalled, and substantial proportions of people who stopped smoking mentioned that the campaign was a significant factor in their decision to quit. What continues to be unclear, however, is how much of the reduction in smoking was due to the effect of the tax, the extensive community programs, or the media campaign. A recent study compared tobacco consumption in California and Nevada, which simultaneously increased its excise tax to the same level but did not use these monies to fund smoking control activities. This comparison suggested that the California media campaign had a major impact on tobacco use above and beyond the effect of the tax increase (S. Glantz, personal communication, 1993).

In sum, comprehensive health communication campaigns have de-monstrated promise in several areas, including tobacco and alcohol. The extensive literature on this topic has produced several key lessons that campaign planners cannot afford to ignore (DeJong 1991):

(1) **Establish a long-term commitment to creating change.** Changing norms, values, and policies is a complex undertaking that may require years to accomplish (Flay and Burton 1990), as evidenced by the evolution of changes in tobacco use.

(2) **Apply behavior change theories to the problem.** Social learning and communication theories can provide the necessary structure for developing interventions that move people from awareness to skill

development to behavior change to behavior maintenance (Farquhar et al. 1984; Flora et al. 1989*b*).

(3) **Apply the consumer orientation of social marketing.** Social marketing uses a consumer perspective to develop, package, and implement interventions, with a stress on consumer benefits (Lefebve and Flora 1988). Audience segmentation, channel analysis, pretesting, and other types of formative research are necessary to develop an effective campaign (Atkin and Freimuth 1989).

(4) **Stimulate interpersonal communication.** The likelihood of behavior change is greatly enhanced by interpersonal communication that reinforces the message and supports the expected change (Rogers 1983).

(5) **Use a variety of mass communication channels.** Television tends to be thought of as the sine qua non of media campaigns, but depending on the audience, it may be the least effective and least economic approach. Reinforcing the message through various communication channels can enhance the message and better ensure that the target population is reached (Atkin and Arkin 1990).

(6) **Take steps to ensure audience exposure to the campaign.** Purchasing media time and space can ensure that the intended audience is exposed to the message. Other strategies include working with local media outlets to get them to sponsor the campaign, thus giving it higher visibility (Wishnow 1983). For some issues, corporate sponsorship might be appropriate.

(7) **Make strategic use of entertainment and news programming.** Several advocacy groups have been effective in getting their message inserted into prime-time entertainment programming (Montgomery 1989). Sometimes groups can key off "social problem" or "disease of the week" television movies to increase audience exposure to their particular topic. Other groups have been able to encourage news stories that give their topic added exposure (Goldman 1984; Wallack et al. 1993).

(8) **Link media strategies with community-based programs.** Virtual-ly every mass media campaign that has shown any evidence of success has been supplemented with community-based programs. The use of media alone, except in rare situations, is unlikely to produce a positive effect.

(9) **Use mass media to focus attention on social, economic, and cultural factors that impact health behavior.** Changing individual behavior may be necessary but not sufficient to stimulate improvements in health status. Alcohol, tobacco, and nutrition groups are increasingly shifting attention to broader social factors as part of the prevention and social change process.

(10) **Use process and outcome evaluation.** Process evaluation helps program managers find out if their intervention is being delivered to the intended audience as planned. Outcome evaluation will let managers know if key goals and objectives are being met (Flay and Cook 1989).

Though far less prevalent than simple public service campaigns, comprehensive health promotion campaigns provide the best model for how media campaigns should be developed and implemented. One of the problems in implementing these campaigns is that they require substantially more commitment, expertise, and resources than typical public service campaigns—factors that may preclude their widespread application to promote health.

MEDIA ADVOCACY

Establishment of the media advocacy approach has been explicitly supported by the National Cancer Institute, which backed the production of *Media Strategies for Smoking Control Guidelines* (U.S. Department of Health and Human Services 1989), the first important document on media advocacy. Prepared by the Advocacy Institute, a Washington-based public interest group, this document defines media advocacy as "the strategic use of mass media to advance a social or public policy initiative." The approach is gaining currency. Erickson et al. (1990), in a review of the role of media in reducing tobacco consumption, noted that media advocacy "is emerging as a powerful tool in the smoking control movement."

To date, there has been relatively little published on media advocacy. Convissor et al. (1990) described media advocacy efforts in Atlanta, Detroit, and San Francisco to localize and frame the 1989 Surgeon General's recommendations to reduce drunk driving. Wallack (1990*a*,*b*) compared the assumptions underlying media advocacy with those of social marketing and described the role of media advocacy in a randomized, controlled community trial to reduce tobacco use (Wallack and Sciandra 1990–91). A recent book provides both a practical rationale and a theoretical basis for media advocacy, and uses a number of case studies on AIDS, handguns, alcohol, and tobacco to illustrate key concepts of this approach (Wallack et al. 1993).

Media advocacy is based on an understanding of public health problems as primarily social, economic, and political. While traditional approaches focus on personal risk factors, media advocacy addresses environmental risk factors through community and policy development. While traditional approaches use media to fill the "knowledge gap" so that people can change personal behavior, media advocacy addresses the "power gap" so that communities can create environmental change through policy development. The goal of media advocacy is not to give people a message but to provide groups with a voice to define problems and promote policy solutions. It may well be the case for some people that getting a finely crafted message to change their personal behavior will be sufficient to motivate them to do so. But the lesson of public health is that, for those most at risk and most in need, this will not be the case. Thus, media advocacy should be seen as a complement to, rather than a replacement for, comprehensive health communication campaigns.

The actual birth and formalization of the media advocacy approach can be traced directly to the tobacco control movement and the development of techniques for gaining media access and framing tobacco issues as policy rather than individual concerns. The tobacco control movement was able to shift its point of access from the public affairs desk to the news desk. As a result, tobacco as a public health issue began to appear on the front pages, business pages, and sports pages as well as in the health section. Tobacco use was redefined as a social issue that needed policy solutions, and the dominant view of smoking as an individual behavioral issue receded into the background. Popular targets of tobacco control advocates have been sales to minors; vending machines; clean indoor air acts; tobacco industry sponsorship of sports, recreational, and cultural events; advertising and marketing; international trade; and the introduction of new tobacco products.

Media advocacy in the alcohol field has focused on the general promotion of an environmental perspective for the prevention of alcohol-related problems. Specific policy issues have included the marketing of malt beverages to low-income communities, advertising, industry sponsorships, excise taxes, warning labels, and local control of alcohol availability. For example, alcohol policy advocates were successful in getting PowerMaster, a high-alcohol-content malt liquor, withdrawn from the market through a combination of community organization and media advocacy strategies.

Media advocacy has two broad objectives. First, media advocacy seeks to *gain access* to the media to tell a particular story. Second, media advocacy seeks to *frame* the story so that it focuses primarily on policy rather than the unhealthy behavior of particular individuals. The successful pursuit of both these functions is dependent on a sophisticated understanding of how news is created and reported and how the agenda-setting process works. Walter Lippmann noted, "Mass media are like the beam of a searchlight that moves restlessly about, bringing one episode and then another out of darkness into vision" (1965[1922], p. 229). The key to media advocacy is to fix the searchlight on public policy issues, hold it there, and consistently advance policy approaches by setting long-term objectives and developing media and community advocacy strategies to reach them.

Media advocacy uses the following general strategies:

(1) **Develop local coalitions.** By including a diversity of groups, local coalitions demonstrate that the issue is of widespread concern, broaden their base for strategy development, and establish legitimacy with media outlets. Such a coalition was recently developed in San Francisco to remove tobacco and alcohol advertising from city buses.

(2) **Cultivate relationships with journalists.** Journalists appreciate ideas for well-thought-out stories that are newsworthy and have local interest (Meyer 1990). A good source who can come up with story ideas with good news value and local interest, solid data, and other informed sources will be very much appreciated by journalists. The process often begins with a simple phone call or letter to a journalist.

(3) **Create news.** Scoop Nisker, a radio news commentator in the San Francisco Bay Area, advises his listeners, "If you don't like the news, go out and make some of your own." The media know that the public has a great appetite for health-related stories with a local angle. A San Diego coalition created a major ongoing news story by raising concerns about the "alcoholization" of Sea World by its new owners, Anheuser-Busch (Wallack et al. 1993). Tobacco researchers created news by reporting that preschool children were as likely to identify Joe Camel as they were Mickey Mouse.

(4) **Use breaking news.** Because health is part of almost any story, breaking news can often be localized and linked to an advocate's issue. For example, when the United States banned the import of produce from Chile because cyanide was found on two grapes, tobacco activists in various communities held press conferences to point out that it would take bushels of these grapes to equal the

cyanide in one cigarette. This tactic highlighted the health risks of tobacco, but also underscored the irrationality of a public health policy that treats tobacco risk so lightly while crippling the economy of another country because of a health risk that was negligible by comparison.

(5) **Use paid advertising.** Paid advertising can ensure that the message gets to the intended audience. For example, at a critical stage in the development of the Tobacco Products Control Act, the Canadian Non-Smokers Rights Association took out a full-page ad in the *Toronto Globe and Mail* to reach a House of Commons committee that was working on the legislation (Mintz 1990). The advertisement included a picture of the prime minister, whose party controlled the committee, and his close friend, who had just been appointed president of the Canadian Tobacco Manufacturers' Council. The headline above the pictures of these two men stated: "How many thousands of Canadians will die from tobacco industry products may be in the hands of these two men." Mintz explains, "The ad devastated [the lobbyist's] influence by personalizing the tobacco lobby and making whatever success it might have politically damaging to [the prime minister]" (1990, p. 31).

In sum, media advocacy focuses on the social, legal, and economic environment as a causative factor in public health problems and develops strategies to advance changes in policy at the community, regional, or national level. Its focus is on the behavior of producers, marketers, and regulators rather than on the behavior of the persons with the health problem. That is, attention is focused on the "victimizers" and their supporters rather than on the "victims." There is growing evidence that media advocacy can be effective in developing policies to alter the community environment, specifically the local availability of alcohol and tobacco products. There have also been some successes at the national level (e.g., Uptown cigarettes, PowerMaster malt liquor). Evaluation of this promising strategy should be a priority.

SUMMARY

The three approaches to mass media and health promotion reviewed here provide clear choices for public health professionals. With public service campaigns, the audience is not involved in defining the problem or its solution. Rather, this is done for them by groups with a vested economic interest, which often results in the most effective prevention approaches being pushed off the public agenda in favor of messages designed to change individual behavior. The role of the community is extremely limited or nonexistent. Such campaigns can occasionally be used to advance a public policy agenda, but only indirectly by creating problem awareness, promoting organizations that are working for change, and presenting supportive factual information.

With the comprehensive health communication approach, the community is invited to participate in the development of programs and to share in tailoring the education and skill development process to meet the needs of their own community. There is some attention to environmental factors, through the promotion of voluntary policy changes in the private sector, changes in social norms, and the integration of additional health promotion services into the community structure.

Media advocacy perceives the world from a social rather than personal point of view, having a primary focus on the environment in which behavior takes place. With this approach, an effort is made to enhance the power of the community, principally by teaching local activists the media and organizing skills they need to define problems, determine solutions, and take action. The key focus is on politics, policy, and social change.

In deciding the best use of media resources, then, researchers need to assess where we stand on the following question: Will improved health status come about *primarily* as a result of (1) individuals obtaining more knowledge about personal health behaviors, or (2) groups getting more power to change social and economic conditions?

If media are used to reinforce nonpolitical definitions of health and social problems, definitions that focus primarily on personal responsibility for health status, such strategies may actually contribute to maintaining the very conditions that give rise to and sustain these problems. On the other hand, if media are used to highlight political and policy issues, they can instead contribute to the significant changes that are necessary to make a difference in public health.

REFERENCES

Alcalay, R. The impact of mass communication campaigns in the health field. *Soc Sci Med* 17:87-94, 1983.

Atkin, C., and Arkin, E. Issues and initiatives in communicating health information. In: Atkin, C., and Wallack, L., eds. *Mass Communication and Public Health: Complexities and Conflicts.* Newbury Park, CA: Sage, 1990. pp. 13-40.

Atkin, C.K.; DeJong, W.; and Wallack, L. *The Influence of Responsible Drinking TV Spots and Automobile Commercials on Young Drivers.* Washington, DC: AAA Foundation for Traffic Safety, 1992.

Atkin, C., and Freimuth, V. Formative evaluation research in campaign design. In: Rice, R., and Atkin, C., eds. *Public Communication Campaigns.* 2d ed. Newbury Park, CA: Sage, 1989.

Bal, D.; Kizer, K.; Felten, P.; Mozar, H.; and Niemeyer, D. Reducing tobacco consumption in California. *JAMA* 264(12):1570-1574, 1990.

Bollier, D. Raise the Halo High. *Channels.* Apr. 1989. pp. 32-38.

Buchanan, D., and Wallack, L. This is the Partnership for a Drug-Free America: Any questions? Mimeo. Washington DC: Partnership for a Drug-Free America, 1994.

Casswell, S., and Stewart, L. A community action project on alcohol: Community organization and its evaluation. *Community Health Stud* XIII(1):39-48, 1989.

Convissor, R.; Vollinger, R.; and Wibur, P. Using national news events to stimulate local awareness of public policy issues. *Public Health Rep* 105(3):257-260, 1990.

Cotts, C. Hard Sell in the Drug War. *The Nation.* Mar. 9, 1992. pp. 300-302.

DeJong, W. On the use of mass communications to promote the public health. *Surgeon General's Workshop on Organ Donation: Background Papers.* Rockville, MD: Office of the Surgeon General, U.S. Department of Health and Human Services, 1991. pp. 37–90.

DeJong, W., and Atkin, C.K. "A Review of National Television PSA Campaigns for Preventing Alcohol-Impaired Driving, 1987-1992." Unpublished manuscript, Harvard School of Public Health, 1992.

DeJong, W.; Atkin, C.K.; and Wallack, L. A critical analysis of "moderation" advertising sponsored by the beer industry: Are "responsible drinking" commercials done responsibly? *Milbank Qtrly* 70:661–678, 1992.

DeJong, W., and Wallack, L. The role of designated driver programs in the prevention of alcohol-impaired driving: A critical reassessment. *Health Educ Qtrly* 19:429–442, 1992.

DeJong, W., and Winsten, J.A. Responding to AIDS: Limits on the strategic use of the broadcast media to effect behavior change. In: Sepulveda, J.; Fineberg, H.; and Mann, J., eds. *AIDS Education and Communication.* New York: Oxford University Press, 1992. pp. 255–272.

Dubos, R. *Mirage of Health.* New York: Harper and Row, 1959.

Erickson, A.; McKenna, J.; and Romano, R. Past lessons and new uses of the mass media in reducing tobacco consumption. *Public Health Rep* 105(3):239–244, 1990.

Farquhar, J. The potential role of the media in public health, education, and health policy. In: Hamner, J., and Jacobs, S., eds. *The Media, Communication, and Health Policy.* Memphis: Center for Health Sciences, University of Tennessee, 1984.

Farquhar, J.; Fortmann, S.P.; and Flora, J. Effects of communitywide education on cardiovascular disease risk factors: The Stanford Five-City Project. *JAMA* 264:359–365, 1990.

Farquhar, J.; Maccoby, N.; and Solomon, D. Community applications of behavioral medicine. In: Gentry, W., ed. *Handbook of Behavioral Medicine.* New York: Guilford Press, 1984.

Farquhar, J.; Maccoby, N.; Wood, P.; and Alexander, J. Community education for cardiovascular health. *Lancet.* Jun. 4, 1977. pp. 1192–1195.

Flay, B.R. *Selling the Smokeless Society: Fifty-Six Evaluated Mass Media Programs and Campaigns Worldwide.* Washington, DC: American Public Health Association, 1987.

Flay, B.R., and Burton, D. Effective mass communication strategies for health campaigns. In: Atkin, C., and Wallack, L., eds. *Mass Communication and Public Health: Complexities and Conflicts.* Newbury Park, CA: Sage, 1990. pp. 129–146.

Flay, B., and Cook, T. Three models for summative evaluation of prevention campaigns with a mass media component. In: Rice, R., and Atkin, C., eds. *Public*

Communication Campaigns. 2d ed. Newbury Park, CA: Sage, 1989.

Flora, J.; Maccoby, N.; and Farquhar, J. Communication campaigns to prevent cardiovascular disease: The Stanford community studies. In: Rice, R., and Atkin, C., eds. *Public Communication Campaigns.* 2d ed. Newbury Park, CA: Sage, 1989*a*. pp. 233–252.

Flora, J.; Maibach, E.; and Maccoby, N. The role of media across four levels of health promotion intervention. *Ann Rev Public Health* 19:181–201, 1989*b*.

Fortmann, S.; Winkleby, M.; Flora, J.; Haskell, W.; and Taylor, C. Effect of long-term community health education on blood pressure and hypertension control. *Am J Epidemiol* 132(4):629–646, 1990.

Freimuth, V. Developing the public service advertisement for nonprofit marketing. *Adv Nonprofit Market* 1:55–93, 1985.

Goldman, J. *Public Relations and the Marketing Mix.* Lincolnwood, IL: NTC Business Books, 1984.

Haan, M.; Kaplan, G.; and Camacho, T. Poverty and health. *Am J Epidemiol* 125:989–998, 1987.

Institute of Medicine. Committee for the Study of the Future of Public Health. *The Future of Public Health.* Washington, DC: National Academy Press, 1988.

Kitagawa, E., and Hauser, P. *Differential Mortality in the United States: A Study in Socioeconomic Epidemiology.* Cambridge: Harvard University Press, 1973.

Lefebve, C., and Flora, J. Social marketing and public health intervention. *Health Educ Qtrly* 15:299–315, 1988.

Lippmann, W. *Public Opinion.* New York: The Free Press, 1965 (originally published in 1922).

Maccoby, N.; Farquhar, J.; Wood, P.; and Alexander, J. Reducing the risk of cardiovascular disease: Effects of a community-based campaign on knowledge and behavior. *J Community Health* 3:100–114, 1977.

Maccoby, N., and Solomon, D. Heart disease prevention: Community studies. In: Rice, R., and Paisley, W., eds. *Public Communication Campaigns.* Beverly Hills, CA: Sage, 1981.

Meyer, P. News media responsiveness to public health. In: Atkin, C., and Wallack, L., eds. *Mass Communication and Public Health: Complexities and Conflicts.* Newbury Park, CA: Sage, 1990. pp. 52–59.

Mintz, M. No Ifs, Ands, or Butts. *The Washington Monthly.* Jul./Aug., 1990. pp. 30–37.

Montgomery, K.C. *Target: Prime Time.* New York: Oxford University Press, 1989.

Pierce, J.; Macaskill, P.; and Hill, D. Long-term effectiveness of mass media led anti-smoking campaigns in Australia. *Am J Public Health* 80(5):565–569, 1990.

Rogers, E. *Diffusion of Innovations.* New York: Free Press, 1983.

Skirrow, J. Influencing adolescent lifestyle: The role of mass media. *Drug Alcohol Depend* 20:21–26, 1987.

Smith, D., and Egger, M. Socio-economic differences in mortality in Britain and the United States. *Am J Public Health* 82:1079–1081, 1992.

Stern, M.; Farquhar, J.; Maccoby, N.; and Russell, S. Results of a two year health education campaign on dietary behavior: The Stanford three community study. *Circulation* 54:826–33, 1976.

Tesh, S. *Hidden Arguments: Political Ideology and Disease Prevention Policy.* New Brunswick, NJ: Rutgers University Press, 1988.

U.S. Department of Health and Human Services. *Media Strategies for Smoking Control: Guidelines.* NIH Pub. No. 89-3013. Washington, DC: Supt. of Docs., U.S. Govt. Print. Off., 1989.

Wallack, L. Improving health promotion: Media advocacy and social marketing approaches. In: Atkin, C., and Wallack, L., eds. *Mass Communication and Public Health: Complexities and Conflicts.* Newbury Park: Sage, 1990*a*. pp. 147–163.

Wallack, L. Social marketing and media advocacy: Two approaches to health promotion. *World Forum* 11:143–154, 1990*b*.

Wallack, L., and Barrows, D. Evaluating primary prevention: The California "Winners" alcohol program. *Int Qtrly Community Health Educ* 3(4):307–335, 1982–83.

Wallack, L.; Dorfman, L.; Jernigan, D.; and Themba, M. *Media Advocacy and Public Health: Power for Prevention.* Newbury Park, CA: Sage, 1993.

Wallack, L., and Sciandra, R. Media advocacy and public education in the community trial to reduce heavy smoking. *Int Qtrly Community Health Educ* 11:205–222, 1990–91.

Wilkinson, R. National mortality rates: The impact of inequality. *Am J Public Health* 82:1082–1084, 1992.

Winkleby, M.; Jatulis, D.; Frank, E.; and Fortmann, S. Socioeconomic status and health: How education, income, and occupation contribute to risk factors for cardiovascular disease. *Am J Public Health* 82:816–820, 1992.

Wishnow, J. *The Activist: A Broadcasters' Step-by-Step Guide to Total Station Public Affairs Projects.* Washington, DC: National Broadcast Association for Community Affairs, 1983.

Chapter 17

The Nature and Effectiveness of Media Advocacy, Counteradvertising, and Health Promotion Messages

Sally Casswell[1]

New Zealand is a small country on the other side of the Pacific. We have been through some very interesting times recently in terms of moving toward a market-driven, individualistically focused society. Not surprisingly, alcohol policy has also gone through some interesting shifts at this time. Wallack's chapter is excellent and instructive for anyone interested in alcohol problem prevention. In my comments, I hope to reinforce many of the points he has made reporting on some of the things that have happened in New Zealand recently.

Wallack focuses on three issues: public service announcements (PSAs), community involvement in problem prevention and the role the paid mass media can have in that, and media advocacy. I have little to say about PSAs, which are peculiarly American in the sense that many other countries have relied on paid-for problem prevention announcements. However, the kind of public relations function that Wallack describes as very much part of the PSAs in the United States can certainly occur in paid advertisements too. It depends on the nature of the organization controlling the advertisements, and on who and what is influencing the organization.

I would like to strongly reinforce Wallack's second point about the value of the integration of community action work and paid mass media. We have heard from marketing experts about synergy—the synergy between all of the aspects of marketing that support mass media advertising in order to sell a product. There is sufficient evidence to suggest that this type of synergy is also possible in alcohol problem prevention. The "mass media umbrella," as it is often referred to, is perceived as very important by community activists. It legitimizes, supports, and reinforces their activities. But there is also synergy in the

[1]Alcohol and Public Health Research Unit, School of Medicine, University of Auckland, Auckland, New Zealand, Private Bag 92019

other direction. Community involvement in the media program can go some way toward reducing the public relations focus of the mass media campaigns that the PSAs epitomize. Sometimes the community actors will be more interested in presenting the issues from a truly public health perspective, compared with the advertising industry's approach or that of the alcohol agencies that often fund these mass media campaigns.

For synergy to occur there needs to be close association, a partnership, between the community and the mass media. This can be illustrated by a recent case from New Zealand. The Alcohol and Public Health Research Unit had been involved with pretesting health promotion advertisements around alcohol issues and had shown the ads in development to a group of Maori (the indigenous people of New Zealand). The Maori are a colonized people who experience relatively high levels of alcohol-related problems, similar in some ways to the situation of Native Americans in the United States. The unit wanted to find out how they received the mass media messages that were being considered for broadcast in New Zealand.

The research showed that some aspects of this new campaign, not specifically to do with alcohol messages but rather with the way food was portrayed, were extremely culturally insensitive. That information was passed on, but the ad agency and the alcohol agency initially did not change the ad. A meeting was held with community workers as part of the alcohol agency's new policy of trying to increase the synergy between community workers and the mass media in New Zealand problem prevention campaigns. At this meeting, community workers were shown the ad prior to its going on the air. They reacted so strongly to the cultural insensitivity in the ad that the alcohol agency decided to change it. The point of this story is not that the ad-agency people behaved inappropriately or were insensitive; rather, it illustrates how the community workers seized ownership of a mass media campaign. What they said was, "That is our public face out there!"

Community ownership of mass media campaigns is likely to increase the strength and power of the mass media because the messages from community groups and commercial advertisers will complement and enhance each other. If community workers feel some ownership of the campaign, they will use the same concepts and slogans in their activities and interactions, increasing the impact because of the synergy of mass media and interpersonal channels of communication.

With this synergy going on, an additional step is to put some of the media budget under the workers' control. Then one might see changes; for example, instead of just using an approach familiar to industry-devised campaigns, community action groups might produce material around the political issues to do with alcohol consumption and the role it plays in the power relations within society. If community workers have media budgets, for example, for local radio productions and local radio campaigns, they will build relations with journalists. This is very useful in the area of media advocacy, which Wallack discussed and which the rest of this chapter is concerned with.

Like Wallack, I regard as a very positive step the change that has happened in the 1980's in the alcohol field—namely, the clearer recognition of the great importance of the social, political, and economic environment in the creation and reinforcement of alcohol-related problems. Strategies based on this understanding are more likely to reduce the level of alcohol-related problems than those utilizing an individual education approach.

Public policy changes can, in fact, encourage individuals to make healthy choices. For example, the Smoke Free Environment Act that has been implemented in New Zealand is supportive of people who want to change their smoking behavior, and it encourages them to go into smoking cessation programs. The same thing probably happens with enforcement of drunk-driving laws, which gives young drivers a justification for changing their behavior. We know from our survey data that a significant proportion of heavy-drinking young men would like to cut down. The enforcement of drunk-driving legislation gives them a justification to provide to their friends. As Wallack points out, problem prevention is a process of changing political behavior in order to make personal behavior change more possible.

Media advocacy is the strategic use of the media to advance such public policy objectives as the smoke-free environment legislation or drinking-driving legislation. Because, as Wallack's chapter states, there is little or no research on the effectiveness of media advocacy approaches, I want to suggest some research directions that could help support and improve the use of media advocacy in the alcohol prevention area.

First, it is important that researchers avoid conceptualizing research in this area as looking for a "yes or no" answer: Is it effective or not effective? We are not looking for a "silver bullet" to prevent alcohol-related problems. Rather, we should frame our evaluation questions to look at the conditions and circumstances in which media advocacy is most likely to be effective, what small gains we can make, and what factors are likely to increase these gains.

Research can play a role in determining the specifics of appropriate policies for media advocacy at a particular historical, political, cultural, and economical moment. Just such a debate arose recently around the specifics of appropriate alcohol advertising policy in New Zealand.

New Zealand is very unusual in that it did not have broadcast media advertising of brands of alcohol until the late 1980's. A new economic climate, along with increasing commercialization of the media, led to a change so that brand advertising of alcohol was allowed on television and radio. Once the change had gone through, public health advocates had to decide on an appropriate policy goal to work toward in the new policy climate. They asked themselves, "Do we work toward a new ban? Do we advocate removing the tax deductibility of alcohol advertising? Do we go for health warnings attached to the advertisements?" Unfortunately, research in this area was not sufficiently advanced to assist with assessment of the relative effectiveness of these approaches. A pragmatic decision was made to attempt health warnings, partly because warnings were felt to threaten the interests of the advertising and media industries less directly, partly because they were novel, and partly because they were being attempted in the United States at the time. Furthermore, this approach was judged more likely to achieve media coverage and political acceptance in the particular social climate of that time. Researchers with expertise in the policymaking process can have a role in helping inform debate around what policy is likely to be feasible in the climate in which the media advocacy is taking place.

A second issue is how media advocacy is affected by the industry structures that are in place. These are documentable issues—issues that media advocates need to understand more about. Wallack's chapter mentions that in the quasi-experimental design evaluation study we conducted in New Zealand, the project used mass media campaign money to run four full-page advertisements on alcohol policy issues. The influence of industry structures on media advocacy can be illustrated by what happened over the policy advertising that was a part of this evaluated demonstration project. The project had been working with the advertising agency for several months on individual-focused "When To Say When" type moderation advertising. We then moved into the policy arena. We did a lot of work with the creative people, and they started to produce some exciting ideas. I was called in by the managing director, who said he was not happy about this sort of approach. The ad agency had a big brewery client and he said that he felt he would have to show the copy for our advertisements to the brewery client before they were published. I said, "That seems fine just as long as the project has a veto on the brewery advertisements." The manager decided not to take that option, and we had an uneasy truce for a little longer. The next policy-directed advertisement, which dealt with the alcohol advertising issue, was refused publication by the Newspaper Publishers Association. At that point, our relationship with the agency broke down, and they withdrew and refused to continue with the account. In many ways this was predictable. Yet better documentation in case studies of these kinds of events could assist in the development of such projects. Clearer understanding of the linkages between different sectors, such as the broadcast media, print media, sports and leisure industries, advertising, and the various sectors of the alcohol industry, could assist with the development of more effective media advocacy strategies.

A third issue that is worth researchers investigating is, What are perceived to be appropriate approaches in media advocacy? Again, the political and economic contexts are relevant, as are the ways in which the issues are conceptualized by the community and how acceptable and appropriate the proposed public policy is. There are important questions, for example, around the appropriateness of moralism in media advocacy messages. It is likely that the public and policymakers would find it more acceptable for public health advocates to take a moralistic approach in the tobacco field than in the alcohol field (although drinking-driving issues may be an exception). The harm associated with tobacco use is more widely recognized, and public policy solutions have greater acceptance (perhaps because of the distribution of tobacco use along class lines). Dan Beauchamp (1988) has warned against approaches that appear to classify industry groups as pariahs and instead favors an approach that holds them responsible. Wallack has shown us media messages that appear to portray the tobacco industry as pariahs. What response do these ads get? How would similar ads dealing with alcohol producers be received? Public health advocates often have a wealth of information about their experiences with responses to different approaches that they exchange informally, and these are also valid issues for the research literature.

The "active audience" that we have heard much about in relation to portrayals of alcohol in the media and alcohol advertising presents another research question. How do the active recipients receive media advocacy messages? What is the action that is the desired outcome for each sector of the active recipient audience—the concerned citizen, professionals, and policymakers? (i.e., How will they respond to media advocacy messages and themselves become advocates?) Defining the audience for media advocacy messages, measuring the response of the recipients, and deciding what action is the desired outcome rely on formative evaluation research (McClintock 1986). Formative evaluation is accepted as an essential part of the development of paid mass media campaigns; it would also be a useful area for research involvement in media advocacy.

Wallack's chapter suggests the need for a series of case studies to document media advocacy campaigns and assess the outcomes. Useful methodology for such case studies has been described by researchers such as Nancy Milio (1988) as research into the policy development process. This requires naturalistic research approaches rather than utilizing experimental design paradigms (Pearsol 1987). Such research, documenting the process and attempting to assess qualitatively the probable outcome of media advocacy campaigns, would be a useful addition to the literature on alcohol and the mass media.

REFERENCES

Beauchamp, D. E. *The Health of the Republic: Epidemics, Medicine, and Moralism as Challenges to Democracy.* Philadelphia: Temple University Press, 1988.

McClintock, C. Toward a theory of formative program evaluation. *Eval Studies Rev Ann* 11:205–223, 1986.

Milio, N. Making healthy public policy; developing the science by learning the art: An ecological framework for policy studies. *Health Promo* 2:263–274, 1988.

Pearsol, J. A. Justifying conclusions in naturalistic evaluations: An interpretive perspective. *Eval Program Plan* 10:335–341, 1987.

A Synthesis of the Issues

Chapter 18

Alcohol and the Mass Media: Issues, Approaches, and Research Directions

Susan E. Martin[1]

The Working Group on the Effects of the Mass Media on the Use and Abuse of Alcohol, which served as a catalyst for this monograph, involved a diverse group of researchers with expertise on alcohol, advertising and mass communications, and public health. The meeting's format provided for an abbreviated oral presentation of the commissioned paper, a formal comment by a discussant, and a group discussion of each topic. Because the group discussions were so impressively rich and lively, we decided to provide a sense of the richness of that debate and the wealth of ideas expressed by identifying the major recurrent themes and presenting a selection of the most cogent comments. To be parsimonious but retain the flavor of the original argument, the comments have been organized thematically rather than in chronological order.

A review of the tapes from the conference indicated how frequently and easily the discussion slipped from research issues to policy questions. Participants tended to move from what we know and need to know from a scientific perspective to the larger political, economic, and sociocultural issues concerning the impact of advertising and the mass media on culture, the goals of advertising and marketing, and policy questions related to the control and availability of alcohol and the impact of such efforts. There were also many alternations in discourse between a microlevel perspective focused largely on individual perceptions and behavior and a macrolevel view focused on group behavior and on the social and cultural implications of advertising and mass communications. Thus, differences in approach that energized the discussion frequently reflected the varying academic disciplines, methodological preferences, interpretations of research findings, and public policy perspectives.

[1]Prevention Research Branch, National Institute on Alcohol Abuse and Alcoholism, 6000 Executive Blvd., Rockville, MD 20892

In addition, it is worth noting that one aspect of the discussion that has been largely omitted from this synthesis, but which played an important part in the conference, was information sharing across communities of scholarship. Alcohol researchers asked many questions about the nature and effects of marketing strategies and communication technologies; health promotion experts whose activities focus on tobacco control asked about alcohol advertising; and advertising experts and econometricians inquired about the effects of alcohol on health.

Several themes emerged from the meeting and are treated as questions or issues below. The first was a question of what the focus of discussion should be. Are we concerned with the effect of advertising on aggregate consumption, or should research focus particularly on vulnerable individuals or groups? This debate highlighted the tension between macrosociological approaches and individual-oriented psychological approaches. A related theme was that of change versus continuity. Has television altered "the stories children learn"? Has it reshaped cultural values related to alcohol or simply mirrored them? How has the shift to nontraditional media and promotion efforts by beer and wine advertisers affected alcohol consumption, abuse, and related outcomes?

A second recurrent theme was the question of what we really know about the effects of alcohol advertising and marketing. Is the frequent finding that advertising has, at best, weak effects attributable to the actual absence of effects or the failure to adequately measure either short-term or long-range outcomes?

A third major focal point of discussion revolved around measurement. Participants grappled with such questions as what is the dependent variable of interest and how can we best measure it? Is the goal of the research to measure drunken incidents (rather than consumption), aggregate consumption, or youth initiation? Should the endpoint of studies be drinking behavior, or is it enough to measure intention to drink and attitudes toward specific brands and drinking situations?

A fourth theme was the role of the viewer in the media equation. How do viewers interpret what they see? In particular, how do children and adolescents select, attend to, and interpret advertising and programming?

A fifth theme was the relationship between commercial alcohol advertising and the activities of public health communicators and advocates. What do advertisers and marketers try to do and how do they accomplish those objectives? Is there a difference between "selling" and "unselling"? If so, does it simply reflect a difference between the economic power of advertisers and that of public health advocates? Does such a difference suggest that public health messages and initiatives require different strategies from those adopted by commercial advertisers? If so, what types of strategies might be useful?

The final set of issues related to future research and policy initiatives. What should we study and how should we study it to arrive at more definitive answers? Even if such studies were completed and alcohol advertising was found to increase alcohol-related problems, what policies might be most effective in addressing these problems?

DEFINING THE ISSUE: ALCOHOL ADVERTISING AND BEYOND

The opening presentations by George Gerbner and Joseph Gusfield led to an initial debate about the nature and scope of the key issues for discussion at the meeting. Gerbner encouraged participants to focus on the ways in which the mass media undercut "community-based drinking values and traditions of long-standing" and to identify the contribution that mass media make or can make to the alleviation of detrimental drinking behaviors. He noted that the traditional practices that ritualized drinking and kept alcohol-related behavior generally within manageable bounds now are threatened by mass media messages, since "with salesmanship there are no limits." He urged the group to frame the issue more broadly than one of measuring the effects of alcohol advertising on aggregate sales or individual drinking behavior. Instead, Gerbner suggested treating advertising and its effects as part of the broader question of the role of the mass media in American culture. Thus, the question becomes one of how to balance commercial interests in marketing dangerous products, First Amendment rights of free speech, and the information needs and health concerns of the public in a global mass media environment.

This desire to look broadly at the effects of marketing and the mass media on culture was echoed by a number of participants throughout the meeting. Some repeatedly sought to put alcohol advertising into a historical and sociocultural perspective, treating it as a commodity with deep cultural roots and meanings which, at the same time, now is driven by global interests. For example, Joseph Gusfield suggested examining the reasons that there is a conference focusing on advertising and the role of the media rather than on *other* public policy issues related to alcohol use and abuse, and the political implications of this choice of a focus. Michael Goodstadt suggested that the issue was one of "control of the marketplace" in the struggle between brewers and distillers. Lawrence Wallack emphasized the importance of framing the questions for discussion at the conference and for subsequent research and warned against "treating advertising in a reductionist way" by focusing on specific effects on specific individuals rather than viewing advertising as part of a larger marketing scheme and larger set of social values. Within this broader framework, some stressed the importance of examining how alcohol is related to marketing innovations and to factors such as price and availability.

Other participants cautioned that while it is useful to adopt a broad conceptual framework, this should not detract from close examination of "the more manageable aspects" of measurement issues and the more "practical action agenda." Enoch Gordis, for example, encouraged the participants to focus on the initiation of drinking, particularly among adolescents, and to address the quality and nature of the evidence related to the contribution of advertising and marketing to underage drinking. Several participants, primarily those who are psychologists, suggested examining the ways that alcohol advertising becomes embedded in and draws on cultural values. This involves exploring cognitions and attitudes of individuals as well as the effects of marketing efforts targeted at particular groups and communities. Others expressed specific concerns about such issues as the use of lifestyle advertising and its relationship to underage drinking and the effects of minimum legal drinking age laws on the use of alcohol in inappropriate contexts and situations.

Another aspect of the definitional issue revolved around the question of research endpoints: Should the focus be on aggregate consumption, on the effects of advertising and other messages on the attitudes and values of individuals and particular groups, or on individuals' actual drinking behavior? Critics of the focus on the individual drinker's behavior noted that framing the issue in this way puts the onus of responsibility for drinking or associated alcohol problems on the individual rather than on cultural roots and the influences that support, maintain, and to some degree control such drinking.

Noting wide variations in consumption across regions and various ethnic and social groups, other participants emphasized the importance of examining the effects of marketing strategies designed to target messages to specific groups in order to sell specific brands, even in the absence of changes in aggregate consumption.

Several of the psychologists and marketing researchers stressed the need to understand how advertising affects social identity and consumer decisionmaking processes as a means of selling products or "unselling" high-risk behaviors. Other participants were wary of all studies of causal effects regardless of whether behaviors or cognitions were the endpoints of interest. As Anders Hansen observed,

> For well over 30 years, the alcohol industry has been successful in defining public debate . . . about the regulation of advertising around the single question of proving direct causal effects. One suspects that as long as the industry can maintain this as the key within which to frame the debate, the industry is unlikely to get too worried because they know that for every study that finds some causal effects, there will be another one that calls the effect into question.

Jerome Williams summarized the apparent difference in perspectives among participants by making a distinction between the goals and primary research concerns of *advertising researchers* and those of *alcohol-advertising researchers.* For the former, the primary goal is altering individual responses to achieve brand shifting or maintaining consumer brand loyalty (i.e., beating the competition). In contrast, the latter (i.e., persons who study the public health effects of alcohol, including the contribution of advertising to consumption) focus on aggregate consumption and drinking problems and seek ways to reduce them. For them, what brand a consumer drinks is of little concern; the nature of alcohol advertising and its effects on the initiation of drinking and the amount consumed are more important, as are public perceptions of alcoholic beverages.

WHAT DO WE REALLY KNOW ABOUT ALCOHOL ADVERTISING EFFECTS?

A central issue for working group participants was what can be said with certainty regarding the effects of alcohol advertising, since there appear to be inconsistent findings and competing interpretations of the data. Resolving the question of the presence and strength of an alcohol advertising effect requires assessment of the validity and reliability of existing studies and consideration of the appropriateness of the methodologies they have used. Participants often found it difficult to disentangle their interpretation of research findings and their concerns about methodological issues both with respect to advertising in general and with regard to advertisements for alcoholic beverages as a specific type of product. The discussion broke into three components: what the current studies say; explanations for the weak and ambiguous findings; and what level of certainty is sufficient to reach "definitive" conclusions regarding the effects of alcohol advertising.

What Do the Data Show?

Several participants stated that in general there is little evidence that even effective advertisements increase product use, although they may affect brand choice. For example, Victor Tremblay asserted that studies of aggregate demand find that advertising has a big effect at the brand level but little or no significant effect at the market level.

David Stewart added that advertising seeks to increase awareness of a product by exposing the public to new products and creating a desire that potential consumers did not have before. Such an effect is indirect rather than direct and is generally limited. For example, research from split-cable studies of advertising effects found that 50 to 75 percent of ads did not increase sales, although they may have reinforced current levels of sales. And the findings from other studies that look generally at consumer behavior clearly indicate that "advertising has an effect, but it is not a particularly strong force." Thus, it seems unlikely that alcohol advertising will have different effects on consumer behavior than do advertisements for other products. Stewart asserted, therefore, that the expectation that there will be "big blips in response to advertising . . . is just not supported by the empirical evidence."

Charles Atkin stated that there does seem to be some causal data showing an impact of advertising on drinking behavior, although the evidence from field surveys and experiments thus far is "suggestive but not yet definitive." Part of the uncertainty is due to inconsistencies in the pattern of findings across various studies, and part is due to methodological limitations. These include inappropriate use of otherwise good techniques and deficiencies in the execution of specific studies. Nevertheless, Atkin concluded,

> I would say at this point that the preponderance of the evidence indicates that alcohol advertising stimulates higher consumption of alcohol by both adults and adolescents. I think any conclusions of null effects are not tenable in the face of numerous positive findings in various kinds of investigations. On the other hand, the evidence does not support the interpretation that the advertising is exerting a powerful influence on drinking behavior. It appears to be a contributing factor that increases drinking to a modest degree rather than being a major determinant.

During the final group discussion, several of the participants sought to determine whether there was a consensus regarding the strength of the research evidence concerning the overall effects of alcohol advertising. For example, Sally Casswell stated that based on the variety of studies that reported an advertising effect (including qualitative research, content analyses, surveys, and correlational and experimental studies) "it appears that there is something there," even if the effects are small. She added, "In my opinion, there is sufficient evidence to say that alcohol advertising is likely to be a contributing factor to overall consumption and other alcohol-related problems in the long term."

Others cautioned that there were substantial differences among participants regarding the adequacy and strength of the research evidence. They noted that neither the econometric research nor the survey research is persuasive, although both are useful and suggestive. Therefore, they called for further research using a variety of approaches.

Why Does Research Show Such Weak Advertising Effects?

Esther Thorson asserted that the absence of alcohol advertising effects is due to the methodological failures of the research. She was particularly critical of laboratory studies, noting that it is not enough for alcohol researchers to show subjects 10 advertisements without paying close attention to their content. Ads are designed with a specific target; if the researcher shows subjects ads that are not aimed at them, their study misses examining "the highly-tuned supports and promises" that sell products. Thorson added that until alcohol researchers "make a proper choice of the stimulus" and examine the mass media messages as they occur in the viewer's real world environment, "there's no reason to expect any effect." If research were designed to take account of what the advertiser is trying to do and if it examined the relationship between the specific structure of the message and the individual or group for whom that message is targeted, investigators probably would find "whopping effects." Such findings would show the inadequacies of the existing studies, as well as identify mass media effects that simply have not been measured.

Enlarging on this view in response to a statement citing the number of liquor stores and billboards in certain areas of Los Angeles, Thorson reiterated, "It is not simply presence but targeted messages that attract people and promote actions." The actual content of the ads is "a critical factor" that has been absent in much of the alcohol research literature. She identified three critical elements of marketing activities that have been ignored: **synergy**, or the combination of public relations, advertising, direct marketing, and packaging designed to have greater impact; **aperture**, or the ways that marketers shape "motivating moments" or use viewers' readiness to have their attitudes changed; and **brand equity**, or "everything a person brings to a brand when they think about it."

David Stewart remained more skeptical. He asserted that evidence for advertising generally shows that it has only a weak effect; therefore, to expect alcohol advertising to have a large and measurable effect is not warranted. Advertising that makes people aware of products is going to increase awareness of something viewers may then want. That is different from creating a desire that they did not have before. What precipitates the use of a product like alcohol probably has far less to do with a youth looking at a Budweiser ad and saying, "Wow, I'm going to go and drink Budweiser" than the peer pressure at a party where beer is available. "If advertising has an effect, it is a much, much smaller effect than some of the other cultural kinds of events that initiate people into the use of alcoholic beverages."

What Level of Certainty is Needed for Various Audiences?

Participants also differed with respect to the required level of confidence in the research before it is deemed credible and definitive. Some asserted that even if researchers were able to do all the research recommended by meeting participants, the findings still might not be seen as credible enough by Congress to affect policy or to be accepted by the alcohol beverage industry.

Charles Atkin conceded that it is unlikely that research evidence would be sufficiently definitive to impress the alcohol beverage industry, particularly if it showed that alcohol advertising is causing some problems in society. Even studies with near-perfect methodology are likely to be subject to criticism, particularly when they touch on regulatory matters. He argued, therefore, for a standard based on what impresses a "reasonable scientist" studying the subject and added that the quantity of the evidence right now is not even close to that on most of the advertising effects issues that have been raised.

Several participants noted that there is a different standard that prevails for research within the world of advertising. Because it is difficult to prove connections between advertising exposure and outcomes that go all the way through behavior, the industry takes the behavioral connection on faith and focuses on cognitive responses.

Charles Atkin cautioned, however, that scientists cannot stop at cognitive data and conclude that because advertising alters attitudes, behavioral changes will correspondingly follow. The impact of advertising on behavior is uncertain because cognitive effects get modified greatly by an organism that has a distinctive value system and by distinct opportunities that exist in a variety of social contexts. These change a straightforward process into one that is much more convoluted. Thus, advertising can have a strong effect at stage one, a moderate effect further down the line, and a relatively modest effect by the time one gets to the final (behavioral) endpoint. And alcohol researchers *do* have to trace these processes all the way through to the end point of primary interest.

Others noted that the "reasonable scientist" standard may apply to NIAAA, but it will not necessarily convince members of Congress and other policymakers for whom the salient attributes of research are not necessarily contributions to confidence. They are more likely to be convinced by studies with large samples than by tight, elegant, small studies that control for all kinds of potentially confounding variables. The latter tend to be ignored because they are small. This is ironic since the larger the sample size, the better the chance that an effect that reaches statistical significance may be of little substantive import.

An additional concern mentioned by several participants was the way that studies are counted in the policy world. Regardless of the methodological rigor of a study or its relevance to the long-term effect of advertising, policymakers tend to base policies on how many studies report an effect compared with the number that suggest no effect.

RESEARCH APPROACHES

Much discussion revolved around how best to study the mass media and their effects. One recurrent concern was which outcome measures should researchers attend to—short-term impacts or longer term, cumulative effects of media messages? Cognitions or behaviors? Aggregate consumption or measures of drinking by groups or individuals? Should one consider other goals of the alcohol beverage industry, such as cultivating good will? Other research concerns were directed toward data limitations, particularly data used in econometric studies and ways to improve such studies.

Using Cognitions and Emotions as Outcome Measures

Most of the studies supported by NIAAA have focused on alcohol consumption or misuse as the criterion or outcome variable. Several participants, particularly those who are familiar with advertising research, observed that focusing constantly on the end states of behavior results in contrived designs that force-fit a problem into "a sort of medical model." The behavioral approach also ignores an important intermediate step between the advertisement and consumption—namely, the processing of the ad by the viewer. In fact, Michael Mazis asserted that until research puts more emphasis on these intermediate outcomes, it is unlikely to make much progress. To understand advertising, it is necessary to study what people do with the information they receive and how they process it. Additionally, he observed, it is not realistic to look for the same magnitude of effect in an advertising study as in medical research due to differences in the types of interventions involved.

Joel Cohen explained that between the exposure to advertising and actual behavior (either purchase or consumption behavior), there is the cognitive realm. Advertising works by associating its product with positive qualities and attributes. Therefore, researchers should explore the object–concept linkage. What is less clear, however, is whether the association between an attribute or concept and a product or object is only with a particular brand or extends to the object class. Does the association of brand X beer with masculinity, for example, sell more beer generally or just more brand X? How can one separate measurement of the product class from the individual brands of products in the class?

Esther Thorson noted that although "we are all cognitivists" and believe that the world runs on facts and figures, studies have found that what a lot of what people do "comes from the gut." Thus, how much people like alcohol ads turns out to be an important predictor of subsequent behavior that is infrequently studied, as is the emotional impact of an ad. Thus, Thorson added, "Researchers need to ask people about their affective responses to the messages."

Jan Howard noted that whether government-supported research focuses on attitudes and expectancies or behavioral outcomes has important implications for its costs. In the past NIAAA has consistently stressed the importance of measuring behavioral outcomes. Perhaps research could use intentions as the measurable outcome. This is particularly appropriate if other studies irrefutably prove that the intention to drink is firmly linked to subsequent drinking and if advertisers and producers in fact "are more than halfway there in getting that person to buy the product" once the target audience has positive expectancies about it.

Aggregate Data and Outcome Measures in Econometric Studies

Several participants argued that aggregate data cannot legitimately measure the possible links between advertising and consumption. Even if research finds that advertising has no effect on overall consumption there may be effects on particular groups and individuals that drink more as a result of new targeting efforts. Such effects are particularly important to identify if they are found in vulnerable groups such as inner city residents and youths. Because aggregate data cannot get at such important issues, some participants suggested that it is preferable to support personal interview and panel data to study individual and group changes in alcohol use rather than continuing to rely on econometric studies based on aggregate data.

Henry Saffer, however, countered that despite its limitations, the econometric research is valuable and could be improved by focusing on a narrower range or a narrower target to more precisely estimate the dependent variable. This can be done by longitudinal research tracking change over time, by focusing on a particular age group, or by using a narrower surrogate outcome measure like single-driver nighttime accidents. Studies might also focus on beer advertising, which is targeted much more to persons in their 20s.

Outcomes Beyond Consumption: Focusing on Advertisers' Goals

John Elder called for research that looks at dependent variables other than consumption, since part of the goal of advertisers is to protect the legitimacy of the industry they are promoting. He noted that tobacco companies have several goals or elements in their strategic planning activities that apply to alcohol producers as well. These were characterized by Robert Miles in *Coffin Nails and Corporate Strategies* as domain offense, domain defense, and domain creation. Domain offense includes efforts to achieve brand switching and to reach persons who are not yet smokers but who may legally purchase cigarettes. Domain defense is designed to protect the legitimacy of tobacco and the tobacco industry and to support the view that it is protecting the American way, free speech, and the First Amendment. Domain creation involves seeking new markets at home and abroad, extending product lines, and weaving them into the economy and culture. According to Elder, many of the advertisements shown in Thorson's article, for example, are not just designed to tell rich yuppies to buy various liqueurs; they are designed to protect the distillers' domain by showing, in essence, that they are legitimate because they advertise to the elite.

Currently most tobacco control research focuses on domain offense, ignoring an important part of what the industry is doing. Elder urged participants to think in much broader terms and consider at least what types of domain defensive measures the public health community is confronting in order to design the countermeasures and interventions that are most effective. He illustrated his concern by citing the sponsorship by Philip Morris of the bicentennial celebration of the adoption of the Constitution and the Bill of Rights by financially supporting the tour of the original document around the country. Recent tobacco control efforts have focused on protecting the nonsmoker from exposure to sidestream smoke. Tobacco companies now are concerned not only with getting nonsmokers to smoke but getting them to "shut up," hence the effort of those companies to link their names to the Bill of Rights (including the rights of smokers).

Limitations of Data Availability

Several researchers, particularly economists who conduct secondary analyses of existing data, observed that their studies were hampered by the lack of available data. Henry Saffer stated that the best econometric data on advertising come from Arbitron and Leading National Advertisers (market research companies) and cover paid advertisements in the traditional media. Data on point-of-purchase advertising (e.g., window displays) and consumer novelties are more difficult to assess. Another problem is that half the advertising dollars now go into what is called unmeasured media. There are no data available on exactly where this money is being spent by the alcohol beverage industry, so it has not been studied in a systematic way.

THE ROLE OF THE VIEWER

One issue on which participants generally agreed was the need to expand understanding of the interaction between the viewer and the media. Rather than treat the viewer as a passive recipient of messages spewed out by the media, participants called for research that recognizes that audiences select the media they use, select the messages to which they pay attention, and interpret those messages in light of their knowledge and experience.

Although there is a useful and growing body of content analyses of TV and film presentations of alcohol, several participants observed that these analyses have been guided by what researchers think is important, without knowing how messages are interpreted by viewers. These content analyses have found the frequency of the presentation of alcohol in entertainment programming to be inescapable and the nature of the presentation to be unrealistic. Nevertheless, far less is known about how portrayals affect audiences.

Jane Brown suggested that research on audience reactions to alcohol portrayals should build on the more extensive body of research on TV and violence; it also should go beyond TV to focus on reactions to videos and movies, which are the preferred media of adolescents. Such studies need to "put the organism back into the picture" using the active audience perspective. This means taking into account that audiences come to viewing situations with motivations, ideas about how the world works, a desire to gain information, and the need to create identities. Moreover, their responses to stimuli depend on their specific developmental stage and information needs. A key focus for this line of research is determining at what age or stage adolescents are open to and seek out information about alcohol and drinking. Such findings then might be used by health educators in developing alternative scripts for youth.

Lawrence Wallack also underscored the importance of studying audience response to portrayals of alcohol use. He noted that some portrayals give a very clear and specific message that excessive drinking is not okay, even if there is a designated driver. However, a number of other designated driver messages seem to presume that the only problem of concern related to drinking is driving. For example, in one episode of "Mr. Belvedere" the son asks his father on New Year's morning, "Did you drive the car into the swimming pool again this year?" The father replies no because somebody else was the designated driver. Wallack wanted to know whether viewers perceive this conversation as permissive of drunken behavior. Similarly, Jan Howard wondered whether showing "new" groups of drinkers in TV advertisements as well as in programming (e.g., little old ladies in tennis shoes) was interpreted as legitimating their drinking.

Both interview and experimental studies find that there is a difference between what people are exposed to and what they report seeing on TV. They recall seeing a car chase, a murder, or other forms of violence because, Esther Thorson asserted, violence is intrinsically salient. If the setting is a bar such as in "Cheers," however, viewers do not report seeing a glass of beer on the bar because it is not unusual or threatening in the same way. If one of the characters in "Cheers" walked around the bar carrying a bottle, as was the case in one episode shown in Jane Brown's presentation, whether such uncharacteristic barroom behavior is salient enough for viewers to notice is uncertain. Agreeing with Thorson, Jerome Williams observed that his content analysis of popular movies has found alcohol and tobacco to be frequently present but often unnoticed in films such as "Superman."

George Balch observed that although advertisers carefully develop strategic plans for communicating messages, they sometimes discover their message was not perceived as intended. He noted that the gap between what individuals remember seeing and what they are exposed to has some interesting regulatory implications regarding alcohol. For instance, there is a regulation that people cannot *drink* in beer commercials shown on television. Yet, viewers exposed to these ads consistently say they believe that people were drinking in the beer commercials. Balch added, "Perhaps we would approach regulation differently if we studied audience perceptions instead of regulating *a priori* without understanding how consumers actually perceive these things."

While some interpreted his statement as suggesting that regulations might be more effective if they were guided by research, other participants took issue with Balch. Joel Cohen noted that the general discussion and Balch's comment illustrate the difference between alcohol research and media research regarding measurement. Media or advertising researchers studying commercials are looking specifically for immediate effects. In contrast, a public health perspective is concerned with small, cumulative longer term effects. To measure short-term effects, the 24-hour recall, which is the standard in advertising, asks consumers what they remember seeing in a program. According to Cohen, this may be a convenient way to ask the question, but it is unrelated to the way people store things in memory. This difference is very important in discussions of assessments of advertising effects becasue the methods used by cognitive psychologists differ substantially from those used by advertisers. Associations formed in memory are not necessarily expressed in response to direct questions or the wrong memory probe.

Sally Casswell, hearing Balch's statement as a suggestion that regulation is ineffective and thus should be eliminated, asserted that such a stance ignores the fact that regulations serve important symbolic functions, signaling to the public that a product is "dangerous" and requires regulation. Reiterating Cohen's point that many of the experimental studies are designed to capture only the short-term effects of advertising, she noted that despite this limitation, in the policy world such studies are counted, and policies are based on the sheer number of studies that may suggest an effect compared with the number that suggest no effect.

ADOLESCENTS AND THE MEDIA

There was also disagreement about how adolescents respond to both advertising and program content. David Stewart claimed that "at best advertising plays a very minor role" in adolescents' patterns of consuming and how they process advertising. Several others asserted that adolescents are quite receptive to messages and that the teenage years are a very vulnerable segment of the lifespan. They noted that despite methodological flaws in consumer research on adolescents, social identity theory suggests that adolescents are strongly influenced by their environment but, if asked, will deny it. Joel Grube added that his study provides some evidence that alcohol advertising can influence children, particularly their beliefs about alcohol and, indirectly, their intentions to drink as adults.

David Stewart agreed that the literature clearly indicates that adolescents are not immune from peer and parental influences but reiterated that the important question is whether advertising is a *particularly* powerful influence and whether teens are *particularly* vulnerable. His reading of the literature indicates that teens learn how to consume alcohol from their parents and that advertising is a weak force.

Jane Brown observed that in her research on the sexuality of adolescent girls from ages 11 to 15, she and her colleagues have found that the girls' rooms were covered with advertising posters. They surmised that the girls use advertising images as a way to "try on different identities" and create a self, relying on the media for direction, guidance, and answers. She added that for the researcher "the trick is to measure how identities change over time and how the process is related to media use and risky health behaviors."

Lorraine Collins observed that Americans have a very ambivalent attitude about alcohol, and this confuses many children. They turn to alcohol advertisements for guidance that they should be getting from parents and other adults. She asserted, therefore, that we need formal education or socialization for drinking like that offered in driver's education courses. However, others took issue with several aspects of Collins' argument. They noted that American culture provides ample information about alcohol and experience with drinkers, both positive and negative, and that Collins' analogy to driver's education and its effectiveness in reducing accidents ignored the research findings. When the driver's education course was made compulsory rather than voluntary (and students could get licenses earlier) the reduction in accidents disappeared.

ADVERTISING: GOALS, EFFECTS, AND POLICY IMPLICATIONS

Clear differences in the perspectives of participants, as well as the policy implications of their viewpoints, arose in discussions of the goals and tactics of alcohol advertisers. Charles Atkin questioned the extent to which their strategies are designed to achieve brand switching as opposed to increasing generic demand for their product category (i.e., stimulating more drinking in general). Thorson responded that it is difficult to determine the answer to Atkin's question, adding that demographics (e.g., the aging of the baby boom generation) suggest that advertisers need to do both and to attract drinkers just as they turn 21. Jerome Williams added that there are two ways to increase consumption: marketers can get more people to drink or get people that are already in their market to drink more per person. Both forces appear to be at work. The mature-markets theory says that advertisers of a new product seek new consumers; once their market matures, advertising just involves brand switching. Since some of the consumers die, however, the marketer also must attract new entrants somehow. Thus, Williams asserted, marketers attempt to attract new consumers as replacements and seek to increase the consumption per entrant in the market at the same time.

Joel Cohen added, "If marketers say there is only brand shifting going on . . . this ignores reality." Generally, a consumer first decides whether to buy a product (e.g., a lawnmower), then decide on the best brand to buy. However, for beer and cigarettes this decisionmaking sequence may not hold. Cohen conceptualized a multidimensional space in which consumers are distributed and which is defined by various psychological (e.g., social identity, self-image) and physical (e.g., product performance-based) needs, wants, and goals. The more closely the marketer can position his or her brand in terms of the desired psychological or physical benefits it provides to the particular group to whom the product is targeted, the greater the likelihood that those people are going to use the brand, and hence the product. Cohen asserted, "I don't know many people who decide to smoke cigarettes. They decide to smoke Marlboros (or another brand) . . . because those particular images or cluster of benefits (associated with the brand) are what they want." He noted that Thorson's presentation suggests that the same process may be operating with beer.

Others responded that if viewers who are exposed to brand X beer ads develop an association between that brand and masculinity, the question remains whether they associate the product class (i.e., all beers) with that characteristic. Someone might say, in effect, "I identify with (the status claims of) brand X but I don't drink beer; that's not me." Therefore, the issue is not simply a social identity associated with a particular brand but with the general product category as well.

Cohen, however, noted that the relationship between the product–object associations and behavior is probablistic. Some may not internalize the associations themselves or may not think that important others make similar product attributions (thereby reducing their social/symbolic value). In a universe of people, some will try the marketer's beer, decide they hate the taste, and never drink it again. For others, the taste of beer will be a secondary consideration, perhaps until a bit later in life. Regardless, the probability of becoming a beer drinker has been increased by each marketer's efforts to develop desired brand-benefit associations. The point is that "the brand is the gateway to the product class."

Cohen observed that in his research on smoking he realized that there is a potential disjuncture between the concept "cigarettes" and what the purchaser thinks about in the store (i.e., "Marlboro"). This observation has important implications for the phrasing and the effects of warning labels, since consumers may think of the brand instead of the generic product class.

Others countered that their research does not support Cohen's observations. Victor Tremblay reported that his study of demand for beer at the firm level found very strong evidence to suggest that advertising increases demand at the firm level but not at the brand level.

George Balch stated that marketers distinguish three sources or types of demand: primary demand, which involves getting people into the product category; secondary demand, which involves brand loyalty or switching (i.e., "my brand instead of yours"); and tertiary demand aimed at increasing the amount a user consumes. Alcohol advertisers do not say "drink more." Their strategy is to increase the number of occasions for drinking rather than the amount consumed at any one drinking occasion. In addition, Balch noted, advertisers attract new drinkers by developing new brands and by designing advertising that is much more precisely targeted toward new groups of potential drinkers. For example, they have created light beer and are designing ads for it to appeal to women, which rarely was done in the past.

There was disagreement about whether the two messages, "drink more" and "drink more often," have the same effect. From the marketers' point of view the effect is quite different; the two messages have an identical effect only if you measure aggregate consumption. But, Balch noted, "aggregate consumption is not the social problem of overconsumption," and he suggested the need for more precise distinctions in identifying alcohol marketing goals and effects.

Speaking from a public health perspective, other participants noted that increasing the number of occasions on which alcohol is used may increase various risks to health and safety, depending on the type of drinking that takes place. If the cultural norm is to binge drink, increasing the number of such occasions may be related to both immediate harm and the long-term physiological effects of the total amount of alcohol consumed over a lifetime.

In response to Joseph Gusfield's question whether the attributes of a product affect the nature and success of advertisers, several participants responded yes and provided examples. Anticonstipation drugs are hard to sell; at the same time, as Jerome Williams noted, there is a multibillion-dollar market for illicit drugs for which there is no advertising but substantial demand. He added, "Obviously, there are some inherent attributes that make products attractive or difficult to sell. One cannot say all products are the same or that an advertising campaign will have the same effect across all product categories."

HEALTH PROMOTION, COUNTER-ADVERTISING, AND MEDIA ADVOCACY

There was considerable debate regarding the comparability between advertising and counter-advertising, including public service messages and/or campaigns. Lawrence Wallack asserted that "unselling is different from selling," which has many more techniques that can be used than are available for unselling. David Stewart disagreed, noting that in both cases the message must be clearly tailored to a particular group in a way to which they can relate.

In explaining health promotion advertising and communication activities, Wallack identified several distinct strategies. Public service announcements, social marketing, and comprehensive public communications campaigns usually treat the individual as the audience to whom messages containing information are directed. In contrast, media advocacy focuses on "promoting healthy public policies and relies more heavily on a political science agenda-setting framework." This includes mobilizing one or several communities to take control of the products being sold in them or the manner in which these products are marketed. Wallack noted that the "spot" antismoking advertisements that he showed in his presentation are part of the California anti-tobacco campaign and are accompanied by extensive community involvement. In mounting that campaign, public health advocates are attempting to reframe the smoking issue by shifting the focus from the individual smoker to the tobacco industry, forcing consumers to question the legitimacy and credibility of the industry, and mobilizing public support for the legislative and public policy battle that is occurring in that state. Wallack added that enabling consumers to determine what products enter their communities is an important aspect of democratization and that "media advocacy is about giving people a voice instead of a message."

Others pointed to parallel changes being adopted in business marketing, which is moving from transaction marketing (i.e., straight buy–sell) to relationship marketing (i.e., establishing long-term ties with clients using tactics such as "just-in-time inventory") and in consumer marketing, which is moving away from a simple economic transaction approach to an emphasis on consumer involvement with the purchase process. The latter change appears to be a response to the efforts of consumer advocates in getting community groups to recognize that marketing is not just a straight economic transaction. More consumers are asking whether the bank in which they put their savings is reinvesting those dollars in their community. Similarly, Jerome Williams asserted, it appears that community activism was responsible for PowerMaster beer being taken off the market and that growing numbers of consumers are engaged in boycotts, which suggests that "perhaps the most effective way of dealing with undesirable advertising" is getting community groups involved.

Lawrence Wallack asserted that the way an issue is framed or defined changes public perception of who has the problem (i.e., the individual or community), what that problem is, and how to solve it. Several participants elaborated on this point. Joseph Gusfield illustrated the importance of framing by citing his recent study of the antismoking movement. He found that initially the movement cast its message so as to make the smoker the victim of the tobacco industry. In the past decade, however, the movement's tactics have shifted from exclusive concern with smoking as detrimental to the health of the *smoker* to something that the smoker does that is detrimental to *other people*. Consequently, the smoker is now more of a villain who has to step outside, to be segregated from the rest of us.

Other discussants reiterated the importance of framing in making clear that "alcohol is not like Bisquick" and the policy implications of the fact that it is a commodity that poses a variety of health and other hazards if it is abused. In this regard, Patricia Taylor identified some of the policy options that the Center for Science in the Public Interest has been supporting. These include eliminating the depiction of risky activities in ads, eliminating Spring Break promotions, and severely restricting college marketing activities. She suggested that all of these approaches probably would be more effective than an outright ban on advertising, as well as be more acceptable to the public and more likely to be implemented. However, she noted that there are a number of barriers to implementing such policies.

Several participants elaborated on these problems. They raised concerns about the effects of political action committees and other sources of campaign contributions from the alcohol beverage industry. They asserted that lawmakers are likely to be less willing to regulate industries on which they depend for campaign contributions. They noted that the alcohol beverage industry is spending a great deal of money on "public service" advertising to create a favorable political climate (e.g., "know when to say when" campaigns), which subtly undermines social and policy change efforts advocated by health promotion and community organizations concerned about alcohol problems.

POLICY-RELEVANT RESEARCH DIRECTIONS

There was general agreement that eliminating all advertising for alcohol would neither stop underage or abusive drinking nor be a desirable policy. Rather, participants from diverse disciplines agreed that it is preferable to treat alcohol advertising as part of the larger issue of commercial marketing of alcoholic beverages, to explore various narrower policy options, and to incorporate regulations within a comprehensive alcohol control policy from the national to the local level. Research can and should play an important role in shaping these policies by providing information in relevant areas.

Although participants differed with respect to research priorities, largely along disciplinary and policy-orientation lines, several areas for future research and key questions were identified as useful in shaping public policy. In addition, there was agreement that alcohol researchers need to examine both behavior and what happens at the cognitive level as people learn and form beliefs about the linkage between alcohol products, the products' attributes, and various outcomes. Both types of research should be pursued simultaneously. The following general questions, drawn largely from the agenda presented in Charles Atkin's paper, with additional issues emerging in other participants' papers and the group discussions, were identified as potentially fruitful avenues for further research:

1. What is the contribution of advertising to the initiation, use, and misuse of alcohol?

Both field experiments and survey research could be used to address such questions as How strong is the causal impact that can be traced to advertising, directly and indirectly? Which independent and intervening variables amplify or attenuate the influence of advertising? And to what extent does advertising affect frequency and/or quantity of consumption?

Longitudinal studies are necessary to address questions related to the role advertising plays in children's learning about alcohol, their predispositions to initiate drinking, and its actual initiation. These studies should focus on how children and adolescents learn about alcohol use, and the role that advertising plays in this learning process, using a developmental perspective that has been beneficial in other areas.

2. What are the specific and differential effects on various audience segments of advertising to general audiences and of targeted marketing?

Of particular interest is the relative impact of alcohol advertising and marketing activities on attitudes and behaviors of various age, gender, race/ethnic, and socioeconomic groups as well as on heavy drinkers. It was suggested, for example, that in developing alcohol advertisements, they be tested using focus groups composed of vulnerable populations such as alcoholics and persons under 21 rather than only on normal healthy adults over 21.

The absence of data on the effects of advertising in specialty media channels and of nontraditional marketing on alcohol consumption and drinking problems, particularly among underage and minority audiences, makes these topics important areas for research. Studies of nontraditional marketing should focus on exploring the effects of high audience-involvement activities such as event marketing.

3. How are viewers affected by content and stylistic factors in alcohol-relevant ads?

It was suggested that in the future alcohol researchers should look far more closely at the content of the ad in experimental studies and use the same outcome variables that advertisers consider in message creation and evaluation. In addition, researchers need to consider such factors as timing or when individuals are open to messages (aperture), the dynamic effects of multiple channels of information (synergy), and the cumulative effects of ad campaigns (brand equity).

Studies also should focus on object–concept associations in order to learn more about how people process ads and what they do with the information. Rather than focusing on alcohol consumption or abuse as outcomes, laboratory research should explore intermediate variables such as perceptions, attitudes, cognitive responses, emotional responses, and the development of associations between alcohol and a particular lifestyle, emotion, or value that is emphasized in advertising or promotions.

Other research suggestions included laboratory experiments to address (1) the extent to which subjects respond to the generic product versus the specific brand; (2) the effects of various types of celebrity endorsers and lifestyle ads; (3) the effectiveness of various types of persuasive appeals (e.g., camaraderie, escape, relaxation, sexuality), particularly their appeal to children; (4) the impact of various presentation styles on various audiences, particularly high-risk groups; (5) the linkage between brand symbols and the generic product associations; and (6) the differential influence of message variables on particular audience segments.

4. What is the role of the viewer in interaction with the media?

Several participants called for research on the dynamic processes through which viewers simultaneously draw on mass media images in making sense of their own lives, and use personal experiences and knowledge to interpret the mass media to which they are exposed. Studies should include examination of how viewers seek and select information and relate to the messages presented in television programming, movies, video, and nontraditional media.

Developmental studies that focus on the effects of media presentations on the beliefs of children should identify at what ages and stages of their drinking history these presentations have the greatest influence. Such research could provide a basis for identifying components of interventions to be implemented at those critical stages of development.

How to study viewers' perceptions, however, was a matter of debate among the participants. Esther Thorson and Jane Brown argued for experimental studies as one important method for investigating how audiences process media messages, suggesting the value of exploring the comparative salience of the events; Anders Hansen, on the contrary, argued against laboratory experiments as a means of studying media influence. He asserted that lab studies focus on direct, immediate measurable effects whereas the real concern is the longer term cumulative effect of advertising. Thus, laboratory approaches ignore the political aspects of framing the advertising issue.

5. What is the optimal mix of varied quantities of product advertising and public service messages dealing with alcohol?

Surveys and field experiments might be used to determine whether drinking problems can be more effectively reduced by decreasing the quantity of advertising or by increasing the quantity of responsible-drinking and drunk-driving messages. What is the relative effectiveness of responsible drinking and antidrunk-driving messages sponsored by alcohol companies compared with those prepared by nonindustry organizations? How effective are the alcohol beverage industry's "goodwill" campaigns such as the "know when to say when" campaign? What do various groups in the population think *when* means? Does this mental marker affect their behavior?

6. What are the most effective strategies and messages for counteracting

harmful effects of alcohol advertising and marketing?

A wide range of studies was suggested for examining how best to address health risks related to the promotion of alcoholic beverages. Suggestions included laboratory examinations of the effects of counter-messages in altering deleterious influences of commercial advertising, evaluations of specific health promotion campaigns, and broader examinations of changing marketing strategies and internal conflicts within the alcohol beverage industry. For example, Michael Goodstadt would encourage study of conflicts within the industry over "control of the marketplace" such as recently occurred between the brewers and distillers in Canada when the latter sought to place ads on TV asserting "an ounce is an ounce." Since the various control strategies currently being supported by the Center for Science in the Public Interest have not been systematically studied, several participants suggested that if any are adopted by a local community or State, the program's implementation and outcomes should be assessed.

Rigorous studies of community mobilization efforts also would be desirable. Such research on political processes will require background work to operationalize variables and outcome measures with more precision than in previous studies.

In concluding the meeting, participants were reminded by Jerome Williams that "when you are in the jungle and trying to keep away the gnats and fleas, don't get swallowed by the tigers." Or, to paraphrase Williams, keep the focus on the larger problem, which, many participants reiterated throughout the meeting, goes well beyond simply measuring the effects of advertising. That larger public policy question, how best to control the harmful effects of alcohol misuse, should certainly include alcohol advertising, but it should do so in conjunction with efforts aimed at a variety of other leverage points, including education, prices, and general accessibility issues.

Appendix

PARTICIPANTS LIST

Dr. Charles Atkin
Department of Communications
Michigan State University
East Lansing, Michigan

Dr. Jane Brown
School of Journalism and Mass Communication
University of North Carolina
Chapel Hill, North Carolina

Dr. Sally Casswell
Alcohol and Public Health Research Unit School of Medicine
University of Auckland
Auckland, New Zealand

Dr. Joel Cohen
Center for Consumer Research
College of Business Administration
University of Florida
Gainesville, Florida

Dr. R. Lorraine Collins
Research Institute on Addictions
Buffalo, New York

Dr. John Elder
School of Public Health
San Diego State University
San Diego, California

Dr. George Gerbner
Annenberg School for Communication
University of Pennsylvania
Philadelphia, Pennsylvania

Dr. Joel Grube
Prevention Research Center
Berkeley, California

Dr. Joseph Gusfield
Department of Sociology
University of California at San Diego
La Jolla, California

Dr. Anders Hansen
Centre for Mass Communication Research
University of Leicester
Leicester, England

Dr. John Lastovicka
Department of Marketing
College of Business
Arizona State University
Tempe, Arizona

Dr. Michael Mazis
Department of Marketing
College of Business
American University
Washington, DC

Dr. Henry Saffer
National Bureau of Economic Research
New York, New York

Dr. David W. Stewart
College of Marketing
School of Business Administration
University of Southern California
Los Angeles, California

Dr. Esther Thorson
School of Journalism
University of Missouri
Columbia, Missouri

Dr. Victor J. Tremblay
Department of Economics
Oregon State University
Corvallis, Oregon

Dr. Lawrence Wallack
School of Public Health
University of California at Berkeley
Berkeley, California

Dr. Jerome Williams
Department of Marketing
Pennsylvania State University
University Park, Pennsylvania

ATTENDEES LIST

Dr. Richard Ashmore
Department of Psychology
Rutgers University
New Brunswick, New Jersey

Dr. Judith Auerbach
Consortium of Social Science Associations
Washington, DC

Dr. George Balch
Prevention Research Center
University of Illinois-Chicago
Chicago, Illinois

Dr. William Bukoski
National Institute on Drug Abuse, NIH
Bethesda, Maryland

Dr. James Callahan
American Society of Addiction Medicine
Chevy Chase, Maryland

Ms. Nancy Chase
Center for Substance Abuse Prevention, SAMHSA
Rockville, Maryland

Mr. Bob Denniston
Center for Substance Abuse Prevention, SAMHSA
Rockville, Maryland

Mr. John Donnelly
Research!America
Alexandria, Virginia

Ms. Janet Flynn
Distilled Spirits Council of the United States
Washington, DC

Ms. Lorraine Gafney
Wine Institute
Washington, DC

Dr. Michael Goodstadt
Alcohol Research Foundation
Toronto, Canada

Dr. Hugh Klein
NOVA Research Company
Bethesda, Maryland

Ms. Linda P. Kaplan
National Association of Alcoholism and Drug Abuse Counselors
Arlington, Virginia

Mr. Robert G. Kirk
American Council on Alcoholism
Baltimore, Maryland

Dr. Roger Kurrus
National Highway Traffic Safety Administration
Washington, DC

Dr. Phyllis Langton
George Washington University
Washington, DC

Dr. Tom Likens
Anheuser-Busch Companies
Williamsburg, Virginia

Ms. Susan Lockhart
Center for Substance Abuse Prevention, SAMHSA
Rockville, Maryland

Ms. Christine Lubinski
National Council on Alcoholism and Drug Dependence
New York, New York

Dr. John McCarthy
Catholic University of America
Washington, DC

Ms. Molly McGinley
Beer Institute
Washington, DC

Ms. Winnie Mitchell
Office of the Surgeon General, DHHS
Washington, DC

Dr. William Modzeleski
Department of Education
Washington, DC

Dr. Susan Newcomber
National Institute on Child Health and Human Development, NIH
Bethesda, Maryland

Dr. Al Pawlowski
Alcoholic Beverage Medical Research Foundation
Baltimore, Maryland

Ms. Carolyn Pinsky
CRTC Legal Branch
Ottawa, Canada

Dr. Barry A. Seekin
Anheuser-Busch Companies
Williamsburg, Virginia

Dr. James W. Swinehart
Public Communication Resources
Pelham, New York

Ms. Pat Taylor
Center for Science in the Public Interest
Washington, DC

Mr. Joel Whitaker
Kane's Beverage Week
Sanwood, New Jersey

Ms. Judith Wilkenfeld
Federal Trade Commission
Washington, DC